THE HISTORY OF AL-ṬABARĪ

AN ANNOTATED TRANSLATION

VOLUME XXXIV

Incipient Decline

THE CALIPHATES OF AL-WĀTHIQ, AL-MUTAWAKKIL, AND AL-MUNTAṢIR

A.D. 841–863/A.H. 227–248

The History of al-Ṭabari

Editorial Board

Ihsan Abbas, University of Jordan, Amman

C. E. Bosworth, The University of Manchester

Jacob Lassner, Wayne State University, Detroit

Franz Rosenthal, Yale University

Ehsan Yar-Shater, Columbia University (*General Editor*)

SUNY

SERIES IN NEAR EASTERN STUDIES

Said Amir Arjomand, Editor

The preparation of this volume was made possible in part by a grant from the National Endowment for the Humanities, an independent federal agency.

Bibliotheca Persica
Edited by Ehsan Yar-Shater

The History of al-Ṭabarī

(Ta'rīkh al-rusul wa'l-mulūk)

VOLUME XXXIV

Incipient Decline

translated and annotated
by

Joel L. Kraemer

Tel Aviv University

State University of New York Press

Published by
State University of New York Press, Albany

For information, address State University of New York
Press, State University Plaza, Albany, N.Y. 12246
Library of Congress Cataloging in Publication Data

Ṭabarī, 838?–923.
[Ta 'rīkh al-rusul wa-al-mulūk. English. Selections]
Incipient decline / translated and annotated by Joel L. Kraemer.
p. cm.—(SUNY series in Near Eastern studies) (Bibliotheca Persica) (The history of al-Ṭabarī = Ta 'rīkh al-rusul wa 'l-mulūk ; v. 34)
Translation from extracts from: Ta 'rīkh al-rusul wa-al-mulūk.
Bibliography: p.
Includes index.
ISBN 0-88706-874-X. ISBN 0-88706-875-8 (pbk.)
1. Islamic Empire—History—750-1258. I. Kraemer, Joel L. II. Title. III. Series. IV. Series: Biblioteca Persica (Albany, N.Y.) V. Series: Ṭabarī, 838?–923. Ta 'rīkh al-rusul wa-al-mulūk. English ; v. 34.
DS38.2.T313 1985 vol. 34
[DS38.6]
909'.1 s—dc19
[909'.0976710] 88-2261
CIP

10 9 8 7 6 5 4 3 2 1

Preface

THE HISTORY OF PROPHETS AND KINGS (*Ta'rīkh al-rusul wa'l-mulūk*) by Abū Ja'far Muḥammad b. Jarīr al-Ṭabarī (839–923), here rendered as the *History of al-Ṭabarī,* is by common consent the most important universal history produced in the world of Islam. It has been translated here in its entirety for the first time for the benefit of non-Arabists, with historical and philological notes for those interested in the particulars of the text.

Ṭabarī's monumental work explores the history of the ancient nations, with special emphasis on biblical peoples and prophets, the legendary and factual history of ancient Iran, and, in great detail, the rise of Islam, the life of the Prophet Muḥammad, and the history of the Islamic world down to the year 915. The first volume of this translation will contain a biography of al-Ṭabarī and a discussion of the method, scope, and value of his work. It will also provide information on some of the technical considerations that have guided the work of the translators.

The *History* has been divided here into 38 volumes, each of which covers about two hundred pages of the original Arabic text in the Leiden edition. An attempt has been made to draw the diving lines between the individual volumes in such a way that each is to some degree independent and can be read as such. The page numbers of the original in the Leiden edition appear on the margins of the translated volumes.

Al-Ṭabarī very often quotes his sources verbatim and traces the chain of transmission (*isnād*) to an original source. The chains of transmitters are, for the sake of brevity, rendered by only a dash

(—) between the individual links in the chain. Thus, According to Ibn Ḥumayd—Salamah—Ibn Isḥāq means that al-Ṭabarī received the report from Ibn Ḥumayd who said that he was told by Salamah, who said that he was told by Ibn Isḥāq, and so on. The numerous subtle and important differences in the original Arabic wording have been disregarded.

The table of contents at the beginning of each volume gives a brief survey of the topics dealt with in that particular volume. It also includes the headings and subheadings as they appear in al-Ṭabarī's text, as well as those occasionally introduced by the translator.

Well-known place names, such as, for instance, Mecca, Baghdad, Jerusalem, Damascus, and the Yemen, are given in their English spellings. Less common place names, which are the vast majority, are transliterated. Biblical figures appear in the accepted English spelling. Iranian names are usually transcribed according to their Arabic forms, and the presumed Iranian forms are often discussed in the footnotes.

Technical terms have been translated wherever possible, but some, such as dirham and imām, have been retained in Arabic forms. Others that cannot be translated with sufficient precision have been retained and italicized as well as footnoted.

The annotation aims chiefly at clarifying difficult passages, identifying individuals and place names, and discussing textual difficulties. Much leeway has been left to the translators to include in the footnotes whatever they consider necessary and helpful.

The bibliographies list all the sources mentioned in the annotation.

The index in each volume contains all the names of persons and places referred to in the text, as well as those mentioned in the notes as far as they refer to the medieval period. It does not include the names of modern scholars. A general index, it is hoped, will appear after all the volumes have been published.

For further details concerning the series and acknowledgments, see Preface to Volume 1.

Ehsan Yar-Shater

Contents

Preface / v

Translator's Foreword / xi

Abbreviations / xxv

Tables 1. Genealogy of ʿAbbāsid Caliphs (A.D. Ninth Century) / xxvi

2. Genealogy of the Khāqānids / xxvii

3. Genealogy of the Ṭāhirids / xxviii

Maps 1. Armenia, Ādharbayjān, Arrān / xxix

2. Sāmarrā / xxx

The Caliphate of Hārūn al-Wāthiq Abū Jaʿfar

The Events of the Year 227 (841/842) (cont'd) / 3

The Events of the Year 228 (842/843) / 5

The Events of the Year 229 (843/844) / 8

The Reason for al-Wāthiq's Action against the Secretaries This Year / 11

The Events of the Year 230 (844/845) / 17

An Account of the Dispatch of Bughā al-Kabīr to the Tribesmen / 17

The Events of the Year 231 (845/846) / 22

The Reason for the Liquidation of the Banū Sulaym and Its Consequences / 22
The Reason for the Rebellion of the Baghdad Group and the Consequence of Their Action and That of Aḥmad b. Naṣr / 27
The Reason for the Prisoner Exchange and How It Took Place / 38

The Events of the Year 232 (846/847) / 45

The Reason for Bughā the Elder's March against the Banū Numayr and What Took Place between Them / 45
An Account of the Illness from Which al-Wāthiq Died / 51
A Portrayal of al-Wāthiq, His Years, and the Extent of His Caliphate / 52
Some Reports about al-Wāthiq / 53

The Caliphate of Jaʿfar al-Mutawakkil ʿalā-llāh

The Events of the Year 232 (846/847) (cont'd) / 61

The Occasion of Jaʿfar's Becoming Caliph and the Period of His Caliphate / 61

The Events of the Year 233 (847/848) / 65

The Reason for al-Mutawakkil's Anger at Muḥammad b. al-Zayyāt and Its Consequences / 65

The Events of the Year 234 (848/849) / 77

The Reason for Muḥammad b. al-Baʿīth's Escape and the Consequences of His Affair / 77
The Reason for Ītākh's Pilgrimage This Year / 81

The Events of the Year 235 (849/850) / 83

How Ītākh Was Killed / 83

The Events of the Year 236 (850/851) / 107

The Killing of Muḥammad b. Ibrāhīm b. Muṣʿab and How It Took Place / 107

The Events of the Year 237 (851/852) / 113

The Cause of the Revolt by the Inhabitants of Armenia against Yūsuf b. Muḥammad / 113

What Was Done with Aḥmad b. Naṣr and the Result of This / 119

The Events of the Year 238 (852/853) / 121

Bughā's Role in the Defeat of Isḥāq b. Ismāʿīl / 121

The Events of the Year 239 (853/854) / 128

The Events of the Year 240 (854/855) / 130

The Cause for the Revolt of the Inhabitants of Ḥimṣ and Its Result / 130

The Events of the Year 241 (855/856) / 133

The Role of the Inhabitants of Ḥimṣ in the Revolt against Muḥammad b. ʿAbdawayh and Its Consequence for Them / 133

The Reason for Flogging ʿĪsā b. Jaʿfar b. ʿĀṣim and the Caliph's Role in This / 135

The Reason for the Prisoner Exchange / 138

The Affair of the Bujah and Its Consequences / 141

The Events of the Year 242 (856/857) / 146

The Events of the Year 243 (857/858) / 149

The Events of the Year 244 (858/859) / 151

The Events of the Year 245 (859/860) / *154*

The Cause of Najāḥ b. Salamah's Demise / 158

The Events of the Year 246 (860/861) / *167*

The Events of the Year 247 (861/862) / *171*

The Reason for al-Mutawakkil's Murder and How It Took Place / 171
Some Things about al-Mutawakkil and His Way of Life / 185

The Caliphate of al-Muntaṣir Muḥammad b. Jaʿfar

The Events of the Year 247 (861/862) (cont'd) / *195*

The Events of the Year 248 (862/863) / *204*

The Reason for Dispatching Waṣīf to Byzantium and His Role / 204
The Abdication of al-Muʿtazz and al-Mu'ayyad / 210
The Illness That Caused al-Muntaṣir's Death, the Time When He Died, and How Long He Lived / 218
Something of al-Muntaṣir's Conduct / 223

Bibliography of Cited Works / 225

Index / 235

Translator's Foreword

Ya'qūbī begins his description of Sāmarrā thus: "We shall now speak of Surra Man Ra'ā ("He who sees it rejoices"), the second capital of the Hāshimite caliphs. Eight caliphs have resided there." The caliphs he mentions, after its founder al-Mu'taṣim, were all sons or grandsons of his. Three of them are treated in this volume, namely, al-Mu'taṣim's son and successor al-Wāthiq, al-Wāthiq's brother al-Mutawakkil, and al-Mutawakkil's son al-Muntaṣir. This was the summit of what has been called "the Sāmarrā period." The massive building projects in the new capital—quarters, palaces, mosques, gardens, markets, thoroughfares, canals, and so on—inaugurated by al-Mu'taṣim and carried on by al-Wāthiq, and especially by al-Mutawakkil, defined Sāmarrā's physical character.

Al-Mu'taṣim is said to have founded Sāmarrā and to have moved upstream to his new capital in order to avoid the perennial clashes and friction between the Turkish troops and the Baghdad populace. In Sāmarrā, with wisdom that grows from experience, al-Mu'taṣim adopted a policy of isolating the Turkish (and related) military elite from the rest of the population. The Turkish officers—men such as Ashnās, Bughā the Elder, Bughā the Younger, Ītākh, Waṣīf, and Sīmā (whom we shall meet on the following pages)—were assigned fiefs, as were civil officers and other members of the ruling elite. High Turkish officers were given palaces. The famous Jawsaq al-Khāqānī, which came to be a caliphal residence, had in fact been the palace of al-Fatḥ b. Khāqān.

The Turkish presence in Sāmarrā cast long shadows. The caliphs of Banū Hāshim came under the dominant influence of the Turkish military class. Al-Muʿtaṣim's policy of segregating the Turkish soldiery, it has been suggested (by J. M. Rogers, "Sāmarrā"), was aimed at achieving his own personal safety. (See also Ayalon, "Mamlūk Military Institution," 54–55). If so, this strategy certainly backfired. For it is more than likely that their isolation contributed to their growing consolidation and power. It is significant that when Ītākh was trapped and murdered in Baghdad by order of al-Mutawakkil, our narrator points out that this never could have happened in Sāmarrā. "Were he not seized in Baghdad, they would have been unable to apprehend him. Had he entered Sāmarrā and wanted his men to kill all his opponents, he would have been able to accomplish this."

The crowning example of Turkish power and Hāshimite frailty was the assassination of al-Mutawakkil by Turkish officers within the precincts of his own palace. The Turks were afterwards not only instrumental in raising al-Muntaṣir to the caliphate—he was, it appears, involved in the assassination plot—they also forced him eventually to depose his two brothers as heirs apparent, and finally they (evidently) had al-Muntaṣir himself killed.

The attempts by the ʿAbbāsid caliphs to counter and alleviate the growing Turkish pressure foundered. Near the beginning of his reign, al-Wāthiq arrested and fined a group of eminent secretaries, that is, administrators and officials. This measure, allegedly prompted by his wazīr Ibn al-Zayyāt, was conceivably aimed at securing funds to pay the salaries of the Turkish military personnel, as some sources say. But a further motive—also mentioned—may have been to strike a blow at these very Turks, such as Ītākh and Ashnās. Many of the leading secretaries arrested were in their service. But this step was isolated and ineffectual. In any case, it is noteworthy that al-Wāthiq was (reportedly) moved to fine and imprison the secretaries by the precedent set by his grandfather, Hārūn al-Rashīd, who had removed the Barmakids from favor because of their alleged control over the caliphate. To be sure, such expropriations were basically predatory. And al-Wāthiq's successor, his brother al-Mutawakkil, shortly after assuming office, removed officials, confiscated property, and executed powerful notables.

The two mainstays of the administration—the military officers and civil officials—worked hand in hand directing the affairs of the far-flung empire. The base of power was a praetorian-bureaucratic condominium, buttressed by the swords of the Turks and the pens of the secretaries. It would be a mistake to view the Turkish military elite as a purely martial force. The Turks often served as government administrators and provincial rulers. The cultural attainments of some members of this military aristocracy are noteworthy. The rapid acculturation of the Turkish immigrants to the ʿAbbāsid realm is indeed striking. Fatḥ b. al-Khāqān, son of a newcomer, was a first-generation, arabicized Turk. (Consider also the famous philosopher Abū Naṣr al-Fārābī [d. 950], who was born in Turkestān, in the district of Fārāb, to a father who came to Baghdad as an army commander.)

Al-Fatḥ b. Khāqān was knowledgeable in the Arabic language, assimilated Arab culture, and amassed a great library that also served his friend and protégé, Abū ʿUthmān ʿAmr b. Baḥr al-Jāḥiẓ. The latter's *Fī manāqib al-Turk (On the Merits of the Turks)* was addressed to al-Fatḥ. In his brief treatise Jāḥiẓ in fact concentrates on the horsemanship, bowmanship and, in general, upon the courage, pride, and military prowess of the Turks, although he cites (van Vloten, *Tria opuscula,* 47) exceptions, noting also that military prowess itself requires other virtues, including technical knowledge, cultural refinement and administrative competence (which al-Fatḥ, we may add, evidently possessed). Ṭabarī does not comment on the cultural pretensions and attainments of the Turks, but neither does he take interest in secular culture in general. This was the age of Ḥunayn b. Isḥāq and his school, translators of Greek science and philosophy into Syriac and Arabic, and yet not a whit of this is mentioned. Ṭabarī does not evince the interest that (the Shīʿite historians) Yaʿqūbī and Masʿūdī exhibit in these matters.

The Turks were apparently the primary cause of al-Mutawakkil's rather mysterious move to reestablish his capital in Damascus, which is described in our narrative. The transfer of the seat of power may be seen as an effort to elude their overwhelming influence. It failed for somewhat obscure reasons—an inclement climate and a mutiny by Turkish troops over pay allotments are alluded to.

In military affairs the Turkish officer class clearly proved itself absolutely indispensable. When revolts broke out in distant provinces, a local commander or an Arab officer from the central government would often be dispatched initially to suppress it. These first efforts were generally futile. As a result, a Turkish general—like Bughā the Elder or Bughā the Younger—was usually called upon to establish order and loyalty to the central government authorities. During the reign of al-Mutawakkil, wars at the periphery of the empire were particularly rampant—in Upper and Lower Egypt, Ādharbayjān, Armenia and Asia Minor—and these energetic Turkish commanders were kept very busy. These military expeditions to maintain government jurisdiction in the remotest regions betoken caliphal authority rather than weakness.

The power and influence of the Turkish praetorian guard invaded the Caliphal Palace itself. Al-Mutawakkil, as stated, was assassinated by a cabal of Turks, with his son al-Muntaṣir taking part in the conspiracy. The latter had cosseted the Turkish officers, much to his father's annoyance and discontent. Caliphs had been assassinated before: regicide was not uncommon in the annals of Islamic history. But never before had regicide taken the form of a patricide. This was indeed shocking and unprecedented. When al-Muntaṣir thereafter succeeded to the caliphate, tongues wagged and heads shook in dismay.

At this place in his narrative, Ṭabarī injects a personal note, a reminiscence from his youth: "I often heard people say," he states, "when the caliphate passed to al-Muntaṣir, that from the time he acceded to rule until his death he would live for six months, the extent of life of Shīrawayh b. Kisrā after he killed his father, and this was spread among the populace and notables alike."

Reading this volume the reader should bear in mind that the swirl of events described on its pages took place during Ṭabarī's lifetime. He was about three years old when al-Wāthiq came to power; about eight when al-Mutawakkil succeeded him; and about twenty-two when al-Muntaṣir supplanted his father. Thus, Ṭabarī lived through these events and had a personal connection with some of the action he describes. And if he did not experience events directly, he knew informants who did or who had their information from informants who did. His reports are often given in vivid and striking detail. Moreover, he knew some of the protagonists personally. For instance, he was tutor to the sons of the wazīr ʿUbaydallāh b. Yaḥyā (for ten dīnārs a month, it is said), and he studied with Yaʿqūb b. Ibrāhīm al-Dawraqī, who supported the revolt of Aḥmad b. Naṣr.

Ṭabarī is, then, writing "contemporary history." And although he did not experience the major events directly, he often reports the testimony of people who did—eyewitnesses and informants who were in touch with eyewitnesses. Thus, our volume, unlike previous ones, lacks *isnād*s (chains of transmission); it contains relatively few anonymous informants—individual and collective—and rather many identified as actual participants in the events reported. A brief survey of sources may illustrate this point and bring out others regarding Ṭabarī's sources and his striking attention to authentic evidence and detail. He was not an ingenuous annalist but a genuine historian who searched for witnesses and documentation. His informants are occasionally very simple people—a singer, a black slave, a Turkish woman, and the ladies of the harem. The most momentous occasion, in fact, the murder of the caliph al-Mutawakkil, is reported by the most ordinary people.

Close to the beginning of his narrative, Ṭabarī describes caliph al-Wāthiq's arrest of government officials and confiscation of their property. For this purpose, he summons the testimony of a certain ʿAzzūn b. ʿAbd al-ʿAzīz al-Anṣārī, who reports (p. 1331) a conversation with the caliph in his court. ʿAzzūn attests that he was in al-Wāthiq's company when a discussion took place on the reason for the fall of the famous Barmakids, namely, their inordinate control over Hārūn al-Rashīd and his purse. Al-Wāthiq reportedly drew a lesson from his ancestor's experience and went on to deflate his own government officials.

During the period of al-Wāthiq and al-Mutawakkil insurrections and disturbances—major and minor—erupted in the center of the empire, and serious revolts broke out in distant provinces. The central government's expedition against the Banū Sulaym tribal group in the Ḥijāz (pp. 1335ff.) is described by a spectator, Aḥmad b. Muḥammad b. Makhlad (pp. 1341, 1358), who marched with the commander Bughā al-Kabīr on his expedition to suppress the revolt. The campaign waged against the Banū Numayr tribal group in al-Yamāmah is reported (p. 1358) by the same Aḥmad b. Muḥammad b. Makhlad, who again rubbed shoulders with Bughā and observed the events. The account is expanded by another spectator, who described Bughā's initial rout at the hands of the tribesmen (p. 1360). The insurgence of the religious leader Aḥmad b. Naṣr in Baghdad is reported (1343) on the authority of "some(one) of our shaykhs." ("Some[one]" renders *baʿḍ,* which may mean "one" or "some.") The source knew a man who visited with Aḥmad, and thus he was able to name his associates.

The revolt of Muḥammad b. al-Baʿīth in Ādharbayjān is reported partly (p. 1379) by an eyewitness, Abū al-Agharr, son-in-law of Ibn al-Baʿīth, who surrendered to the government forces and was brought to Sāmarrā, as was Ibn al-Baʿīth after his capture. The poet ʿAlī b. al-Jahm was on hand (p. 1387) when Ibn al-Baʿīth was presented to al-Mutawakkil, and quotes Ibn al-Baʿīth's poetry recited on the occasion, noting the man's literary talent. Another (anonymous) spectator is also cited. Some accounts of prominent revolts are not assigned to a witness or authority, for instance, the revolt of the inhabitants of Armenia against Yūsuf b. Muḥammad (p. 1408) and its aftermath, namely, Bughā's defeat of Isḥāq b. Ismāʿīl in Tiflis and the burning of the town (p. 1414). As a sequel to Aḥmad b. Naṣr's rebellion, Ṭabarī relates how his body was taken down from the gallows in Sāmarrā and sent with his friends to Baghdad (p. 1412). In this case, Ṭabarī cites a report by the postmaster of Baghdad to the caliph concerning the behavior of the populace and a letter from al-Mutawakkil to Muḥammad b. ʿAbdallāh b. Ṭāhir instructing him how to behave toward the crowds. The revolt of the inhabitants of Ḥimṣ against their chief of security police is related without reliance on (named) informants (p. 1420). The revolt of the Bujah tribesmen in Africa is described without a source for the events, but only a reference to the fact that Yaʿqūb b. Ibrāhīm, chief of Egyptian Post and Intelligence, wrote to al-Mutawakkil about the uprising (p. 1429). The Byzantine raid on Damietta, a memorable event, is related (p. 1417) without authorities, as is most of Ṭabarī's (often fascinating) information concerning Byzantium. For instance, the Byzantine raid on Samosata is reported without an informant (p. 1447), as is the account telling that the inhabitants of Lulon prevented their (Byzantine) governor from entering the town. The caliph al-

Muntaṣir's dispatching Waṣīf the Turk on a summer expedition to Byzantine territory is reported without source (p. 1480), although Ṭabarī preserves a long letter of al-Mutawakkil to Muḥammad b. ʿAbdallāh b. Ṭāhir concerning Waṣīf's campaign. The letter, containing pious sentiments about the holy war, was written by the wazīr Aḥmad b. al-Khaṣīb (p. 1485).

The prisoner exchanges that took place in our period between the Muslims and Byzantines are reported in engrossing detail and on the basis of eyewitness testimony. The prisoner exchange of 231 (845–46) is related primarily (p. 1351) on the authority of Aḥmad b. Abī Qaḥṭabah, an associate of Khāqān al-Khādim, the Muslim representative at the exchange. In addition, Aḥmad b. al-Ḥārith's attestation is cited (p. 1353)—he had questioned Ibn Abī Qaḥṭabah and had also visited the Byzantine emperor. Muḥammad b. ʿAbdallāh al-Ṭarsūsī, a Muslim prisoner released by the Byzantines, describes (p. 1354) how the ransoming was actually carried out. A slightly different version (p. 1355) is offered by al-Sindī, *mawlā* of Ḥusayn al-Khādim, while Muḥammad b. Karīm, another Muslim prisoner, adds important details (p. 1356). The prisoner exchange of 246 (860) reported (p. 1449) by Naṣr b. al-Azhar al-Shīʿī ("the Shīʿite"), the emissary of al-Mutawakkil to the Byzantine emperor, contains a charming description of Naṣr's visit to Constantinople and his audience with the emperor Michael III. The Shīʿite ambassador relates (correctly) that Bardas, maternal uncle of the emperor, was in charge of the affairs of the realm.

The rather frequent occasions when officials—even high officers such as wazīrs—were arrested and tortured to death are communicated by our historian with great care and precision. The famous wazīr Ibn al-Zayyāt, for instance, was tortured in an iron maiden, an instrument of his own design. A certain al-Dandānī communicates details of the wazīr's discomfort (p. 1374) on the basis of the torturer's own authoritative account. Further detail is provided by Mubārak al-Maghribī, who was also close to the scene.

The murder of Turkish commander Ītākh is told by Ibrāhīm b. al-Mudabbir (p. 1384). Ibrāhīm says that he had gone out with the chief of security police, Isḥāq b. Ibrāhīm, to meet Ītākh on his return from Mecca, and he gives a careful eyewitness account of the process leading to the murder. A man named Turk, a *mawlā* of Isḥāq, reported (p. 1386) on a conversation he had with Ītākh while the latter was in prison.

The long account of Najāḥ's demise is related by (p. 1400) al-Ḥārith b. Abī Usāmah—historian and traditionist—and others. Al-Ḥārith gives details of the punishment (p. 1442).

Ṭabarī diligently preserves *literatim* documents concerning the events he portrays. While these documents, in a narrative setting, are not the same as archival records, their value is appreciable. Al-Mutawakkil's decree concerning Dhimmīs, for example, is presented (p. 1389) in its official form, and his letter concerning these regulations (p. 1390), sent to district governors, is also preserved. It was written by the secretary Ibrāhīm b. al-ʿAbbās al-Ṣūlī. Ṭabarī was presumably in touch with circles of government officials, like al-Ṣūlī, who were in a position to make this kind of material available to him. The letter of investiture by al-Mutawakkil to his three sons (p. 1396) was made in four copies, three for the sons and one for the library of the caliph. Ibrāhīm b. al-ʿAbbās al-Ṣūlī recited a poem about the investiture (p. 1402), and it appears that he also wrote these letters. To be sure, investiture documents were formularies and thus of less interest than some other records. Private correspondence of the caliph is also preserved, such as al-Mutawakkil's letter of condolence to Ṭāhir b. ʿAbdallāh b. Ṭāhir (p. 1406) on the occasion of the death of his relative, Muḥammad b. Ibrāhīm. The account of the abdication of the princes al-Muʿtazz and al-Mu'ayyad, brothers and heirs apparent of the caliph al-Muntaṣir (p. 1486), is accompanied by the text of the abdication (p. 1489), which had been read aloud by the wazīr Aḥmad b. al-Khaṣīb. And the text of the long letter, signed by Aḥmad, which al-Muntaṣir writes to Abū al-ʿAbbās Muḥammad b. ʿAbdallāh b. Ṭāhir, pertaining to the abdication, is also presented. It is a pity that al-Mutawakkil's letters to the provinces prohibiting debate concerning the Qur'ān and the like have not been preserved (p. 1412).

Ṭabarī evidently had access to police records and information of the Bureau of Post and Intelligence (*barīd*). For instance, the notice on the death of al-Ḥasan b. Sahl (p. 1406) is derived from a report of al-Qāsim b. Aḥmad al-Kūfī. Al-Qāsim was in the service of al-Fatḥ b. Khāqān, who was in charge of Intelligence in Sāmarrā and the Hārūnī Palace. Another source for this notice was Ibrāhīm b. ʿAṭā', supervisor of Intelligence in Sāmarrā. A day later, Ṭabarī writes, a dispatch came from the chief of Intelligence in Baghdad (Madīnat al-Salām) announcing the death of Muḥammad b. Isḥāq b. Ibrāhīm (p. 1407). In describing (p. 1424) the flogging of ʿĪsā b. Jaʿfar b. ʿĀṣim, a Shīʿite who had defamed Abū Bakr, ʿUmar, ʿĀ'ishah and Ḥafṣah, in the Sharqiyyah Quarter of Baghdad, Ṭabarī tells how the information about ʿĪsā got to the authorities. The postmaster of Baghdad conveyed details to the wazīr ʿUbaydallāh b. Yaḥyā, who transmitted them to al-Mutawakkil. The report of the judge in ʿĪsā's trial was evidentally included in the postmaster's communication. Ṭabarī preserves the detailed letter of the wazīr ʿUbaydallāh in response to the judge's report, spelling out exactly how Ibn ʿĀṣim should be punished. Ṭabarī's account of the appearance of Maḥmūd al-Naysabūrī in Sāmarrā (p. 1394), a man who claimed to be Dhū al-Qarnayn and a prophet, was probably based on police or intelligence records.

Ṭabarī relates accounts of the death of the three caliphs treated in this volume and the transition of power predominantly on the basis of participants' reports. The death of al-Wāthiq is based upon information (p. 1363) derived from a number of "our colleagues," but reports about al-Wāthiq's conduct prior to his death (p. 1365) are assigned to the poet al-Ḥusayn b. al-Ḍaḥḥāk, who was present. The transition from al-Wāthiq to al-Mutawakkil is told (p. 1368) by more than one authority, although Saʿīd the Younger reports (p. 1370) on Mutawakkil's relations with al-Wāthiq and events which preceded his being elevated to the caliphate. When al-Wāthiq placed his brother al-Mutawakkil in custody, Saʿīd was taken along with him.

The portrayal of the murder of al-Mutawakkil (p. 1452) is an outstanding narrative. On the fateful day, Ibn al-Ḥafṣī, the Singer, attended an audience with the caliph, and so was in a position to report (p. 1455) vital details. Ibn al-Ḥafṣī was accompanied by ʿAthʿath al-Aswad, a black slave, and a certain Naṣr b. Saʿīd al-Jahbadh ("the Government Banker"). He describes the caliph's cheer that day and his gloomy premonitions. Ibn al-Ḥafṣī also reports on caliph's ridicule of his son al-Muntaṣir one day earlier. Details of this treatment are assigned to Hārūn b. Muḥammad b. Sulaymān al-Hāshimī, who was informed by some(one) of the women in the curtained off area. Then Bunān, a page and close associate of al-Muntaṣir, gives a report concerning al-Muntaṣir and his reaction to news of the caliph's assassination, hinting that he was taken by surprise (p. 1459). The black slave ʿAthʿath is the main observer who actually describes the assassination. His own role in defending the caliph, he says, was limited by the circumstance that he was struck by a blow on his head. An alternate description by Zurqān, deputy of the chamberlain Zurāfah, has it that ʿAthʿath fled headlong. Zurqān does not depict al-Muntaṣir as having been surprised (p. 1462). According to another report, a Turkish woman delivered a note regarding what the group planned to al-Fatḥ b. Khāqān. Thus, he and the wazīr ʿUbaydallāh knew of the plot but were overconfident and did not prepare a defense.

Abū ʿUthmān b. Saʿīd the Younger (p. 1471) places full responsibility for the murder plot on al-Muntaṣir, but says that it was a defensive act. He tells of the aftermath of the assassination, al-Muntaṣir's announcement of the murder, and the oath of allegiance to him. Al-Muntaṣir's final illness is reported (pp. 1495ff.) by some(one) of the informants, with versions or details by Ibrāhīm b. Jaysh, Ibn Dihqānah, and Saʿīd b. Salāmah al-Naṣrānī.

Although Ṭabarī may have been affected by many of these events, personal accents are rarely audible. His primary task qua historian, as he conceived it, was to be a reliable transmitter of information, of tradition. He prefers just to give the facts without comment and fanfare. He does this conscientiously and with fine detail.

Although Ṭabarī's orientation was that of a Baghdadian, a supporter of the central government and a Sunnī Muslim (see Rosenthal, *History,* 134), these points of view are not intrusive in the narrative. If Ṭabarī held a personal position on Muʿtazilism, it is not reflected in our text. He tells dispassionately how al-Wāthiq made confession of the Muʿtazilite creed a condition for ransoming Muslim captives in the hands of the Byzantines—a policy that must have scandalized many Muslims. He describes with detachment the abortive revolt of Aḥmad b. Naṣr al-Khuzāʿī and his Traditionist supporters against al-Wāthiq and his pro-Muʿtazilah policy.

Indeed, his most intimate note is struck in connection with the death of Aḥmad b. Ḥanbal, which took place in 241 (856–57). Ṭabarī simply does not report it. His silence is eloquent. Ṭabarī's opinion of Ibn Ḥanbal was allegedly reserved, and his relations with the Ḥanbalī school were marred by strain and conflict. The discord brought on his head the wrath and abuse of Ḥanbalīs and their many supporters among the populace (who eventually, it is reported, refused him a decent burial). Ṭabarī's passing over the death of Ibn Ḥanbal in total silence was surely not accidental. Other historians took note. And Masʿūdī, duly registering the event, even recorded the popular belief that the world had dimmed on the occasion, mentioning a meteor storm that took place during that year. Ṭabarī reports the meteor storm, which he says was visible in Baghdad, but no more. Indeed, a later historian, Ibn Kathīr, noting Ṭabarī's silence, includes in his *Bidāyah* a long biographical encomium of Ibn Ḥanbal, almost by way of compensation. Ibn Kathīr observes that Ṭabarī did not in fact mark the death of *any* Ḥadīth scholars in 241, intimating that he went this far so as to avoid having to mention Ibn Ḥanbal.

We would not expect Ṭabarī, who was after all a pious Muslim, to have had much affection or sympathy for al-Mutawakkil. The caliph was a notorious tippler, sensual and ruthless, hardly an exemplar of God's vicegerent on earth. Ṭabarī recounts his cruel destruction of the wazīr Ibn al-Zayyāt and the Turk Ītākh, as well as his virtually systematic elimination of men who had helped his father found Sāmarrā. But he does not express a whit of criticism or bend his narrative to insinuate disapproval. On the contrary, he describes very movingly the scene when al-Mutawakkil returned to his palace after having viewed the populace that turned out to view him when he appeared in public. He took a handful of earth, Ṭabarī says, and sprinkled it upon his head, remarking, "I saw this great throng and, realizing that they were under my sway, I wished to humble myself before God." And Ṭabarī describes the assassination of al-Mutawakkil with some sympathy for the victim, it seems. When he notes that al-Mutawakkil's palace was demolished after his death, and that his canal project was never completed, this comes more as a statement of fact and sad comment on the frailty of grand human designs than as a judgment upon al-Mutawakkil himself.

Ṭabarī studiously transmits the material he received, preserving different points of view, various aspects and possibilities. He does not strain to give a consistent account; he strives to give conflicting versions a hearing. He is, of course, selective, as any historian must be. For example, he admits that he did not wish to relate unseemly things about al-Mutawakkil, which his son al-Muntaṣir had told a group of jurisprudents. And he states that he recounted the story of al-Mutawakkil's assassination only in part. Some things the reader is not supposed to know.

As for the rest, the reader must often draw his own conclusions and offer his own interpretation. Ṭabarī gives different accounts of the same event much as he offers diverse interpretations of a verse in his Qur'ān commentary. A true interpretation, a final authorized version, need not be spelled out. It may be elicited from the various traditions and reports that are handed down, if at all. The historian, like the Ḥadīth scholar, is primarily obliged to preserve traditions for posterity. Ṭabarī was no more disturbed by contradictions in rival accounts than was the Biblical narrator. The value of this technique was commented upon by I. Goldziher long ago: "[Ṭabarī's] method of ranking together, in an Oriental manner, the various and often contradictory items of his information, instead of amalgamating his inferences from them into a compact unity, is sure to diminish its literary value but for that it enhances its usefulness in the matter of sources, by having preserved many of them in their literal texts, without which we should be compelled to use unilateral information only" (Goldziher, "Historiography," *Gesammelte Schriften,* III, 361).

Ṭabarī occasionally nudges the reader gently to understand the significance of events. He demonstrates his brand of sophistication by clever juxtaposition of material and by subtle understatement. The final anecdote in our narrative is a trivial one, like the final "trivial item [that] concludes [his] majestic work that deals with events that are among the greatest in world history" (Franz Rosenthal, *The History of Ṭabarī,* Vol. XXXVIII, 207, n. 978). He tells that al-Muntaṣir had promised something to his most intimate confidant—Bunān. The caliph's untimely demise left Bunān empty-handed. Ṭabarī deftly records Bunān's lament: "He died . . . and did not give me anything."

The basis of the translation is the Leiden edition. The text from

III, 1329 to 1367 was edited by M. J. de Goeje. He used two manuscripts, referred to by sigla C and O.

C = Constantinople, Köprülü 1041.
O = Oxford Bodleiana Pocock 354.

The text from III, 1367 to 1501 was edited by V. G. Rosen on the basis of the same manuscripts.

There is a considerable lacuna in Ms. O from 1358.12 to 1410.8 (232–237 A.H.).

Professor Stephen Humphreys kindly shared with me information about pertinent manuscripts found in Istanbul.

Ms. Ahmet III 2929, vol. 12, preserved in the Topkapi Saray, a thirteenth century manuscript, is said by Humphreys to be "of superb quality and in very good condition." This manuscript was used by Muḥammad Abū al-Faḍl Ibrāhīm for his edition of the text that concerns us (Cairo edition, vol. IX). The manuscript preserves some valuable readings as well as material that does not appear in Mss. C and O. For example, it contains a long passage at III, 1497 that does not appear in the recension preserved by Mss. C and O. There is reason to believe that the passage properly belongs to the text and is not an addition. I have used Ibrāhīm's edition for variant readings from this manuscript, to which Ibrāhīm gives the siglum A.

Esad Efendi 2085, housed in the Süleymaniye, covers the years 224–251, which is pertinent to our material (the years 227–248). However, according to Humphreys, it is late (fourteenth century?) manuscript and does not add anything of importance, while abbreviating personal names and omitting some lines of poetry.

Ibrāhīm also used Ms. Dār al-Kutub 1602 Ta'rīkh, to which he gives the siglum D.

The notes in the Leiden edition begin to give variant readings at III, 1353.6 from Abū Bakr al-Ṣūlī's *Kitāb al-awrāq fī akhbār āl al-ʿAbbās wa-ashʿārihim*, preserved in a Leningrad manuscript that was identified and used in connection with Ṭabarī by V. R. Rosen. (See V. I. Belayev, in the *Proceedings of the 24th International Congress of Orientalists*, held in Munich in 1957.)

The *Kitāb al-awrāq* covers the years from 227 to 256, and is therefore most relevant to our text. I have cited al-Ṣūlī from the notes to the Leiden edition.

In addition, readings from al-ʿAynī's *ʿIqd al-jumān fī taʾrīkh ahl al-zamān* are cited (from manuscript) beginning at III, 1369.18 and will be cited from the Leiden edition apparatus.

Fragmenta historicorum arabicorum, II, ed. M. J. de Goeje, which covers the years 196 to 251, follows Ṭabarī's text very closely and is useful for variant readings, as is Ibn al-Athīr's *al-Kāmil fī al-taʾrīkh*.

Several friends and colleagues were generous with aid and advice, and I wish to express my gratitude to them. Professor Jacob Lassner was helpful in many ways. He clarified points of terminology, lent me books from his library in an hour of need, and edited the manuscript with professional skill. Professor Franz Rosenthal made many valuable improvements. A discussion with him was enlightening vis-à-vis the manuscript situation. This was then supplemented by Professor Stephen Humphreys, whose information about manuscripts in Istanbul is gratefully acknowledged here. My colleague Professor Joseph Sadan sat over the poetry with me and made many beneficial suggestions.

The project could not have been completed without the help and support of my wife, Roberta.

Joel L. Kraemer

Abbreviations

BSOAS: *Bulletin of the School of Oriental and African Studies*
EI[1]: *Encyclopaedia of Islam*, first edition
EI[2]: *Encyclopaedia of Islam*, new edition
GAS: *Geschichte des arabischen Schrifttums*. See Sezgin
IJMES: *International Journal of Middle East Studies*
JESHO: *Journal of the Economic and Social History of the Orient*
JSS: *Journal of Semitic Studies*
JRAS: *Journal of the Royal Asiatic Society*
RSO: *Rivista degli studi orientali*
SI: *Studia Islamica*
WZKM: *Wiener Zeitschrift für die Kunde des Morgenlandes*
ZDMG: *Zeitschrift der Deutschen Morgenländischen Gesellschaft*

Table 1. Genealogy of ʿAbbāsid Caliphs (A.D. Ninth Century)

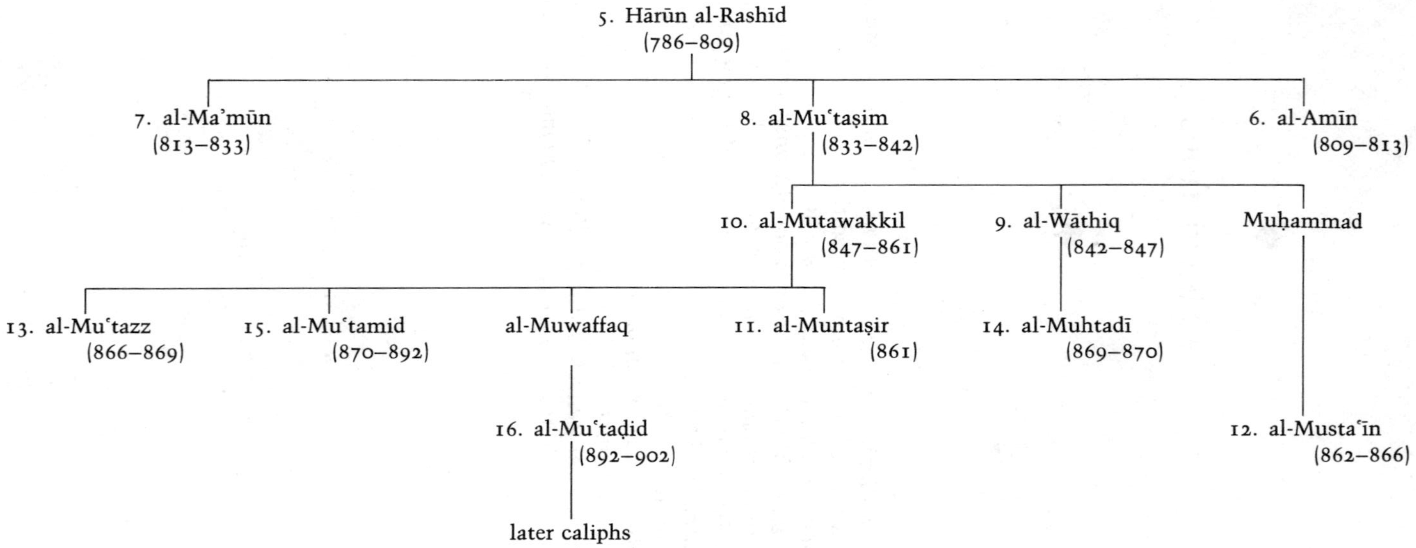

Table 2. Genealogy of the Khāqānids

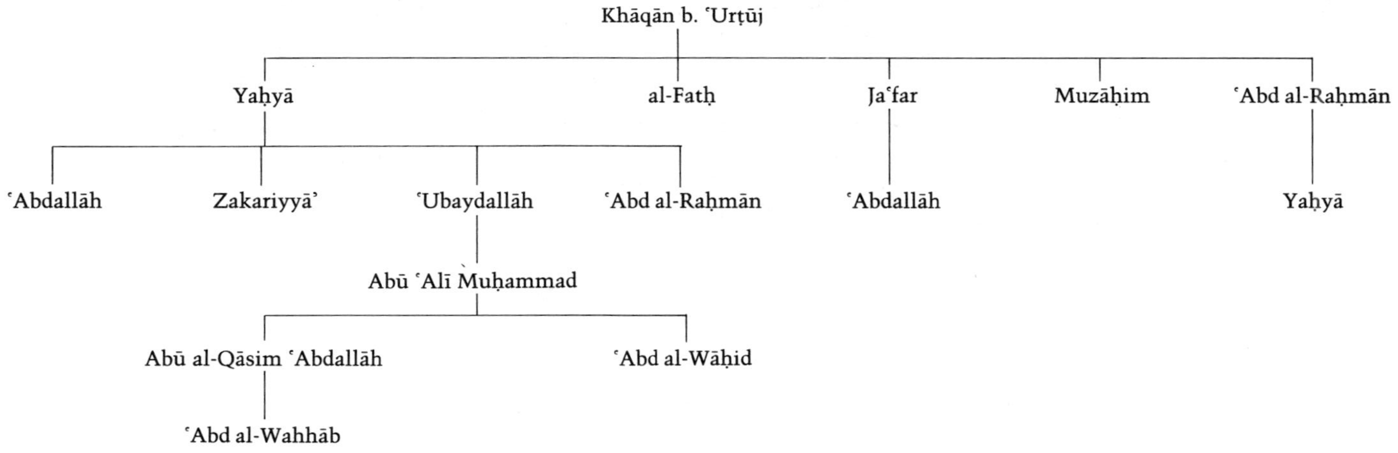

Table 3. Genealogy of the Ṭāhirids

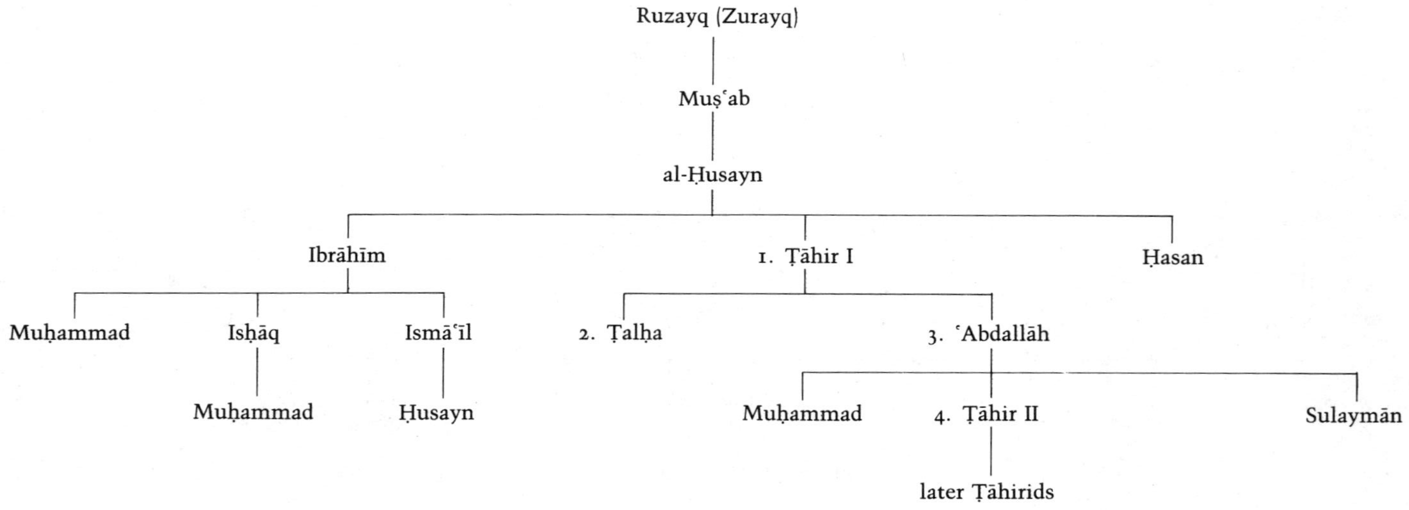

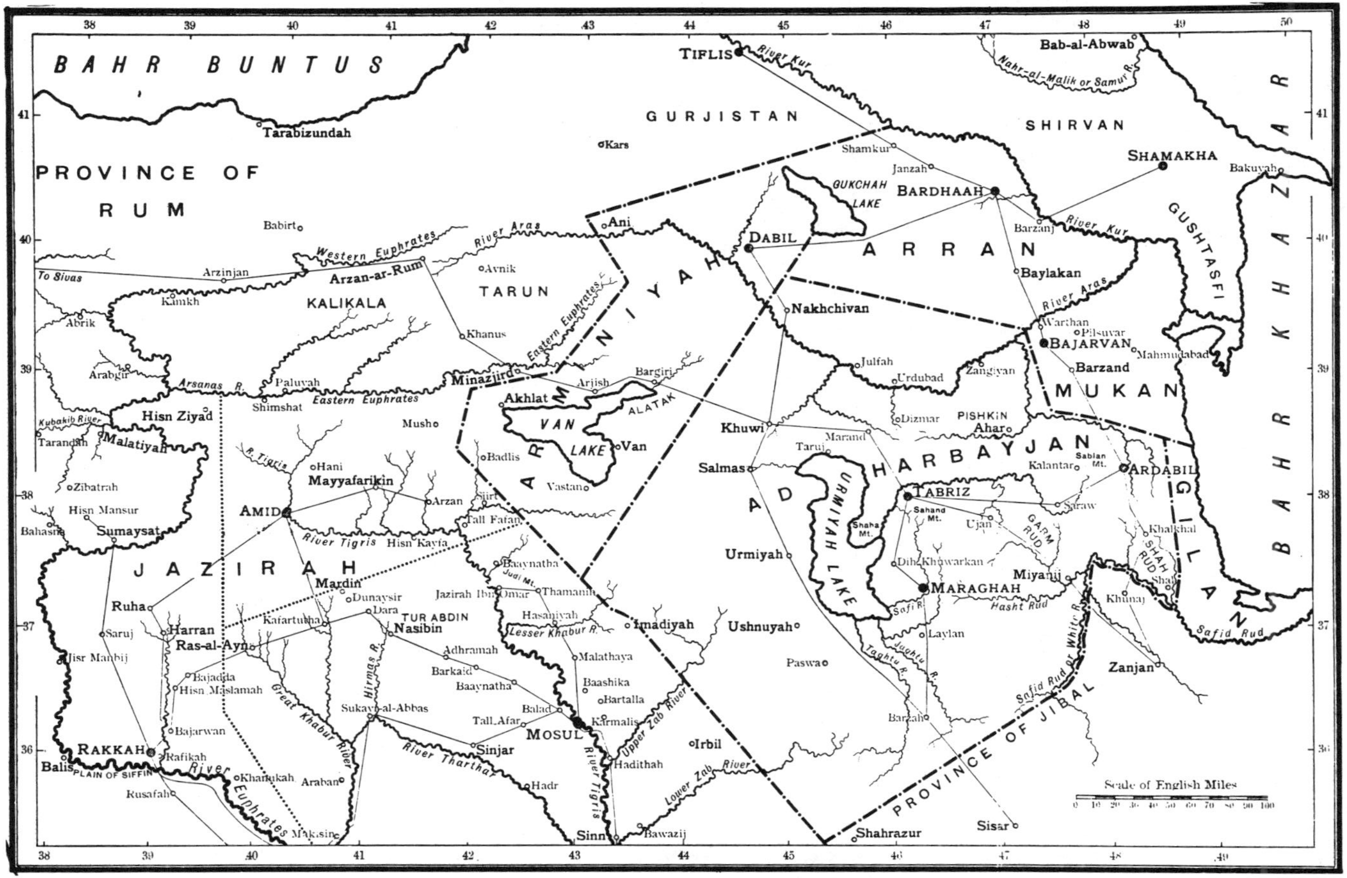

Map 1. Armenia, Ādharbayjān, Arrān. After G. Le Strange, *The Lands of the Eastern Caliphate*

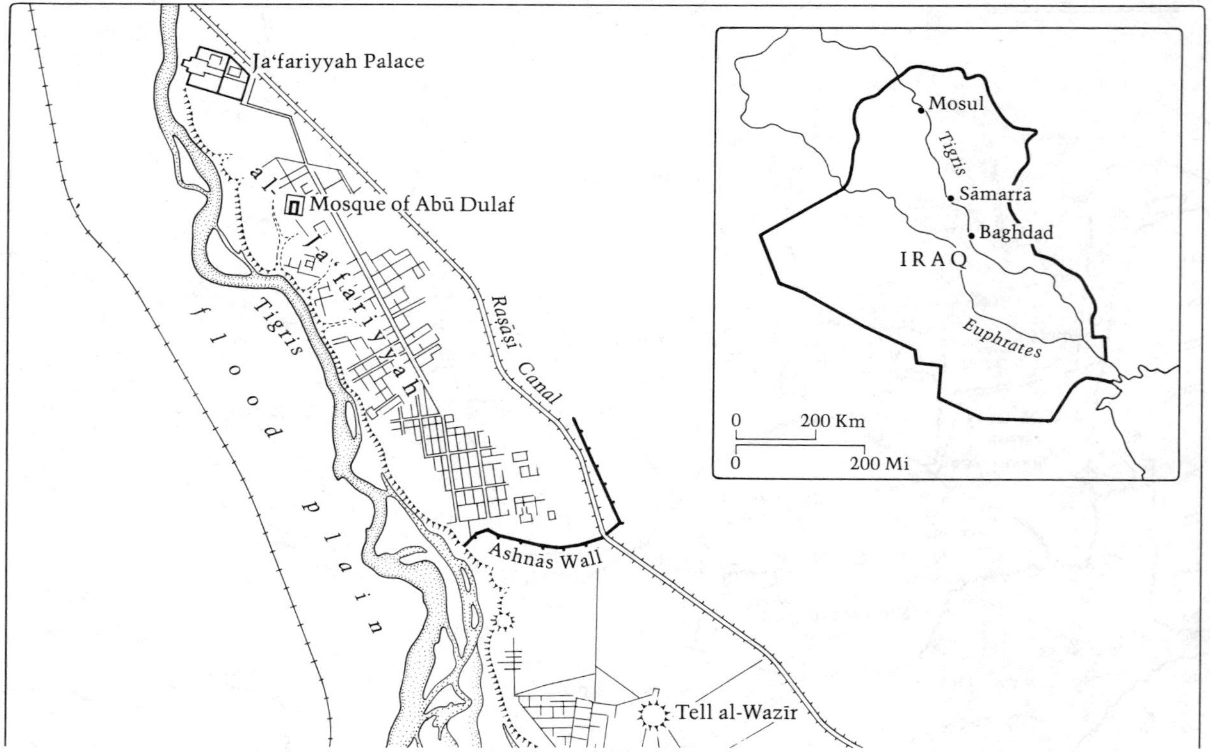

Ja'fariyyah Palace
Mosque of Abū Dulaf
al-Ja'fariyyah
Tigris
flood plain
Raṣāṣī Canal
Ashnās Wall
Tell al-Wazīr
Mosul
Tigris
Sāmarrā
Baghdad
IRAQ
Euphrates
0 200 Km
0 200 Mi

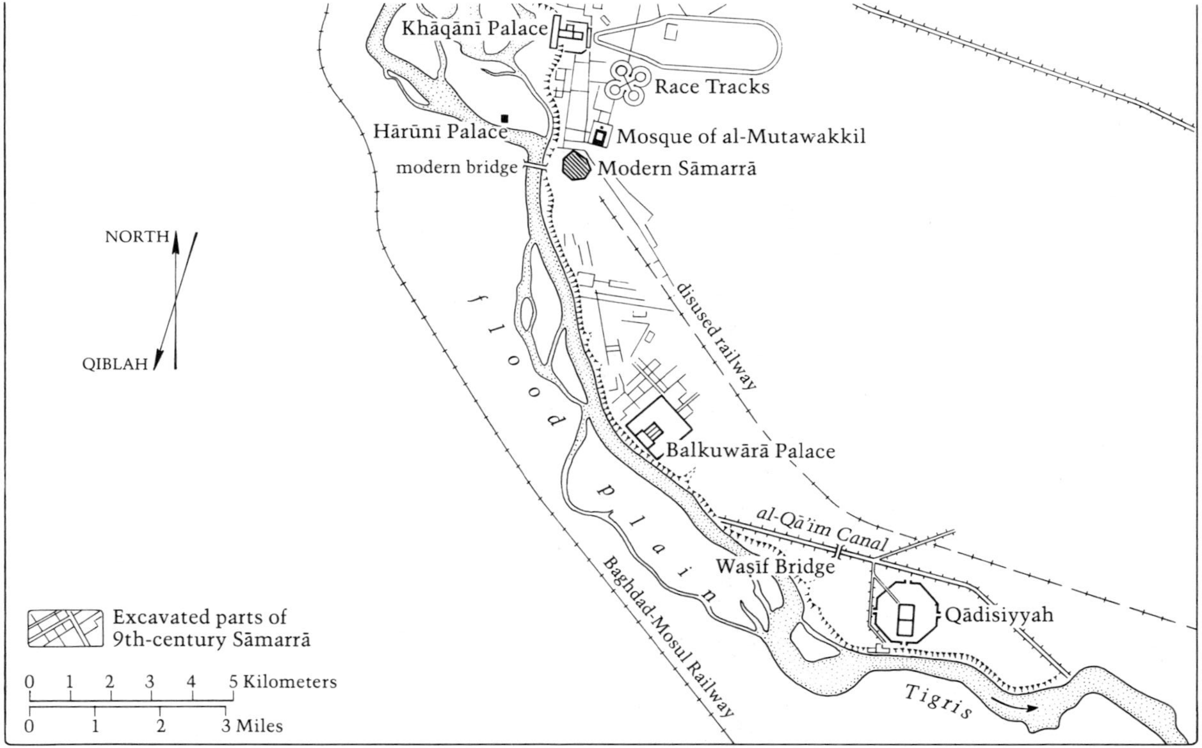

Map 2. Sāmarrā. Map drawn by George Colbert after E. Herzfeld, *Geschichte der Stadt Samarra.*

The Caliphate of Hārūn al-Wāthiq
Abū Jaʿfar

The Events of the Year 227 (cont'd)

(October 21, 841–October 9, 842)

On the day that al-Muʿtaṣim died, his son Hārūn al-Wāthiq b. Muḥammad al-Muʿtaṣim received the oath of allegiance. This was on Wednesday, 8 Rabīʿ I, 227 (December 26, 841).[1] He was given the teknonym Abū Jaʿfar. His mother was a Byzantine slave named Qarāṭīs.[2] [1329]

In this year the Byzantine emperor Theophilus died following a reign of twelve years. His wife Theodora reigned after him, her son Michael son of Theophilus being but a youth.[3]

---

1. 8 Rabīʿ I, 227, actually fell on a Monday. The day of the week given by Ṭabarī does not always correspond to the date mentioned.

2. An *umm (al-)walad* was a female slave, or concubine, who bore children to her master and was thus entitled to certain rights; see *EI*[1], s.v. Quite a few ʿAbbāsid caliphs were the offspring of slave mothers; See Thaʿālibī, *Laṭā'if*, 102. *Qarāṭīs* is the plural of *qirṭās* ("papyrus"), which is derived from Greek *khartēs*.

3. Theophilus, son of Michael II, reigned 829–42, and was succeeded by his son Michael III (842–67). They belonged to the Amorian, or Phrygian, dynasty. Michael ruled for fourteen years along with his mother, Theodora, and for ten years on his own. See Bury, *History*, Appendices, VI–VII, 465–71. According to C. Mango, "When Was Michael III Born?" his birth date was January 9/10, 840. Thus, he was two years old when his father died (January 20, 842), and he was crowned in the same year. See also below, n. 264.

[1330] Leading the pilgrimage this year was Ja'far b. al-Mu'taṣim.[4] Al-Wāthiq's mother accompanied him, intending to make the pilgrimage, but she died in al-Ḥīrah on 4 Dhū al-Qa'dah (August 16, 842) and was buried in al-Kūfah in the palace of Dāwūd b. 'Īsā.[5]

---

4. Ja'far b. al-Mu'taṣim, brother of al-Wāthiq, became the tenth caliph of the 'Abbāsid dynasty with the regnal title al-Mutawakkil; see below, pp. 61–191.

5. Dāwūd b. 'Īsā b. Mūsā b. Muḥammad, an 'Abbāsid prince, was son of the famous 'Īsā b. Mūsā, nephew of al-Saffāḥ and al-Manṣūr; see *EI*[2], s.v. He had been governor of Mecca and Medina at the time of al-Amīn and al-Ma'mūn. See Ṭabarī, III, 709; Zambaur, *Manuel*, 20, 25, 193; and see Ṭabarī, III, 981–83 (Bosworth, *Reunification*, 19–21).

The Events of the Year

228

(October 10, 842–September 29, 843)

Al-Wāthiq bestowed a crown upon Ashnās and adorned him with two ornamental belts in Ramaḍān (June–July 843).[6]

---

6. Abū Ja'far Ashnās (d. 230/844–45) was a Turkish army commander who had been purchased by al-Mu'taṣim and served during the caliphates of al-Mu'taṣim and al-Wāthiq; see Ṭabarī, III, 1236–67 (Marin, *Reign*, Index, 134); Ya'qūbī, Buldān, 256=Wiet, *Les pays*, 45. He led the vanguard in the battle of Amorium; III, 1236 (Marin, 61). Ya'qūbī, *Ta'rīkh*, II, 585, makes the ceremony mentioned here an act of appointment, said to be al-Wāthiq's first, and states that Ashnās was put in charge of territories from Sāmarrā (*min bābihi*) to the Maghrib. Ashnās was governor of Egypt from 219 (834–35) to 230 (844–45); Kindī, *Wulāh*, 192, 194–96; Abū al-Maḥāsin, *Nujūm*, II, 231, 255; Zambaur, *Manuel*, 27; see also Balādhurī, *Futūḥ*, 364. Abū Ja'far Ashnās al-Turkī is not to be confused with Abū Ja'far Ashnās, Turkish page of Abū Isḥāq b. al-Rashīd (Ṭabarī, III, 1017) or with Ashnās, a page of Ismā'īl b. Aḥmad; Ṭabarī, III, 2203 (see Rosenthal, *Return*, 95). Al-Mu'taṣim had presented his Turkish *mawlā*s with brocade, belts, and gold ornaments, attiring them differently from other soldiers; Mas'ūdī, *Murūj*, VII, 118; Ṭabarī, III, 1169 (Marin, 7, n. 62). Hilāl al-Ṣābī, *Rusūm*, 93 (tr. Salem, 75), gives a list of honorary insignia bestowed upon army commanders. Crowns were occasionally presented to wazīrs; Sourdel, *Vizirat*, 295, 677. For *wishāḥ* ("ornamental belt"), see Dozy, *Vêtements*, 429. Compare the Byzantine insignia, which included diplomas, gold-handled swords, tunics, and colored mantles and belts; Bury, *Imperial Administrative System*, pp. 22f.

In this year Abū al-Ḥasan al-Madāʾinī died in the residence of Isḥāq b. Ibrāhīm al-Mawṣilī.[7]

In this year the poet Abū Tammām Ḥabīb b. Aws al-Ṭāʾī died.[8]

Leading the pilgrimage this year was Sulaymān b. ʿAbdallāh b. Ṭāhir.[9]

In this year the prices on the Mecca Road were so high that a *raṭl* of bread cost a dirham, and a water skin cost forty dirhams.[10] At the Place for Standing (Mawqif) people were first stricken by intense heat and then by heavy rain mixed with hail, so that severe heat and cold afflicted them within a single hour.[11] The downpour at Minā on the Day of Sacrifice (Yawm al-Naḥr) was

7. Abū al-Ḥasan al-Madāʾinī, the famous historian and traditionist, was born in al-Baṣrah, then went to al-Madāʾin, and thereafter to Baghdad, where he joined Isḥāq b. Ibrāhīm al-Mawṣilī, who was his patron; *EI*[2], s.v. al-Madāʾinī; Sezgin, *GAS*, I, 314. The date of his death is variously given as 215, 225, 231, 234, 235. Sezgin accepts 235 (849–50). He does not mention the date given here. Isḥāq b. Ibrāhīm al-Mawṣilī, noted musician and composer, son of Ibrāhīm al-Mawṣilī, also a famous musician, died in Baghdad in 235 (849–50). He was a companion of the caliphs Hārūn al-Rashīd, al-Wāthiq, and al-Mutawakkil; see *EI*[2], s.v. Isḥāq b. Ibrāhīm al-Mawṣilī; Sezgin, *GAS*, I, 371; Farmer, *History*, 124–26 *et passim*.

8. Abū Tammām Ḥabīb b. Aws al-Ṭāʾī, famous poet and anthology editor, died in 231 (845–46), according to his son, or in 232 (846–47), according to other sources, although Ṭabarī and others dependent upon him give 228 (842–430); *EI*[2], s.v. Abū Tammām Ḥabīb b. Aws.

9. Sulaymān b. ʿAbdallāh b. Ṭāhir, d. 265 (878–79), belonged to the Ṭāhirid family/dynasty, which produced governors of Khurāsān and Baghdad in the third/ninth century, and participated actively in its cultural life; see Bosworth, "The Ṭāhirids and Arabic Culture." He became governor of Baghdad in 255 (868–69); see Ṭabarī, III, 1506, etc.; Zambaur, *Manuel*, 197–98. See Table 3.

10. A *raṭl* (<Gr. *litra*) in the early Islamic period in Mecca was = 1.5 kg.; in Medina in the tenth century = 625 gr.; Hinz, *Masse und Gewichte*, 28. The standard weight of a dirham (silver) was 3.125 grams; Hinz, 3. Nominally, 13 dirhams = 1 dīnār. To be sure, the exchange rate always varied. Ashtor, *Prix*, 49–50, notes that a similar quantity of bread in ninth- or tenth-century Iraq cost merely 1/20 dirham. See also *EI*[2], s.v. Dirham.

11. The Place for Standing is the place of halting, or station (*wuqūf*), in the valley of ʿArafāt, in front of Jabal al-Raḥmah, during the pilgrimage celebrations. The halting takes place on the ninth of Dhū al-Ḥijjah. The Day of Sacrifice, on the tenth of Dhū al-Ḥijjah, is commemorated by the sacrifice of animals, usually sheep and goats, at Minā. Jamrat al-ʿAqabah is a construction on the western side of the valley of Minā. The *jamrah* is stoned by pilgrims on the Day of Sacrifice prior to the festival sacrifice.

unprecedented. A mountain slide at Jamarat al-ʿAqabah killed a number of pilgrims.

Leading the pilgrimage this year was Muḥammad b. Dāwūd.[12]

---

12. The ʿAbbāsid Muḥammad b. Dāwūd b. ʿĪsā b. Mūsā, son of Dāwūd b. ʿĪsā b. Mūsā (above, n. 5), was governor of Mecca during the caliphates of al-Amīn and al-Ma'mūn (221–33/835–47), and led pilgrimages during the caliphates of al-Muʿtaṣim and al-Wāthiq. He was governor of Mecca, 221–33 (835/6–847/8); Ṭabarī, III, 982 (Bosworth, *Reunification*, 20–21); Marin, *Reign*, Index, 136; Zambaur, *Manuel*, 20.

The Events of the Year 229

(September 30, 843–September 17, 844)

In this year al-Wāthiq bi-llāh imprisoned and fined the secre-
[1331] taries.[13] He remanded Aḥmad b. Isrā'īl to Isḥāq b. Yaḥyā b. Muʿādh, captain of the guard, and ordered that Isḥāq flog him ten

13. A number of sources ascribe al-Wāthiq's measures against the secretaries to the initiative of his wazīr Ibn al-Zayyāt; see, for instance, Tanūkhī, *Faraj*, 102–03; Ibn al-Abbār, *Iʿtāb*, 136–37. And see Pseudo-Tanūkhī, *Mustajād*, 141. According to Tanūkhī, Ibn al-Zayyāt had the property of the secretaries confiscated in order to secure funds to maintain the Turks. Yaʿqūbī, *Ta'rīkh*, II, 587, stresses the misdemeanors of the secretaries who were punished. See also Ibn Kathīr, *Bidāyah*, X, 301. As the secretaries were often in the employ of the Turkish military commanders and officials, the steps taken against them may have been aimed indirectly against the Turks as well. See also Iṣfahānī, *Aghānī*, XXI, 162, where a version is given according to which al-Wāthiq's caliphate depended upon the Turks Ītākh (or Aytākh) and Ashnās and their secretaries Sulaymān b. Wahb and Aḥmad b. al-Khaṣīb. According to this version, Ibn al-Zayyāt wrote an ode, which he ascribed to a military figure, denouncing the excessive wealth and power of Sulaymān b. Wahb and Aḥmad b. al-Khaṣīb, and inciting al-Wāthiq to take action against the secretaries. This was done by comparing the caliph's relationship to the secretaries to that of Hārūn al-Rashīd and the Barmakids. This version, as far as the analogy is concerned, is consistent with the account given below. In our text, however, Ibn al-Zayyāt is not presented as an instigator of the attack, but only as hostile to Ibn Abī Du'ād and others in charge of the *maẓālim* courts.

lashes daily.[14] He is said to have flogged him about a thousand lashes, whereupon he handed over 80,000 dīnārs.[15] Al-Wāthiq seized 400,000 dīnārs from Sulaymān b. Wahb,[16] secretary of Ītākh;[17] 14,000 dīnārs from al-Ḥasan b. Wahb;[18] and he seized

14. Abū Ja'far Aḥmad b. Isrā'īl al-Anbārī was later wazīr of al-Mu'tazz; 252–55 (866/67–868/69). He was arrested and killed along with Abū Nūḥ 'Īsā b. Ibrāhīm in 255/869; see Ṭabarī, III, 1720–23; Tanūkhī, *Faraj*, 52, 142, 173–74; Sourdel, *Vizirat*, 281, 290, 295–99; Index, 753. Isḥāq b. Yaḥyā b. Mu'ādh was governor of Damascus in 191 (806–807) and of Egypt in 235 (849–50); Kindī, *Wulāh*, 198–99; Maqrīzī, *Mawā'iẓ*, I, 338; Ṭabarī, III, 1133 (Bosworth, *Reunification*, 223); Zambaur, *Manuel*, 27, 28. He became captain of the caliphal guard in 225 (839–40), replacing Afshīn; Ya'qūbī, *Ta'rīkh*, II, 590; Ṭabarī, III, 1303 (Marin, *Reign*, 110). For his grant in Sāmarrā, see Ya'qūbī, *Buldān*, 260, 272=Wiet, *Les pays*, 52, 79. His father had been a commander in the war against Bābak (Ṭabarī, III, 1233; Marin, *Reign*, 56). On Isḥāq b. Yaḥyā and his genealogy, see also Crone, *Slaves on Horses*, 183–84. For his brother Aḥmad, see below, n. 587.

15. The standard weight of a dīnār (gold) was 4.233 grams; see Hinz, *Masse und Gewichte*, 1; Goitein, *A Mediterranean Society*, I, 359. Goitein put the purchasing power of a dīnār in medieval Egypt (ca. A.D. 1000) at about a hundred U.S. dollars (1967). See also *EI*², s.v. Dīnār.

16. Sulaymān b. Wahb b. Sa'īd, of the Banū Wahb, served as secretary of al-Ma'mūn, then of Ītākh and Ashnās, and thereafter as wazīr under al-Muhtadī and al-Mu'tamid. He was arrested with Ītākh in 235 (849–50; Ṭabarī, III, 1386; below, p. 85). And he was arrested under al-Muwaffaq and died in prison in 271 (884–85) or 272 (885–86); Ṭabarī, III, 1315; Marin, *Reign*, 120, 123; Ibn al-Abbār, *I'tāb*, 138–44 (138, n. 2); Ibn al-Jawzī, *Muntaẓam*, V, 45; *EI*¹, s.v. Sulaimān b. Wahb; Amedroz, "Tales," 418ff.; Sourdel, *Vizirat*, 300–03, 310–13; Index, 782.

17. Ītāk (Aytākh), a Turkish army commander, had been a Khazar slave, a cook, who belonged to Sallām al-Abrash al-Khādim. He was purchased by al-Mu'taṣim from Sallām in 199 (814–15; below, 1383, p. 81 and n. 281). He served as chief of the security police at Sāmarrā under al-Mu'taṣim and al-Wāthiq, then as *ḥājib* (chamberlain) of al-Mutawakkil and commander of the royal guard. Ītākh was made governor of the Yemen by al-Wāthiq in 229 (843–44), and after the death of Ashnās, in 230 (844–45), he became governor of Egypt. According to Ya'qūbī, *Ta'rīkh*, II, 585, al-Wāthiq also made him governor of Khurāsān, Sind, and the sub-provinces of the Tigris. He was later imprisoned by al-Mutawakkil and killed in 235 (849–50); see below, pp. 83–86. See Ṭabarī, III, 1195; Marin, *Reign*, 27 and n. 162; Index, 135; Kindī, *Wulāh*, 196–97; Abū al-Maḥāsin, *Nujūm*, II, 255–56, 275; Zambaur, *Manuel*, 27; Sourdel, *Vizirat*, 264, n. 2; Index, 769.

18. Al-Ḥasan b. Wahb was a brother of the more influential Sulaymān b. Wahb; see the family tree of the Banū Wahb in Sourdel, *Vizirat*, 745; and see 256, n. 3; Index, 765. He was the main *aide de camp* of the wazīr Ibn al-Zayyāt. He was also a poet, and was in touch with Abū Tammām and al-Buḥturī; some of his poetry is preserved by Mas'ūdī, *Murūj*, VII, 149, 152, 167. See also Iṣfahānī, *Aghānī*, XX, 54–55; Ibn al-Abbār, *I'tāb*, 138, n. 2.

one million dīnārs from Aḥmad b. al-Khaṣīb and his secretaries;[19] 100,000 dīnārs from Ibrāhīm b. Rabāḥ and his secretaries;[20] 60,000 dīnārs from Najāḥ;[21] and 140,000 dīnārs from Abū al-Wazīr by way of settlement.[22] This was aside from what he seized from financial agents on the basis of their revenues.[23]

Muḥammad b. ʿAbd al-Malik[24] evinced hostility to Ibn Abī

---

19. Aḥmad b. al-Khaṣīb al-Jarjarā'ī belonged to the famous Jarjarā'ī family of government officials and wazīrs. His father had been governor of Egypt. Under al-Wāthiq he was secretary to Ashnās. He became wazīr to al-Muntaṣir (247–48/861–63) after the latter became caliph, having served formerly as his tutor and secretary. He was later exiled to Crete, in 248 (862–63), as a result of the enmity he aroused among Turkish military commanders in Sāmarrā, and he died there in 265/878–799; see Ṭabarī, III, 1262 (Marin, *Reign*, 80, and n. 379, 81); 1471–73 (below, p. 195ff.); 1508 (Saliba, 7); *Fragmenta*, 557; Ibn Abbār, *Iʿtāb* 136, 138–39, 141, 166; Sourdel, *Vizirat*, 287–89, Index, 753; *EI²*, s.v. al-Djardjarā'ī.

20. Ibrāhīm b. Rabāḥ b. Shabīb al-Jawharī was appointed over the Bureau of Expenditure under al-Ma'mūn. Under al-Wāthiq he was in charge of administration of the Bureau of Estates. His name is variously given as Ibn Rabāḥ or Ibn Riyāḥ (an orthographic variant—one diacritic marks the difference). See Dhahabī, *Mushtabih*, 302–03 (cited in Leiden edition, note *ad loc.*). Dhahabī notes that the name was common among *mawlā*s (cf., *inter alios*, Rabāḥ, who was a *mawlā* of Muḥammad). Ibrāhīm died in 245 (859–60); see below, 1440 (p. 158); Ibn al-Abbār, *Iʿtāb*, 145; Sourdel, *Vizirat*, 240, n. 1, 262–63, 733.

21. Abū al-Faḍl Najāḥ b. Salamah was secretary under al-Wāthiq, and later secretary and in charge of inspection of fiscal officials under ʿUbaydallāh b. Yaḥyā, wazīr of al-Mutawakkil. He was executed in 245 (859–60) after a falling out with ʿUbaydallāh; below, 1440 (p. 157); Yaʿqūbī, *Ta'rīkh*, II, 601; Ibn Khallikān, *Wafayāt*, III, 59, 61, 493; Sourdel, *Vizirat*, 262–63, 272, n. 5, 280, Index, 776.

22. Abū al-Wazīr Aḥmad b. Khālid was fiscal prefect of Egypt in 226 (840–41); Kindī, *Wulāh*, 449; Sourdel, *Vizirat*, 263, n. 2, citing A. Grohmann, *Arabic Papyri in the Egyptian Library* (Cairo, 1938), III, 143. Abū al-Wazīr was involved in purchasing land for the construction of Sāmarrā, along with Ibn al-Zayyāt, Ibn Abī Du'ād, and ʿUmar b. Faraj; Yaʿqūbī, *Buldān*, 258 = Wiet, *Les pays*, 48; Herzfeld, *Samarra*, 93. The four disappeared from public life at about the same time; Wiet, *Les pays*, 48, n. 5. And see Ṭabarī, III, 1179 (Marin, *Reign*, 15). He was briefly wazīr under al-Mutawakkil in 233 (847–48). In the same year he fell from grace, and was removed from office; below 1378 (p. 74); Yaʿqūbī, *Ta'rīkh*, II, 592; Masʿūdī, *Murūj*, VII, 148, 197; Zambaur, *Manuel*, 6; Amedroz, "Tales," 423; Sourdel, *Vizirat*, 257, n. 1, 263, 268, 271.

23. For *ʿumālāt* = "revenues," see Glossarium, CCCCLXXVII; Lane, *Lexicon*, 2159. Dozy, *Supplément*, II, 177, gives also "financial administration, district, province."

24. Muḥammad b. ʿAbd al-Malik b. al-Zayyāt, at first chancellery secretary at the end of the caliphate of al-Ma'mūn, served as wazīr under al-Muʿtaṣim, al-Wāthiq, and al-Mutawakkil. The name al-Zayyāt means oil merchant, a profession that his grandfather and father practiced. It is both a family name (Ibn al-Zayyāt) and a personal cognomen (al-Zayyāt), as he himself was apparently an oil

Du'ād[25] and others in charge of the *maẓālim* [courts], as a result of which they were investigated and imprisoned. Called upon to preside, Isḥāq b. Ibrāhīm[26] deliberated their case. They were publicly displayed and treated harshly.

The Reason for al-Wāthiq's Action against the Secretaries This Year

ʿAzzūn b. ʿAbd al-ʿAzīz al-Anṣārī[27] reportedly said: We were in al-Wāthiq's company one evening this year. He remarked, "I have no desire for wine tonight; let's have a discussion instead." He sat in his middle portico in the Hārūnī [Palace],[28] in the first edifice,

---

merchant. He was later arrested and his property confiscated under al-Mutawakkil in 232 (846–47), and he died in 233 (847–48); see Ṭabarī, III, 1183; Marin, *Reign*, 19 and n. 119, Index, 136; below, pp. 65ff.; Amedroz, "Tales," 416ff.; Sourdel, *Vizerat*, 252–69, esp. 254, n. 3; Index, 788; Sezgin, *GAS*, II, 576; *EI*², s.v. Ibn al-Zayyāt.

25. Abū ʿAbdallāh Aḥmad b. Abī Du'ād, the famous judge, who served under the caliphs al-Ma'mūn and al-Muʿtaṣim (who appointed him chief judge) and al-Wāthiq, was a leading Muʿtazilite. He played an active role in the *miḥnah* (inquisition) and in the interrogation of Aḥmad b. Ḥanbal, and had considerable influence upon al-Wāthiq, a strong upholder of Muʿtazilite doctrine. He and Ibn al-Zayyāt were staunch rivals. He died in 240 (854–55); below, 1421 (p. 131); and see earlier, Ṭabarī, III, 1139. See also Sourdel, *Vizirat*, 258–60; Index, 753; *EI*², s.v. Aḥmad b. Abī Du'ād.

26. The Ṭāhirid Isḥāq b. Ibrāhīm b. Muṣʿab, governor of Baghdad under al-Ma'mūn, was appointed chief of security police (*ṣāḥib al-shurṭah*) of Baghdad by al-Muʿtaṣim, and served thereafter during the reigns of al-Wāthiq and al-Mutawakkil. When al-Muʿtaṣim went to Sāmarrā, Isḥāq served as his deputy in Baghdad. He participated actively in the inquisition of al-Ma'mūn. Isḥāq's father Ibrāhīm was a brother of Ṭāhir I, and he was therefore occasionally called al-Ṭāhirī. He died in 235 (849–50). See Bosworth, *Reunification*, Index, 274; Marin, *Reign*, Index, 135; below 1403 (p. 105); Ibn Ṭayfūr, *Baghdād* 18–19, 37–38; Shābushtī, Diyārāt, Index, 437; Zambaur, *Manuel*, 44, 197–98; Patton, *Aḥmed ibn Ḥanbal*, 70ff. *et passim*; Sourdel, *Vizirat*, 260, n. 4, 265–66; Index, 769 (234, n. 1, is not relevant); Bosworth, "The Ṭāhirids and Arabic Culture," 46, 67–68; *idem*, "The Ṭāhirids and Ṣaffarids," 90ff., 101. See Table 3.

27. ʿAzzūn b. ʿAbd al-ʿAzīz al-Anṣārī's name is given by Ibn al-Athīr, *Kāmil*, VII, 6, as ʿArūd (with variants). Ṭabarī Ms. C has ʿAzūr; Ms. O reads ʿArūz. Shābushtī, *Diyārāt*, 56, says that he was a boon campanion of al-Muʿtaṣim and al-Wāthiq. Ṭabarī, III, 1503 (Saliba, 4) mentions a street named for Zurāfah (or Zarāfah) and ʿAzzūn; see Herzfeld, *Samarra*, 119, n. 1 (*dār* ʿAzzūn). ʿAzzūn's account of the reason for the fall of the Barmakids is not noted by Ṭabarī in his description of this episode, where he lists different versions.

28. The Hārūnī was a palace complex that al-Wāthiq constructed in Sāmarrā and named after himself. His full name was Abū Jaʿfar b. al-Muʿtaṣim Hārūn al-

[1332] which Ibrāhīm b. Rabāḥ had erected. Over one of the sections of this portico was a very high dome that was white as an egg, except for what appears[29] to be a cubit-thick[30] belt around the middle, which was teak plated with lapis lazuli and gold. It was called the Dome of the Girdle, and the portico was called the Portico of the Dome of the Girdle.

ʿAzzūn said: We conversed the whole evening. Al-Wāthiq inquired, "Who among you knows the reason why my ancestor [Hārūn] al-Rashīd assailed the Barmakids and removed them from favor (*niʿmah*)?"[31]

ʿAzzūn said that he responded: By God, I'll tell you, Commander of the Faithful. The reason for this was that a slave girl (*jāriyah*) belonging to ʿAwn al-Khayyāṭ[32] was mentioned to al-Rashīd, whereupon he sent for her and had her presented. Pleased by her beauty, intelligence, and cultural refinement, he asked ʿAwn what price he proposed.

ʿAwn replied, "Commander of the Faithful, the issue of her price is well-known. I have taken an irrevocable oath to free her and all my slaves and to donate my property to charity. I summoned legal representatives to witness that I would not set her price any lower than 100,000 dīnārs, and I cannot circumvent this

---

Wāthiq. He was named Hārūn after his grandfather Hārūn al-Rashīd. Al-Wāthiq's successor, al-Mutawakkil, also dwelled in the Hārūnī. (Another Hārūnī Palace, named for Hārūn al-Rashīd, existed in Baghdad.) The Hārūnī was situated near the Dār al-ʿĀmmah (Public Audience Hall), south of the caliph's residence on the Tigris River. See Yaʿqūbī, *Buldān*, 264–65 = Wiet, *Les pays* 57–58; *Taʾrīkh*, II, 590; Balādhurī, *Futūḥ*, 364; Yaqut, *Muʿjam*, IV, 946; Herzfeld, *Samarra*, 95, 104, 118–19. See also *EI*¹, s.v. Sāmarrā; Le Strange, *Lands*, 154; Creswell, *Early Muslim Architecture*, II, 228, 254. and Rogers, "Samarra," 148–49; al-ʿAmid, *Architecture*, 16 (Fig. 1), 134.

29. The words "what appears" render *fīmā tarā al-ʿayn*; see Glossarium, CCCLXXXIV.

30. The *dhirāʿ* (cubit) was of various lengths (ca. 50 cm.), depending upon time and place; see Hinz, *Masse und Gewichte*, 55ff.

31. The term *niʿmah* relates to "benefit" and "ties created by benefit"; see Mottahedeh, *Loyalty*, 73–79, 82–84. The decline of the Barmakids (Ṭabarī, III, 674ff.) has been a subject of speculation from their time until today; *EI*², s.v. ʿAbbāsa, and s.v. Barāmika. The account given here traces their fall to the pecuniary, or perhaps rather circumspect, behavior of Yaḥyā b. Khālid, and implies an inordinate degree of control over the caliph and his purse. See also Ibn Khaldūn, *Muqaddimah*, I, 28ff., especially p. 30.

32. Ibn al-Athīr, *Kāmil*, VII, 6–7, gives the name as ʿUdūl al-Khayyāṭ (with the variant Ghawn, which differs from ʿAwn by a single diacritical point).

by any legal subterfuge. This is her legal status." The Commander of the Faithful responded that he was ready to purchase her for 100,000 dīnārs.

He then wrote to Yaḥyā b. Khālid[33] informing him about the slave girl and ordering Yaḥyā to send him 100,000 dīnārs. Yaḥyā commented that this was a bad precedent, because if al-Rashīd dared request 100,000 dīnārs to pay for a single slave girl, he was liable to go on requiring commensurate sums of money. Thus, Yaḥyā wrote back informing him that he could not do it. Al-Rashīd then became angry with Yaḥyā and exclaimed, "Aren't there 100,000 dīnārs in the treasury?" And he reiterated to Yaḥyā that he had to have the money. [1333]

Yaḥyā gave word that the sum should be drawn up in dirhams so that upon seeing it al-Rashīd would consider it excessive and perhaps return it. Yaḥyā then sent the money in dirhams, stating that it was the equivalent of 100,000 dīnārs. He ordered that the dirhams be placed in al-Rashīd's portico,[34] which he passed through on the way to the place of the ritual ablution for the noon prayer.

ʿAzzūn said: Al-Rashīd went out around this time and came upon a pile of coins. When he asked what it was, he was told that it was the payment for the slave girl, and that as dīnārs were unavailable an equivalent sum of dirhams was delivered. Al-Rashīd thought that this was excessive. He summoned one of his servants (*khādim*)[35] and asked him to take the money into his custody and to make a treasury (*bayt māl*) for him so that he

33. The famous Yaḥyā b. Khālid al-Barmakī, former governor of Ādharbayjān, became tutor and secretary to al-Rashīd while he was still a prince, and ascended to power alongside him. When al-Rashīd became caliph, Yaḥyā was appointed wazīr, with his sons al-Faḍl and Jaʿfar b. Yaḥyā serving in the government with him. He served as wazīr from 170 (786–87) to 187 (802–03); *EI*[1], s.v. Yaḥyā b. Khālid; *EI*[2], s.v. Barāmika.

34. The portico was presumably in the Khuld Palace (Qaṣr al-Khuld), where al-Rashīd usually stayed when he was in Baghdad.

35. The word *khādim* may mean "eunuch," and this is the primary and virtually universal meaning for the term as suggested by Prof. David Ayalon in many publications. The evidence adduced by Ayalon points in this direction, but as not every *khādim* was a eunuch, I have left the cognomen untranslated in the case of high-ranking officers (e.g. Ītākh al-Khādim) and have otherwise rendered the noun *khādim* as "servant." Whether the servant (or: slave) was a eunuch or not I therefore leave undetermined.

might store there what he wished. He called it the Treasury of the Bride (Bayt Māl al-ʿArūs). And he ordered that the slave girl be returned to ʿAwn.

He then began to investigate the treasury and discovered that the Barmakids had squandered it. Consequently, he began to suspect them but held back.

It was al-Rashīd's custom to send for companions and for a number of cultured men so as to pass the evening in conversation and repast with them. Among the attendants was a man renowned for his cultural refinement, known by his teknonym, Abū al-ʿŪd.[36] He was among those in attendance one night, and his conversation impressed al-Rashīd. He thereupon ordered one of his servants (*khādim*) to go to Yaḥyā b. Khālid when the latter arose in the morning and order Yaḥyā to give him 30,000 dirhams. He did so.

Yaḥyā said to Abū al-ʿŪd, "I'll do it, but we have no ready cash today. Tomorrow, when money is available, we'll give it to you, God willing." He then put him off to the point of tediousness. Abū al-ʿŪd began to angle for an opportunity to incite al-Rashīd against the Barmakids. Al-Rashīd's suspicions concerning their conduct had become public knowledge.

Abū al-ʿŪd visited al-Rashīd one night, and as they conversed,
[1334] Abū al-ʿŪd kept turning the conversation deftly until he got al-Rashīd to the saying of ʿUmar b. Abī Rabīʿah:[37]

Hind promised and it wasn't her custom to promise.
Would that Hind had fulfilled to us her promise.

Would that she had acted independently for once!
It is the weakling who does not act independently.

Al-Rashīd commented, "Yes, by God, only the weakling does not act independently." He went on this way until the session ended.

Yaḥyā had procured one of al-Rashīd's servants (*khādim*) to provide him with information about the caliph. When Yaḥyā

36. Abū al-ʿŪd is a nickname, *ʿūd* meaning "lute."

37. For the verses by ʿUmar b. Abī Rabīʿah, in slightly different form, see his *Dīwān*, ed. P. Schwarz, 115; ed. Beirut, 101–02; *Sharḥ Dīwān ʿUmar b. Abī Rabīʿah* of al-Makhzūmī, 312–13; Arberry, *Arabic Poetry*, 40/41. Hind, often mentioned by the poet, is Hind bt. al-Ḥārith of the Banū Murrah.

called upon al-Rashīd in the morning, al-Rashīd proclaimed upon seeing him, "I wanted to send you a poem yesterday that someone in my company recited to me, but then I refrained from disturbing you." He then recited the two verses to him. Yaḥyā remarked, "How beautiful they are, O Commander of the Faithful!"—wondering what it was that he intended. Having departed, Yaḥyā sent a message to this servant, inquiring about the recitation of the poem. The servant replied that Abū al-ʿŪd had recited it.

The wazīr Yaḥyā thereupon summoned Abū al-ʿŪd and said to him, "We withheld your money, but now we have funds ready at hand." He then told one of his servants (*khadam*), "Go and give him 30,000 dirhams from the treasury of the Commander of the Faithful, and give him 20,000 dirhams from my own funds for our having put him off. Go also to al-Faḍl and Jaʿfar and tell them, 'This man deserves to be treated well. The Commander of the Faithful ordered that he be given money but I put him off. When the funds were available I ordered that they be handed over. I also gave him a donation from my own resources. I should like you to give him a contribution as well.'" When they asked how much the contribution should be, Yaḥyā replied: "20,000 dirhams." Whereupon each one gave him 20,000 dirhams, and Abū al-ʿŪd left for his residence with all this money. [1335]

Al-Rashīd applied himself in earnest to the matter of the Barmakids until he eventually assailed them and removed them from favor (*niʿmah*). He had Jaʿfar killed as he did with all the rest.

Al-Wāthiq remarked, "By God, my ancestor was right. The weakling does not act independently." And he launched into a discussion of disloyalty and what its perpetrators deserve.

ʿAzzūn said: "I reckon that he will assault his secretaries." In less than a week he did so. He seized Ibrāhīm b. Rabāḥ, Sulaymān b. Wahb, Abū al-Wazīr, Aḥmad b. al-Khaṣīb and the whole lot of them.

ʿAzzūn said: Al-Wāthiq ordered that Sulaymān b. Wahb, secretary of Ītākh, be imprisoned, and he confiscated 200,000 dirhams from him, or according to another version—dīnārs.[38] Sulaymān

---

38. According to the account above (p. 9), 400,000 dīnārs were confiscated from Sulaymān b. Wahb. A description of Sulaymān b. Wahb's arrest and torture (by Ibn al-Zayyāt) appears in Pseudo-Tanūkhī, *Mustajād*, 85. See also Iṣfahānī, *Aghānī*, XXI, 162.

was fettered and dressed in a woolen sailor's tunic,[39] whereupon he handed over 100,000 dirhams, and requested that the balance be deferred for twenty months. Al-Wāthiq acceded to this. He ordered that he be set free and returned to the secretariat of Ītākh, authorizing him to don black [garments].[40]

In this year Shār Bāmiyān governed the Yemen for Ītākh.[41] He departed for there in Rabīʿ II (December 28, 842–January 25, 843).

In this year Muḥammad b. Ṣāliḥ b. al-ʿAbbās became governor of Medina.[42]

Leading the pilgrimage this year was Muḥammad b. Dāwūd.

---

39. The *midraʿah* was a woolen sleeveless tunic worn by slaves and the lower classes; Dozy, *Vêtements,* 181; *EI*[2], s.v. Libās.

40. Dignitaries in the ʿAbbāsid court customarily wore black garments, and wearing black thus signified that an official was in caliphal service; see, e.g., Hilāl al-Ṣābi', *Rusūm,* 91 (tr. Salem, 74); Ahsan, *Social Life,* 51–52.

41. Harthamah Shār Bāmiyān, an associate of Ītākh, is mentioned also below, 1373 (p. 69). Ibn al-ʿAdīm, *Ta'rīkh Ḥalab,* I, 71–72, gives a list of the places he governed. See Zambaur, *Manuel,* 114. *Shēr (Shīr* or *Shār)* is a Persian word meaning "king," and was the title of the rulers of Bāmiyān, a city in the Hindu Kush. In the ʿAbbāsid period descendants of the Bāmiyān dynasty served in the ʿAbbāsid court; see *EI*[2], s.v. Bāmiyān.

42. For Muḥammad b. Ṣāliḥ b. al-ʿAbbās b. Muḥammad b. ʿAlī al-Hāshimī, ʿAlid governor of Medina, see also below, 1336, 1341 (pp. 18 and 25); Zambaur, *Manuel,* 25. Al-Wāthiq tended to favor ʿAlids.

The Events of the Year 230

(September 18, 844–September 6, 845)

One of the events was al-Wāthiq's dispatching Bughā al-Kabīr[43] to the Arab tribesmen who had created havoc in Medina and its environs.

An Account of the Dispatch of Bughā al-Kabīr to the Tribesmen

It is reported that the trouble began when the Banū Sulaym[44] behaved insolently toward the people around Medina. Whenever [1336]

43. Bughā al-Kabīr (the Elder) was a military commander of Turkish descent (Bughā = "bull") active during the reigns of al-Muʿtaṣim, al-Wāthiq, and al-Mutawakkil. He died in 248 (862–63); Ṭabarī, III, 1174; Marin, *Reign*, 11 and n. 91; Index, 134; *EI*², s.v. Bughā al-Kabīr. Another Bughā, called al-Ṣaghīr ("the Younger"), makes his appearance below.

44. The Banū Sulaym were a northern tribe, descendants of Qays ʿAylān, very powerful east of the Medina-Mecca line. They consisted of both sedentary and nomadic (or seminomadic) elements; Caskel, *Das genealogische Werk*, I, 92; II, 517; *Jamharah*, 120a; *EI*¹, s.v. Sulaim. See also Tanūkhī, *Taʾrīkh*, II, 586–87. Dr. Michael Lecker has kindly answered a number of my queries about the Banū Sulaym.

the Banū Sulaym came to a market in the Ḥijāz they would fix its prices according to their whim. This matter went so far that they attacked members of the Banū Kinānah[45] and Bāhilah[46] in al-Jār,[47] injuring some and killing others. This was in Jumādā II, 230 (February 13–March 13, 845). Their chief was ʿUzayzah b. Qaṭṭāb al-Sulamī. As a result, Muḥammad b. Ṣāliḥ b. al-ʿAbbās al-Hāshimī, then governor of Medina—the city of the Messenger—dispatched Ḥammād b. Jarīr al-Ṭabarī against them.

Al-Wāthiq had sent Ḥammād to Medina along with an armed party[48] consisting of 200 Shākiriyyah horsemen to prevent the Arab tribesmen from infiltrating into the town. Ḥammād set out against them with a contingent of regular army troops and with volunteers from the Quraysh, the Anṣār and their clients, along with residents of Medina. While Ḥammād was heading for the Banū Sulaym, their scouts encountered him. The Banū Sulaym were reluctant to fight, but Ḥammād b. Jarīr gave orders to do combat with them. He attacked them at a place called al-Ruwaythah, three days march from Medina.[49]

The Banū Sulaym and their reinforcements then came from the desert, 650 altogether, along with all who joined them from those Banū ʿAwf[50] belonging to the Banū Sulaym, including Ashhab b.

---

45. The Banū Kinānah b. Khuzaymah were related to Asad. They lived in the mountains north and northeast of Mecca and on the coast. Many were indigent and tended to indulge in plunder and warfare. See Caskel, *Das genealogische Werk,* I, 3; II, 371; *Jamharah,* 4b; *EI*², s.v. Kināna b. K͟huzayma.

46. The Bāhilah were a sedentary and semisedentary tribe in middle Arabia. Their center was Sūd (Sawd). They occupied both sides of the road from Riyāḍ to Mecca; Caskel, *Das genealogische Werk,* I, 92, 137; II, 220; *EI*², s.v.

47. Text: bi-l-Jār; Ms. C and Cairo ed.: bi-l-Ḥijāz (and cf. Ibn al-Athīr, Kāmil, VII, 8). Jār, half on the mainland and half on an island, was the port of Medina; see *EI*², s.v. al-D͟jār. "Al-Jār" is the *lectio difficilior*; and "Ḥijāz" may be influenced by the occurence of this word two lines above.

48. Literally, "as an armed party" (*maslaḥatan*). For the term, see Glossarium, CCXCCV; Lane, *Lexicon,* 1403. It may also refer to one person. The function of a *maslaḥah* is to occupy an observation point, to go before an army and warn of an enemy approach, to look for spies, and to prevent enemies from entering Muslim territory. It is, then, a reconnaissance patrol or scouting unit.

49. Al-Ruwaythah, diminutive of al-Rawthah, was a station for watering animals on the pilgrimage route between Mecca and Medina in the territory of the Banū Sulaym; Yāqūt, *Muʿjam,* II, 875; Hamdānī, *Ṣifat Jazīrat al-ʿArab,* 171, 180, 181, 184; Bakrī, *Muʿjam,* II, 685, x.v. Ruwaythah.

50. The Banū ʿAwf were a northern tribe, descendants of Sulaym; Caskel, *Das genealogische Werk,* I, 265; II, 212; *Jamharah,* 205.

Duwaykil b. Yaḥyā b. Ḥimyar al-ʿAwfī, his paternal uncle Salamah b. Yaḥyā, and ʿUzayzah b. Qaṭṭāb al-Labīdī of the Banū Labīd b. Sulaym. These were their commanders. Their cavalry[51] consisted of 150 horses. Ḥammād and his forces fought them. Then 500 of their reinforcements[52] joined the Banū Sulaym, having come from a place where their bedouins[53] were located, called the heights of al-Ruwaythah, four *mīl* (eight km.)[54] from the battlefield. They fought fiercely. The blacks (*sūdān*) of Medina[55] were thoroughly routed, whereas Ḥammād and his entire force, along with the Quraysh and the Anṣār, stood firm. They engaged in battle until Ḥammād and his entire force were killed, along with a substantial number of the Quraysh and Anṣār who had stood firm. The Banū Sulaym gained possession of sheep and oxen, weapons, and clothing. [1337]

The matter of the Banū Sulaym now became grave. The villages and watering places that lay between them and Mecca and Medina were looted to the point that no one could travel along this route. In addition, the bedouin tribes that were allied to them interdicted the roads.[56]

Consequently, al-Wāthiq sent Bughā the Elder, Abū Mūsā the Turk, against them, along with the Shākiriyyah, the Turks, and the Maghāribah. Bughā proceeded at their head to Ḥarrat Banī Sulaym,[57] with Ṭardūsh the Turk at his vanguard, in Shaʿbān, 230 (April 13–May 11, 845), a few days before the end of the month. He encountered them at one of the watering places of the Ḥarrah. The skirmish took place at Shaqq al-Ḥarrah,[58] beyond al-Suwāri-

51. Instead of "their cavalry" (*khayluhum*), Ms. O reads *jumlatuhum*, "all of them," which the note in the Leiden edition prefers.

52. Ms. O reads: *wa-amdāduhā* instead of *amdāduhā*, i.e., "Then the Banū Sulaym and their reinforcements came."

53. The Banū Sulaym, as stated (above, n. 44), consisted of nomadic (or semi-nomadic) bedouins and a settled population.

54. See Hinz, *Masse und Gewichte*, 63.

55. The *sūdān* al-Madīnah were black slaves who formed a kind of fighting force; see also Shaban, *Islamic History*, I, 110.

56. For *taṭarraqa* "infiltrate, penetrate," see Glossarium, CCCCXXXIX; Lane, *Lexicon*, 1847, "found a way, sought to gain access."

57. Ḥarrat Banū Sulaym was the large bed of lava in the area of the Sulaym settlements; See Yāqūt, *Muʿjam*, II, 248; Hamdānī, *Ṣifat Jazīrat al-ʿArab*, 170, 185; Bakrī, *Muʿjam*, II, 436.

58. Shaqq al-Ḥarrah is the eastern part of Ḥarrat Banī Sulaym.

qiyyah—their village where they would take refuge.[59] Al-Suwāriqiyyah consists of strongpoints. Most of the Banū Sulaym who encountered Bughā were of the Banū ʿAwf, including ʿUzayzah b. Qaṭṭāb and Ashhab, their two commanders-in-chief at the time. Bughā killed about fifty of their men, taking captive a like number, and the remainder were routed. As a result, the Banū Sulaym became vulnerable, and after the skirmish Bughā invited them to accept a guarantee of safe conduct under the jurisdiction of the Commander of the Faithful al-Wāthiq.

Bughā remained in al-Suwāriqiyyah, and the Banū Sulaym
[1338] came and rallied to him. He mustered them by the tens and fives and singly,[60] and seized from among those gathered at al-Suwāriqiyyah, aside from the Banū Sulaym, people of unknown origin. The lightly equipped among the Banū Sulaym fled, except for a few. These were the ones who would assail people and interdict the roads. Most of those who came into Bughā's custody were of the Banū ʿAwf who had remained steadfast. The last of those seized belonged to the Banū Ḥubshī of the Banū Sulaym. Those marked as evil and vicious—about 1,000 men—were imprisoned under Bughā's jurisdiction. The rest he freed.

Bughā then left al-Suwāriqiyyah for Medina along with the Banū Sulaym captives and those given a guarantee of safe-conduct. This was in Dhū al-Qaʿdah, 230 (July 10–August 9, 845). He incarcerated the captives in Medina in the palace complex named after Yazīd b. Muʿāwiyah.[61] Bughā made the pilgrimage to Mecca in Dhū al-Ḥijjah (August 9–September 6, 845). When the festive season ended, he headed for Dhāt ʿIrq.[62] He dispatched someone

59. Al-Suwāriqiyyah was a populous settlement on the pilgrimage route northeast of Mecca, in the territory of the Banū Sulaym. It was also called Qāriyat Banī Sulaym. Some of the Banū Sulaym resided in the town and some lived as bedouins in the surrounding area and infiltrated into the Ḥijāz and Najd pilgrim road; Yāqūt, Muʿjam, III, 180; Bakrī, *Muʿjam*, III, 764; Samhūdī, *Wafā*, II, 325.

60. For the distributive sense of the numbers given here, see Glossarium, CDXCIV. Ms. O omits "two," which occurs in the text but appears out of place.

61. A palace named after ʿAtīka bt. Yazīd b. Muʿāwiyah is mentioned by Samhūdī, *Wafāʾ*, II, 725.

62. Dhāt ʿIrq is a town near ʿIrq, a mountain slightly northeast of Mecca and on the Mecca Road. An *ʿirq* is a vein formed by sand; see Yāqūt, *Muʿjam*, III, 651; Hamdānī, *Ṣifat Jazīrat al-ʿArab*, Index, 45; Bakrī, *Muʿjam*, s.v.

to the Banū Hilāl,[63] who proposed to them something along the lines of what was offered the Banū Sulaym. When the Banū Hilāl approached, he seized about 300 of their insurgents and violent men and freed the rest. He then returned from Dhāt ʿIrq. It is a day's journey from al-Bustān (the Garden),[64] and it is a two-day journey from Dhāt ʿIrq to Mecca.

In this year Abū al-ʿAbbās ʿAbdallāh b. Ṭāhir died in Naysābūr, on Monday,[65] 11 Rabīʿ I (December 26, 844), nine[66] days after the death of Ashnās the Turk. ʿAbdallāh b. Ṭāhir died. He had been in charge of the security police (*al-ḥarb wa-l-shurṭah*),[67] al-Sawād, Khurāsān and its districts, al-Rayy, Ṭabaristān and its adjacent territories, and Kirmān. The tax of these districts was, on the day he died, forty-eight million dirhams. Al-Wāthiq appointed ʿAbdal- [1339]
lāh's son Ṭāhir[68] governor of all the districts of ʿAbdallāh b. Ṭāhir.

Isḥāq b. Ibrāhīm b. Muṣʿab went on the pilgrimage this year and was in charge of the events of the festive season.

Leading the pilgrimage this year was Muḥammad b. Dāwūd.

---

63. The Banū Hilāl were descendants of the eponymous ancestor Hilāl, whose genealogy is traced back to Muḍar, ʿAylān, and Qays. Some of the tribe emigrated to Egypt with the Banū Sulaym in the eighth century. In the tenth century they fought alongside the Carmathians. In the eleventh, they invaded North Africa along with the Banū Sulaym. They are related to the Banū Numayr; Caskel, *Das genealogische Werk,* I, 92; II, 282; *Jamharah,* 121a; *EI*², s.v. Hilāl.

64. The Garden is the Bustān Ibn ʿĀmir (or Ibn Maʿmar); Yāqūt, *Muʿjam,* I, 611.

65. But 11 Rabīʿ I was a Wednesday. For the Ṭāhirid Abū al-ʿAbbās ʿAbdallāh b. Ṭāhir, army commander, poet, companion of caliphs, and patron of the arts, son of the founder of the dynasty, See Ṭabarī, III, 1044ff; Rothstein, "Zu aš-Šābuštī's Bericht über die Ṭāhiriden," 162–65; Zambauer, *Manuel,* 197, and Index, 318; Bosworth, "The Ṭāhirids and Arabic Culture," 58ff.; *idem,* The Ṭāhirids and Ṣaffarids," 97–101. His greatest protégé was the poet Abū Tammām al-Ṭāʾī. See Table 3.

66. Ms. C reads "Seven," as do Cairo edition Mss. A and D.

67. Chiefs of the security police (*shurṭah*) are occasionally called "chiefs of war," or "chiefs of war and police" (*wulāt al-ḥarb wa-l-shurṭah*); Tyan, *Histoire,* 578.

68. For Ṭāhir b. ʿAbdallāh b. Ṭāhir, i.e. Ṭāhir II, see Bosworth, "The Ṭāhirids and Arabic Culture," 69–70; *idem,* The Ṭāhirids and Ṣaffarids, 98, 101. Ibn al-Athīr, *Kāmil,* VII, 9–11, adds here a long passage on ʿAbdallāh b. Ṭāhir. In the Cairo edition, a note suggests that the material may have gone back to Ṭabarī, but this is doubtful. See Table 3.

The Events of the Year 231

(September 7, 845–August 28, 846)

A prisoner exchange was carried out between the Muslims and the Byzantines by Khāqān al-Khādim in Muḥarram (September 7–October 6, 845).[69] The number of Muslims allegedly came to 4,362.

It was in this year that members of the Banū Sulaym were killed in Medina in Bughā's prison.

The Reason for the Liquidation of the Banū Sulaym and Its Consequences

It is reported that, when the Banū Hilāl came to Bughā in Dhāt ʿIrq, and he seized those I mentioned, he went on the small pilgrimage (*ʿumrah*) of al-Muḥarram. He then departed for Medina. All of the Banū Hilāl whom he had seized he imprisoned in his

69. A Khāqān al-Khādim had served Hārūn al-Rashīd; Ṭabarī, III, 1140; Baladhurī, *Futūḥ*, 381 (Kāqān al-Khādim al-Ṣughdī). On the prisoner exchange, see below, pp. 38ff. The number of Muslims given there is 4,460.

custody along with the members of the Banū Sulaym whom he had previously apprehended. He assembled all of them, in fetters and chains, in the palace complex named after Yazīd b. Muʿāwiyah. The Banū Sulaym had previously been incarcerated for several months.

Bughā then went to the Banū Murrah.[70] In the prison of Medina there were about 1,300 men belonging to the Banū Sulaym and Hilāl. They breached the palace in order to escape. But a Medinese woman noticed the breach and alarmed the inhabitants of Medina, who thereupon approached. The Medinese discovered [1340] that the prisoners had assaulted the prison custodians, killing one or two, and that some or all had come out, having seized the custodians' weapons. The Medinese, free (*aḥrār*) and slave (*ʿabīd*), rallied against them—the governor of Medina at the time being ʿAbdallāh b. Aḥmad b. Dāwūd al-Hāshimī[71]—and prevented their escape. Their besiegers passed the night surrounding the palace until the morning.

Their assault had been on Friday evening. This was because ʿUzayzah b. Qaṭṭāb had said to the prisoners that he foresaw an evil omen for Saturday.

The Medinese kept pressing the battle, and the Banū Sulaym fought back. But the Medinese defeated them and killed every last one of them. ʿUzayzah would recite in *rajaz* verse:

A push is needed be the gate narrow.
 I indeed am ʿUzayzah b. Qaṭṭāb.

Death is preferable to disgrace for a true man.
 This, my Lord, is the gatekeeper's work.

He freed the fetter on his hand, and was then shot in the leg, falling over prostrate. They were all killed. The blacks of Medina killed the tribesmen they encountered in the lanes of Medina—those who had entered in order to bring provisions—until they met a tribesman emerging from the tomb of the Prophet and killed

70. On the Banū Murra, see Caskel, *Das genealogische Werk,* I, 125; II, 433; *Jamharah,* 162b.

71. An ʿAbdallāh b. *Muḥammad* b. Dāwūd b. ʿIsā b. Mūsā was governor of Mecca in 239 (853–54); see below, 1420 (p. 129); Zambaur, *Manuel,* 20.

him. He was one of the Banū Abī Bakr b. Kilāb,[72] a descendant of 'Abd al-'Azīz b. Zurārah.[73]

Bughā was away. When he arrived and discovered that they had been killed, he was deeply distressed. It is reported that the gatekeeper had accepted a bribe from the prisoners in exchange for a promise that he would open the gate for them, but they came too soon, before the appointed time.

They would recite in *rajaz* verse while fighting:

Death is preferable to disgrace for a true man.
The gatekeeper took a thousand dīnārs.

[1341] And they set about reciting when Bughā seized them:

O finest benefit (*bughyah*), sword of the vigilant,
Remover of wrongdoing, remote and perverse,

I do not hold with whoever of us is delinquent.
Do—may God guide you—what you are commanded.

He replied, "I have been commanded to kill you."

When the comrades of 'Uzayzah b. Qaṭṭāb, chief of the Banū Sulaym, were killed, he fled and entered a well. A Medinese fellow went in after him and killed him. The dead were heaped one on top of the other over the Gate of Marwān b. al-Ḥakam.

I have received an account on the authority of Aḥmad b. Muḥammad[74] that the muezzin of the Medinese summoned the Banū Sulaym to prayer during the night when they were under guard in order to warn them that the dawn was breaking, but that they had already been awake. The Arab tribesmen began to laugh, saying, "O tipplers of barley soup,[75] you teach us about the night. We know it better than you."

---

72. For the Banū Abī Bakr b. Kilāb, a subtribe of Kilāb, see Caskel, *Das genealogische Werk*, I, 93, 94; II, 222; *Jamharah*, 121b.

73. For 'Abd al-'Azīz b. Zurārah, see Caskel, *Das genealogische Werk*, I, 94.

74. He is Aḥmad b. Muḥammad b. Makhlad. See also below, 1358 (p. 45), and note 169.

75. *Sawīq* is dried wheat or barley, usually made into a heavy soup by mixing water, butter, honey, oil, etc. It was also eaten dry. *Sawīq* was often taken by travelers on journeys or by troops on campaigns. A skirmish between the Muslims and Meccans after the battle of Badr was called Ghazwat al-Sawīq. In our text, the Medinese, who indulged in this repast, are the butt of the bedouins' derision; see Glossarium, CCCII; Lane, *Lexicon*, s.v.; Dozy, *Supplément*, s.v.; *EI*[1], s.v. Sawīq; *EI*[2], s.v. Ghidhā', II, 1059.

A man of the Banū Sulaym recited:

When Ibn ʿAbbās[76] was amīr,
The mere gnashing of his canine teeth clamored.

He oppressed with impunity,
And attacked what was weak[77] against his blow.

We were such as to repel oppression
With swords unsheathed in our hands.

The Commander of the Faithful rose against us
Like a lion bestirring from the thicket.

If he be gracious, we hope for God's pardon,
And if he kills, at least our killer is noble.

The reason for Bughā's absence was that he had gone to Fadak to combat the Banū Fazārah[78] and Murrah there who had conquered it. When he could see them, he sent a Fazārī to offer them a guarantee of safe conduct and to get information about them. When the Fazārī came to them, he warned them of Bughā's impending assault and suggested that they escape, whereupon they fled for the open country, abandoning Fadak, except for a few who remained. Their destination was Khaybar and Janafā'[79] and the surrounding areas. [1342]

Bughā overcame some of them and offered a guarantee of safe conduct to others, the rest having fled with a chief of theirs called al-Rakkāḍ ("the Runner") to a place in al-Balqā',[80] in the district of Damascus. Bughā remained for about forty nights in Janafā', a village on the border of the district of Syria, adjacent to the Ḥijāz.

---

76. Ibn ʿAbbās is Muḥammad b. Ṣāliḥ b. al-ʿAbbās, ʿAlid governor of Medina, mentioned above, 1335 (p. 16). "ʿAbbās" is one of the Arabic terms for "lion," and also means "stern, austere, morose" (Lane, *Lexicon,* s.v.). Thus the images in our poem are quite apposite.

77. The word *ḍaʿīf* is used here as a substantive; see Glossarium, CCCXXXIV.

78. The Banū Fazārah were a subtribe of Ghaṭafān; Caskel, *Das genealogische Werk,* I, 92, 130; II, 246; *Jamharah,* 166b; *EI*², s.v. Fazāra.

79. Janafā' is an oasis in the region of Syria, near the Ḥijāz; Yāqūt, *Muʿjam,* II, 133; Thilo, *Ortsnamen,* 45.

80. Yāqūt, *Muʿjam,* I, 728; *EI*², s.v. al-Balḳā'.

He then departed for Medina with the Banū Murrah and Fazārah who had fallen into his hands.

During this year, a contingent from the tribes of Ghaṭafān,[81] Fazārah, and Ashja'[82] came to Bughā. He had sent emissaries to them and to the Banū Tha'labah.[83] When they came to him, it is reported, he ordered Muḥammad b. Yūsuf al-Ja'farī[84] to have them swear a firm oath that they would not fail to show up when he summoned them; they did so.

Bughā then headed for Ḍariyyah[85] to pursue the Banū Kilāb.[86] He sent his emissaries to them, and it is alleged that about 3,000 of their men rallied to him. He imprisoned about 1,300 of them, of those who were miscreants, and freed the rest. Bughā then brought them to Medina in Ramaḍān, 231 (May, 846) and imprisoned them in the palace complex of Yazīd b. Mu'āwiyah. After that he went to Mecca and remained there until he witnessed the festive season.

[1343] The Banū Kilāb remained in custody. Nothing happened to them during the period of Bughā's absence until he returned to Medina. Then, when he arrived in Medina, he sent for the members of Tha'labah, Ashja' and Fazārah, and he required them to swear the oath. They did not respond, however, but dispersed throughout the countryside. He had them pursued, but not[87] one was overtaken.

In this year a group rebelled in Baghdad, in the suburb (*rabaḍ*) of 'Amr b. 'Aṭā', rendering the oath of allegiance to Aḥmad b. Naṣr al-Khuzā'ī.[88]

---

81. See *EI*^{2}, s.v. Ghaṭafān.

82. The Ashja' were a principal tribe of Ghaṭafān; see Caskel, *Das genealogische Werk*, I, 92, 135; II, 201; *Jamharah*, 166a; *EI*^{2}, II, 1023, s.v. Ghaṭafān.

83. See Caskel, *Das genealogische Werk*, I, 141; II, 552; *Jamharah*, 195a; *EI*^{1}, s.v. Tha'laba.

84. On Muḥammad b. Yūsuf al-Ja'farī, see below, 1358–62 (pp. 46–50). He was a guide of Bughā in the campaign against the Banū Numayr and, according to the account, a member of that tribe.

85. Ḍariyyah is a village of the Banū Kilāb on the road from al-Baṣrah to Mecca; *EI*^{2}, s.v.

86. Banū Kilāb b. Rabī'ah are a tribe of 'Āmir b. Ṣa'ṣa'ah, ultimately of Qays 'Aylān; see Caskel, *Das genealogische Werk*, I, 92, 93; II, 371; *Jamharah*, 121a; *EI*^{2}, s.v. 'Āmir b. Ṣa'ṣa'a.

87. For *kathīr aḥad* in this sense, see Glossarium, CVI.

88. On the rebellion of Aḥmad b. Naṣr, see Ya'qūbī, *Ta'rīkh*, II, 589; Mas'ūdī, *Murūj*, VII, 169; Abū al-Ḥusayn, *Ṭabaqāt al-Ḥanābilah*, I, 80–82; Khaṭīb, *Ta'rīkh Baghdād*, V, 173–84; Ibn al-Athīr, *Kāmil*, VII, 13–15; Ibn Kathīr, *Bidāyah*, X, 303–

The Reason for the Rebellion of the Baghdad Group and the Consequence of Their Action and That of Aḥmad b. Naṣr

The reason for this was that Aḥmad b. Naṣr b. Mālik b. al-Haytham al-Khuzāʿī[89] . . . Mālik b. al-Haytham was one of the *naqībs* of the ʿAbbāsids, and his son was occasionally visited by Ḥadīth scholars, such as Yaḥyā b. Maʿīn,[90] Ibn al-Dawraqī,[91] and Abū Khaythamah.[92] Aḥmad b. Naṣr would openly express disagreement with the exponents of the doctrine of the Qur'ān's creation, notwithstanding the position his father held with the governing authorities of the ʿAbbāsid regime.[93] He would excoriate those

---

06. And see Patton, *Aḥmed ibn Ḥanbal,* 116ff.; Laoust, *Ibn Baṭṭa,* xxxiv–xxxv; *idem, Schismes,* 110; Lapidus, "Separation," 381–82.

89. Aḥmad b. Naṣr's father was a close associate of the ʿAbbāsids. The Market (*suwayqah*) of Naṣr, on the Mahdī Canal below the Rūm Quarter, named for him, was given to him by al-Mahdī as a grant; Khaṭīb, *Ta'rīkh Baghdād,* V, 173; Le Strange, *Baghdad,* 214–15; Lassner, *Topography,* 78, 79, 104. Aḥmad's grandfather, Mālik b. al-Haytham, an agent (*naqīb*) of the ʿAbbāsids in Khurāsān, was governor of Mosul in 142 (759–60); Azdī, *Ta'rīkh Mawṣil,* Index, 465; Zambaur, *Manuel,* 36. The sentence is an anacoluthon; part of the text may be lacking at this point, perhaps a comment on Naṣr b. Mālik; see the note in the Leiden edition. For Aḥmad b. Naṣr and his ancestry, see Crone, *Slaves on Horses,* 181–83; Kennedy, *The Early Abbasid Caliphate,* 80–81; Daniel, *Political and Social History,* Index, 219.

90. Abū Zakariyyā' Yaḥyā b. Maʿīn b. ʿAwn was a famous Ḥadīth scholar, an associate of Aḥmad b. Ḥanbal; died in 233 (847) in Medina; see Sezgin, *GAS,* I, 106.

91. Abū ʿAlī Aḥmad b. Ibrāhīm b. Kathīr al-Dawraqī, a Ḥadīth scholar, died in 246 (860–61); Sezgin, *GAS,* I, 112. *Fragmenta,* 529, has here *ibnā* al-Dawraqī, i.e., the two Ibn al-Dawraqīs. According to the Khaṭīb, *Ta'rīkh Baghdād,* V, 174, both Aḥmad and Yaʿqūb al-Dawraqī were associated with Aḥmad b. Naṣr. On Yaʿqūb b. Ibrāhīm al-Dawraqī, the older brother, see Khaṭīb, XIV, 277–80. Ṭabarī is said to have studied with Yaʿqūb al-Dawraqī; see Introductio, LXIX.

92. Text: Ibn Khaythamah. But *Abū* Khaythamah Zuhayr b. Ḥarb b. Shaddād al-Nasā'ī is obviously intended. He died in 234 (848–49); Sezgin, *GAS,* I, 107. *Fragmenta,* 529, has correctly Abū Khaythamah. Al-Ma'mūn had summoned Yaḥyā b. Maʿīn, Abū Khaythamah and Aḥmad b. al-Dawraqī, *inter alios,* for interrogation concerning the question of the Qur'ān's creation. They responded, under intimidation, that it is created; Ṭabarī, III, 1116 (Bosworth, *Reunification,* 204); Ibn Ṭayfūr, *Baghdād,* 187; Patton, *Aḥmed ibn Ḥanbal,* 64; Lapidus, "Separation," 379. Ibn al-Athīr, *Kāmil,* VII, 14.1, adds an Abū Zuhayr (variant: Zuhr); but this appears to be a truncated version of Abū Khaythamah Zuhayr.

93. From the time of al-Ma'mūn until al-Mutawakkil, the Muʿtazilite view that the Qur'ān is created was followed by ʿAbbāsid caliphs, and a supporter of the regime was expected to embrace this doctrine. Aḥmad b. Naṣr, however, adopted the Ḥanbalite position advocating the Qur'ān's eternity. See Patton, *Aḥmed ibn Ḥanbal, passim;* Madelung, "Origins."

who held this doctrine, despite al-Wāthiq's severity toward those who professed this, the inquisition he directed against them, and the prevailing influence Aḥmad b. Abī Du'ād had upon him.[94]

I received an account from some(one) of our shaykhs, on the authority of the one who reported it. He had dropped in on Aḥmad b. Naṣr one of those days. A group of people was with Aḥmad, and al-Wāthiq was mentioned in his presence, whereupon he launched into saying, "Didn't this pig do . . . . ?" Or he said, "This infidel (*kāfir*)." This behavior of his was bruited
[1344] about. People made him afraid of the government authorities[95] by saying they have learned of your business, and he got afraid of them.

Among his visitors there was reportedly a man named Abū Hārūn al-Sarrāj:[96] another called Ṭālib; and another, who was a Khurāsānī and associate of Isḥāq b. Ibrāhīm b. Muṣʿab, chief of the security police. These men openly professed to him adherence to his doctrine. The Ḥadīth scholars who surrounded him, namely, Aḥmad b. Naṣr and those Baghdadīs who denied the doctrine of the Qur'ān's creation, incited Aḥmad and induced him to agitate against this doctrine. In this matter they had recourse to him in particular because of the influence his father and grandfather had with the ʿAbbāsid regime and on account of his assets in Baghdad.

He was one of those to whom the residents of the East Side had given the oath of allegiance concerning "the promotion of the good, the discouraging of evil and obedience to Him." This was in 201 (816–17), when dissolute people were rampant in Madīnat al-Salām and corruption out in the open, al-Ma'mūn being then in Khurāsān—we gave an account of this above.[97] He persisted in

94. Masʿūdī, *Murūj*, VII, 146, says that al-Wāthiq followed his father (al-Muʿtaṣim) and uncle (al-Ma'mūn) on the question of justice (a Muʿtazilite principle); and see *Murūj*, VI, 21. Aḥmad b. Abī Du'ād, a staunch supporter of Muʿtazilism, is often said to have had great influence upon al-Wāthiq.

95. Text: *fa-khuwwifa bi-l-ṣultān.* Leiden O and Cairo edition D read *fa-khawwafa al-sulṭān.* The term *sulṭān,* usually translated "government authorities," may mean "caliph" here, as it occasionally does in historical writings of the ninth and tenth centuries.

96. The text of Ibn al-Athīr, *Kāmil,* VII, 14, gives the name pointed as al-Saddākh (variant: al-Sarrāj).

97. Aḥmad b. Naṣr received the oath of allegiance in 201, according to Khatīb, *Ta'rīkh Baghdād,* V, 176; but Ibn Kathīr says it was his father *Naṣr b. Mālik;*

this undertaking until al-Ma'mūn came to Baghdad in 204 (819–20). They had hoped that the general populace would respond to his call, as he had acted for the reasons that have been mentioned.

It is reported that Aḥmad b. Naṣr reacted favorably to those who requested this of him, that those who strove on his behalf by summoning people to him were the two men whose names I mentioned previously, and that Abū Hārūn al-Sarrāj and Ṭālib distributed money among people, giving a dīnār to each person.

Aḥmad b. Naṣr fixed with them an appointed night when a drum would be beaten, signaling a rallying together the next morning for an assault against the government authorities. Ṭālib [1345]
was on the West Side of Baghdad together with those in league with him, and Abū Hārūn was on the East Side together with those in league with him. Ṭālib and Abū Hārūn gave dīnārs to two sons of the commander Ashras, among others, for distribution among their neighbors. Some of them drank wine (*nabīdh*), and a number of them gathered around to partake of it. Having become drunk, they beat the drum on the night of Wednesday, one night before the appointed time. The set time for this was the night of Thursday, 3 Sha'bān, 231 (April 4, 846). They thought that it was the night of Thursday, the one that they had set for the uprising. They beat the drum vigorously, but no one responded.

Isḥāq b. Ibrāhīm was away from Baghdad, his proxy there being his brother, Muḥammad b. Ibrāhīm.[98] The latter dispatched to them a page (*ghulām*) of his by the name of Rakhsh,[99] who came and questioned them concerning their story. None of those men-

---

Bidāyah, X, 303. According to Ṭabari, Naṣr b. Ḥamzah b. Mālik al-Khuzā'ī, was appointed governor over the East Side in 201; Ṭabarī, III, 1002 (Bosworth, *Reunification,* 47). The Khaṭīb states that Aḥmad b. Naṣr acted (in 201) along with Sahl b. Salāmah al-Anṣārī. See Ṭabarī, III, 1009 (Bosworth, 57), where Sahl, Khālid al-Daryūsh, and other "good citizens" (*ṣulaḥā'*) are said to have defended their neighborhoods from criminal elements and self-styled protectors. See Lapidus, "Separation," 375, 379–81, on the movement of *al-amr bi-l-ma'rūf*; and Kennedy, *Early Abbasid Caliphate,* 81.

98. The Ṭāhirid Muḥammad b. Ibrāhīm b. [al-Ḥusayn b.] Muṣ'ab, brother of Isḥāq b. Ibrāhīm, died in 236 (850–51); see below, 1404 (p. 107); and see Ṭabarī, III, 1236; Marin, *Reign,* 61 and n. 304; Index, 136; Zambaur, *Manuel,* 46, 197, 198; Bosworth, "The Ṭāhirids and Ṣaffarids," 101, 102. See Table 3.

99. Rakhsh, a Persian name, means "lightning, the rainbow, reflection of light," etc., and "happy, fortunate, prosperous," as well as "mottled or swift horse" (the name of Rustam's steed); Steingass, *Dictionary,* 572.

tioned as having beaten the drum showed up. A man was pointed out who was a bathhouse attendant, afflicted in his eye, by the name of 'Īsā al-A'war ("the One-Eyed"). Rakhsh threatened to have him beaten. He consequently informed on the two sons of Ashras, on Aḥmad b. Naṣr b. Mālik and others whom he named.

Rakhsh searched for the group that very night, apprehending some of them. He seized Ṭālib, whose residence was in the suburb on the West Side, and Abū Hārūn al-Sarrāj, whose residence was on the East Side. And he pursued for several days and nights those whom 'Īsā al-A'war had named. They were taken into cus-
[1346] tody on the East Side and the West Side, each group being seized in its own section. Abū Hārūn and Ṭālib were each shackled with seventy[100] *raṭl*s of iron. In the residence of the two sons of Ashras two green banners with red on them were found in a well.[101] One of the supporters of Muḥammad b. 'Ayyāsh brought them up. He was prefect of the West Side. The prefect of the East Side was al-'Abbās b. Muḥammad b. Jibrīl al-Qā'id ("the Commander") al-Khurāsānī.[102] Afterwards a eunuch (*khaṣī*) of Aḥmad b. Naṣr was seized and threatened. He thereupon confirmed what 'Īsā al-A'war had confessed.

Rakhsh went to Aḥmad b. Naṣr, who was then in the bath. He said to the government officers, "This is my residence. If you come upon a banner or equipment, or weapons for rebellion, you are free to expropriate them and to shed my blood with impunity." The residence was searched, but not a thing was found in it, whereupon he was brought to Muḥammad b. Ibrāhīm b. Muṣ'ab. Two of his eunuchs and two of his sons were seized, as well as a man who often visited him by the name of Ismā'īl b. Muḥammad b. Mu'āwiyah b. Bakr al-Bāhilī, whose residence was on the East Side.

---

100. Ms. O and Cairo edition Ms. D: ninety.

101. Green was actually the color that had been adopted by al-Ma'mūn after he appointed the 'Alid 'Alī al-Riḍā as heir apparent. The choice of green may have signified paradise (*al-janna*) or the beginning of a new era. It was later used by the Ottomans, who claimed an 'Abbāsid precedent. See Fārūq 'Umar, *Buḥūth*, 242ff. Red was a color used by rebels (e.g. al-Muḥammirah) against government authority; Hilāl al-Ṣābi, *Rusūm*, 75 (to Salem, 61).

102. For al-'Abbās b. Muḥammad and his ancestry, see Crone, *Slaves on Horses*, 179–80.

These six were brought on mules, having saddles without cushions underneath, to the Commander of the Faithful al-Wāthiq, who was in Sāmarrā. Aḥmad b. Naṣr was shackled in a pair of fetters. They were brought out from Baghdad on Thursday, 28 Shaʿbān, 231 (April 29, 846).

Al-Wāthiq was informed about their whereabouts. He invited Ibn Abī Du'ād and his partisans and convened a public assembly for them so that they might undergo an open inquisition (*imtiḥān*). The group was assembled in his presence. Aḥmad b. Abī Du'ād was reportedly averse to having Aḥmad b. Naṣr killed in [1347]
public.[103]

When Aḥmad b. Naṣr was brought in, al-Wāthiq did not argue with him about the uprising, nor about the report of his intention to rebel against him. He asked him instead, "What do you have to say concerning the Qur'ān?"

He replied, "It is the word of God." Defying death, Aḥmad b. Naṣr had smeared himself with a depilatory (*tanawwara*)[104] and perfumed himself.

When al-Wāthiq asked, "Is the Qur'ān created?" Aḥmad replied, "It is the word of God."[105]

When he asked, "What is your view concerning your Lord? Will you see Him on the Day of Resurrection?" Aḥmad replied, "O Commander of the Faithful, according to traditions of the Messenger of God, he said, 'You will see your Lord on the Day of Resurrection as you see the moon. You will not be harmed by viewing Him.' We follow the tradition."[106] He went on to say,

---

103. Ibn Abī Du'ād's reluctance may indicate that Naṣr had wide public support in Sāmarrā, as he did in Baghdad. Aḥmad b. Abī Du'ād's hesitancy here (and see below, 1348, p. 33) is occasionally adduced as a sign of his moderation.

104. See Glossarium, DXXXIV. And see Lane, *Lexicon*, s.v. *nāra*.

105. This is the very response that Aḥmad b. Ḥanbal and his supporters gave under the inquisition in the days of al-Ma'mūn; Patton, *Aḥmed ibn Ḥanbal*, 70–72. Note, however, that the reply dodges the question, as it is not stated that the Qur'ān is the *uncreated* or *eternal* word (or speech) of God.

106. The question relates to the vision of God (*ru'yat Allāh*) and ultimately to the issue of *tashbīh* ("anthropomorphism"). One of the principles of Aḥmad b. Ḥanbal was the vision of God on the day of Resurrection and the belief that the Prophet saw his Lord. See, for instance, McCarthy, *Theology*, *Kitāb al-lumaʿ*, pars. 68–81; and Appendix IV, p. 242 (from al-Ashʿarī, *Maqālāt al-Islāmiyyīn*, I, 292): "They [Aṣḥāb al-Ḥadīth, Ahl al-Sunnah] hold that God will be seen by eyes on the Day of Resurrection as the moon is seen on the night of full moon." The Muʿta-

"And I have received a tradition on sound authority from Sufyān b. ʿUyaynah[107] that 'the heart of a human being is between two of God's fingers; He scrutinizes it.' The Prophet would pray, 'Scrutinizer of hearts, make my heart steadfast in your religion.' "[108]

Isḥāq b. Ibrāhīm[109] said to Aḥmad b. Naṣr, "Watch what you are saying." He replied, "You ordered me to say this." Disturbed by his remark, Isḥāq asked, "Did I really order you to say this?" He replied, "Yes, you ordered me to give sincere counsel to him, as he is the Commander of the Faithful. My sincere counsel to him is not to controvert a tradition of the Messenger of God."

Al-Wāthiq asked those around him what they had to say concerning Aḥmad b. Naṣr. They went on quite a bit. ʿAbd al-Raḥmān b. Isḥāq[110] said—he had been a judge on the West Side who was removed from office, and he was present, and Aḥmad b. Naṣr was devoted to him—"O Commander of the Faithful, his blood may be shed with impunity." Abū ʿAbdallāh al-Armanī, an associate of Ibn Abī Du'ād, said, "Give me his blood to drink, O Commander of the Faithful." Whereupon al-Wāthiq said, "He
[1348] will be killed as you wish."

But Ibn Abī Du'ād commented, "O Commander of the Faithful,

---

zilites, on the other hand, held that God cannot be seen. For the tradition, *tarawna rabbakum fī yawm al-qiyāmah . . .*, see Wensinck, *Concordance*, II, 202; Bukhārī, Mawāqīt, 16, 26; Adhān, 129; Tafsīr 50, 2, etc. And see below, 1353–54 (p. 40), where it is reported that Muslim captives in Byzantine hands were interrogated on these two questions prior to their being ransomed.

107. Sufyān b. ʿUyaynah b. Maymūn al-Hilālī, the famous Ḥadīth scholar, jurist and exegete, died in 196 (811) in Mecca; Sezgin, *GAS*, I, 96. Aḥmad b. Ḥanbal studied with him. For his view that the Qur'ān is the speech of God, see Madelung, "Origins," 511.

108. For the tradition, *inna qalb ibn ādam bayn uṣbuʿayn . . .*, see Wensinck, *Concordance*, V, 454; Ibn Ḥanbal, *Musnad*, II, 173. In Ibn Ḥanbal's version, the epithet *al-jabbār* appears instead of *Allāh* as here; and it ends *idhā shā'a an yuqallibahu qallabahu*. In the version of Tirmidhī, Daʿwat, 89, 60 (Wensinck, *loc. cit.*): *laysa ādamī illā wa-qalbuhu . . . .* The *ḥadīth* continues, in the version of Ibn Ḥanbal: *yā muṣarrif al-qulūb* (instead of *yā muqallib al-qulūb*, as in our text). And see the versions in Wensinck, V, 459, from *Musnad*, II, 168, etc.

109. Isḥāq b. Ibrāhīm had been one of the leaders of the inquisition at the time of al-Ma'mun; see above, n. 26.

110. ʿAbd al-Raḥmān b. Isḥāq al-Qāḍī had been a judge in Baghdad at the time of al-Ma'mūn and al-Muʿtaṣim; Ṭabarī, III, 1120, 1128 (Bosworth, *Reunification*, 209, 218), 1235 (Marin, *Reign*, 60 and n. 295); Massignon, "Cadis et naqībs," 107.

an infidel is asked to rescind thrice in case he has some infirmity or mental derangement."[111] He was apparently loath to have Aḥmad b. Naṣr killed on his account.

Al-Wāthiq said, "When you see that I have gotten up to go toward him, let no one else rise along with me. I shall reckon my steps toward him."[112] He called for al-Ṣamṣāmah, the sword of ʿAmr b. al-Maʿdī Karib al-Zubaydī. It was in the storeroom, having been presented to Mūsā al-Hādī, who ordered Salm al-Khāsir, the poet, to describe it for him, which he did, whereupon the caliph gave him a present.[113]

Al-Wāthiq took hold of al-Ṣamṣāmah. It had a wide blade, joined at the base by three nails that connected the blade with the joint of the hilt. Al-Wāthiq approached Aḥmad, who was in the middle of the palace. He called for a leather mat, in the middle of which Aḥmad b. Naṣr was placed, and a rope. Aḥmad's head was bound and the rope stretched. Al-Wāthiq gave him a blow that fell upon the rope that was on his shoulder. Then he gave him another blow on his head. At this point, Sīmā al-Dimashqī unsheathed his sword and struck the nape of Aḥmad's neck, severing his head.[114] Bughā al-Sharābī reportedly gave him another

---

111. An unbeliever (*kāfir*) who is an apostate (*murtadd*), as opposed to an unbeliever by birth (*kāfir aṣlī* = *mushrik*), who is confined to a choice of death or slavery if captured, must be asked to rescind three times according to Islamic law; see *EI*[1], s.v. Murtadd.

112. That is, go slowly and deliberately. Abū al-Ḥusayn, *Ṭabaqāt*, I, 81, adds "to this infidel who worships a Lord we neither worship nor recognize by the attributes which he ascribes to Him."

113. Abū Thawr ʿAmr b. al-Maʿdī Karib al-Zubaydī, a renowned Arab poet and warrior, fought with his famous sword named "al-Ṣamṣāmah" in the Jāhiliyyah and continued wielding his weapon after converting to Islam; *EI*[2], s.v. ʿAmr b. Maʿdīkarib. Salm b. ʿAmr al-Khāsir, d. 186 (802) (Sezgin, *GAS*, II, 511), was a panegyrist of al-Mahdī and al-Hādī. According to Balādhurī, *Futūḥ*, 143, al-Wāthiq had a polisher temper the sword.

114. Sīmā al-Dimashqī (the Damascene), also called Sīmā al-Turkī ("the Turk"), was purchased by al-Muʿtaṣim from the wazīr Faḍl b. Sahl; Ṭabarī, III, 1325 (Marin, *Reign*, 129); Yaʿqūbī, *Taʾrīkh*, II, 591; *Buldān*, 256, 262 = Wiet, *Les pays*, 45, 54; Masʿūdī, *Murūj*, VII, 307; Iṣfahānī, *Aghānī*, XVIII, 93. In the version of Abū al-Ḥusayn, *Ṭabaqāt*, I, 81, it is the caliph himself who kills Aḥmad b. Naṣr, but the account there appears to be telescoped. Abū al-Ḥusayn adds "a marvelous report" according to which the severed head uttered, "There is no God but Allāh . . ." and relates other stories about the head reciting Qurʾān verses.

blow.[115] Al-Wāthiq stabbed him with the point of al-Ṣamṣāmah in his abdomen.

He was then carried seated backward to the enclosure in which Bābak[116] was. There he was suspended, with a pair of fetters on his feet, dressed in trousers (*sarāwīl*) and a shirt (*qamīṣ*).[117] His head was brought to Baghdad, where it was displayed first on the East Side and then on the West Side, and thereafter returned to the East Side. The head was placed in an enclosure, a pavilion erected about it, and a guard placed over it. This spot was known as Ra's Aḥmad b. Naṣr. A note was placed upon Aḥmad's ear, on which was written:

> This is the head of the infidel, polytheist, and deviant,
> [1349] namely, Aḥmad b. Naṣr b. Mālik. He was of those killed by God at the hands of ʿAbdallāh Hārūn al-Imām al-Wāthiq bi-llāh, Commander of the Faithful, after the latter had given him proof concerning creation of the Qur'ān and denial of anthropomorphism (*tashbīh*). He offered Aḥmad repentance, making possible return to the truth. But he refused, save open opposition. Praise to God who dispatched him to His fire and to His grievous punishment. When the Commander of the Faithful interrogated him about this, he confirmed anthropomorphism and uttered infidelity, whereupon the Commander of the Faithful regarded his blood as licit and cursed him.

Al-Wāthiq ordered that whoever was named as belonging to the associates of Aḥmad b. Naṣr, who was reported to be a follower of his, should be interrogated. They were put into prisons. After-

115. For Bughā al-Ṣaghīr al-Sharābī, see *EI*², s.v.; Sourdel, *Vizirat*, Index. His cognomen al-Sharābī apparently means "the Cupbearer" (and not "the Tippler," as occasionally rendered). A *sharābī* is also a seller of juice or a preparer or seller of potions; Goitein, *Mediterranean Society*, I, 151; II, 46, 253, 261. On the cognamen, see also Shaban, *Islamic History*, II, 82–83 (< Shārbāmyānī).

116. Bābak is the famous heresiarch who revolted during the period of al-Muʿtaṣim; Marin, *Reign*, esp. 8–15, 21–57, 59; *EI*², s.v. He was killed and suspended on a gibbet in Sāmarrā, which became a favored spot for hanging religious deviants and criminals.

117. Sirwāl means "underdrawers," and in the later Islamic period the term "included also pantaloons, kneebreeches, long trousers, and close-fitting drawers"; *EI*², s.v. Libās, V, 733. A *qamīṣ* is a body shirt; *ibid.*; see also Ahsan, *Social Life*, 45–46, 55, 60 (*sirwāl*); 10, 34, 36–39 (*qamīṣ*).

wards, about twenty men who had been named were placed in dark dungeons. They were prevented from receiving the alms given to prisoners and from having visitors, and were encumbered with irons. Abū Hārūn al-Sarrāj was brought along with others to Sāmarrā. They were thereafter taken back to Baghdad and imprisoned.

The cause for apprehending the men who were seized on account of Aḥmad b. Naṣr was that a certain man, a fuller, who was in the suburb, came to Isḥāq b. Ibrāhīm b. Muṣʿab and proclaimed that he would name the followers of Aḥmad b. Naṣr. Isḥāq sent men along with the fuller to pursue them. When they were rounded up, the pursuers found cause for imprisoning the fuller along with them. He had date palms in al-Mihrizār,[118] which were cut down, and his residence was plundered. Among those imprisoned [1350]
on account of Aḥmad b. Naṣr was a group of people who were the offspring of ʿAmr b. Isfandiyār. They died in prison.

One of the poets recited the following concerning Aḥmad b. Abī Du'ād:

Whenever you stray from Iyād
You become a punishment against mankind.[119]

You belong, as you claim, to Iyād,
So be gentle to these men, Iyādite.

In this year, al-Wāthiq intended to go on the pilgrimage and prepared himself for it. He sent ʿUmar b. Faraj[120] on ahead to put

118. For Mihrizār, Ms. O has M-h-d-r-ā-n. Read perhaps Mihrijān. See Schwarz, *Iran* (IV), 170; (V), 546. A place called Mihrawān is mentioned by Yāqūt, *Muʿjam*, IV, 697; Le Strange, *Lands*, 375.

119. The word for mankind is *ʿibād*, lit. "servants" (of God). There may be an allusion here to the connection of the tribe of Iyād with the Christian community of al-Ḥīrah called ʿIbād; see note in Leiden edition. Some members of the tribe of Iyād had settled in al-Ḥīrah. Aḥmad b. Abī Du'ād claimed to belong to Iyād.

120. ʿUmar b. Faraj al-Rukhkhajī was one of the officials who had purchased land for the founding of Sāmarrā. He was later punished by al-Mutawakkil and his property confiscated in 233 (847–48); see below, 1377–78 (pp. 73–74). See also Balādhurī, *Futūḥ*, 357; Yaʿqūbī, *Ta'rīkh*, II, 592; *Buldān*, 258 = Wiet, *Les pays*, 48 and n. 4; Masʿūdī, *Murūj*, VII, 148 (read ʿUmar), 228; Tanūkhī, *Nishwār*, II, 12–18, 20; Ibn al-Abbār, *Iʿtāb*, 145; Pellat, "Une charge," 38–39; Sourdel, *Vizirat*, 237, 257, n. 1, 259, n. 3, 263, 268, 280, n. 1. A palace in Baghdad was named for his father, Faraj al-Rukhkhajī; Lassner, *Topography*, 79. And see Crone, *Slaves on Horses*, 190, on both father and son.

the route in order. 'Umar returned and notified him that water was scarce, whereupon al-Wāthiq changed his mind.[121]

Leading the pilgrimage this year was Muḥammad b. Dāwūd.

In this year al-Wāthiq appointed Ja'far b. Dīnār governor of the Yemen.[122] He went there in Sha'bān (April 2–May 1, 846). He and Bughā the Elder went on the pilgrimage. Bughā the Elder presided over the events of the festive season. Ja'far went to the Yemen accompanied by 4,000 horsemen and 200 infantry, and was given six[123] months of service allotments.

In this year, Muḥammad b. 'Abd al-Malik al-Zayyāt appointed, in the Caliphal Palace, Isḥāq b. Ibrāhīm b. Abī Khamīṣah, client of the Banū Qushayr, of the people of Uḍākh, over al-Yamāmah, al-Baḥrayn, and the Mecca Road adjacent to al-Baṣrah.[124] Aside from the caliph, no one except Muḥammad b. 'Abd al-Malik al-Zayyāt is reported to have made appointments in the Caliphal Palace.[125]

In this year, a group of brigands broke into the treasury, which was in the Public Palace (Dār al-'Āmmah) situated in the interior
[1351] of the palace complex.[126] They took 42,000 dirhams and a small

121. Text; *fa-bada'a lahu.* Addenda, DCCLXXV: *fa-badā lahu.*

122. Ja'far b. Dīnār al-Khayyāṭ was an army commander who served under al-Mu'taṣim and governed the Yemen from 224 (838–39) until he was deposed in 225 (839–40). He was later reinstated by al-Wāthiq, as we have it in our text; see on him, Ṭabarī, III, 1103; Marin, *Reign,* 27 and n. 161; Index, 135; Ya'qūbī, *Ta'rīkh,* II, 593; Zambaur, *Manuel,* 114. He became supervisor of the Mecca Road and the events of the festive season in the years 241–43 (1433–36; below, pp. 145–50).

123. Ms. C: seven.

124. Isḥāq b. Ibrāhīm b. Abī Khamīṣah was of the Banū Qushayr b. Ka'b b. Rabī'ah, a northern tribe, descendants of Qays 'Aylān (Caskel, *Das genealogische Werk,* I, 101; II, 473; *Jamharah,* 129b). Uḍākh is a village of the Banū Numayr in al-Yamāmah; Yāqūt, *Mu'jam,* I, 303. Al-Baḥrayn in the pre-Islamic and early Islamic period was on the Eastern Arabian coast, southwest of the present-day island of Baḥrayn; Yaqut, *Mu'jam,* I, 148, 506; Thilo, *Ortsnamen,* 34; *EI*², s.v. al-Baḥrayn.

125. On the Caliphal Palace in Sāmarrā, also known as al-Jawsaq al-Khāqānī, see Ya'qūbī, *Buldān,* 261 = Wiet, *Les pays,* 53; Herzfeld, *Samarra,* 104; Sāmarrā'ī, *Ta'rīkh,* I, 78; Creswell, *Early Muslim Architecture,* II, 230; Rogers, "Samarra," 137. And see al-'Amid, *Architecture,* 91ff. It was excavated by H. Viollet and thereafter by F. Sarre and E. Herzfeld. It should not be confused, of course, with the Caliphal Palace (Dar al-Khilāfah or Khalīfah) in Baghdad (see Le Strange, *Baghdad,* 233, 243, 314; Lassner, *Topography,* Index, 317).

126. The Public Palace, or Public Audience Hall (Dār al-'Āmmah), containing the public treasury (*bayt al-māl*), was the open palace of the Caliphal Palace complex, in which the caliph would sit on Mondays and Thursdays. The treasury storehouses were in the northeast corner of the palace, which was bordered on the north by the Sarījah Road. See Ya'qūbī, *Buldān,* 261 = Wiet, *Les pays,* 53;

amount of dīnārs. They were subsequently apprehended. Yazīd al-Ḥulwānī, chief of the security police and deputy of Ītākh, relentlessly pursued the brigands until he apprehended them.[127]

In this year, Muḥammad b. ʿAmr al-Khārijī, of the Banū Zayd b. Taghlib, along with thirteen men, rebelled in Diyār Rabīʿah.[128] Ghānim b. Abī Muslim b. Ḥumayd al-Ṭūsī went out to engage him with a like number [of fighters]—the latter was responsible for the security police of Mosul.[129] Four of the rebels were killed. Muḥammad b. ʿAmr was taken captive and sent to Sāmarrā, and subsequently to the Maṭbaq [Prison] of Baghdad.[130] The heads of his followers and his banners were raised [for public display] near Khashabat Bābak.[131]

In this year, Waṣīf, the Turk, arrived from the area of Iṣbahān, al-Jibāl, and Fārs.[132] He had gone in pursuit of the Kurds, for they had been trying to infiltrate into these areas. About 500 of the Kurds came with him, including young slaves (*ghilmān*), bound together in chains and fetters. Waṣīf ordered that they be impris-

---

Herzfeld, *Samarra,* 104–5; Creswell, *Early Muslim Architecture,* II, 230; Samarrāʾī, *Taʾrīkh,* I, 82, 91; al-ʿAmid, *Architecture,* 98ff.

127. Yazīd b. ʿAbdallāh al-Ḥulwānī (al-Turkī) became governor of Egypt under al-Fatḥ b. Khāqān in 242 (856–57); Kindī, *Wulāh,* 199, 202–04, 206–10; Maqrīzī, *Mawāʿiẓ,* I, 249; Abū al-Maḥāsin, *Nujūm,* II, 308, 314; Zambaur, *Manuel,* 27.

128. See Yaʿqūbī, *Taʾrīkh,* II, 589 (Muḥammad b. ʿAmr al-Shaybānī al-Khārijī). Ibn al-Athīr, *Kāmil,* VII, 16, gives the name as Muḥammad b. ʿAbdallāh al-Khārijī al-Thaʿlabī (Taghlibī?). Khārijite "revolts" in Diyār Rabīʿah were fairly common; see also Ṭabarī, III, 1500 (below, p. 224), where the same man is said to have revolted in the area of Mosul. He was finally killed in Diyār Rabīʿah in 252 (866); III, 1685 (Saliba, 144). The frequent Khārijite uprisings in the area of the Jazīrah were often no more than disturbances by Arab nomads and seminomads; see Kennedy, *Early Abbasid Caliphate,* 21.

129. Ibn al-Athīr, *Kāmil,* VII, 16, reads: Ghānim b. Abī Muslim b. Aḥmad al-Ṭūsī; Zambaur, *Manuel,* 37. For his family affiliation, see Crone, *Slaves on Horses,* 174–75.

130. The Maṭbaq was a formidable prison built by al-Manṣūr in southwest Baghdad on the road leading to the al-Baṣrah and al-Kūfah gates; Le Strange, *Baghdad,* 27; Lassner, *Topography,* 243.

131. Khashabat Bābak was a section of Sāmarrā named after the gibbet where Bābak was hanged; Yaʿqūbī, *Buldān,* 259 = Wiet, *Les pays,* 51; Herzfeld, *Samarra,* 101, 103; Samarrāʾī, *Taʾrīkh,* I, 44. See above, n. 116.

132. Waṣīf, a slave purchased by al-Muʿtaṣim, was a Turkish army commander who served under him and later became a chamberlain (*ḥājib*) for al-Wāthiq and al-Mutawakkil; Ṭabarī, III, 1237; Marin, *Reign,* 62, and n. 313; Yaʿqūbī, *Taʾrīkh,* II, 591; *Buldān,* 256, 258, 262, 264 = Wiet, *Les pays,* 45, 52, 54, 58. Masʿūdī, *Murūj,* VII, 255, 300; *Tanbīh,* 361–63. The name *waṣīf* means "servant" or "page." Waṣīf had estates in Iṣbahān and the Jabal that al-Mutawakkil later sequestered in favor of al-Fatḥ b. Khāqān; below, 1452 (p. 171).

oned. He was awarded 75,000 dīnārs and invested with a sword and apparel.

In this year, the prisoner exchange between the Muslims and the Byzantine ruler was carried out.[133] The Muslims and Byzantines met near the Lamos River at Seleucia, a one day march from Tarsus.[134]

The Reason for the Prisoner Exchange and How It Took Place

It is reported on the authority of Aḥmad b. Abī Qaḥṭabah,[135] an
[1352] associate of Khāqān al-Khādim, a servant (*khādim*) of al-Rashīd—he had been raised in a frontier town (*thaghr*)—that this Khāqān presented himself to al-Wāthiq, together with a group of prominent people of Tarsus and other places, lodging grievances against an official over them in charge of complaints (*maẓālim*) whose teknonym was Abū Wahb. The official was summoned, and Muḥammad b. 'Abd al-Malik kept confronting him with Khāqān and the others in the Public Audience Hall on Mondays and Thursdays after the notables had departed. They would remain until noon, when Muḥammad b. 'Abd al-Malik and they would leave. The official was deposed.

Al-Wāthiq ordered that the inhabitants of the frontier towns (*ahl al-thughūr*) be subjected to an inquisition (*imtiḥān*) concern-

---

133. On the prisoner exchange of 231 (845–46), notable because the Muslims made confession of the Mu'tazilite creed a condition for release of Muslim captives, see Ya'qūbī, *Ta'rīkh*, II, 589; Mas'ūdī, *Tanbīh*, 190–91; Ibn al-Athīr, *Kāmil*, VII, 16–17; Ibn Kathīr, *Bidāyah*, X, 307; Bury, *History*, 274–75; Ostrogorski, *History*, 196; Vasiliev, *History*, 276–77; *idem*, *Byzance*, I, 198–204, 310–15. Ṭabarī's report is particularly valuable for its detail and eyewitness accounts.

134. The Lamos River, on the border between Islamic and Byzantine territory, between Cilicia Trachea and Arab Cilicia, was the locale of prisoner exchanges on various occasions; the first between al-Rashīd and Nicephorus I in 189–90 (805); the second in 192 (808); and the third, the one treated here. See also below, *anno* 241, p. 140; Marin, *Reign*, 61, n. 306, 62, 63, 66; Rosenthal, *Return*, 33, n. 175; *EI*², s.v. Lamas-Ṣū.

135. Aḥmad b. Abī Qaḥṭabah is mentioned here and on p. 1353 (Ibn Abī Qaḥṭabah) as an associate of Khāqān al-Khādim. On p. 1354 an Abū Qaḥṭabah is mentioned as the emissary of Khāqān to the Byzantines, and Abū Qaḥṭabah al-Maghribī al Ṭurṭūsī is cited in connection with the prisoner exchange of 241 (855-56) on 1427 (below, p. 139 and n. 462). But we assume that the same person is intended.

ing the Qur'ān. All except four individuals declared its createdness, whereupon al-Wāthiq ordered that the four be decapitated unless they acknowledged it. He ordered that all the inhabitants of the frontier towns be given grants (*jawā'iz*) as Khāqān saw fit. The inhabitants of the frontier towns hastened to their places, Khāqān tarrying a bit after them.

Emissaries of the Byzantine ruler—he was Michael son of Theophilus, son of Michael, son of Leo, son of George[136]—came to al-Wāthiq, requesting that the caliph ransom Muslim captives who were under the Byzantine ruler's jurisdiction. Al-Wāthiq consequently sent Khāqān to carry out the transaction. Khāqān and his companions left in order to ransom the Muslim captives at the end of 230 (844–45), in keeping with the appointed time set between Khāqān and the emissaries of the Byzantine ruler, which was the Day of the ʿĀshūrā',[137] that is, 10 Muḥarram, 231 (September 16, 845).

Al-Wāthiq thereafter appointed Aḥmad b. Saʿīd b. Salm b. Qutaybah al-Bāhilī[138] governor over the frontier towns (*thughūr*) and provinces (*ʿawāṣim*), and ordered him to be present at the prisoner exchange. He departed with seventeen[139] postal couriers. There was a dispute between the Byzantine emissaries who came to request the prisoner exchange and Ibn al-Zayyāt concern- [1353]
ing the matter at hand. The Byzantines stated that they would not accept in exchange old women, old men, or children.[140] This dispute went on between the emissaries and Ibn al-Zayyāt for a number of days until they consented to an equal exchange.

Al-Wāthiq sent to Baghdad and al-Raqqah in order to buy

136. See above, n. 3, for Michael III (842–67), son of Theophilus (829–42), son of Michael II (820–29). Michael II was preceded by Leo V, the Armenian (813–20), who was, however, not his father, and Leo V was preceded by Michael I Rangabé (811–13).

137. The ʿĀshūrā' is a voluntary fast day on the tenth of Muḥarram.

138. For Aḥmad b. Saʿīd b. Salm b. Qutaybah al-Bāhilī and his ancestry, see Crone, *Slaves on Horses*, 136–38, and sources cited there; and see also Ibn al-ʿAdīm, *Ta'rīkh Ḥalab*, I, 70. Ibn al-Athīr, *Kāmil*, VII, 17, has Muslim instead of Salm, an obvious error.

139. Ms. O: fifteen.

140. According to Bar Hebraeus, *Chronography*, 140–41, the Christian ambassador claimed that the Arab prisoners were all soldiers captured in battle, but that the Christian prisoners taken by the Arabs included, aside from soldiers, old men and women and very young boys and girls who were apprehended in villages.

mamlūk slaves available for sale. He purchased all those that he could, but the requisite number [for the prisoner exchange] was not reached. Al-Wāthiq therefore brought from his palace elderly Byzantine women[141] and others until the right number was met. He then sent two men who were associated with Ibn Abī Du'ād, one named Yaḥyā b. Ādam al-Karkhī, who had the teknonym Abū Ramlah, and [the other] Ja'far b. al-Ḥadhdhā'.[142] He sent with them one of the secretaries of the military administration[143] by the name of Ṭālib b. Dāwūd. Al-Wāthiq ordered Ṭālib and Ja'far to interrogate the captives. Whoever professed that the Qur'ān was created was to be ransomed, and whoever denied this was to be left in the hands of the Byzantines. Al-Wāthiq ordered that Ṭālib be given 5,000 dirhams, and that all those ransomed professing that the Qur'ān was created be given one dīnār from the money[144] brought with them. The group then departed.

It is reported on the authority of Aḥmad b. al-Ḥārith:[145] I questioned Ibn Abī Qaḥṭabah, an associate of Khāqān al-Khādim—he was the intermediary between the Muslims and the Byzantines who had been sent to determine the number of Muslims in Byzantine territory. Aḥmad had come to the Byzantine ruler and calculated their number prior to the ransoming. He reported that their number came to 3,000 men and 500 women.

Al-Wāthiq subsequently ordered that they be ransomed. He dispatched Aḥmad b. Sa'īd posthaste to carry out the prisoner exchange, and he sent as well men to interrogate the Muslim
[1354] prisoners. Those who professed that the Qur'ān was created, and that God cannot be seen in the Afterlife, were ransomed, and those who did not profess this were left in the hands of the Byzantines. There had not been a prisoner exchange since the days of Muḥammad b. Zubaydah in 194 (809–10) or 195 (810–11).[146]

141. Ms. O: Byzantine women and old women.

142. Text: al-Ḥadā'. In Ṭabarī, Index, 102, the name is given as Ja'far b. (Aḥmad) al-Hadhā'. Ya'qūbī, *Ta'rīkh* (II, 588), has Ja'far b. Aḥmad al-Ḥadhdhā' ("Shoemaker") and says that he was *ṣāḥib al-jaysh* ("army commander"). See also Addenda, DCCLXXV.

143. The *kuttāb al-'arḍ* served in the *dīwān al-jaysh; EI²*, II, 507, s.v. *Djaysh;* Glossarium, CCCCLVII.

144. Text: *min māl.* Cairo edition Ms. A: *min mālihi.*

145. An Abū Ja'far Aḥmad b. al-Ḥārith b. al-Mubārak, historian and pupil of al-Madā'inī, died in 258 (871–72); Sezgin, *GAS,* I, 318.

146. That is, the caliph al-Amīn, Muḥammad, son of Hārūn al-Rashīd by Zubaydah.

Aḥmad b. al-Ḥārith said: On the Day of the ʿĀshūrāʾ, on 10 Muḥarram, 231 (September 16, 844), the Muslims and the non-Arab peasants (*ʿulūj*)[147] with them met with two Byzantine officers, one called Anqās and the other, Telesios.[148] The Muslims and the volunteers numbered 4,000, including horsemen and infantry.[149] They met at a place called Lamos.

It is reported that Muḥammad b. Aḥmad b. Saʿīd b. Salm b. Qutaybah al-Bāhilī received a letter from his father[150] that stated that the Muslims and the Dhimmīs[151] with them who were ransomed numbered 4,600. Six hundred of them were women and children and fewer then five hundred were Dhimmīs. The rest were men from various regions.

Abū Qaḥṭabah reported—he was the emissary of Khāqān al-Khādim to the Byzantine ruler whose task was to examine the number of prisoners and to ascertain the accuracy of what Michael, the Byzantine ruler, claimed—that the number of Muslims prior to the exchange was 3,000 men, 500 women, and children who were in Constantinople and elsewhere, save those whom the Byzantines brought forth and Muḥammad b. ʿAbdallāh al-Ṭarsūsī[152] who was in their custody.

Abū Saʿīd b. Salm sent Muḥammad b. ʿAbdallāh al-Ṭarsūsī and Khāqān, along with a number of prominent captives, to al- [1355]
Wāthiq. Al-Wāthiq placed each one of them upon a horse and gave him 1,000 dirhams.

---

147. The term *ʿulūj* is polysemous and thus difficult to translate by a single word. It means, according to Kazimirski, s.v., someone ignorant, savage, rustic, barbarian, or a non-Arab who is not a Muslim. One may say that the term refers to the autochthonic, as yet not arabicized, population. Thus, the terms "peasants" and "infidels" are occasionally employed to render the sense. *ʿUlūj* occasionally means "peasants" in the pejorative sense, even when referring to Muslims, like English "rube" or "yokel."

148. The first name may also be read Ayqās; Ms. C: Nifās? The second—Ṭalsiyūs or the like—yields Telesios; Vasiliev, *Byzance*, I, 313.

149. Yaʿqūbī, *Taʾrīkh*, II, 589, gives the number as more than 70,000 men.

150. Muḥammad b. Aḥmad's father is mentioned above, 1352 (p. 39); and see n. 138.

151. The Dhimmīs are the non-Muslim minorities, primarily Christians and Jews, living under Muslim protection, the beneficiaries of a contract (*dhimmah*) with the Muslims stipulating their obligations in return for this protection. See *EI*², s.v. Ahl al-Dhimma.

152. Leiden Ms. O gives his toponymic *nisbah* as Ṭurṭūsī. The difference determines whether he, or his family, hailed from Tarsus in Asia Minor (which is most likely) or from Tortosa in Spain; see also below, n. 462.

This same Muḥammad reported that he had been a captive in the custody of the Byzantines for thirty years, and that he was taken captive in the raid of Rāmiyah.[153] He had been one of the sellers of provender when he was taken captive, and was among those ransomed in this exchange.

Muḥammad b. 'Abdallāh said: We were ransomed on the Day of the 'Āshūrā', on the Lamos River at Seleucia, near the sea. The number of ransomed captives came to 4,460. There were 800 women, with their husbands[154] and children, and more than one hundred Dhimmīs of the Muslims. The exchange took place on a one-to-one basis, whether young or old. Khāqān endeavored to evacuate[155] all the Muslims that could be located in Byzantine territory.

Muḥammad b. 'Abdallāh continued: When they were assembled for the exchange, the Muslims stood on the east side of the river, the Byzantines on the west side. The river was fordable. Each party would send forth a man, and the two would meet in the middle of the river. When a Muslim reached the Muslims, he and they would exclaim, "God is the greatest." And when a Byzantine reached the Byzantines, they said something in their language equivalent to "God is the greatest."

It is reported on the authority of al-Sindī, *mawlā* of Ḥusayn al-Khādim:[156] The Muslims and Byzantines built bridges over the river. We would send a Byzantine over our bridge, and the Byzantines would send a Muslim over their bridge. The one would come to us and the other to them. He denied that the river was fordable.

[1356] It is reported on the authority of Muḥammad b. Karīm: When

---

153. The Index gives Rāmiyah as a toponym. For a Rāmiyah ca. 22 km, southeast of Tyre, see Dussaud, *Topographie,* 11; *Pauly-Wissowa,* s.v. Rama. Vasiliev, on the other hand (*Byzance,* I, 313), translates: "expédition de troupes légères."

154. The phrase "with their husbands" is omitted in Ibn al-Athīr, *Kāmil,* VII, 17. Ṭabarī cites conflicting accounts of the number of Muslims freed: p. 1339 (4,362), 1354 (4,600), 1355 (4,460). Ya'qūbī gives a low number of 500 men and 700 women. Other sources stay in the neighborhood of 4,000; see Vasiliev, *Byzance,* I, 202, n. 4.

155. The words "endeavored to evacuate" render *istafragha;* see Glossarium, CDI.

156. Perhaps Ḥusayn al-Khādim 'Araq al-Mawt; see Ṭabarī, III, 1841; Ya'qūbī, *Ta'rīkh,* II, 621; Jahshiyārī, *Wuzarā',* 82.

we were restored to the Muslims, Jaʿfar and Yaḥyā interrogated us. We responded appropriately and were given two dīnārs apiece.

Muḥammad b. Karīm said: The two Byzantine Patrikioi who brought forth the captives did not mind associating[157] with Jaʿfar and Yaḥyā.

He said: The Byzantines were disturbed by the number of Muslims, as they were few and the Muslims many, but Khāqān reassured them in this regard. He established a truce of forty days between the Byzantines and the Muslims, during which time the Byzantines would not be raided, so that they could reach their territory and place of safety. The exchange went on for four days. A large number of Byzantine captives remained with Khāqān, whom the Commander of the Faithful had designated for ransoming the Muslims. Khāqān turned over to the Byzantine ruler one hundred persons of those who remained with him. Thus, the Byzantines would be in arrears owing to the difference, thereby assuring an exchange for the Muslims who might be captured before the ransom period expired. He returned the rest to Tarsus, where he sold them.

Muḥammad b. Karīm said: About thirty ransomed Muslims who had converted to Christianity in Byzantine territory departed with us. When the forty-day period of truce between Khāqān and the Byzantines elapsed, Aḥmad b. Saʿīd b. Salm b. Qutaybah undertook a winter raid. Snow and rain afflicted the men, and approximately 200 died. Many drowned in the Podandos [River],[158] and about 200 were taken prisoner. The Commander of the Faithful al-Wāthiq was angry with Aḥmad b. Saʿīd for this. The total number of men who died and were drowned came to 500.

A Patrikios who was one of the Byzantine commanders advanced upon Aḥmad b. Saʿīd, who was accompanied by 7,000 [1357]
men. Aḥmad b. Saʿīd withdrew before him, whereupon the [Muslim] notables said to him. "An army of 7,000 men should not be frightened away. If you cannot face them head on, then at least

---

157. Text: *lā ba'sa bi-himā fī muʿāsharatihimā*; see Glossarium, CXXVI.

158. Badandūn or Budandūn (Budhandūn) = Podandos of the Romans and Byzantines, now called Bozanti (Pozanti), is ca. 13 km. north/northwest of the Cilician Gates; Le Strange, *Lands*, 133–35; Honigmann, *Ostgrenze*, Index, 253; Minorsky, *Ḥudūd*, 78, 220; *EI*² s.v. Bozanti.

infiltrate their territory." So he seized about 1,000 head of cattle and 10,000 sheep and departed. As a result, al-Wāthiq deposed him and appointed Naṣr b. Ḥamzah al-Khuzā'ī,[159] on Tuesday, 16 Jumādā I of this year (January 18, 846).

In this year, al-Ḥasan b. al-Ḥusayn, brother of Ṭāhir b. al-Ḥusayn, died in Ṭabaristān in Ramaḍān (May, 846).[160]

In this year, al-Khaṭṭāb b. Wajh al-Fals died.[161]

In this year, Abū 'Abdallāh b. al-A'rābī al-Rāwiyah died on Wednesday, 13 Sha'bān (April 14, 846) at the age of 80.[162]

In this year, Umm Abīhā bt. Mūsā, sister of 'Alī b. Mūsā al-Riḍā, died.[163]

In this year, Mukhāriq al-Mughannī ("the Singer")[164] died, as did Abū Naṣr Aḥmad b. Ḥātim, the transmitter of al-Aṣma'ī,[165] 'Amr b. Abī 'Amr al-Shaybānī,[166] and Muḥammad b. Sa'dān al-Naḥwī.[167]

---

159. For Naṣr b. Ḥamzah, a cousin of Aḥmad b. Naṣr, see Crone, *Slaves on Horses,* 183. He was appointed governor of Baghdad in 201 (816–17); Ṭabarī, III, 1002 (Bosworth, *Reunification,* 47); and was later governor of Damascus.

160. For the Ṭāhirid al-Ḥasan b. al-Ḥusayn b. Muṣ'ab, see Ṭabarī, III, 1066, etc.; Marin, *Reign,* 91, 93–106; Zambaur, *Manuel,* 198 (Ṭāhirids); Bosworth, "The Ṭāhirids and Ṣaffarids," 97, 100. And see Table 3.

161. Al-Khaṭṭāb b. Wajh al-Fals, a *mawlā* of Banū Umayyah, supported the revolt of the Sufyānid 'Alī b. 'Abdallāh b. Khālid b. al-Yazīd b. Mu'āwiyah against al-Amīn; Ibn al-Athīr, *Kāmil,* VI, 172, *anno* 195 (810–11).

162. He was a transmitter of poetry (*rāwiyah*), grammarian, poet, etc. See Iṣfahānī, *Aghānī,* III, 131–32, 138; Shābushtī, *Diyārāt,* 15–16, and n. 9 *ad loc.* for additional sources.

163. Umm Abīhā bt. Mūsā was the daughter of Mūsā al-Kāẓim, seventh *imām* of the Imāmī/Twelver Shī'ites. 'Alī b. Mūsā al-Riḍā, her brother, is the eighth *imām,* who had been designated by al-Ma'mūn as heir apparent.

164. Mukhāriq b. Yaḥyā al-Mughannī, a famous court musician, was active from the time of al-Amīn to that of al-Wāthiq; Ṭabarī, III, 967, etc., Guidi, *Tables,* 613; Farmer, *History,* 121–22, Index, 254; Neubauer, *Musiker,* 199–201; Stigelbauer, *Sängerinnen,* 36, 81, 111–13, especially 81, n. 537.

165. See Ibn al-Nadīm, *Fihrist,* 121; Suyūṭī, *Bughyat al-wu'āh,* 130; Sezgin, *GAS,* II, Index, 728; *EI*[2], I, 718, s.v. al-Aṣma'ī;

166. 'Amr b. Abī 'Amr al-Shaybānī, a philologist, was son of the philologist and poetry expert, Abū 'Amr Isḥāq b. Mirār al-Shaybānī; Ibn al-Nadīm, *Fihrist,* 150; Sezgin, *GAS,* II, 88, 183, 354;

167. Abū Ja'far Muḥammad b. Sa'dān al-Naḥwī, a philologist and Qur'ān reader, was son of the philologist Ibrāhīm b. Muḥammad b. Sa'dān b. al-Mubārak; Ibn al-Nadīm, *Fihrist,* 154; Sezgin, *GAS,* IX, 135.

The
Events of the Year
232
(August 28, 846–August 16, 847)

One of the events was Bughā the Elder's march against the Banū Numayr and his attack upon them.

The Reason for Bughā the Elder's March against the Banū Numayr and What Took Place between Them [1358]

I was informed[168] by Aḥmad b. Muḥammad b. Makhlad[169] concerning most of their account. He was said to be with Bughā on this journey. But the rest of the account derives from someone else.

It is reported that the reason for Bughā's march against the Banū Numayr was that ʿUmārah b. ʿAqīl b. Bilāl b. Jarīr b. al-Khaṭafī[170] eulogized al-Wāthiq in an ode, and then visited him

168. O begins with "Abū Jaʿfar said," i.e., Ṭabarī.
169. Text: Aḥmad b. Muḥammad b. Khālid. C reads Makhlad (without points); and see also Index and Addenda, DCCLXXV; and Cairo edition (on basis of A and D).
170. A panegyrist of al-Wāthiq, ʿUmārah was son of the poet ʿAqīl b. Bilāl; Iṣfahānī, *Aghānī,* XX, 183–88; Sezgin, *GAS,* II, 559.

and recited the ode to him, whereupon al-Wāthiq ordered that he be given 30,000 dirhams and lodging. ʿUmārah told al-Wāthiq about the Banū Numayr, informing him about their mockery and corruption upon earth, and about their making raids upon people, including al-Yamāmah and its adjacent territories. Al-Wāthiq thereupon wrote commanding Bughā to wage war against them.

Aḥmad b. Muḥammad reported that when Bughā was ready to march against the Banū Numayr from Medina he brought with him Muḥammad b. Yūsuf al-Jaʿfarī as a guide along the way. He headed for al-Yamāmah, and encountered a contingent of theirs in a place called al-Shurayf.[171] They engaged him in battle, and Bughā killed about fifty of their men, taking forty captive.

Bughā then went to Ḥuẓẓayyān, and thereafter to a village of the Banū Tamīm called Marʾah in the district of al-Yamāmah.[172] He encamped there, and then dispatched his emissaries to propose to the Banū Numayr a guarantee of safe-conduct, summoning them to obedience. They refused him, however, reviling his emissaries, and slipped away to do combat with him. This went
[1359] on until he dispatched two last emissaries, one of the Banū ʿAdī of Tamīm and the other of the Banū Numayr. They killed the Tamīmī and wounded the Numayrī.

Consequently, Bughā set out for them from Marʾah. His march against them was on 1 Ṣafar, 232 (September 27, 846). He came to Baṭn Nakhl and kept marching until he entered Nukhaylah, whereupon he sent word to them that they should come to him.[173]

The Banū Ḍabbah of Numayr broke camp and ascended their mountain—on the left side of the Sawd Mountain—it was a mountain to the rear of al-Yamāmah, most of whose inhabitants

---

171. There were two places named Shurayf, one in al-Yamāmah and the other in the Yemen. For the Yamāmah Shurayf, where the Banū Numayr were located, see Yāqūt, *Muʿjam*, III, 285.

172. For Ḥuẓẓayyān, see Yāqūt, *Muʿjam*, II, 292; for Banū Tamīm, see *EI*[1], s.v. Tamīm; for Marʾah in al-Yamāmah, see Yāqūt, *Muʿjam*, IV, 481; Hamdānī, *Ṣifat Jazīrat al-ʿArab*, 140, 181.

173. For Baṭn Nakhl, see Yāqūt, *Muʿjam*, I, 667; Hamdānī, *Ṣifat Jazīrat* al-ʿArab, 180, 189. There were many locations named Nukhayl (diminutive of *nakhl*, "date palm") or Nukhaylah, including the well-known Nukhaylah close to al-Kūfah (Yāqūt, *Muʿjam*, IV, 771).

were of the Bāhilah.[174] Bughā sent emissaries to them, but they refused to come to him, so he sent a detachment against the Banū Numayr, which, however, failed to overtake them. As a result, he sent detachments that eventually caught up with them and took captives. Bughā then sent in their wake one of the contingents accompanying him. It consisted of about 1,000 men, aside from the weak (*ḍuʿafāʾ*)[175] and attendants who stayed behind in the army camp. He encountered the Banū Numayr, and they rallied to fight him, numbering then about 3,000 men. They were in a place called Rawḍat al-Abān and Baṭn al-Sirr, two days journey from al-Qarnayn and one day from Uḍākh.[176] They routed his vanguard and put his left wing to flight, killing about 120 or 130 men of Bughā's force and hobbling about 700 camels and 100 riding animals in his army camp, as well as plundering the impedimenta and some of the material that was with him.

I was informed by Aḥmad b. Muḥammad: Bughā encountered them and attacked them, but the night came over him. Bughā thereupon began to implore and summon them to return to obedience[177] of the Commander of the Faithful. Muḥammad b. Yūsuf al-Jaʿfarī argued this with them.

They set about saying to him, "By God, Muḥammad b. Yūsuf, we brought you into the world,[178] but you have not respected your blood relations. Now you come to us with these slaves and peasants (*ʿulūj*) with whom you fight us. By God, we'll show you hot tears"—and such kind of talk.

When morning approached, Muḥammad b. Yūsuf said to Bughā, "Attack them before the light of dawn when they see how few we are and move boldly against us." But Bughā refused him. [1360]
When dawn broke and the Banū Numayr took notice of the number of men with Bughā—they had placed their infantry in

174. Yāqūt, *Muʿjam,* III, 183, and Hamdānī, *Ṣifat Jazīrat al-ʿArab,* 149, 169, mention Sawd (or Sūd) Bāhilah as a village belonging to the Bāhilah.

175. The term *ḍuʿafāʾ* (pl. of *ḍaʿīf*), meaning "weak, infirm," refers in this context to women, children, slaves, etc.

176. For Baṭn al-Sirr, see Yāqūt, *Muʿjam,* I, 666; Hamdānī, *Ṣifat Jazīrat al-ʿArab,* 174, 176. And for al-Qarnayn (the Two Peaks), named for two small mountains, see Yāqūt, *Muʿjam,* IV, 73.

177. Text: *wa-ilā ṭāʿah.* Addenda, DCCLXXV; *ilā ṭāʿah* . . . .

178. The word *waladnāka,* lit. "we gave birth to you," has the sense of "your mother is of our folk"; see Glossarium, DLXVI.

front of them and their horsemen at their rear, with their livestock—they attacked and routed us, all the way to our camp, and we were certain to be wiped out.

Aḥmad b. Muḥammad said: Bughā learned that some of the horses of the Banū Numayr were located at a certain place in their territory, and so he sent there about 200 horsemen from his force. Just as we were about done for, Bughā and his men having been routed, the contingent that Bughā had dispatched at night to these horses came on the scene. Coming from the place to which they had been sent from the camp, they arrived at the rear of the Banū Numayr, who had routed Bughā and his forces. Bughā's men blew their trumpets. And when the Banū Numayr heard the clarion, and spotted those who emerged against them at their rear, they exclaimed, "By God, the slave has deceived us!"[179] They turned their backs in flight, their horsemen abandoning their infantrymen after having protected them to the utmost.

I was informed by Aḥmad b. Muḥammad: Not more than one of their infantrymen survived; every last one of them was killed. But the horsemen took off in flight on the backs of their steeds.

Someone aside from Aḥmad b. Muḥammad said that the rout of Bughā and his force went on from morning to noon, on Tuesday, 13 Jumādā II, 232 (February 4, 847). The Banū Numayr were then engaged in plundering and in hobbling the camels and horses until Bughā's men who had been put to flight returned to him, and those who were separated from him rejoined him. This force attacked and routed the Banū Numayr, and from noon until afternoon killed about 1,500 of their men. Bughā stayed at the site of the skirmish at the watering place known as Baṭn al-Sirr[180] until
[1361] the heads of the Banū Numayr who were killed were gathered for him. He and his companions then rested for three days.

I was also informed by Aḥmad b. Muḥammad that the Numayrī horsemen who fled from the skirmish sent messengers to Bughā requesting a guarantee of safe conduct, which he granted them. Thus, they came to him; he bound them in fetters and went off with them.

---

179. Text: *'udhr.* Addenda, DCCLXXV; *ghadara;* see Glossarium, CCCIV; so Cairo edition on basis of D. "The slave" is pejorative for Bughā.

180. See Hamdānī, *Ṣifat Jazīrat al-'Arab,* 145.

However, someone other than Aḥmad b. Muḥammad said: Bughā went from the place of the skirmish in pursuit of those who had eluded him, but he overtook only the weak who were exhausted and some livestock, and then returned to the fortress of Bāhilah.

He said: Those of the Banū Numayr whom Bughā fought were the Banū ʿAbdallāh b. Numayr, the Banū Busrah and Bilḥajjāj, the Banū Qaṭan, the Banū Salāh, the Banū Shurayḥ, and clans that remained behind who belonged to the Banū ʿAbdallāh b. Numayr.[181] Only a few of the Banū ʿĀmir b. Numayr participated in the fighting. The Banū ʿĀmir b. Numayr are cultivators of date palms and ewes, and not horsemen. [The Banū] ʿAbdallah b. Numayr are the ones who fought the Arab tribesmen. ʿUmārah b. ʿAqīl recited to Bughā:

You left the rough ones and rugged clan,
    And filled the prisons with refuse.

I was informed by Aḥmad b. Muḥammad that after Bughā had bound, arrested, and taken with him the Banū Numayr who received his guarantee of safe-conduct, they rioted along the way and tried to break their fetters and escape. He ordered that they be brought forward one at a time. As each one was presented, he had him beaten about 400 to 500 lashes. Aḥmad[182] b. Muḥammad claimed that he witnessed their beating, and that not one of them gave vent to his pain. A shaykh of theirs was brought forth who had hung a text of the Qur'ān on his neck.[183] Muḥammad b. Yūsuf, who was seated next to Bughā, laughed at him, saying, [1362]
"This is the most offensive thing that has happened—may God give you prosperity." This was when he hung the text on his neck. He then beat him 400 or 500 lashes but the shaykh did not give in to his pain or appeal for help.

---

181. On the Banū ʿAbdallāh b. Numayr, see Caskel, *Das genealogische Werk,* I, 228; II, 116, *Jamharah,* 354. For the Banū Busrah and Bilḥajjaj of Numayr b. ʿĀmir, see *ibid.,* I, 92; II, 450; *Jamharah,* 121a. And for Banū Qaṭan, see *ibid.,* I, 290; II, 468. On Shurayḥ and Salāh, see Kaḥḥālah, *Muʿjam,* II, 590, 529.

182. Text: *aḥad.* Cairo edition (on the basis of Mss. A and D): Aḥmad.

183. For other instances of Qur'ān texts suspended from the neck, see, for example, Ibn ʿAbd Rabbihi, *ʿIqd,* I, 212; al-Mubarrad, *Kāmil,* III, 946 (ʿAbdallāh b. Khabbāb), which were brought to my attention by Dr. Khalil Athamina.

It is reported that a horseman of the Banū Numayr, called[184] "the Madman" (*al-majnūn*), encountered Bughā and stabbed him in the course of the skirmish that I have described. One of the Turks shot the Madman, but he escaped and lived for three days before succumbing to his wound.

Then Wājin al-Ushrūsanī al-Ṣughdī[185] joined Bughā, along with an auxiliary force of 700 men of the Ushrūsaniyyah-Ishtīkhaniyyah.[186] Bughā sent Wājin and Muḥammad b. Yūsuf al-Jaʿfarī after the Banū Numayr. They pursued the latter relentlessly until they penetrated deep into the territory of the Banū Numayr, coming to Tabālah[187] and its environs at the border of the district of the Yemen, but the Banū Numayr eluded him.

Bughā departed, having apprehended only six or seven of them, and then stayed at the fortress of Bāhilah. Bughā sent detachments from Halān, Sawd, and other places in the district of al-Yamāmah to the mountains and plains of the Banū Numayr to fight those who accepted the guarantee of safe conduct and then held out. The detachments killed one contingent and took another captive. A number of the leaders of the Banu Numayr began to request a guarantee of safe conduct, each one for himself and for his own clan. Bughā acceded to them, and was magnanimous and conciliatory. He remained until all those suspected of being in these regions were rounded up for him. Seizing about 300 men, he fettered them with irons and brought them to al-Baṣrah, in Dhū al-Qaʿdah, 232 (June 19–July 18, 847).

---

184. Text: *bi-duʿā'*. Addenda, DCCLXXV and Cairo edition (Ms. D): *yudʿā*.

185. Wājin (or: Wājan) al-Ushrūsani al-Ṣughdī (the Ṣughdian) was from Ushrūsanah, the name of a province and a town east of Samarqand in Transoxania; Le Strange, *Lands*, 474–76. See also Ṭabarī, III, 1306–07 (Marin, *Reign*, 113) and 1503 (Saliba, 3); Yaʿqūbī; *Ta'rīkh*, II, 602.

186. Text: Al-Ushrūsaniyyah al-Ishtīkhaniyyah. Ishtīkhan is a town slightly to the north of Samarqand; Le Strange, *Lands*, 466. The compound term may refer to citizens of the town of Ishtīkhan in the province of Ushrūsanah. But the two formed separate elements in the mixed population of military personnel living in Sāmarrā, that is, the Farāghinah, Ushrūsaniyyah, Ishtīkhanjiyyah and others, from various districts of Khurāsān; see, e.g., Yāqūt, *Muʿjam*, 263 = Wiet, *Les pays*, 55. Perhaps the word "and" must be supplied or understood.

187. Tabālah is in northwest Yemen, in the interior of ʿAsīr; Yāqūt, *Muʿjam*, I, 816; *EI*[1], s.v.

Bughā sent a dispatch to Ṣāliḥ al-ʿAbbāsī[188] to march with those of the Banū Kilāb, Fazārah, Murrah, Thaʿlabah, and others who were with him in the city and to meet up with him. Ṣāliḥ al-ʿAbbāsī overtook Bughā in Baghdad, and both of them went to Sāmarrā in al-Muḥarram, 233 (August 17–September 15, 847).

The number of Arab tribesmen whom Bughā and Ṣāliḥ [1363] al-ʿAbbāsī brought, aside from those who died, fled, and were killed in these skirmishes that we have described, were 2,200, including men of the Banū Numayr, Banū Kilāb, Murrah, Fazārah, Thaʿlabah, and Ṭayyiʾ.[189]

In this year, the pilgrims were stricken upon the return journey by fierce thirst at four stations to al-Rabadhah.[190] A drink fetched the price of a few dīnārs. Many people died of thirst.

In this year, Muḥammad b. Ibrāhīm b. Muṣʿab was appointed governor of Fārs.

In this year, al-Wāthiq gave orders to desist from tithing seagoing vessels.

In this year, the cold was so severe in Nīsān (April) that water froze on the fifth day of the month.

In this year, al-Wāthiq died.

An Account of the Illness from Which al-Wāthiq Died

A number of our colleagues informed me that the illness from which al-Wāthiq died was dropsy. He was treated by being seated in a heated oven, where he found relief and comfort.[191] Al-Wāthiq ordered them the next day to increase the heat of the oven. This was done, and he sat in it longer than on the previous day. But he

188. On Ṣāliḥ al-ʿAbbāsī (al-Turkī), see also below 1422 (p. 134), where the governor of Damascus sends him with troops to quell a revolt in Ḥimṣ. Yaʿqūbī, *Buldān,* 262 = Wiet, *Les pays,* 55, notes a street and palace named for him in Sāmarrā. See Herzfeld, *Samarra,* 112.

189. See Caskel, *Das genealogische Werk,* I, 176; II, 555, *Jamharah,* 87.

190. Al-Rabadhah was an important station on the Mecca Road near Medina, about 6 km. from Dhāt ʿIrq; Yaʿqūbī, *Buldān,* 312 = Wiet, *Les pays,* 146; Yāqūt, *Muʿjam,* II 748; Hamdānī, *Ṣifat Jazīrat al-ʿArab,* 142, 171, 185.

191. According to Yaʿqūbī, *Taʾrīkh,* II, 590, the ground was dug out to form a cavity, which was then heated with tamarisk wood.

was overcome with heat, and was then removed from the oven and placed on a litter. Al-Faḍl b. Isḥāq al-Hāshimī, 'Umar b. Faraj, and others were present. Then Ibn al-Zayyāt and Ibn Abī Du'ād arrived. They were unaware of the caliph's death until his face struck the litter, at which point they realized that he had died.

According to another version, Aḥmad b. Abī Du'ād attended him, and was with him when he lost consciousness[192] and died, whereupon Aḥmad approached to close his eyelids[193] and fit him out [for burial].[194] His death was on 23 Dhū al-Ḥijjah (August 10,
[1364] 847). He was buried in his palace in the Hārūnī. The one who recited funeral prayers, attended to his burial, and took care of his affairs was Aḥmad b. Abī Du'ād. Al-Wāthiq had ordered Aḥmad b. Abī Du'ād to lead the public prayer on the Day of Sacrifice (10 Dhū al-Ḥijjah) in the oratory. Aḥmad led the festival prayers, for al-Wāthiq was very ill, and could not attend the oratory. He died of this illness.

A Portrayal of al-Wāthiq, His Years, and the Extent of His Caliphate

Someone who knew him personally reported that al-Wāthiq was fair, tending to a ruddy complexion, and was handsome, of medium height and well-built. His left eye was paralyzed and had a white fleck.[195] He died, as some claim, at the age of thirty-six; according to others, he succumbed at the age of thirty-two. Those who claim that he was thirty-six say that he was born in 196

192. Text: *a'mā 'alayhi.* Addenda, DCCLXXV and Cairo edition (Mss. A and D): *ghumiya 'alayhi.*

193. The word *ghammaḍa* means "to close the eyelids of a dead person"; Glossarium, CCCXCII; Introductio, LXXXIX.8, and note d, which refers to Ṭabarī, III, 1136.13; see also Dozy, *Supplément,* II, 227.

194. For *yuṣliḥu min sha'nihi* in the sense of "fit him out" or the like, see Glossarium, CCCXXVI.

195. A fair (*abyaḍ*) complexion connoted nobility, and ruddy (*aḥmar*) was often used for northern people (Byzantines and Greeks), according to Fischer, *Farb- und Formbezeichnungen,* 338–39. For similar physical descriptions of al-Wāthiq, see also Mas'ūdī, *Tanbīh,* 361; Abū al-Maḥāsin, *Nujūm,* II, 263; Suyūṭī, *Ta'rīkh,* 342 = tr. Jarrett, 356. William Beckford, in his famous novel *Vathek* (1786), calls particular attention to al-Wāthiq's terrible eye that no one could bear to behold. Beckford's source was D'Herbelot's reference to al-Wāthiq's "oeil si terrible" in *Bibliothèque Orientale* (1697), 912. On al-Wāthiq's awesome glare, see, for example, Tha'ālibī, *Laṭā'if,* 111.

(811–12) and that his caliphate lasted five years, nine months, and five days. And some of them say seven days and twelve hours. He was born along the route of the Mecca Road. His mother was a Byzantine slave named Qarāṭīs. His name was Hārūn, his teknomyn, Abū Jaʿfar.

It is reported that when he was stricken with the sickness from which he died—his abdomen had become afflicted with dropsy—he ordered that the astrologers be brought into his presence, and they were. Among those in attendance were al-Ḥasan b. Sahl, the brother of al-Faḍl b. Sahl;[196] al-Faḍl b. Isḥāq al-Hāshimī;[197] Ismāʿīl b. Nawbakht;[198] Muḥammad b. Mūsā al-Khwārazmī; al-Majūsī al-Quṭrabbulī;[199] Sanad, the associate of Muḥammad b. al-Haytham;[200] and all those engaged in astrology. They considered his illness, star, and horoscope, and predicted that he would live a long time, estimating fifty years in the future. But in less than ten days he died.

Some Reports about al-Wāthiq [1365]

Al-Ḥusayn b. al-Ḍaḥḥāk[201] reported that he saw al-Wāthiq a few days after al-Muʿtaṣim died. He was seated at the first soirée that

---

196. Al-Ḥasan b. Sahl was court astrologer and finance minister and governor for al-Ma'mūn; d. 236 (850–51); Bosworth, *Reunification*, Index, 272; Sourdel, *Vizirat*, Index, 766, and especially 215–18; Sezgin, *GAS*, VII, 122; *EI*², s.v. His brother al-Faḍl b. Sahl, Dhū al-Riyāsatayn, was court astrologer for Hārūn al-Rashīd and then wazīr of al-Ma'mūn, who had him killed in 202 (817–18) or 203 (818–19); Bosworth, Index, 271; Sourdel, Index, 761, and especially 196–213; Sezgin, *GAS*, VII, 115; *EI*², s.v. Sezgin cites our passage on p. 119.

197. Al-Faḍl b. Isḥāq al-Hāshimī was presumably the son of Isḥāq b. Sulaymān al-Hāshimī, who served in the court of al-Ma'mūn; Ibn Ṭayfūr, *Baghdād*, 1, 79; Sezgin, *GAS*, VII, 119.

198. See on him, Ibn Ṭayfūr, *Baghdād*, 164.

199. The mathematician-astronomer Muḥammad b. Mūsā b. al-Khwārazmī was born in Khwārazm and served in the court of al-Ma'mūn; Ṭabarī, III, 1085 (Bosworth, *Reunification*, 158); Ibn Ṭayfūr, *Baghdād*, 29, 79, 116, 192; Ibn al-Nadīm, *Fihrist*, 652; Ibn al-Qifṭī, *Ta'rīkh*, 286; Sezgin, *GAS*, V, 228; *EI*², s.v. Khʷārazmī, Abū Djaʿfar. Al-Majūsī al-Quṭrabbulī is unidentified.

200. For the mathematician and astronomer/astrologer Sanad (or Sind) b. ʿAlī Abū al-Ṭayyib, see Sezgin, *GAS*, V, 242; VI, 138; VII, 119. For Muḥammad b al-Haytham b. ʿAdī al-Ṭā'ī, see Ṭabarī, III, 1141, 1156 (Bosworth, *Reunification*, 232, 249); and Ibn Ṭayfūr, *Baghdād*, 89, 144.

201. Text: al-Ḥasan. Addenda, DCCLXXV, and Cairo edition (Mss. A and D): al-Ḥusayn. Al-Ḥusayn b. al-Ḍaḥḥāk al-Bāhilī al-Ashqar al-Khalīʿ ("the Dissolute"), a

he convened. The first song at this soirée was rendered by Shāriyah, the slave girl of Ibrāhīm b. al-Mahdī:[202]

When the bearers raised his bier they knew not
If it be for abiding or perdition.

May your female mourners say about you what they wish,
Morning and night.[203]

Al-Ḥusayn b. al-Ḍaḥḥāk said: He wept and, by God, we wept to the point that the weeping totally possessed us. Then one of the singers proceeded to sing:[204]

Bid farewell, Hurayrah, for the cavalcade is departing.
O man, can you endure saying farewell?[205]

Al-Ḥusayn b. al-Ḍaḥḥāk said: And the caliph wept, by God, even more, exclaming, "I have never heard a condolence[206] for a father or an elegy as I did today." Then the soirée dispersed.

Al-Ḥusayn b. al-Ḍaḥḥāk reported on the authority of ʿAbdallāh b. al-ʿAbbās b. al-Faḍl b. al-Rabīʿ that ʿAlī b. al-Jahm recited concerning al-Wāthiq after he became caliph:[207]

---

well-known Baṣrian poet, court poet of ʿAbbāsid caliphs, confidant of al-Amīn, was a panegyrist of al-Wāthiq; d. 250 (864–65); *EI*², s.v. al-Ḥusayn b. al-Ḍaḥḥāk; Sezgin, *GAS*, II, 518–19.

202. Shāriyah al-Jāriyah, a famous singing girl, was freed by the ʿAbbāsid prince Ibrāhīm b. al-Mahdī, who then married her; Iṣfahānī, *Aghānī*, XIV, 109–114; Shābushtī, *Diyārāt*, 8,100,110-11, 154; Ibn al-Zubayr, *Dhakhā'ir*, par. 144; Farmer, *History*, 134; Stigelbauer, *Sängerinnen*, Index, 173, especially 39–49.

203. Text: *wa-waqt*. Read *wa-ʿinda* (with Ibn al-Athīr and Ṣūlī). At this point the Leiden edition begins to cite variants from Abū Bakr al-Ṣūlī, *Kitāb al-awrāq* (see Translator's Foreword).

204. Ṣūlī: *fa-ghannā Mukhāriq* ("Mukhāriq sang").

205. This is the beginning of one of the most famous odes in Arabic literature. See Geyer, *Zwei Gedichte von al-'Aʿšâ*, II, 10. Hurayrah, a singing girl of Bishr b. ʿAmr of Ḥīrah, is the beloved of the poet al-Aʿshā.

206. Text: *wa-baghī*. Addenda, DCCLXXV, and Cairo edition: *wa-naʿī*.

207. ʿAbdallāh b. al-ʿAbbās b. al-Faḍl b. al-Rabīʿ was a singer and composer of melodies in caliphal courts from the time of Hārūn al-Rashīd to that of al-Muntaṣir; d. 227 (841–42); Iṣfahānī, *Aghānī*, XVII, 121–41; Farmer, *History*, 160; Neubauer, *Musiker*, 161. ʿAlī b. al-Jahm b. Badr was a well-known poet and sometime judge; d. 249 (863). He was court poet during the reign of al-Mutawakkil; *EI*², s.v. ʿAlī b. al-Djahm; Sezgin, *GAS*, II, 580–81. For the poem, see Iṣfahānī, *Aghānī*, XII, 117, and ʿAlī b. al-Jahm, *Dīwān*, 188.

Both the worldly and the pious
Thrive during the regime of al-Wāthiq Hārūn.

He abounds with justice and generosity,
Sustaining this world along with religion.

Goodness prevails through his kindness,[208]
And people are at comfort and ease.

How many wish him a long life [1366]
And how many intone "amen."

ʿAlī b. al-Jahm also recited concerning him:[209]

People trust (*wathiqat*) the king al-Wāthiq bi-llāh.
With this monarch wealth is wretched, not the companion.[210]

The sword is congenial to him,
The precious object alien.

A lion he, stern battle smiles at his might.
Sons of al-ʿAbbās, God wills that only you govern.[211]

Qalam, the slave girl of Ṣāliḥ b. ʿAbd al-Wahhāb, sang these two songs, and she rendered the song of Muḥammad b. Kunāsah:[212]

I may be respectful and timid,
But when I sit with people of faith and honor

---

208. Text: *qad ʿamma bi-l-iḥsān fī faḍlihi.* Iṣfahānī, *Aghānī,* XII, 117 (cited in note): *wa-ʿamma bi-l-iḥsān min fiʿlihi.*

209. Iṣfahānī, *Aghānī,* XII, 117, has the poem with slight variants; see also ʿAlī b al-Jahm, *Dīwān,* 13.

210. The meaning is that his generosity puts the wealthy to shame, while his companion benefits.

211. Text: *ya'bī...illā.* Addenda, DCCLXXV: *ya'ba...illā,* Note the association here of the lion metaphor with the name ʿAbbās. See above, n. 76.

212. On Qalam, or Qalam al-Ṣāliḥiyyah—Qalam means "Reed Pen"—the slave girl of Ṣāliḥ b. ʿAbd al-Wahhāb, see Iṣfahānī, *Aghānī,* XII 115–117, VIII, 173; Herzfeld, *Samarra,* 162. For Abū Yaḥyā Muḥammad b. Kunāsah, see Ibn al-Nadīm, *Fihrist,* 198, 362; Iṣfahānī, *Aghānī,* XII, 111–16. The poem and the following account appear in *Aghānī,* XII, 116.

I let my soul behave naturally
And say what I like without being shy.

When her tune was sung in al-Wāthiq's presence,[213] he liked it and sent a message to Ibn al-Zayyāt: "Woe unto you, who is this Ṣāliḥ b. ʿAbd al-Wahhāb? Summon him and have him bring along his slave girl." Ṣāliḥ brought her to al-Wāthiq, and she was introduced to him. Pleased with her singing, he sent to Ṣāliḥ asking that he state his price. Ṣāliḥ replied, "100,000 dīnārs, O Commander of the Faithful, as well as the governorship of Egypt." So the caliph returned her. Then Aḥmad b. ʿAbd al-Wahhāb, brother of Ṣāliḥ, recited concerning al-Wāthiq:

The house of the lovers does not wish you to separate,[214]
What you see has made you a new helper for them.

The souls of those who loved Laylā[215] were tormented
And remained unrequited and uncompensated.

Qalam, the slave girl of Ṣāliḥ, composed this song. And Zurzur
[1367] the Elder[216] sang it for al-Wāthiq. The caliph asked whose song it was, and Zurzur responded that it was composed by Qalam. Al-Wāthiq sent word to Ibn al-Zayyāt to bring Ṣāliḥ and Qalam along with him.

When she entered, al-Wāthiq asked her if she had composed the song, and she replied, "Yes, O Commander of the Faithful." He said, "May God bless you." And he sent a message to Ṣāliḥ asking him to name a reasonable price.

Ṣāliḥ replied by message, "I give her as a gift to the Commander of the Faithful, and may God bless the Commander of the Faithful through her," The caliph replied, "I accept her. [And turning to

---

213. Text: *fa-ghannathu*. The translation follows the reading suggested in the note (*fa-ghunniya laḥnuhā bayn yaday*). In Iṣfahānī, *Aghānī*, XII, 116, where the poem is cited and the following anecdote related, the caliph immediately asks who composed the music and is told that it was Qalam.

214. The translation is uncertain.

215. The allusion is to Laylā, the beloved of Majnūn, in the popular romance Majnūn Laylā. A certain Qays b. al-Mulawwaḥ loved Laylā bt. Saʿd, but he could not have her and thus lost his mind. See *EI*², s.v. Madjnūn Laylā.

216. Zurzur or Zurzūr ("Starling") b. Saʿīd al-Kabīr was a page (*ghulām*) of Jaʿfar b. Mūsā al-Hādī and court singer during the caliphates of al-Maʾmūn, al-Muʿtaṣim and al-Wāthiq; Iṣfahānī, *Aghānī*, XII, 92–93; Neubauer, *Musiker*, 210.

Ibn al-Zayyāt, he said,] "Muḥammad, pay him 5,000 dīnārs." He called her Ightibāṭ ("Delight").

Ibn al-Zayyāt put Ṣāliḥ off, and she went on singing, "The house of the lovers does not wish. . ."

Al-Wāthiq said to her, "May God bless you and the one who taught you."

She replied, "Sir, and how does the one who taught me benefit?" You have ordered that he be given something that he has not received." Al-Wāthiq said, "Sammānah, the inkwell!"[217] He wrote to Ibn al-Zayyāt: "Pay Ṣāliḥ b. ʿAbd al-Wahhāb the price for Ightibāṭ, 5,000 dīnārs, and double it."

Ṣāliḥ said: I went to Ibn al-Zayyāt, who received me well. He said, "Take this first 5,000. As for the other 5,000, I shall pay you in a week. If you are asked [about this], say that you have received the money."

Ṣāliḥ said, "I didn't want to be asked and have to acknowledge that I received the money, so I hid in my house until he paid me. When Sammānah asked me if I had received the money, I said yes."

Ṣāliḥ left government service and used the money for business ventures until he died.

---

217. Text: Saymānah. Addenda, DCCLXXV, and Cairo edition: Sammānah. Iṣfahānī, *Aghānī*, XII, 116.22, mentions here only an anonymous servant (*khādim*).

The Caliphate of Jaʿfar al-Mutawakkil ʿalā-llāh

Portrait of al-Mutawakkil from a medallion dated 241/855. Photo courtesy Kunsthistorisches Museum, Vienna

The Events of the Year 232 (cont'd)

(August 28, 846–August 16, 847)

In this year Jaʿfar al-Mutawakkil was given the oath of allegiance as caliph. He is Jaʿfar b. Muḥammad b. Hārūn b. Muḥammad b. ʿAbdallāh b. Muḥammad Dhū al-Thafināt b. ʿAlī al-Sajjād b. ʿAbdallāh b. al-ʿAbbās b. ʿAbd al-Muṭṭalib.[218] [1368]

The Occasion of Jaʿfar's Becoming Caliph and the Period of His Caliphate

I was informed by more than one authority that when al-Wāthiq died Aḥmad b. Abī Du'ād, Ītākh, Waṣīf, ʿUmar b. Faraj, Ibn al-Zayyāt, and Aḥmad b. Khālid Abū al-Wazīr were present in his

218. Dhū al-Thafināt means "The Callused," referring to calluses on the knees caused by frequent praying. Sajjād is "The Worshipper," designating one who prostrates himself often. Thus, the two are virtually synonomous in meaning, and it is not surprising that the nicknames of Muḥammad and ʿAlī are occasionally reversed. See, for instance, Ibn Qutaybah, *Maʿārif,* 54; Mubarrad, *Kāmil,* II, 573; Ibn Khallikān, *Wafayāt,* II, 216–20; 592–94; Abū al-Faraj b. al-Jawzī, *Kitāb al-alqāb,* s.v. And see Ṭabarī, III, 2497. On the caliphate of al-Mutawakkil, see M. Shamsuddin Miah, *The Reign of al-Mutawakkil.*

palace.[219] They decided to render the oath of allegiance to Muḥammad b. al-Wāthiq, who was a beardless lad.[220] They dressed him in a black lined robe (*durrāʿah*)[221] and a Ruṣāfī cap.[222] It turned out that he was too small.

Waṣīf said to them, "For God's sake, can you assign the caliphate to someone like this, who is not even permitted to lead public prayer?"

My authorities said: They went on arguing about whom they would appoint, mentioning several candidates. One of those present in the palace with them reportedly said, "I left the place where I was and passed by Jaʿfar al-Mutawakkil, who was dressed in a shirt and trousers, sitting with the sons of the Turks. He asked me what news there was, and I replied that their deliberation was still going on. They thereafter summoned him."

Bughā al-Sharābī gave him the news and brought him. Al-Mutawakkil responded that he feared that al-Wāthiq had not died.

My authorities said: Al-Mutawakkil passed by al-Wāthiq and saw that he was garbed in a shroud, whereupon he came and sat. Aḥmad b. Abī Du'ād dressed Jaʿfar with a tall hat,[223] affixed a
[1369] turban and kissed him between his eyes, saying, "Peace upon you, O Commander of the Faithful, and God's mercy and blessings." Then al-Wāthiq was washed, the funeral prayer was offered, and he was buried. Following this, they went immediately to the Public Audience Hall. Al-Mutawakkil had not yet been given his regnal title.

On the day that al-Mutawakkil received the oath of allegiance, he was reportedly twenty-six years old. He set aside pay allot-

---

219. Note in this company the combination of government officials/secretaries (Aḥmad b. Abī Du'ād, ʿUmar b. Faraj, Ibn al-Zayyāt, Aḥmad b. Khālid) with Turkish army commanders (Ītākh, Waṣīf). For this passage, see also Chejne, *Succession,* 121–22.

220. Muḥammad b. al-Wāthiq later became caliph with the throne name al-Muhtadī.

221. Ahsan, *Social Life,* 39–40, infers from our passage that caliphs occasionally wore a *durrāʿah* at their installation. On *durrāʿah,* see also *EI*², s.v. Libās, V, 737.

222. For *qalansuwah Ruṣāfiyyah,* see Dozy, *Vêtements,* 188, citing Ibn Khallikān, *Wafayāt,* I, 315; Ahsan, *Social Life,* 30, 52; *EI*², s.v. Libās, V, 734–35. The *qalansuwah* was at first a close-fitting cap, but it may also be a cowl or hood.

223. The word *al-ṭawīlah* is short for *al-qalansuwah al-ṭawīlah*; Glossarium, CCCXLIV. It was "a tall, conical Persian hat"; see Ahsan, *Social Life,* 15, 30, 55; *EI*², s.v. Libās, V, 737.

ments for the regular army for a period of eight months. Muḥammad b. ʿAbd al-Malik al-Zayyāt drafted the oath of allegiance for him. He was responsible at the time for the Bureau of the Chancellery (*dīwān al-rasāʾil*).

They assembled afterward to choose a regnal title for the caliph. Ibn al-Zayyāt suggested that they call him al-Muntaṣir billāh. The notables discussed the matter thoroughly until they came to a definite conclusion. Aḥmad b. Abī Du'ād came to al-Mutawakkil early the next day and said, "I've come up with a regnal title that I hope will be appropriate, God willing. It is al-Mutawakkil ʿalā-llāh." Al-Mutawakkil then gave word that this regnal title should be adopted. He summoned Muḥammad b. ʿAbd al-Malik and ordered that this be conveyed in writing to the notables. Letters were dispatched to them bearing the following text:

> In the name of God, the merciful, the compassionate. The Commander of the Faithful, may God give him long life, has ordered, may God preserve you, that his official title be on his pulpits[224] and in his letters to his judges, secretaries, officials, and functionaries in his government bureaus and others with whom he is customarily in correspondence, "From ʿAbdallāh Jaʿfar al-Imām al-Mutawakkil ʿalā-llāh, Commander of the Faithful." I await your response indicating your readiness to execute this order and informing me of my letter's successful arrival, God willing.

It is reported that when the caliph ordered that the Turks be given service allotments for four months, and that the regular army, the Shākiriyyah, and those of a like status among the Hāshimites be given allotments for eight months, he ordered that [1370]
the Maghāribah be given allotments for three months. They, however, refused to accept.[225] He wrote to them, "Whoever

224. For *aʿwād manābirihi* in this sense, see Glossarium CCCLXXXII; Dozy, *Supplément*, II, 186.

225. The translation follows the Leiden text. But in the Mss. used for the Leiden edition the Shākiriyyah appear after the words "eight months." The reading of the Leiden text is based upon a collation of Ibn al-Athīr, *Kāmil*, 23; *Fragmenta*, 536, ll. 12–13; and ʿAynī, *ʿIqd al-Jumān* (which the notes begin to cite here from manuscript). In these sources, however, it is stated: "He commanded to give the Shākiriyyah of the regular army [allotments] for eight months."

among you is a slave (*mamlūk*) shall go to Aḥmad b. Abī Du'ād to be sold, and whoever is free will be treated by us along the lines of the regular army." They accepted this. Waṣīf persuaded them until they were brought around. They were given three months' service allotments, and then were paid along the lines of the Turks.

Al-Mutawakkil received the notables' oath of allegiance at the hour of al-Wāthiq's death, and [he received] the public oath of allegiance at sunset on the same day.

It is reported on the authority of Sa'īd the Younger[226] that before al-Mutawakkil was made caliph he told Sa'īd and a number of people who were with him that he dreamt that Sulaymānī sugar[227] would descend upon him from heaven, on which was written "Ja'far al-Mutawakkil 'alā-llāh." He discussed the dream's significance with us. We said, "It is, by God, O amīr—may God strengthen you—the caliphate."

Sa'īd said: When al-Wāthiq learned of this, he held Ja'far in custody, and Sa'īd along with him, and harassed Ja'far because of it.

Leading the pilgrimage this year was Muḥammad b. Dāwūd.

---

226. Abū 'Uthmān Sa'īd al-Ṣaghīr appears below as confidant of al-Muntaṣir; below, 1471ff. (pp. 195ff.); see also p. 1743, where he is mentioned as belonging to al-Muntaṣir.

227. Sugar is called *sukkar Sulaymānī* at the second stage of preparation, according to *EI*[1], s.v. Sukkar. See also Ahsan, *Social Life,* 100ff., especially 101, n. 208 (citing N. Dear, *The History of Sugar,* London, 1949, I, 68ff., 74ff.; Rodinson, *EI*[2], s.v. Ghidhā'; *idem, JESHO,* 7 [1964], 57–72).

The Events of the Year 233

(August 17, 847–July 7, 848)

One of the events was al-Mutawakkil's anger at Muḥammad b. ʿAbd al-Malik al-Zayyāt and his incarcerating him.

The Reason for al-Mutawakkil's Anger at Muḥammad b. al-Zayyāt and Its Consequences

The reason for al-Mutawakkil's anger at him was reportedly as follows:

Al-Wāthiq had made Muḥammad b. ʿAbd al-Malik al-Zayyāt wazīr and delegated affairs to him. Al-Wāthiq had become angry with his brother Jaʿfar al-Mutawakkil for certain things and authorized ʿUmar b. Faraj al-Rukhkhajī and Muḥammad b. al-ʿAlāʾ al-Khādim to observe him at all times and record information [1371]
about him.[228]

---

228. Muḥammad b. al-ʿAlāʾ al-Khādim is said to have been active under al-Maʾmūn along with the police chief ʿAyyāsh; Herzfeld, *Samarra*, 174, n. 2. Al-Wāthiq's annoyance was presumably triggered by the suspicion that his brother Jaʿfar wished to follow him in the line of succession, thus displacing al-Wāthiq's own son.

Jaʿfar went to Muḥammad b. ʿAbd al-Malik to request that he intercede with his brother al-Wāthiq on his behalf so that he might be restored to favor. After entering, Jaʿfar remained standing before Muḥammad for a while without being addressed. Then Muḥammad motioned for him to be seated, at which point he sat down. When Muḥammad was finished going over his correspondence, he turned to Jaʿfar in a menacing way and inquired why he had come.

He replied, "I came so that you might ask the Commander of the Faithful to look upon me with favor."

Muḥammad commented to those around him, "Look at this one. He infuriates his brother and then asks me to restore him to favor. Go, and if you make amends, then you will be reinstated."

Jaʿfar rose, dejected and morose as result of the poor audience and his having been slighted. He left Muḥammad's company and approached ʿUmar b. Faraj to request that he sign his chit for receipt of pay allotments. But ʿUmar b. Faraj let him down. He took the chit and tossed it into the courtyard of the mosque. It was ʿUmar's custom to sit in a mosque.

Abū al-Wazīr Aḥmad b. Khālid was present. When he got up to depart, Jaʿfar rose along with him. Jaʿfar inquired, "O Abū al-Wazīr, did you see what ʿUmar b. Faraj did with me?" Abū al-Wazīr replied, "What may I do for you?"

Jaʿfar said, "I am ʿUmar's steward,[229] and yet he does not sign my chit without my importuning and groveling. Send me your agent." Abū al-Wazīr sent Jaʿfar his agent and paid him 20,000 dirhams, telling him, "Use this for spending until God straightens out your affairs."

Jaʿfar took the money and sent Abū al-Wazīr's messenger back to him a month later asking Abū al-Wazīr for help. Abū al-Wazīr sent him 10,000 dirhams.

Immediately after leaving ʿUmar, Jaʿfar went to Aḥmad b. Abī Du'ād. When he entered, Aḥmad rose to meet him. He received him at the door of the house, kissed him, and acted obligingly toward him.

229. Text: *zammām*. Addenda, DCCLXXV: *zimām*. See Glossarium, CCLXXIX ("inspector, controller"). The *zimām* was the Bureau of Control, that is, an auditing body, as of taxes or expenditures; see Hilāl al-Ṣābī, *Wuzarā'*, 284, 380; Sourdel, *Vizirat*, Index, 759.

Aḥmad asked him, "Why have you come? What may I do for you?" Jaʿfar replied, "I have come to try and secure the favor of the Commander of the Faithful." Aḥmad said, "It is my pleasure and honor to do it [for you]."

Aḥmad b. Abī Du'ād then spoke to al-Wāthiq about this, and, although he promised [to restore Jaʿfar to favor], he was still not [1372] receptive to him. On the day of the races, Aḥmad b. Abī Du'ād spoke with al-Wāthiq.[230]

Aḥmad said, "I am ever-mindful of al-Muʿtaṣim's kindness, and Jaʿfar is his son. I have spoken to you about him, and you promised to extend your grace. You owe it to al-Muʿtaṣim, O Commander of the Faithful, to show favor to him." Al-Wāthiq immediately showed kindness to him and attired him. Al-Wāthiq then departed. As Aḥmad b. Abī Du'ād had spoken flatteringly of Jaʿfar, causing his brother to show him favor, Aḥmad b. Abī Du'ād was in good stead with Jaʿfar when the latter assumed rulership.

Muḥammad b. ʿAbd al-Malik had reportedly written to al-Wāthiq when Jaʿfar left him: "Commander of the Faithful, Jaʿfar b. al-Muʿtaṣim came to me, requesting that I ask the Commander of the Faithful to be kind to him. He was, however, dressed in an effeminate fashion and had long hair in the back."

Al-Wāthiq wrote to Muḥammad, "Send for him and have him presented. Order someone to cut the hair in the back, then give word to someone to take some of his hair[231] and strike his face with it, and send him back to his residence."

It is reported on the authority of al-Mutawakkil: When al-Wāthiq's emissary came to me, I was wearing a new black garment, and I came to him, hoping that he would be favorably disposed toward me.

When I arrived he said, "Page, summon me a cupper (*ḥajjām*)," whereupon one was summoned. He said, "Cut his hair[232] and gather it together." The cupper sheared it upon the new black

---

230. On *ḥalbah* ("races"), see Mercier, *La chasse,* 200–04. A hippodrome in Sāmarrā stood slightly to the southeast of the Great Mosque of al-Mutawakkil.

231. The expression *akhadha min shaʿrihi,* lit. "to take (from) his hair," may mean "to cut his hair"; Glossarium, CVII; Lane, *Lexicon,* 28. But here the first sense fits better.

232. See previous note.

garment, not bothering to catch it on a piece of cloth (*mandīl*).[233] He took Jaʿfar's hair, including the hair from the back, and struck him in the face with it.

Al-Mutawakkil said: I was never so distressed by anything as I was when al-Wāthiq had my hair sheared upon the new black garment. I came to him so attired, hoping to please him, but he had my hair cut upon it.

When al-Wāthiq died, Muḥammad b. ʿAbd al-Malik nominated al-Wāthiq's son as his successor.[234] The matter was discussed[235] while Jaʿfar was in another room, not where they were deliberating the investiture.[236] [Jaʿfar remained in that other room] until
[1373] he was sent for, and he was invested [with the symbol of the caliphate] there. [His preference for al-Wāthiq's son] was the cause of Ibn al-Zayyāt's demise. Bughā al-Sharābī was the emissary who summoned Jaʿfar. On the way, he greeted him as caliph, and they invested him [with the symbol of the caliphate] and rendered him the oath of allegiance.

Jaʿfar bided his time until Wednesday, 7 Ṣafar, 233 (September 22, 847). Resolved to hurt Ibn al-Zayyāt, al-Mutawakkil ordered Ītākh to seize and punish him. So Ītākh sent for him. Ibn al-Zayyāt thought that he was being summoned [for an audience]. He rode out early the next day, supposing that the caliph had summoned him, but, when he was opposite the residence of Ītākh, he was told to turn in the direction of Abū Manṣūr's (Ītākh's) residence. He turned apprehensively, and, when he came to Ītākh's residence, he was diverted to the right,[237] and thus he sensed something ominous. Ibn al-Zayyāt was then brought into a room. His sword, ornamental belt, cap, and lined robe (*dur-*

233. A *mandīl* (from Latin *mantellum*; cf. Spanish *mantilla* and English mantle) is a small or medium-size kerchief or piece of cloth, occasionally used as a head veil; see Rosenthal, *Four Essays*, 63ff., especially 67; Ahsan, *Social Life*, 53; *EI*[2], s.v.

234. This act is consistent with Muḥammad b. ʿAbd al-Malik's previous coolness toward Jaʿfar.

235. Text: *wa-takallama dhālika fī dhālika.* Omit first *dhālika* with note *ad loc.* (see also Addenda, DCCLXXV) and Cairo edition.

236. Text: *yaqʿudūna.* Cairo edition (Ms. A): *yaʿqidūna.*

237. Text: *ʿanhu* ("he was diverted from it"); Cairo edition, Mss. A and D: *yamnatan* ("to the right"). A vaulted cellar (Persian: *serdāb*) in Ītākh's residence was occasionally used as a prison; Ṭabarī, III, 1267 (Marin, *Reign*, 85). See below, n. 282.

rāʿah)[238] were confiscated. His pages were paid and told to leave, which they did, confident that he was staying with Ītākh to drink wine.

[My informant] said: Ītākh had prepared for the arrival of Muḥammad b. ʿAbd al-Malik two of his eminent companions, named Yazīd b. ʿAbdallāh al-Ḥulwānī and Harthamah Shār Bāmiyān. When Muḥammad b. ʿAbd al-Malik arrived, they galloped off to his palace with their troops and Shākiriyyah. Muḥammad's pages asked them, "Where do you want to go? Abū Jaʿfar [Muḥammad b. ʿAbd al-Malik] has ridden off." At that, they fell upon his palace and seized everything in it.

Ibn al-Ḥulwānī reportedly said: I came to the house in which Muḥammad b. ʿAbd al-Malik usually resided, and I noticed that it was shabby in appearance and sparsely furnished. I beheld there four carpets (*ṭanāfis*)[239] and flasks (*qanānī ruṭliyyāt*) that contained a beverage. I also saw a house where his slave girls slept, in which there were mats (*būriyyān*)[240] and cushions (*makhādd*) stacked at its side, although his slave girls slept there without household effects.

It is reported that on the same day al-Mutawakkil sent someone to seize the contents of Muḥammad's residence, including [1374] furniture, livestock, slave girls, and pages. He had all of this brought to the Hārūnī [Palace]. The caliph sent Rāshid al-Maghribī[241] to Baghdad to confiscate Muḥammad's property and slaves that were there. And he ordered Abū al-Wazīr to seize his estates and those belonging to his family wherever they were located. What was in Sāmarrā was brought to the storehouses of Masrūr Sammānah[242] after it was purchased for the caliph.

---

238. Ahsan, *Social Life*, 39, points out that the *durrāʿah* was the main part of the vizier's garb, along with an ornamental belt (*wishāḥ*) and sword.

239. For *ṭanāfis* (sg. *ṭinfisah* or *ṭanfasah*), see Lane, *Lexicon*, 1886; Sadan, *Mobilier*, 113, note 440, Index, 176 ("tapis, selle, coussin [?]").

240. *Būrī* is an arabicized form for Persian *būriyā/būriya*, meaning a woven mat made of reeds; see Lane, *Lexicon*, s.v. Bāra; Steingass, *Dictionary*, s.v.

241. For Rāshid al-Maghribī's grant in Sāmarrā, see Yaʿqūbī, *Buldān*, 261 = Wiet, *Les pays*, 53. And on him, see Ṭabarī, III, 1749; Herzfeld, *Samarra*, 103, 107. He had a brother named Mubārak al-Maghribī; see below, n. 246.

242. Masrūr Sammānah al-Khādim had a grant and was in charge of the storehouses in Sāmarrā, according to Yaʿqūbī, *Buldān*, 261 = Wiet, *Les pays*, 53. He may be identical with Masrūr al-Khādim al-Kabīr, an official of Hārūn al-Rashīd. See below, n. 567. The storehouses are also known as the *bayt al-māl*; see above, 1350 (p. 36); Herzfeld, *Samarra*, 91, 103, 104; Sāmarrāʾī, *Taʾrīkh*, 82, 91.

Muḥammad b. ʿAbd al-Malik was told to delegate an agent to sell his furnishings. They brought to him al-ʿAbbās b. Aḥmad b. Rashīd, the secretary of ʿUjayf,[243] and Muḥammad made him his agent. Muḥammad remained in prison for several days unfettered. Then it was ordered that he be bound, and so he was. He refrained from eating; he would not taste a thing. He was extremely despondent in prison, wept copiously, talked little, and pondered much. He remained this way for a few days, and then was forced to stay awake and prevented from sleeping. This was done by pricking him with a large needle. Then he was left alone for a day and night, and he slept. When he awoke, he expressed a desire for fruit and grapes, and so they were brought in and he took refreshment. He was then forced to stay awake again, and after that it was ordered that he be placed in a wooden oven-like chest that had iron spikes.[244]

It is reported on the authority of Ibn Abī Du'ād and Abū al-Wazīr that Muḥammad had been the first to order use of [an iron maiden]. He tortured Ibn Asbāṭ al-Miṣrī with it to the point that he extracted from him all that he had.

Ibn al-Zayyāt was then afflicted and tortured in [the iron maiden] for a few days. Al-Dandānī[245] reports on the authority of the keeper deputized to torture Ibn al-Zayyāt: I would go out and lock
[1375] the door on him, and he would stretch both hands upward so that his shoulders were narrowed. Then he would enter the chest and sit. The chest had iron spikes in it, and in the middle there was a cross board on which the victim would sit when he wanted some

243. ʿUjayf b. ʿAnbasah was an army commander who served under al-Muʿtaṣim; see Marin, *Reign*, Index, 137, and p. 4, n. 32. He was governor of Ādharbayjān in 217 (832–33); Zambaur, *Manuel*, 177. And see Ibn Ṭayfūr, *Baghdād*, 146–47; Yaʿqūbī, *Ta'rīkh*, II, 570ff.; *Buldān*, 260, 294 = Wiet, *Les pays*, 52, 112; Iṣfahānī, *Aghānī*, V, 74–75; XVIII, 179; etc. (Guidi, *Tables*, 478); Herzfeld, *Samarra*, 107.

244. According to several sources, the *tannūr* (lit. "oven") was made of iron. See, for instance, Masʿūdī, *Murūj*, VII, 194; Khaṭīb, *Ta'rīkh Baghdād*, II, 343; Ibn Khallikān, *Wafayāt*, III, 254; and Ibn al-Ṭiqṭaqā, *Fakhrī*, 235. The poetic justice of Ibn al-Zayyāt's fall became thematic in historical and belletristic literature; see e.g. (in addition to the above) Yaʿqūbī, *Ta'rīkh*, II, 591; Ibn ʿAbd Rabbihi, *ʿIqd*, I, 147; Ibn al-Nadīm, *Fihrist*, 268; Tanūkhī, *Faraj*, 102–03; *Nishwār*, I, 17; Iṣfahānī, *Aghānī*, XX, 49; Ibn Khallikān, *Wafayāt*, IV, 187; and Yāqūt, *Irshād*, VI, 57.

245. Text: al-Dandānī. Mss. used in the Leiden edition have al-Ladhaydānī (?), which the note *ad loc.* says may also represent al-Raydānī or al-Kuzburānī.

relief. He would sit on the board for a while. Then the keeper would come, and, when the victim heard the sound of the door opening, he would stand as before. Then they would intensify the torture.

His torturer said: I fooled him one day, I led him to think that I had locked the door without actually doing so. I merely closed it with the bolt and waited for a while, at which point I pushed the door by accident, and seeing that he was sitting in the chest on the board I commented, "I see that you are doing this thing!" When I went out afterward, I tightened his strangling cord so that he was unable to sit, and I pulled out the board so that it would be between his legs. He tarried after that for only a few days before he died.

There were different opinions concerning the cause of death. One version had it that he was thrown prostrate and whipped fifty times on his abdomen, and was then turned over and beaten likewise on his posterior, and thereby died under the beating without their being aware. He died, his neck having been twisted and his beard pulled out. According to another version, he died without having been beaten.

It is reported on the authority of Mubārak al-Maghribī:[246] I think that during the entire time of his incarceration he ate only one loaf of bread, and he would eat one or two grapes.

[His torturer] said: I would hear him talking to himself, this being two or three days before he died, "O Muḥammad b. ʿAbd al-Malik, you were not content with prosperity, choice horses, fine palaces, and splendid clothes. You were in wonderful shape until you sought the wazīrate. Now taste what you have brought upon yourself." He would go on repeating this to himself. A day before he died his self-reproach ceased and he merely recited the confession of faith and invocation of God. When he died, his two sons, [1376]
Sulaymān and ʿUbaydallāh, were present.[247] They too were under arrest. He had been thrown upon a wooden door in the shirt that

246. On Mubārak al-Maghribī, see Yāqūt, *Buldān*, 261 = Wiet, *Les pays*, 53 (his grant and small market in Sāmarrā). Mubārak's residence became the scene of an attack by the populace against the Turks in 248 (862–63), III, 1505 (Saliba, 5). He was brother of Rāshid al-Maghribī; above, n. 241.

247. Text: *aḥḍarahu*; Cairo edition, Ms. A: *iḥḍirā*.

he wore when he was imprisoned. It had become filthy. His sons said, "Praise God who has given relief from this criminal." His corpse was turned over to them, and they washed it on the wooden door and buried him in a shallow grave. It is reported that dogs dug him up and ate his flesh.

Ibrāhīm b. al-ʿAbbās was governor of Ahwāz, and Muḥammad b. ʿAbd al-Malik was a friend of his.[248] Muḥammad sent to him Aḥmad b. Yūsuf Abū al-Jahm,[249] who made a public example of Ibrāhīm,[250] so that the latter reached a settlement with him at the cost of 1,500,000 dirhams.

Ibrāhīm recited:[251]

You were my brother in the brotherhood of fate,[252]
    But when the time came, you became constant war.

I used to complain of fate to you,
    And now it is because of you that I complain of fate.

I used to consider you for help in adversity,
    Now I seek safety from you.

And he recited:[253]

Because of the opinion of Abū Jaʿfar
    I have fallen into a state boding loss.

Without any crime save
    Enmity of the heretic to the Muslim.

After Muḥammad b. ʿAbd al-Malik's property was confiscated [in Sāmarrā], he was brought with Rāshid al-Maghribī to Baghdad

248. Ibrāhīm b. al-ʿAbbās b. Muḥammad b. Ṣūl (al-Ṣūlī), of a Turkish *mawlā* family, a great-uncle of Abū Bakr al-Ṣūlī, was a well-known secretary and poet. He died in Sāmarrā in 243 (857–58); Sourdel, *Vizirat,* Index, 767; Sezgin, *GAS,* II, 578.

249. For the poet Aḥmad b. Yūsuf Abū al-Jahm, see Ibn al-Nadīm, *Fihrist,* 367; Iṣfahānī, *Aghānī,* XIII, 23.

250. The expression *aqāmahu li-l-nās* stands for *aqāmahu ʿalā al-bulūs*; Glossarium, CDXXXXIX; Lane, s.v. *bulūs.*

251. The poem appears in Iṣfahānī, *Aghānī,* IX, 28, with minor variations (not noted in apparatus of Leiden edition). See also Ibrāhīm b. al-ʿAbbās al-Ṣūlī, *Dīwān,* 166.

252. The "you" here is Muḥammad b. ʿAbd al-Malik.

253. See *Dīwān,* 165.

in order that his property there might also be confiscated. When he arrived, he took Rawḥ, his page, who was also his household manager (*qahramān*), in charge of his funds, with which he did business. He also took a number of his family and with them the packload of a mule. Buildings of his were discovered in Baghdad containing all kinds of merchandise, including wheat, barley, flour, grain, olive oil, raisins, figs, and one filled with garlic. Everything that was confiscated of his, along with the value of what was found, was assessed at 90,000 dīnārs.

Al-Mutawakkil had Muḥammad arrested on Wednesday, 7 Ṣafar (September 22, 847), and he died on Thursday, 19 Rabīʿ I (November 2, 847). [1377]

In this year, al-Mutawakkil turned his wrath upon ʿUmar b. Faraj, in the month of Ramaḍān (April 9–May 8, 848). ʿUmar was turned over to Isḥāq b. Ibrāhīm b. Muṣʿab and was imprisoned in his custody. The caliph sent word to have ʿUmar's estates and property sequestered. Najāḥ b. Salamah went to his house but found there only 15,000 dirhams. Masrūr Sammānah, who was present, seized his female slaves. ʿUmar was fettered with thirty *raṭl*s [of chain], and his *mawlā* Naṣr brought from Baghdad. The former had 30,000 dīnārs of his own property delivered, and Naṣr delivered 14,000 dīnārs more. Forty thousand dīnārs belonging to ʿUmar were also found in Ahwāz, along with 150,000 dīnārs belonging to his brother Muḥammad b. Faraj. Sixteen camel loads of furnishings (*furūsh*) were delivered from his palace along with jewels worth 40,000 dīnārs. His provisions and furnishings were brought on fifty camels that made several return trips. ʿUmar was dressed in a woolen long-sleeved robe (*farajiyyah*)[254] and fettered, and remained this way for a week before being released. His palace was confiscated and the members of his family were seized and searched. There were one hundred slave girls. A settlement was then made for ten million dirhams on condition that only his estates seized in Ahwāz would be returned to him. The woolen tunic (*jubbah*) and fetters were removed. This was in Shawwāl (May 9–June 6, 848).

254. For *farajiyyah*, see Dozy, *Vêtements*, 327, where it is said to be a long cloak with sleeves beyond the fingers and lacking slits. See also Hilāl al-Ṣābī, *Rusūm*, 96–97 (tr. Salem, 77); *EI*[2] s.v. Libās, V, 741.

'Alī b. al-Jahm b. Badr recited to Najāḥ b. Salamah, inciting him against 'Umar b. Faraj:[255]

Bring a message to Najāḥ, hero of the secretaries,
Which the wind will carry to and fro.

The property will not depart from 'Umar's hands on its own,
[1378] Unless a sword be sheathed in his temples.

The Rukhkhajī men will not fulfill what they promised,
Nor will the Rukhkhajī women fail to keep an appointed time.[256]

And 'Alī b. al-Jahm also recited, satirizing 'Umar:[257]

You joined two things which together effaced prudence
The vanity of kings (*mulūk*) and the behavior of slaves (*mamālīk*).

You wished to receive thanks without showing kindness and generosity;
You have indeed traveled an untrodden path.

You thought your honor would not meet calamity,[258]
But I see that you will not be passed over.

In this year, al-Mutawakkil ordered that Ibrāhīm b. al-Junayd al-Naṣrānī, the brother of Ayyūb, secretary of Sammānah, be beaten with poles. [This was done] until he confessed to [having stashed away] 70,000 dīnārs. Al-Mutawakkil sent Mubārak al-Maghribī along with him to Baghdad to appropriate the sum from his residence. Ibrāhīm was brought [back to Sāmarrā] and incarcerated.

In this year, al-Mutawakkil turned his wrath upon Abū al-

255. See Iṣfahānī, *Aghānī*, IX, 114; and 'Alī b. al-Jahm, *Dīwān*, 124.

256. 'Umar b. Faraj was from Rukhkhaj (in Sijistān). For the place, see Le Strange, *Lands*, 339, 345.

257. 'Alī b. al-Jahm, *Dīwān*, 161.

258. The note in the Leiden edition cites Ṣūlī who has: *za'amta annaka lā tu'lā bi-dāhiyah* "You thought that a calamity would not befall you." Ms. C and Iṣfahānī, *Aghānī*, have *yurmā* for *yuqra'* of the text.

Wazīr, in Dhū al-Ḥijjah (July 7–August 4, 848), and ordered that accounts be settled with him. About 16,000 dīnārs were delivered, and tens of thousands of dirhams and jewelry. Sixty-two baskets of Egyptian furnishings were confiscated, as well as thirty-two pages (*ghulām*) and many carpets. Because of Abū al-Wazīr's betrayal, Muḥammad b. ʿAbd al-Malik—he was the brother of Mūsā b. ʿAbd al-Malik—as well as al-Haytham b. Khālid al-Naṣrānī and his nephew Saʿdūn b. ʿAlī were all arrested. A settlement was made with Saʿdūn for 40,000 dīnārs, and with his two nephews, ʿAbdallāh and Aḥmad, for about 30,000 dīnārs. Their estates were simultaneously confiscated.

In this year, al-Mutawakkil made Muḥammad b. al-Faḍl al- [1379]
Jarjarā'ī secretary.[259]

In this year, on Wednesday, 17 Ramaḍān (April 25, 848), al-Mutawakkil removed al-Faḍl b. Marwān[260] from the Bureau of Taxation (*dīwān al-kharāj*) and appointed over it Yaḥyā b. Khāqān al-Khurāsānī, a *mawlā* of the Azd.[261] On the same day, he appointed Ibrāhīm b. al-ʿAbbās b. Muḥammad b. Ṣūl over the Bureau of Controlling Expenditures (*dīwān zimām al-nafaqāt*) and removed Abū al-Wazīr.

In this year, al-Mutawakkil appointed his son Muḥammad al-Muntaṣir over the two sanctuaries [Mecca and Medina], the Yemen and al-Ṭā'if, tying the banner of his office for him on Thursday, 11 Ramaḍān (April 19, 848).

In this year, Aḥmad b. Abī Du'ād had a paralytic stroke on 6 Jumādā II (January 17, 848).

259. That is, wazīr. For Muḥammad b. al-Faḍl al-Jarjarā'ī, d. 250 (864–65), see Zambaur, *Manuel,* 6; Sourdel, *Vizirat,* 271–73, 275–76, 293; *EI*², s.v. Djardjarā'ī [1]. A gifted poet and writer, he had been secretary to al-Faḍl b. Marwān. He returned to the wazīrate in the days of al-Mustaʿīn in 249 (863).

260. Abū al-ʿAbbās al-Faḍl b. Marwān, a secretary of Christian origins, had been wazīr under al-Muʿtaṣim; d. 250 (864–65); Ṭabarī, III, 1181–86, 1326, 1329; Marin, *Reign,* 17–21, 130, 132; Sourdel, *Vizirat,* Index 761, and esp. 233–34, 246–53; *EI*², s.v. al-Faḍl b. Marwān.

261. Yaḥyā b. Khāqān al-Khurāsānī, *mawlā* Azd, was a member of the Khāqānid family, brother of al-Fatḥ and Jaʿfar; see Zambaur, *Manuel,* 12; Sourdel, *Vizirat,* 273 and n. 3; Index, 787. He had been secretary of al-Ḥasan b. Sahl during the caliphate of al-Ma'mūn. For the circumstances of this appointment, see Yaʿqūbī, *Ta'rīkh,* II, 592–93. See Table 2.

In this year, Yaḥyā b. Harthamah[262] came to Mecca from Medina, along with 'Alī b. Muḥammad b. 'Alī al-Riḍā b. Mūsā b. Ja'far.[263] Yaḥyā was in charge of the Mecca Road.

In this year, Michael, son of Theophilus, assailed his mother, Theodora, exposed her, and placed her in a convent. He also killed the Logothete (al-Lughuthīṭ), for it was on his account that Michael suspected her. She had ruled for six years.[264]

Leading the pilgrimage this year was Muḥammad b. Dāwūd.

---

262. Yaḥyā b. Harthamah, son of Harthama b. A'yan (Crone, *Slaves on Horses*, 177–78), was later rewarded for a steadfast stand against the Turks in 251 (III, 1560; Saliba, 47). And in the same year (III, 1621; Saliba, 91) we find him defeating Abū al-Ḥusayn b. Quraysh. See on him, Qummī, *Ta'rīkh Qumm*, 103, 185, 201.

263. 'Alī b. Muḥammad b. 'Alī al-Riḍā b Mūsā b. Ja'far, or Abū al-Ḥasan 'Alī al-Hādī, was the tenth *imām* of the Shī'ites. He died on 25 Jumādā II, 254 (June 21, 868), according to Ṭabarī, III, 1697 (Saliba, 155). See Ya'qūbī, *Ta'rīkh*, II, 591–92, where Yaḥyā b. Harthamah is said to have escorted him from Medina to Baghdad, whence he was brought to Sāmarrā. According to Ya'qūbī, al-Mutawakkil summoned him from Medina because of popular support there for his cause.

264. Ṭabarī alludes here to the fall of the Byzantine empress Theodora. This took place when her son Michael became old enough to conspire (with the backing of his uncle Bardas) against his mother and her chief minister, Theoktistos the Logothete. A plot was hatched in 856, which led to Theoktistos' murder and Theodora's deposition and banishment to a monastery. Michael had ruled for fourteen years along with Theodora; Bury, *History*, 157ff., 469ff. Theodora's fall was in 856–58 not, as here, in 847–48. Note also that Ṭabarī has Theodora as empress in 241 (855–56); below, 1426 (p. 138 and n. 456).

The Events of the Year 234

(August 5, 848–July 26, 849)

One of the events was the escape of Muḥammad b. al-Baʿīth b. Ḥalbas. He had been brought as a prisoner from Ādharbayjān and was subsequently incarcerated.[265]

The Reason for Muḥammad b. al-Baʿīth's Escape and the Consequences of His Affair

It is reported that the reason for this was [as follows]: Al-Mutawakkil had taken ill this year. Now there was a man who served [1380] Ibn al-Baʿīth by the name of Khalīfah.[266] Khalīfah informed Ibn al-Baʿīth that al-Mutawakkil had died, and prepared horses for him. Ibn al-Baʿīth and Khalīfah, who had given him the news, fled to Ibn al-Baʿīth's place of residence in Ādharbayjān, namely, Ma-

---

265. Muḥammad b. al-Baʿīth b. Ḥalbas, a brigand and rebel chief, followed in the footsteps of his ancestors and fortified Marand. Once an ally of the rebel heresiarch Bābak, he later contributed to his defeat; Ṭabarī, III, 1171–72, 1190, 1193 (Marin, *Reign*, 9, 10, 24–26); and see Yāqūt, *Muʿjam*, IV, 503.

266. On the slave Khalīfah, who belonged to Muḥammad b. al-Baʿīth, see also below, 1387 (p. 86).

rand.[267] It is said that he had two fortresses, one called Shāhī and the other Yakdur.[268] Yakdur was outside the lake, and Shāhī was in the midst of it. The lake is about fifty *farsakh*s (three hundred km.),[269] [extending] from the border of Urmiya toward the district (*rustāq*) of Dākharraqān,[270] the country of Muḥammad b. al-Rawwād.[271] Shāhī is a fortified stronghold of Ibn al-Baʿīth, surrounded by water. People sail by way of Lake Urmiya from the outer limits of Marāghah[272] to Urmiya. It is a lake lacking fish and resources.[273]

It is reported that Ibn al-Baʿīth had been in the prison of Isḥāq b. Ibrāhīm b. Muṣʿab. Bughā al-Sharābī spoke in his favor and secured about thirty guarantors [of good behavior] on his behalf, including Muḥammad b. Khālid b. Yazīd b. Mazyad al-Shaybānī,[274] such that Ibn al-Baʿīth could move about freely in Sāmarrā. Afterward he escaped to Marand, where he hoarded food, and where springs of

---

267. Marand is north of Lake Urmiya. Balādhuri, *Futūḥ*, 405, says that Ḥalbas Abū al-Baʿīth was the first to settle there and that it was fortified by al-Baʿīth, father of Muḥammad. Balādhurī also mentions Muḥammad's revolt and its suppression by Bughā; see also *EI*², s.v. Marand. Marand is described briefly below, 1381 (p. 79).

268. Text: Shāhī and Yakdur. Ms. C: Bakdur. Shāhī is mentioned by Ṭabarī, III, 1171 (above, n. 265). It is the name of the peninsula on Lake Urmiya. See *EI*¹, IV, 1037, s.v. Urmiya, where there is a reference to the fortresses of Shāhī and Yakdur (Bakdur), which, it is proposed, may be related to the mountain of Bakyir (Bakdir). Ṭabarī, III, 1171–72 (Marin, *Reign*, 9) calls the fortresses Shāhī and Tabrīz.

269. *Fragmenta*, 539, says that the lake was twenty *farsakh*s (120 km.) from the border of Urmiya.

270. Dākharraqān (Dihkharghān; in local speech of Turks, according to Minorsky—Tukharghan) is in Ādharbayjān between Tabrīz and Marāghah; Le Strange, *Lands*, 164; Minorsky, *Ḥudūd*, 395.

271. Muḥammad b. al-Rawwād was a member of the house of local rulers of the Rawwādid dynasty of Ādharbayjān, descendants of al-Rawwād al-Azdī; see, for instance, Balādhurī, *Futūḥ*, 405; Minorsky, *Ḥudūd*, 395–96; Bosworth, *Islamic Dynasties*, 88–89. Cf. also Ibn Khurradādhbih, *Masālik*, 119.

272. Marāghah, east of Lake Urmiya, is the old capital of Ādharbayjān, see Yāqūt, *Muʿjam*, IV, 476; Le Strange, *Lands*, 164; *EI*², s.v.

273. The lack of life is due to Lake Urmiya's salt water. But Muslim geographers and travelers mention a fish there called "water dog"; Yāqūt, *Muʿjam*, I, 513; Le Strange, *Lands*, 160.

274. Ṭabarī, III, 1577–78 and 1615 (Saliba, 59, 87), describes two encounters in which Muḥammad b. Khālid fled from battle. Zambaur, *Manuel*, 181, lists him as Shīrwānshāh, i.e. as belonging to the lords of Shīrwān (= Shīrvān, Sharvān); Minorsky, *History*, Index, 183. He had been governor of Ādharbayjān, Armenia, and Arrān. See also Crone, *Slaves on Horses*, 170. He was a descendant of Maʿn b. Zāʾida al-Shaybānī/Rabīʿah.

water were also available. Ibn al-Ba'īth repaired its dilapidated walls. Those seeking to rebel—about 2,200 men—came to him from all sides, from the Rabī'ah and others.[275]

The governor of Ādharbayjān, Muḥammad b. Ḥātim b. Harthamah,[276] failed in his pursuit of Ibn al-Ba'īth. Al-Mutawakkil then appointed Ḥamdawayh b. 'Alī b. al-Faḍl al-Sa'dī governor of Ādharbayjān,[277] sending him from Sāmarrā posthaste. When Ḥamdawayh arrived there, he rallied the regular army and the Shākiriyyah and those who responded to his call. They numbered 10,000 men.

Ḥamdawayh advanced toward Ibn al-Ba'īth, forcing him to take [1381] refuge in the town of Marand. It is a town whose circumference is two *farsakh*s (twelve km.). There are many gardens within the town, and outside it is surrounded by trees, except for where its gates are located. Ibn al-Ba'īth amassed siege instruments inside the town, where there were springs of water.

After Ibn al-Ba'īth had held out for a long time, al-Mutawakkil sent Zīrak the Turk[278] against him along with 200,000 Turkish horsemen, but Zīrak accomplished nothing. Al-Mutawakkil then sent against him 'Amr b. Saysil (?) b. Kāl[279] along with 900 of the Shākiriyyah, but to no avail. Al-Mutawakkil thereupon sent against him Bughā al-Sharābī, along with 4,000 troops, comprising Turks, Shākiriyyah, and Maghāribah. Ḥamdawayh b. 'Alī, 'Amr b. Saysil and Zīrak advanced upon the city of Marand. They cut down about 1,000 trees surrounding it, as well as other trees of the thicket, and they set up twenty mangonels against the city. Opposite the city they erected a parapet. Ibn al-Ba'īth set up mangonels in a similar manner. The non-Arab peasants (*'ulūj*) in his districts would shoot with slingshots, preventing anyone from

275. Ya'qūbī, *Ta'rīkh,* II, 594, describes Ibn al-Ba'īth's supporters as lawbreakers or brigands (*ṣa'ālīk*). Muḥammad's family was of the tribe of Rabī'ah.

276. See Zambaur, *Manuel,* 177, who makes him governor of Ādharbayjān as of 233 (847–48; following Ibn al-Athīr). For his family ties, see Crone, *Slaves on Horses,* 177–78.

277. See Zambaur, *Manuel,* 177. And for a similar account, see Ya'qūbī, *Ta'rīkh,* II, 594.

278. Zīrak al-Turkī makes his first appearance here; see also below 1414–16 (pp. 122ff); and see Ya'qūbī, *Ta'rīkh,* II, 594.

279. Ms C: Sasīl; Ibn al-Athīr, *Kāmil,* VII, 28: Saysīl; *Fragmenta,* 540: 'Umar b. Saysil.

approaching the walls of the town. In the course of eight months, about one hundred supporters of the central government were killed fighting Ibn al-Baʿīth, and about four hundred were wounded. A similar number of Ibn al-Baʿīth's forces were killed and wounded.

Ḥamdawayh, ʿAmr, and Zīrak kept pressing the battle. The wall in front of the city was low, about twenty *dhirāʿ* (ca. ten meters) from the foundation. A contingent of Ibn al-Baʿīth's men, bearing spears, were lowered by ropes and gave battle. When the forces of the central government attacked them, they retreated to the wall.
[1382] They occasionally opened a gate called the Water Gate, from which a number of men would exit, fight, and then return.

When Bughā al-Sharābī approached Marand, he reportedly sent ʿĪsā b. al-Shaykh b. al-Salīl al-Shaybānī,[280] bearing letters of safe-conduct for the prominent followers of Ibn al-Baʿīth and for Ibn al-Baʿīth, on condition that they and he surrender to the authority of the Commander of the Faithful. If not, Bughā would fight them, and if he defeated them no one would be spared. Whoever surrendered, however, would be granted safe-conduct. The vast majority of those who were with Ibn al-Baʿīth belonged to the Rabīʿah, of the folk of ʿĪsā b. al-Shaykh. Many of them came down [the walls] by ropes. Ibn al-Baʿīth's son-in-law Abū al-Agharr surrendered.

It is reported on the authority of this Abū al-Agharr: They then opened the gate of the city, and the forces of Ḥamdawayh and Zīrak entered. Ibn al-Baʿīth fled from his house trying to escape from another direction, but a contingent of the army caught up with him. They had along with them Manṣūr, his household manager. Ibn al-Baʿīth was riding a horse, with a sword about his neck, and he was attempting to get to a river, near which was a millstone, so that he could hide therein. They took him prisoner, and the regular troops plundered his house, the houses of his companions, and some of the houses of the townsmen.

When the people had finished plundering, it was announced that the perpetrators would be exempt from responsibility. They seized two of Ibn al-Baʿīth's sisters, three daughters, and his maternal aunt, the rest being female slaves. The central government

280. ʿĪsā b. al-Shaykh died in 269 (882–83); Ṭabarī, III, 2048.

authorities acquired possession of thirteen women of his female entourage. And, of his eminent companions who have been mentioned, they seized about two hundred men, the rest having fled.

Bughā al-Sharābī showed up the next day, and his herald announced that plunder was forbidden. Bughā al-Sharābī took personal credit for the victory.

In this year, al-Mutawakkil went out to al-Madā'in in Jumādā I (December, 848).

Leading the pilgrimage this year was Ītākh. He was in charge of [1383] Mecca and Medina and the festivities, and his name was invoked on the pulpits.

The Reason for Ītākh's Pilgrimage This Year

Ītākh was reportedly a Khazar slave (*ghulām*), a cook, belonging to Sallām al-Abrash. Al-Muʿtaṣim bought Ītākh from Sallām in 199 (814–15).[281] As Ītākh was manly and intrepid, al-Muʿtaṣim, and al-Wāthiq after him, promoted him to the position where many of the administrative functions (*aʿmāl*) of the central government were assigned to him. Al-Muʿtaṣim appointed him governor of the security police (*maʿūnah*) of Sāmarrā along with Isḥāq b. Ibrāhīm. Both Ītākh and Isḥāq b. Ibrāhīm were represented by deputies. Whoever al-Muʿtaṣim or al-Wāthiq wished to have killed would be imprisoned and killed by Ītākh. Among them were Muḥammad b. ʿAbd al-Malik al-Zayyāt, the sons of al-Ma'mūn whose mother was Sundus, Ṣāliḥ b. ʿUjayf, and others.[282]

When al-Mutawakkil took office, Ītākh retained his rank, being responsible for the regular army, the Maghāribah, the Turks, the *mawlās*, the Postal and Intelligence Service (*barīd*), the office of

---

281. Ītākh was, then, one of the first Turkish slaves acquired by al-Muʿtaṣim, who made them into a formidable military unit; see Kennedy, *Early Abbasid Caliphate,* 167. Sallām al-Abrash is cited as a translator of scientific works by Ibn al-Nadīm, *Fihrist,* 587; Qifṭī, *Ta'rīkh,* 196 (al-Abrash). But a Sallām al-Abrash al-Khādim is mentioned by Ṭabarī as having led an army uprising in Jumādā I, 207 (III, 1065; Bosworth, *Reunification,* 134). See also Yaʿqūbī, *Buldān,* 256 = Wiet, *Les pays,* 45. Abrash = "Speckled" (or for Abraṣ, "Leprous").

282. Al-Muʿtaṣim had turned over sons of al-Ma'mūn born to Sundus to Ītākh, who incarcerated them in a vaulted cellar of his residence; Ṭabarī, III 1267 (Marin, *Reign,* 85). Ṣāliḥ, mentioned only here, maybe a son of ʿUjayf b. ʿAnbasa, mentioned above, 1374 (p. 70).

chamberlain, and the Caliphal Palace. Once firmly ensconced in the office of the caliphate, al-Mutawakkil went out for a vacation to the district of al-Qāṭūl.[283] While drinking one night, the caliph picked a quarrel with Ītākh, as a result of which the latter thought to kill him. When al-Mutawakkil awoke the next morning, he was told what had taken place. He apologized to Ītākh and was conciliatory toward him, saying, "You are my father and you have reared me."

When al-Mutawakkil returned to Sāmarrā, he got someone to suggest that Ītākh ask permission to go on the pilgrimage. He did so, and was given permission. Al-Mutawakkil made him amīr of every town he entered [on the way to Mecca] and bestowed a robe of honor upon him. All the army commanders rode with him. Many of the Shākiriyyah, army commanders, and pages went out with him, aside from his own pages and retinue. After he departed, the office of chamberlain was turned over to Waṣīf. This
[1384] was on Saturday, 18 Dhū al-Qa'dah (June 13, 849).

Another version holds that this episode concerning Ītākh took place in 233 (847–48), and that al-Mutawakkil turned over the office of chamberlain to Waṣīf on 17 Dhū al-Ḥijjah, 233 (July 23, 848).

Leading the pilgrimage this year was Muḥammad b. Dāwūd b. 'Īsā b. Mūsā.[284]

---

283. The Qāṭūl district, according to Ya'qūbī, *Buldān*, 256 = Wiet, *Les pays*, 46, was north of Shammāsiyyah and south of Sāmarrā. See also Yāqūt, *Mu'jam*, IV, 922; Herzfeld, *Samarra*, 71; and the discussion by Rogers, "Samarra," 130, n. 21.

284. Text: Muḥammad b. Dāwūd b. Mūsā b. 'Īsā. Addenda, DCCLXXV, and Cairo edition: 'Īsā b. Mūsā, followed here.

The Events of the Year 235

(July 26, 849–July 14, 850)

One of them was the killing of Ītākh al-Khazarī.[285]

How Ītākh Was Killed

It is reported that, when Ītākh left Mecca heading back to Iraq, al-Mutawakkil sent to him Saʿīd b. Ṣāliḥ the Chamberlain[286] with attire and precious gifts, ordering Saʿīd to meet Ītākh in al-Kūfah or somewhere along his route. Al-Mutawakkil had already broached his order concerning Ītākh to his chief of security police in Baghdad.

Ibrāhīm b. al-Mudabbir reportedly said:[287] I went out with Isḥāq

285. The episode of Ītākh's murder is related by Yaʿqūbī, *Taʾrīkh*, II, 593, in a slightly different way.

286. Saʿīd b. Ṣāliḥ, at this point a chamberlain, was later made chief of the police; III, 1549 (Saliba, 39).

287. Abū Isḥāq Ibrāhīm b. Muḥammad b. al-Mudabbir (d. 279 [892]), a well-known secretary and poet, was later wazīr under al-Muʿtamid: see Masʿūdī, *Murūj*, VII, 160–64; Ibn al-Nadīm, *Fihrist*, 270, 321, 367; Iṣfahānī, *Aghānī*, XIX, 114–27; Ibn al-Abbār, *Iʿtāb*, 159–63; Sourdel, *Vizirat*, 316.

b. Ibrāhīm as Ītākh was approaching Baghdad. Ītākh intended to take the Euphrates Road to Anbār and then proceed to Sāmarrā. Isḥāq b. Ibrāhīm wrote to him: "The Commander of the Faithful—may God give him long life—has ordered that you come to Baghdad, that the Hāshimites and notables meet you, and that you hold an audience for them in the palace of Khuzaymah b. Khāzim,[288] and have rewards given to them."

Ibrāhīm b. al-Mudabbir said: We went as far as al-Yāsiriyyah.[289]
[1385] Ibn Ibrāhīm stationed the regular army and the Shākiriyyah on the bridge and went out with his special commanders. A bench (*ṣuffah*) was set down for him at al-Yāsiriyyah, upon which he sat, until he was told that Ītākh was approaching. Isḥāq b. Ibrāhīm then rode out to receive him. When Isḥāq saw Ītākh, he was ready to dismount, but Ītākh implored him not to do so.

Ibrāhīm b. al-Mudabbir continued: Ītākh was accompanied by 300 of his men and pages. He was wearing a white sleeved robe (*qabā'*),[290] and was girded with a sword and sword belts. Both Isḥāq b. Ibrāhīm and Ītākh marched as far as the bridge.[291] Isḥāq then preceded him and passed over [the bridge], going to the door of [the palace of] Khuzaymah b. Khāzim. He said to Ītākh, "Enter, may God cause the amīr to prosper." Whenever one of Ītākh's pages passed by the guards at the bridge, they let him proceed until Ītākh remained with his intimate pages. A group of men then moved in front of Ītākh. The palace of Khuzaymah had been fitted out for him.

Isḥāq remained behind and ordered that only three or four of

288. The palace of Khuzaymah b. Khāzim was located where the road begins at the Main Bridge (*al-jisr*) connecting the West Side of Baghdad with Bāb al-Ṭāq. The land had been granted as an allotment by al-Mahdī to Khuzaymah b. Khāzim, for whom see Crone, *Slaves on Horses,* 180; Kennedy, *Early Abbasid Caliphate,* Index, 235; see Le Strange, *Baghdad,* 218 and Map V, facing p. 107, no. 59; Lassner, *Topography,* 76, 78, 280, n. 1, 281, n. 6.

289. Al-Yāsiriyyah is said by Yāqūt (*Muʿjam,* IV, 1002) to be a large village on the bank of Nahr ʿĪsā, 6 km. from Baghdad. He notes its fine masonry bridge (*qanṭarah*). Ṭabarī mentions here a pontoon bridge (*jisr*). *Fragmenta,* 543, speaks of "the two pontoon bridges" (*jisrayn*). One might suppose that what was a pontoon bridge at the time of Ṭabarī became a masonry bridge by the time of Yāqūt. On the other hand, sometimes *jisr* and *qanṭarah* mean the same thing.

290. The *qabā'* was a sleeved, close-fitting coat, and was typical attire of the Turks, according to Ahsan, *Social Life,* 41–42.

291. The Main Bridge in Baghdad is intended, not the bridge in al-Yāsiriyyah.

Ītākh's pages should enter the palace, and that the doors be seized. And he ordered his guardian escort on the side of the river embankment to wreck all the stairs leading to the palace of Khuzaymah b. Khāzim. When Ītākh entered, Isḥāq locked the door behind him, at which point Ītākh looked around and, realizing that only three pages were with him, he exclaimed, "They have done it!"

Were he not seized in Baghdad, they would have been unable to apprehend him. Had he entered Sāmarrā and wanted his men to kill all his opponents, he would have been able to accomplish this.

Ibrāhīm b. al-Mudabbir went on: Food was brought around evening, and Ītākh ate. He stayed for two or three days. Then Isḥāq came, sailing in a fast boat (*ḥarrāqah*), and prepared another for Ītākh.[292] He sent Ītākh a message for him to come to the boat, and ordered that Ītākh's sword be confiscated. They lowered him into the vessel, and Isḥāq sent an armed escort with him. Isḥāq then traveled upstream as far as his residence. Reaching Isḥāq's palace, Ītākh was taken out [of the boat] and brought into a section of it. He was thereafter bound and fettered, irons being placed on his neck and feet.

At that, Ītākh's two sons, Manṣūr and Muẓaffar, and his two [1386] secretaries, Sulaymān b. Wahb and Qudāmah b. Ziyād al-Naṣrānī, were brought to Baghdad.[293] Sulaymān was responsible for the administrative functions (*aʿmāl*) of the central government; Qudāmah, for the estates of Ītākh in particular. They were imprisoned in Baghdad, and Sulaymān and Qudāmah were flogged. Qudāmah embraced Islam; Manṣūr and Muẓaffar were imprisoned.

Turk, *mawlā* of Isḥāq, reportedly said:[294] I stood at the door of

292. A *ḥarrāqah* is a light all-purpose craft, used in warfare as a fire ship. It was convenient for travel on the Tigris; *Kindermann, "Schiff,"* 22. Ītākh and his captors had to travel upstream on the Tigris from the area of the Main Bridge to that of the Upper Bridge.

293. Sulaymān b. Wahb is mentioned above (n. 16). His arrest and torture are related in detail by Tanūkhī, *Faraj*, I, 51, on the basis of Sulaymān's own report transmitted by his son ʿUbaydallāh. Qudāmah b. Ziyād, a Christian secretary, was father of the distinguished secretary Jaʿfar b. Qudāmah and grandfather of the famous Qudāmah b. Jaʿfar; *EI*², s.v. Ḳudāma b. D̲jaʿfar.

294. For Turk, the *mawlā* of Isḥāq b. Ibrāhīm, see Ṭabarī, III, 1194 (Marin, *Reign*, 27); Ibn Ṭayfūr, *Baghdād*, 147.

the chamber in which Ītākh was imprisoned. He called to me, "O Turk." I replied, "What do you want, Abū Manṣūr?" He said, "Give the amīr greetings and tell him, 'You know what al-Mu'taṣim and al-Wāthiq ordered me to do in your case. But I protected you as far as I could. This should put me in good stead with you. As far as I am concerned, I have experienced adversity and comfort, and I don't care about what I eat and drink. But these two young men have lived in luxury and are not used to misery. So give them soup and meat and something from which to eat.'"

Turk continued: I stood at the entrance to the audience hall of Isḥāq. He asked me, "What is it, Turk? Do you wish to discuss something?" I answered that I did, and that Ītākh had said to me such and such.

Turk went on: The rations of Ītākh were a loaf of bread and a cup of water. Isḥāq ordered that Ītākh's sons be given a table on which were seven loaves of bread and five ladles of water. This remained in effect during Isḥāq's life. I do not know what was done with them afterward. As for Ītākh, he was shackled with eighty *raṭl*s [of iron] about his neck and a heavy fetter. He died on Wednesday, 5 Jumādā II, 235 (December 21, 849). Isḥāq called Abū al-Ḥasan Isḥāq b. Thābit b. Abī 'Abbād[295] to attest to his death, along with the chief of the Post and Intelligence of Baghdad and the judges. He showed them that Ītākh had not been beaten or marked.

I was informed by some(one) of our shaykhs that Ītākh's death
[1387] resulted from thirst. That is, he was fed, and when he asked for water it was withheld until he died from the lack of drink. His two sons remained in prison during the lifetime of al-Mutawakkil. When al-Muntaṣir acceded to rule, he freed them. Muẓaffar lived after he was freed from prison for only three months before he died, Manṣūr surviving him.

In this year, Bughā al-Sharābī delivered Ibn al-Ba'īth in Shawwāl (April 18–May 16), as well as Khalīfah and Abū al-Agharr[296] and

295. An Abū al-Ḥasan b. Abī 'Abbād, a secretary, is mentioned by Ṭabarī, III, 1180 (Marin, *Reign*, 16).

296. Text: *wa-bi-khalīfatihi Abī al-Agharr* ("and with his deputy Abū al-Agharr"). Ms. C (without points); *wa-bi-Khalīfah.* The note suggests *wa-bi-Khalīfah wa-Abī al-Agharr* ("and with Khalīfah and Abū al-Agharr"). Ṭabarī, Index, 172, implicitly identifies this Khalīfah with Khalīfah, the *ghulām* of Ibn al-

the two brothers of Ibn al-Baʿīth, Ṣaqr and Khālid—they had surrendered in return for a guarantee of safe-conduct—and a son of Ibn al-Baʿīth called al-ʿAlā' who gave himself up for a guarantee of safe-conduct. Bughā al-Sharābī delivered about 180 of the prisoners, the rest of them having died before they arrived. When they approached Sāmarrā, they were placed upon camels so that the people could view them. Al-Mutawakkil ordered that Ibn al-Baʿīth and the others be imprisoned, and he had Ibn al-Baʿīth shackled in irons.

ʿAlī b. al-Jahm reportedly said: Muḥammad b. al-Baʿīth was brought to al-Mutawakkil. He ordered that he be decapitated, whereupon he was thrown down upon a leather mat. The swordsmen came and brandished their swords at him.

Al-Mutawakkil spoke to him harshly, "What prompted you to do what you did, Muḥammad?"

He replied, "Distress. You are the rope stretched between God and His creatures. I have two notions concerning [what] you [will do]. And I consider preferable what is most proper for you, namely, a pardon." He then launched into the following:[297]

People wish only that you be my killer today,
  Imām of right guidance, whereas forgiving people[298] is better.

I am merely a sinful creature, [1388]
  While your pardon is created of the light of prophecy.

Baʿīth, mentioned on 1380 (p. 77). A certain Abū al-Agharr Khalīfah b. al-Mubārak al-Sulamī (Ṭabarī, Index, 47) is mentioned in Rosenthal, *Return*, but (*inter alia*) he died in 303 (916); see Rosenthal, Index, 220.

297. The poem appears also, with variants, in Ṣulī, *Awrāq*; Masʿūdī, *Murūj*, VII, 279; *Fragmenta*, 541; and Ibn al-Athīr, *Kāmil*, VII, 32; see note in the Leiden edition. For Ibn al-Baʿīth's literary talent and the significance of his Persian poetry as evidential of Persian poetry in northwestern Iran in the ninth century, see Barthold, "Early Persian Poetry."

298. Text: *bi-l-nās*. Masʿūdi, *Murūj* VII, 279: *bi-l-ḥurr* = "for a free man." *Fragmenta*: *fi-llāh*. Ibn al-Athīr, *Kāmil*: *bi-l-mar'* = "for a man." Both *bi-l-ḥurr* and *bi-l-mar'* fit here. Ṣūlī: *wa-l-ṣulḥ awlā wa-ajmal* = "but reconciliation is more fit and finer," and he then adds another line of verse: "My sin is diminished a bit by your pardon/ Whoever is pardoned by you finds pardon better."

You are the best of those who proceed to glory,
And the best of the two options you shall surely carry out.

ʿAlī b. al-Jahm said: Then al-Mutawakkil turned to me and said that Ibn al-Baʿīth possessed literary talent (*adab*). I hastened to say [to Ibn al-Baʿīth], "The Commander of the Faithful will carry out the best of the two [options] and will favor you." Al-Mutawakkil said, "Return to your residence."

I have received a report on the authority of . . . . :[299] "A group of shaykhs in Marāghah recited to me Persian poems by Ibn al-Baʿīth, and they noted his literary talent and courage. There are many stories about him."

I was informed by someone who reportedly was a witness when Ibn al-Baʿīth was brought to al-Mutawakkil, and Ibn al-Baʿīth spoke with him as he did. Al-Muʿtazz interceded for him while sitting with his father, al-Mutawakkil. Al-Muʿtazz asked that Ibn al-Baʿīth be turned over to him, which he was, and he was pardoned.

When Ibn al-Baʿīth fled he recited:[300]

How many things have I achieved that others have shirked,
And now that failure has begun to stifle me,

Do not rebuke me with what does not avail me.
Go, leave me, my fate is already sealed.

I shall squander money whether in hardship or in ease;
The generous person gives though having nothing.

[1389] When Ibn al-Baʿīth fled, he left behind in his residence three sons of his, called al-Baʿīth, Jaʿfar, and Ḥalbas, as well as slave girls. They were imprisoned in Baghdad in the Gold Palace (Qaṣr al-Dhahab).[301] After the death of Ibn al-Baʿīth—he died a month after he entered Sāmarrā—Bughā al-Sharābī spoke on behalf of Abū al-Agharr, his son-in-law, whereupon the latter was released.

299. There is a lacuna in the text at this point instead of the informant's name.

300. See *Les Séances de Ḥarīrī*, ed. S. De Sacy (Paris, 1847), 75–76, note (on *bi-l-kaẓm*) (cited in note *ad loc.* in Leiden edition).

301. The Gold Palace was in the Round City; Lassner, *Topography*, 49; Index, 322.

A maternal aunt of Ibn al-Baʿīth was released from the prison and died from joy that very day. The rest [of his household] remained in prison.

A hundred *raṭl*s [of iron] had reportedly been placed upon the neck of Ibn al-Baʿīth, and he remained bent over face forward until he died.

When Ibn al-Baʿīth was seized, those who were imprisoned as his guarantors were released. Some of them had died in prison. The rest of his family was thereafter freed. His sons—Ḥalbas, Baʿīth, and Jaʿfar—joined the number of of Shākiriyyah who were with ʿUbaydallah b. Yaḥyā b. Khāqān.[302] They were treated as guests.

In this year, al-Mutawakkil ordered[303] that the Christians and all other Dhimmīs wear yellow hoods (*ṭayālisah*)[304] and *zunnār* belts,[305] ride on saddles with wooden stirrups, affix two pommels at the rear of their saddles, and place two buttons to the caps

302. Abū al-Ḥasan ʿUbaydallāh b. Yaḥyā b. Khāqān, of the Banū Khāqān (Zambaur, *Manuel*, 12; Sourdel, *Vizirat*, 746), appears here for the first time. ʿUbaydallāh later became wazīr under al-Mutawakkil (236–47) and then under al-Muʿtamid (256–63). He died, according to Ibn al-Jawzī (*Muntaẓam*, V, 45), from a blow received in a polo match, on 10 Dhū al-Qaʿdah, 262 (August 5, 876). See also Zambaur, *Manuel*, 7–8, 12; Herzfeld, *Samarra*, 213; Sourdel, *Vizirat*, 274–86, 305–09, etc. (Index, 785). Ṭabarī was employed as a tutor for his sons. See Table 2.

303. The type of restriction imposed upon the Dhimmīs by al-Mutawakkil was first enacted by ʿUmar II, and was thereafter refined and systematized by Hārūn al-Rashīd; see Abū Yūsuf, *Kitāb al-kharāj*, 127–28; tr. Fagnan, 195–97; Fattal, *Statut légal*, 69, 96. See also Lichtenstädter, "Distinctive Dress"; Ashtor, "Social Isolation"; and Tritton, *Caliphs*, 117ff. Our text (up to the caliph's letter to his governors) is translated by Lewis, *Islam*, II, 224–25. And see his translation (pp. 225–26) of Mutawakkil's degree in Qalqashandī, *Ṣubḥ al-aʿshā* (Cairo, 1331–37 [1913–18]), XIII, 368. See also the translation by N. A. Stillman, *Jews of Arab Lands*, 167–68. Bar Hebraeus, *Chronography*, 141, noting al-Mutawakkil's "hatred for Christians," relates the following decrees with his leveling the tomb of al-Ḥusayn b. ʿAlī (see below, 1407, p. 110). In other words, the caliph's decrees vis-à-vis the Dhimmī minority were, in his view, connected with his hostility toward Shīʿites.

304. *Ṭayālisah* (sg. *ṭaylasān*) is translated here as "hoods." Ashtor, "Social Isolation," uses "mantle." According to Y. Stillman, *EI*², s.v. Libās, the *ṭaylasān* in this period was evidently a cowl. See also A. Arazi's Introduction to Suyūṭī, *Aḥādīth*; Ahsan, *Social Life*, 42–43. According to Ibn Qayyim al-Jawziyyah, *Aḥkām ahl al-dhimmah*, II, 738 (cited by Ahsan, 63), Jews were permitted to wear the *ṭaylasān* because it was traditional gear of theirs.

305. On *zunnār* (< Greek *zonarion*), see Dozy, *Vêtements*, 196; N. A. Stillman, *Jews of Arab Lands*, 167, n. 2; Ahsan, *Social Life*, 61–63 (where the dress of the Dhimmī is treated in general).

(*qalānis*)[306] of those who wore them, which were to be of a different color from the cap worn by Muslims. [He also ordered them] to put two patches on their slaves' outer garment, the color of which was to differ from that of the outer garment, that one of the patches be in front of his chest and the other on his back, and that each patch be four finger spans (eight cm.)[307] in diameter and be yellow. [Those Dhimmīs] who wore a turban (*ʿimāmah*) should wear one whose color was also yellow. The [Dhimmī] women
[1390] who went out and showed themselves in public should only appear in a yellow wrap (*izār*).[308] Al-Mutawakkil also ordered that their slaves wear *zunnār* belts and prohibited them from wearing those of a decorative variety (*manāṭiq*).[309] In addition, he ordered that their renovated places of worship be destroyed, and that one-tenth of their residences be seized.[310] If the location was sufficiently spacious, it was to be turned into a mosque. If it was not suitable for a mosque, it was to be [destroyed and] the area made an open tract of land.

And he ordered that wooden images of devils[311] be nailed to the doors of their houses in order to distinguish between their residences and those of the Muslims.[312]

Al-Mutawakkil prohibited the employment of Dhimmīs in government bureaus and in official functions, in which their authority would be exercised over Muslims. He prohibited their children from studying in Muslim elementary schools (*katātīb*), or being taught by Muslims. And he prohibited their displaying

306. The *qalansuwah* (pl. *qalānis*) might be a close-fitting cap or a tall cap of conical shape; see above, n. 222.

307. An *iṣbaʿ* ("finger") = 2.078 or 2.252 cm. (Hinz, *Masse und Gewichte,* 54).

308. On *izār,* see Dozy, *Vêtements,* 24; N. A. Stillman, *Jews of Arab Lands,* 167, n. 4; Lichtenstädter, "Distinctive Dress," 41, n. 22; Ashtor, "Social Isolation," 80. Y. Stillman, *EI²*, s.v. Libās, V, 732, describes it as "a large sheet-like wrap worn both as a mantle and a long loin cloth or waist cloth." She compares the term to late-Biblical *ēzōr.*

309. Dozy, *Vêtements,* 420, explains *minṭaqah* as being a girdle or waist belt fastened by a buckle or clasp; see also Lichtenstädter, "Distinctive Dress," 41, 22; N. A. Stillman, *Jews in Arab Lands,* 167, n. 5; Ahsan, *Social Life,* 62.

310. Tritton, *Caliphs,* 50, claims that al-Mutawakkil was the first caliph to ban renovation of Christian and Jewish places of worship by law. See also Ashtor, "Social Isolation," 86.

311. For *shayāṭīn,* ʿAynī (citing Sibṭ b. al-Jawzī, *Mirʾat al-zamān*) has *asāṭīn* ("columns"). See also Ashtor, *loc cit.*

312. See Tritton, *Caliphs,* 23.

crosses on their Palm Sundays and holding religious processions. In addition, he ordered that their graves be made level with the ground so as not to resemble the graves of the Muslims.[313]

Thus, he wrote to his district governors:

> In the name of God, the Merciful, the Compassionate. Now then, God—may He be blessed and exalted—by His might which cannot be gainsaid and by His power to do whatever He wills has chosen Islam and wished it for Himself. Through Islam He has honored His angels, sent His messengers, and assisted His saints. He embraced Islam with righteousness, encompassed it with succor, protected it from infirmity. He gave Islam victory over other religions, and made it free from doubts, immune from faults, endowed with outstanding virtues. He distinguished it among the religious laws by making it the most pure and virtuous, among precepts by making it the most pristine and noble, among statutes by making it the most just and convincing, and among actions by making it the most beautiful and fitting. He has honored its professors by what he has permitted and prohibited for them. He expounded for them His laws and statutes, set [1391]
> down for them His rules and customs, and prepared for them His expansive reward and recompense.
>
> He says in His Book, by which He commands and prohibits, urges and counsels: "Verily Allāh commands justice and kindness, and giving to kindred, and He forbids indecency and disreputable conduct and greed: He admonishes you, mayhap you will be reminded."[314]
>
> He says, prohibiting His people from partaking of offensive food,[315] drink and sexual relations, exalting them above this, purifying their religion, and making His people superior over others: "Forbidden to you are the dead (carcass), blood, the flesh of swine, that over which any

313. Muslim graves were supposed to be made level with the earth, but were in fact more often raised and even constructed in the form of mausoleums.

314. Qur'ān 16:90/92. The Qur'ān translations throughout are from R. Bell.

315. Text: *ʿumiṭa.* Addenda, DCCLXXV, suggests *ṭuʿima.* Cairo edition *ghumiṭa* is followed here.

other (name) than Allāh has been invoked, that which has been strangled," etc.[316]

Then He concludes, referring to what He prohibits them to partake of, with this verse, protecting His religion from whoever opposed it and perfectly benefiting His chosen people. God—may He be powerful and exalted—says: "Today those who have disbelieved despair of your religion; fear them not but fear you Me. Today I have perfected your religion for you," . . . etc.[317]

God—may He be powerful and exalted—also says: "Forbidden to you are your mothers, your daughters," etc.[318]

And God says: "O you who have believed, wine, *maysir,* stone altars, and divining arrows are simply an abomination, some of Satan's work," etc.[319]

God thereby forbids Muslims to partake of the most abominable and impure foods of members of other religions and to imbibe the drink of theirs that most arouses enmity and hatred and that most impedes mentioning God's name and praying. And He forbids the most sinful and the most unlawful of their marriages in the eyes of the discerning.

He gives Muslims good qualities and noble virtues, and makes them professors of faith, fidelity, virtue, mercy, certainty, and veracity. And He has not posited in their religion division and opposition, nor fanaticism, haugh-
[1392] tiness, treachery, perfidy, oppression, and injustice. He rather commands the former and forbids the latter, and promises for them His paradise and fire, His reward and punishment.

The Muslims, through God's favor by which He has elected them, and the superiority He gave them by the religion He chose for them, are distinguished from members of other religions by their righteous laws, their fine

316. Qur'ān 5:3/4.
317. Qur'ān 5:3/4–5.
318. Qur'ān 4:23/27.
319. Qur'ān 5:90/92.

and upright statutes, and their evident proof. They are distinguished through God's purifying their religion by what He permits and forbids them, by God's decree to strengthen His religion, by His determination to manifest His truth decisively, and by His volition to perfect His benefit to His people, "and that those who perished might perish because of an Evidence (of Allāh's intervention) and that those who remained alive might remain alive because of an Evidence";[320] and that God may give victory and a fortunate outcome to the pious and disgrace in this world and the next to the unbelievers.

The Commander of the Faithful decided—may his success and guidance be through God—that he would compel all the Dhimmīs, elite and common, in his presence and in his near and distant provinces, to make their hoods (*ṭayālisah*)—which some of their merchants, secretaries, their old, and young wear—the color of yellow clothing. None of them shall evade this.

And those of their humble followers beneath these in station, whose circumstance prevents them from wearing hoods, shall affix two pieces of cloth of the same color [to their clothing]. The circumference of each piece shall be a complete span,[321] and shall be affixed in like manner on the outer cloak that he wears, front and rear. And all of [the Dhimmīs] shall fasten buttons to their caps having a color different from that of the caps. They shall protrude where they are fastened, so that they not adhere and be hidden, and so that what is affixed by plaiting not be concealed. [1393]

They shall also attach wooden stirrups to their saddles and fix protruding pommels to their saddlebows. They shall not be permitted to remove the pommels from their saddle bows and place them farther back on their sides. What they do shall be inspected to ensure that the orders of the Commander of the Faithful are carried out by their

320. Qur'ān 8:42/44.
321. A span (of the hand; *shibr*) = about 10 cm.

clear compliance. The inspector should be able to spot compliance readily, it being immediately apparent.

Their male and female slaves, and those of this class who wear girdles, shall wear *zunnār* belts and *kustīj* girdles[322] in place of the girdles that were on their waists.

You shall instruct your officers concerning the orders of the Commander of the Faithful, and do so in such a way that they are motivated to carry out their examinations as commissioned. And you shall warn them about circumventing and deviating from [these regulations], and about punishing whoever of the Dhimmīs contravenes these regulations, be it by opposition, neglect or whatever, so that all of them, regardless of class or profession, hew to the path that the Commander of the Faithful has ordered, God willing.

Know this, whoever considers the Commander of the Faithful and his order. And dispatch to your officers in the regions of your province the letter of the Commander of the Faithful, that is, the letter that you have received concerning what you shall do, God willing.

The Commander of the Faithful asks God, his Lord and Patron, to bless His servant and Messenger Muḥammad and His angels, and to preserve him, having made him caliph for His religion. May he carry out God's commission, which he rightly executes only with God's help, so that he fulfills what God has appointed him to do, and
[1394] attains his consummate reward and most excellent recompense. For God is the Noble, the Compassionate.

Ibrāhīm b. al-ʿAbbās wrote this in Shawwāl, 235 (April 18–May 17, 850).

ʿAlī b. al-Jahm recited:[323]

The yellow things divide
  Between the righteous and the errant,

---

322. For *kasātīj*, pl. of *kustīj* (<Persian *kustī*), meaning belt, girdle, see Glossarium, CDLI; Steingass, *Dictionary*, 1029.

323. See ʿAlī b. al-Jahm; *Dīwān*, 192.

What cares the wise if the errant increase?[324]
All the more for the booty!

In this year, a man named Maḥmūd b. al-Faraj al-Naysābūrī appeared in Sāmarrā. He claimed to be Dhū al-Qarnayn.[325] He had with him twenty-seven men in the vicinity of Khashabat Bābak. Two of his companions appeared at the Public Gate (Bāb al-ʿĀmmah). And in Baghdad, in the mosque of its administrative center, there were two others who claimed that Maḥmūd was a prophet and that he was Dhū al-Qarnayn. He and his companions were remanded to al-Mutawakkil, who ordered that Maḥmūd be beaten with scourges. He was flogged severely and died thereafter from this beating.

Maḥmūd's companions were imprisoned. They had come from Naysābūr and had with them some [text] that they recited. They brought their families with them. Among them was a shaykh who bore witness to Maḥmūd's prophecy, claiming that the latter had received a revelation from Gabriel.

Maḥmūd was flogged one hundred strokes, but did not disclaim his prophecy under the beating. The shaykh who had vouched for him was flogged forty times, whereupon he disavowed Maḥmūd's prophecy under the whipping. Maḥmud was brought to the Public Gate (Bāb al-ʿĀmmah), where he recanted.

The shaykh declared that Maḥmūd had duped him, and ordered Maḥmūd's companions to slap him, which each of them did ten times. A text was taken from Maḥmūd containing words that he composed. He stated that it was his Qur'ān, and that Gabriel—peace upon him—had revealed it to him. He died thereafter on Wednesday, 3 Dhū al-Ḥijjah of this year (June 18, 850), and was buried in the Jazīrah.

In this year, al-Mutawakkil confirmed the oath of allegiance for his three sons as heirs apparent:[326] Muḥammad, whom he called

---

324. For *kathura* in the sense of "increase," see Glossarium, CDXLVIII.

325. Dhū al-Qarnayn ("the Two-Horned") appears in Qur'ān 18:83/82ff. and is often identified with Alexander the Great by both Muslim exegetes and Western scholars. Muslims regard Dhū al-Qarnayn as a believer who warned people of God's reward and punishment. See Paret, *Koran: Kommentar,* p. 318. Maḥmūd b. al-Faraj presumably regarded Dhū al-Qarnayn as a prophet.

326. Nabia Abbott, "Arabic Papyri," discusses the appointment of the three sons of al-Mutawakkil as heirs apparent and the division of the empire. Muḥam-

[1395] al-Muntaṣir; Abū ʿAbdallāh b. Qabīḥah—there was a difference of opinion concerning his proper name: according to one view his name was Muḥammad; according to another it was al-Zubayr—whom he gave the honorific title al-Muʿtazz; and Ibrāhīm, whom he called al-Mu'ayyad.

This was said to have been on Saturday, 26 Dhū al-Ḥijjah (July 11, 850), or, according to another version, on 27 Dhū al-Ḥijjah (July 12, 850).[327] He tied two banners for each, one black, as the banner of investiture, the other white, as the banner of the province. He assigned to each of his sons the province that I shall mention.

The caliph assigned to his son Muḥammad al-Muntaṣir: Ifrīqiyah and the entire Maghrib, from ʿArīsh Miṣr to where his sovereignty extended in the west; the district (*jund*) of Qinnasrīn; the Syrian and Jazīrah border provinces and towns; Diyār Muḍar, Diyār Rabīʿah, Mosul, Hīt, ʿĀnāt, al-Khābūr, and Qarqīsiyā; the districts of Bājarmā and Takrīt; the subdistricts of the Sawād; the districts of the Tigris, the two holy places, the Yemen, ʿAkk, Ḥaḍramawt, al-Yamāmah, al-Baḥrayn, al-Sind, Makrān, Qandābīl, and Farj Bayt al-Dhahab; and the districts of al-Ahwāz. He also gave him the annual income from produce in Sāmarrā; Māh al-Kūfah, Māh al-Baṣrah, Māsabadhān, Mihrajān Qadhaq, Shahrazūr, Darabādh, al-Ṣāmighān, Iṣbahān, Qumm, Qāshān, Qazwīn; the affairs of al-Jabal and the estates affiliated to al-Jibāl; and the income from alms taxes of the Arab tribesmen in al-Baṣrah.

He assigned to his son al-Muʿtazz: The districts of Khurāsān and its affiliated territories, Ṭabaristān, al-Rayy, Armenia, Ādharbayjān, and the districts of Fārs. In 240 (845–855), al-Mutawakkil

---

mad al-Muntaṣir received the largest share, and Ibrāhīm, the last in line of succession, the smallest. See the accounts in Yaʿqūbī, *Ta'rīkh II*, 594–95; Ibn al-Athīr, *Kāmil*, VII, 32–33; Abū al-Maḥāsin, *Nujūm*, II, 280; Ibn Khaldūn, *ʿIbar*, III, 275. They differ in details concerning the provinces assigned to each. Muḥammad al-Muntaṣir was thirteen (see below, 1471, where he is said to be twenty-five years old in 274/861–62); Ibrāhīm had not reached puberty; and al-Zubayr was only three. This meant that agents had to be appointed to administer their territories. The papyri published by Abbott concern village surveys ordered by Aḥmad b. al-Mudabbir, agent for the Syrian region assigned to Ibrāhīm al-Mu'ayyad. Aḥmad b. al-Mudabbir was a brother of Ibrāhīm b. al-Mudabbir (above, n. 287).

327. Ṣūlī gives the date as 1 Muḥarram, 236 (July 15, 850).

assigned to al-Muʿtazz the contents of the treasuries in all the districts, and the mints, and ordered that his name be stamped on dirhams.

He assigned to his son al-Mu'ayyad the districts (*jund*) of Damascus, Ḥimṣ, al-Urdunn and Filasṭīn. [1396]

Abū al-Ghuṣn al-Aʿrābī recited:[328]

The majestic rulers of the Muslims
Are Muḥammad, then Abū ʿAbdallāh.

Then there is Ibrāhīm, disdainful of baseness,
Blessed among the sons of God's caliph.

Al-Mutawakkil wrote a letter to his sons, the text of which is as follows:

> This is a letter written by the Servant of God, Jaʿfar al-Imām al-Mutawakkil ʿalā-llāh, The Commander of the Faithful, calling upon God and those who were present, including the members of his household, partisans (*shīʿah*), army commanders, judges, trusted deputies, jurists, and other Muslims, to witness its entire contents.[329]
>
> To Muḥammad al-Muntaṣir bi-llāh, and to Abū ʿAbdallāh al-Muʿtazz bi-llāh, and Ibrāhīm al-Mu'ayyad bi-llāh, sons of the Commander of the Faithful, in the full competence of his judgment, complete health of his body, thorough understanding, free volition, and striving for obedience to his Lord and the well-being of his subjects, their compliance and the amplitude and integrity of their community.
>
> This was in Dhū al-Ḥijjah 235 (June 16–July 14, 850).[330]
>
> To Muḥammad al-Muntaṣir bi-llāh, son of Jaʿfar al-

328. For the poet Abū al-Ghuṣn al-Aʿrābī, see, for instance, Ibn Qutaybah, *ʿUyūn*, IV, 22.

329. The word *shīʿah* in this context has the sense of "followers, assistants, officers, etc."; Dozy, *Supplément*, I, 811. The letter is also translated by Chejne, *Accession*, 123ff.

330. Cairo edition adds *annahu jaʿala*, on the basis of Mss. A and D, according to which the translation would be: "It was in Dhū al-Ḥijjah . . . that he made Muḥammad al-Muntaṣir. . . ."

Imām al-Mutawakkil 'alā-llāh, the Commander of the Faithful, heir apparent of the Muslims during al-Mutawakkil's life and caliph over them after him:

Al-Mutawakkil commended to al-Muntaṣir piety, which protects whoever cleaves to it, saves whoever takes refuge in it, and is the might and glory[331] of whoever contents himself with it. Good favor is attained by obedience to God, and mercy flows from God. God is forgiving and merciful.[332]

The Servant of God, Ja'far al-Imām al-Mutawakkil 'alā-llāh, Commander of the Faithful, invested as [future] caliph after Muḥammad al-Muntaṣir bi-llāh, son of the
[1397] Commander of the Faithful, Abū 'Abdallāh al-Mu'tazz bi-llāh, son of the Commander of the Faithful. Following Abū 'Abdallāh al-Mu'tazz bi-llāh, son of the Commander of the Faithful, he ordered that the caliphate be transferred to Ibrāhīm al-Mu'ayyad bi-llāh, son of the Commander of the Faithful.

And the Servant of God, Ja'far al-Imām al-Mutawakkil 'alā-llāh, Commander of the Faithful, imposed upon Abū 'Abdallāh al-Mu'tazz bi-llāh and Ibrāhīm al-Mu'ayyad bi-llāh, the two sons of the Commander of the Faithful, obedience and sincere counsel, alliance with [al-Muntaṣir's] friends and enmity toward his foes, secretly and publicly, whether in anger or favor, whether withholding or giving. He also enjoined them to uphold their oath of allegiance to al-Muntaṣir and to show loyalty to his investiture. They should not seek his ruin, nor should they endeavor to deceive him or make common cause against him. They should not act independently of al-Muntaṣir in any way that violates his investiture by the Commander of the Faithful as heir apparent, either while al-Mutawakkil lives or as caliph after him.

The Servant of God, Ja'far al-Imām al-Mutawakkil 'alā-

331. Text: *'izz.* The note *ad loc.* suggests *'izzah,* which may mean "glory" here, but the terms are virtually identical in meaning. I have used two words to encompass the possible semantic range.

332. Qur'ān 2:173/168 and parallels.

llāh, the Commander of the Faithful, has imposed [the following] upon Muḥammad al-Muntaṣir bi-llāh, son of the Commander of the Faithful, with respect to Abū ʿAbdallāh al-Muʿtazz bi-llāh and Ibrāhīm al-Mu'ayyad bi-llāh, the two sons of the Commander of the Faithful: Fidelity to what al-Mutawakkil has appointed for them and invested them with, namely, the caliphate after Muḥammad al-Muntaṣir bi-llāh, son of the Commander of the Faithful, the living succession being Ibrāhīm al-Mu'ayyad bi-llāh, son of the Commander of the Faithful, becoming caliph after Abū ʿAbdallāh al-Muʿtazz bi-llāh, son of the Commander of the Faithful. Al-Mutawakkil enjoins fulfillment of this.

Al-Muntaṣir, in turn, should not renounce any one of them, nor make an investiture excluding any one of them, be it by rendering the oath of allegiance to a son of his or to anyone else among all mankind. The order of succession shall not be altered. Al-Muntaṣir shall not violate any [of the arrangements] concerning the offices that the Servant [1398] of Allāh Jaʿfar al-Imām al-Mutawakkil ʿalā-llāh has assigned to each of them, including: [the supervision of] prayer, police services,[333] judgeships, *maẓālim* courts, taxes, estates, booty, income from alms taxes, and other privileges of their offices, and the office of each of them, including post,[334] [the monopoly on] embroidery (*ṭuruz*),[335] the treasury, subsidies, the mint houses, and all the offices that the Commander of the Faithful has assigned and will assign to each of them.

And al-Muntaṣir shall not transfer anyone servicing them in their districts, including commanders, troops, Shākiriyyah, *mawlā*s, pages, etc. And he shall not interfere with them by reducing anything of their estates and fiefs and other properties and treasures and all that they

333. For the term *maʿāwin* in this sense, see Bosworth, *Reunification*, 99, n. 313. For *maʿāwin* in the sense of "payments" or "subsidies," see Glossarium, CCCLXXXIII.

334. Or: post and intelligence; see *EI*², s.v. Barīd.

335. For *ṭirāz* (sg. of *ṭuruz*), see R. B. Serjeant, "Islamic Textiles," *Ars Islamica*, 9 (1942), 60ff.; *EI*¹, s.v.; Ahsan, *Social Life*, 68–70.

possess, as well as what they own of inherited and newly acquired wealth, old and renovated property, and all that they will acquire and will be acquired for them. And he shall not dispossess, harass, or interfere with any one of his partisans (*shīʿah*), secretaries, judges, slaves, agents, followers, and all their circumstances by [demands for] supervision and accounting or in any other way. And he shall not nullify what the Commander of the Faithful confirmed for the two of them in this contract and investiture by altering it, postponing its execution, or contradicting anything of it.

The Servant of God, Jaʿfar al-Mutawakkil ʿalā-llāh, the Commander of the Faithful, imposed upon Abū ʿAbdallāh al-Muʿtazz bi-llāh, son of the Commander of the Faithful, the same conditions regarding Ibrāhīm al-Mu'ayyad bi-llāh, son of the Commander of the Faithful, as he imposed upon Muḥammad al-Muntaṣir bi-llāh, son of the Commander of the Faithful, should the caliphate pass to him after Muḥammad al-Muntaṣir bi-llāh, son of the Commander of the Faithful. As caliph after Muḥammad al-Muntaṣir bi-llāh, son of the Commander of the Faithful, Abū ʿAbdallāh al-Muʿtazz bi-llāh must behave toward Ibrāhīm al-Mu'ayyad bi-llāh, son of the Commander of the Faithful, according to the conditions al-Mutawakkil set down for Muḥammad al-Muntaṣir bi-llāh, son of the Commander of the Faithful, including all that al-Mutawakkil designated in this letter, according to what he
[1399] expounded, concerning loyalty on the part of Abū ʿAbdallāh al-Muʿtazz bi-llāh, son of the Commander of the Faithful.

Inasmuch as the Commander of the Faithful al-Mutawakkil assigned the caliphate to Ibrāhīm al-Mu'ayyad bi-llāh, son of the Commander of the Faithful, Abū ʿAbdallāh al-Muʿtazz bi-llāh must see to it that the agreement is fully carried out, in accordance with what he owes God and with what the Commander of the Faithful ordered him to do. He must not violate the agreement by dismissing it or substituting [provisions with it].

God threatens whoever opposes His command and deviates from His path in His perfect Book: "Then if any alter it having heard it, the guilt rests upon those who alter it; verily God is One Who hears and knows."[336]

Abū ʿAbdallāh al-Muʿtazz bi-llāh, son of the Commander of the Faithful, and Ibrāhīm al-Mu'ayyad bi-llāh, son of the Commander of the Faithful, have a guarantee of safe-conduct from Muḥammad al-Muntaṣir bi-llāh, son of the Comander of the Faithful, whether one or both of them are staying with him or are absent from him. That is, while Abū ʿAbdallāh al-Muʿtazz bi-llāh, son of the Commander of the Faithful, is not in his governorship of Khurāsān and its adjacent dependencies, those falling within the jurisdiction of Khurāsānī rule, and Ibrāhīm al-Mu'ayyad bi-llāh, son of the Commander of the Faithful, is not in his governorship in Syria and its districts (*ajnād*).

It is incumbent upon Muḥammad al-Muntaṣir bi-llāh, son of the Commander of the Faithful, to transfer Abū ʿAbdallāh al-Muʿtazz bi-llāh, son of the Commander of the Faithful, to Khurāsān and its adjacent dependencies, those falling within the jurisdiction of Khurāsānī rule, and to deliver to him the governorship of Khurāsān and all of its provinces (*aʿmāl*) and districts (*ajnād*), as well as the subdistricts (*kuwar*) included in what Jaʿfar al-Imām al-Mutawakkil ʿalā-llāh, the Commander of the Faithful, has assigned Abū ʿAbdallāh al-Muʿtazz bi-llāh, son of the Commander of the Faithful.

Al-Muntaṣir shall not keep Abū ʿAbdallāh from them or detain him in his presence or in any land except Khurāsān and the districts and subdistricts falling under [1400] Khurāsānī rule. He must see to it that Abū ʿAbdallāh gets to Khurāsān as governor over it and all its provinces, serving independently, with all its provinces assigned to him, so that he may reside where he wishes in the subdistricts of his province. Al-Muntaṣir shall not transfer al-Muʿtazz from them. All those whom the Commander of the Faithful has attached and will attach to his service shall go with him, including his *mawlā*s, commanders,

336. Qur'ān 2:181/177.

Shākiriyyah, companions, secretaries, agents, slaves, and the various people who follow him, along with their wives, children, families, and property. Al-Muntaṣir shall not detain anyone from going to al-Mu'tazz nor cause anyone else to share in anything of his administrative offices. He shall not send [to oversee him] a confidant, secretary, or courier. He shall not chastise him for any reason.

And Muḥammad al-Muntaṣir bi-llāh shall free Ibrāhīm al-Mu'ayyad bi-llāh, son of the Commander of the Faithful, to go out to Syria and its districts, along with those whom the Commander of the Faithful has attached and will attach to his service, including his *mawlā*s, commanders, slaves, troops, Shākiriyyah, companions, agents, female slaves, and the various classes of people who follow him, including their wives, children, and property. He shall not detain anyone from going to them. He shall deliver to him his governorship (*wilāyah*), and all its provinces (*a'māl*), and districts (*junūd*). Al-Muntaṣir shall not prevent al-Mu'ayyad from having access to them or detain him in his presence, nor in any of the lands aside from them. He shall see to it that al-Mu'ayyad gets to Syria and its districts (*ajnād*) to govern them, and he shall not transfer him from them. He is responsible to him for those he attached to his service, including commanders, *mawlā*s, pages, troops, Shākiriyyah, and various classes of people in all circumstances. His responsibilities are governed by conditions similar to those set for Muḥammad al-Muntaṣir bi-llāh, son of the Commander of the Faithful, with regard to Abū 'Abdallāh al-Mu'tazz bi-llāh, son of the Commander of the Faithful, in Khurāsān and its provinces, according to what
[1401] has been prescribed, elucidated, adumbrated, and expounded in this letter.

If the caliphate passes to Abū 'Abdallāh al-Mu'tazz bi-llāh, son of the Commander of the Faithful, and Ibrāhīm al-Mu'ayyad bi-llāh stays in Syria, al-Mu'tazz must confirm Ibrāhīm there, whether he is in his presence or is absent from him. He must let Ibrāhīm go to his province ('*amal*) in Syria, and hand over to him its districts (*ajnād*), governorship (*wilāyah*), and all of its provinces (*a'māl*).

He shall not keep Ibrāhīm from them nor detain him in his presence nor in any land aside from it. He must see to it that Ibrāhīm gets to Syria quickly so as to govern it and all its provinces, in accordance with the conditions set down for Muḥammad al-Muntaṣir bi-llāh, son of the Commander of the Faithful, with regard to Abū ʿAbdallāh al-Muʿtazz bi-llāh, son of the Commander of the Faithful, in Khurāsān and its provinces, that is, according to what was prescribed, described, and stipulated as a condition in this letter.

The Commander of the Faithful will not permit any of those to whom these stipulations apply—Muḥammad al-Muntaṣir bi-llāh, Abū ʿAbdallāh al-Muʿtazz bi-llāh, and Ibrāhīm al-Mu'ayyad bi-llāh, sons of the Commander of the Faithful—to expunge anything that we have made a condition in this letter and affirmed. Fidelity to it is incumbent upon all of them. God will accept only this from them. Adherence is accepting God's compact concerning this matter and that alone.

Jaʿfar al-Imām al-Mutawakkil, Commander of the Faithful, called God, Lord of worlds, and the Muslims who were in his presence as witnesses to all that is in this letter, that he (al-Mutawakkil) will execute what pertains to Muḥammad al-Muntaṣir bi-llāh, Abū ʿAbdallāh al-Muʿtazz bi-llāh, and Ibrāhīm al-Mu'ayyad bi-llāh, sons of the Commander of the Faithful, along with all that he designated in it. God is sufficient as witness and helper to whoever obeys hopefully and is faithful to His compact out of fear and after taking careful measure. God punishes those who oppose Him or strive to shun His command. [1402]

This letter was written in four copies. The attestation of the witnesses in each copy was made in the presence of the Commander of the Faithful. There was a copy in the library of the Commander of the Faithful, a copy in the possession of Muḥammad al-Muntaṣir, son of the Commander of the Faithful, a copy in the possession of Abū ʿAbdallāh al-Muʿtazz bi-llāh, son of the Commander of the Faithful, and a copy in the possession of Ibrāhīm al-Mu'ayyad bi-llāh, son of the Commander of the Faithful.

Jaʿfar al-Imām al-Mutawakkil made Abū ʿAbdallāh al-Muʿtazz bi-llāh, son of the Commander of the Faithful, governor of the provinces of Fārs, Armenia, and Ādharbayjān, as well as the provinces and subdistricts of Khurāsān, its adjacent dependencies, and those falling within the jurisdiction of Khurāsānī rule. Al-Mutawakkil imposed on Muḥammad al-Muntaṣir bi-llāh, son of the Commander of the Faithful, protection of al-Muʿtazz's life and firm commitment to the provinces in his jurisdiction and all the people who have recourse to him in Khurāsān and its adjacent dependencies and those falling within the jurisdiction of Khurāsānī rule, according to what is designated in this letter.

Ibrāhīm b. al-ʿAbbās b. Muḥammad b. Ṣūl recited, praising the three sons of al-Mutawakkil—al-Muntaṣir, al-Muʿtazz, and al-Mu'ayyad:[337]

The bonds of Islam, linked with
Victory, power and confirmation,

Join now a Hāshimite caliph and three
Heirs apparent surrounding the caliphate.

He is a moon (*qamar*) around which satellites (*aqmār*) turn,
Surrounding the ascent of its good fortune with good fortunes.

The ancestors protect them and are protected by them,[338]
They are distinguished by their noble souls and ancestry.[339]

[1403] He is also the author of a poem about al-Muʿtazz bi-llāh:[340]

The rising light of the east becomes bright
by [the presence of] al-Muʿtazz bi-llāh.[341]

---

337. See Iṣfahānī, *Aghānī,* IX, 32. And see Ibrāhīm al-Ṣūlī, *Dīwān,* 131, which omits the third verse, as does Abū Bakr al-Ṣūlī, *Kitāb al-awrāq.*

338. *Aghānī* has "Fate has elevated them, and they are raised by it [read: *bihā*]."

339. The word *judūd* is a double entendre (*jinās*), meaning both "ancestors" and "good luck."

340. Ibrāhīm al-Ṣūlī, *Dīwān,* 130.

341. Abū Bakr al-Ṣūlī, *Kitāb al-awrāq,* adds: "the investiture became so bright that it caused dawn to break at night,/ By it God has bestowed on the nation justice and kindness."

Al-Muʿtazz is indeed perfume
Sent to mankind giving fragrance.

And he is the author of another poem about them:[342]

It is God who has made his religion victorious
And strengthened it with Muḥammad.[343]

God ennobled with the caliphate
Jaʿfar b. Muḥammad.[344]

And God confirmed his investiture
Of Muḥammad and Muḥammad.[345]

And the one confirmed (Muʾayyad) by those two confirmed,
Back to the Prophet Muḥammad.

In this year, Isḥāq b. Ibrāhīm, Supervisor of the Bridge, died.[346] This was on Tuesday, 23 Dhū al-Ḥijjah (July 8, 850) or, according to another version, on 22 Dhū al-Ḥijjah (July 7, 850). Isḥāq had appointed his son as his successor. The latter was bedecked with five robes and girded with a sword. When al-Mutawakkil heard news of Isḥāq's illness, he sent his son al-Muʿtazz to visit him along with Bughā al-Sharābī and a contingent of commanders and soldiers.

The waters of the Tigris reportedly turned yellow[347] this year for three days. People were alarmed at this. They then turned to the color of flood water. This was in Dhū al-Ḥijjah (June 16–July 14).

In this year, al-Mutawakkil brought Yaḥyā b. ʿUmar b. al-Ḥu-

---

342. Ibrāhīm al-Ṣūlī, *Dīwān*, 132.

343. Muḥammad is apparently the caliph Abū Isḥāq Muḥammad al-Muʿtaṣim (rather than the Prophet Muḥammad).

344. Jaʿfar b. Muḥammad is al-Mutawakkil, son of Muḥammad al-Muʿtaṣim.

345. The two Muḥammads are Abū Jaʿfar Muḥammad al-Muntaṣir and Abū ʿAbdallāh Muḥammad al-Muʿtazz. The next line alludes to their brother Muʾ-ayyad.

346. Text: *ṣāḥib al-jisr.* Isḥāq b. Ibrāhīm b. Muṣʿab was chief of security police (*ṣāḥib al-shurṭah*), as Ibn al-Athīr, *Kāmil*, VII, 35, notes here, as though this were the correct reading. On the other hand, Ṭabarī reports, III, 1062 (Bosworth, *Reunification*, 129), that in 206 (821–22) he was put in charge of "the two bridges." Thus, he was called *ṣāḥib al-jisr.*

347. The color *aṣfar/ṣufrā* may be yellow, beige, orange, or yellowish brown; Fischer, *Farb- und Formbezeichnungen*, 358.

sayn b. Zayd b. ʿAlī b. al-Ḥusayn b. ʿAlī b. Abī Ṭālib[348] from one of
[1404] the provinces. He had reportedly assembled a group [of supporters]. ʿUmar b. Faraj flogged him eighteen lashes, and he was incarcerated in Baghdad in the Maṭbaq [Prison].

Leading the pilgrimage this year was Muḥammad b. Dāwūd.

---

348. Text: Yaḥyā b ʿUmar b. Yaḥyā b. Zayd b ʿAlī b. al-Ḥusayn b. ʿAlī. Cairo edition, following Ms. D, has Yaḥyā b. ʿUmar b. Ḥusayn b. Zayd. But cf. Ṭabarī, III, 1515 (Saliba, 15), where his name is given as Yaḥyā b. ʿUmar b. Yaḥyā b. Ḥusayn b. Zayd, etc. And see Addenda, DCCXXV. He was called Abū al-Ḥusayn. Ṭabarī, III, 1515–24 (Saliba 15–21), describes his abortive uprising in al-Kūfah in 250 (864–65). His revolt had an interesting sequel in 255 (868–69; III, 1745), when a leader of the Zanj rebellion claimed to be the incarnated form of Yaḥyā b. ʿUmar.

The Events of the Year 236

(July 15, 850–July 4, 851)

Among them was the killing of Muḥammad b. Ibrāhīm b. Muṣʿab b. Zurayq, brother of Isḥāq b. Ibrāhīm, in Fārs.

The Killing of Muḥammad b. Ibrāhīm b. Muṣʿab and How It Took Place

I have been informed by more than one authority that when Muḥammad b. Isḥāq b. Ibrāhīm's father, Isḥāq, learned that Muḥammad was an insatiable glutton, who demanded exorbitant amounts of food, Isḥāq sent a message summoning him.[349] Isḥāq ordered Muḥammad to eat, explaining, "I want to see how you consume food." He devoured a quantity that astounded Isḥāq. Then, when it seemed that he had reached his surfeit, a roast lamb was served, which he ravaged until only the bones remained. When he had consumed it, Isḥāq remarked, "My son, your father's money will not suffice to feed your belly. Go and associate with the Commander of the Faithful; he can better afford to support you than I."

349. For the Ṭāhirid Muḥammad b. Isḥāq b. Ibrāhīm, see Table 3.

Isḥāq sent Muḥammad to the gate [of the caliph][350] and made him stay there. Muḥammad was in the service of the central government during the lifetime of his father and was his father's proxy at the gate [of the caliph] until his father Isḥāq died.

Al-Mu'tazz appointed Muḥammad b. Isḥāq over Fārs, and al-Muntaṣir appointed him over al-Yamāmah, al-Baḥrayn, and the Mecca Road in Muḥarram (July 15–August 13, 850) of this year. Al-Mutawakkil assigned him all the districts of his father. Al-Mun-
[1405] taṣir added the governorship of Egypt. This was because he reportedly delivered to al-Mutawakkil and his heirs apparent the contents of his father's storehouses, including jewelry and precious objects, thus gaining their favor so that they elevated his rank.

When Muḥammad b. Ibrāhīm[351] learned what was done in the case of his nephew Muḥammad b. Isḥāq, he became hostile to the central government, and al-Mutawakkil discovered objectionable things about him.

I was told by some(one) of my informants that Muḥammad b. Ibrāhīm's hostility was directed only against his nephew Muḥammad b. Isḥāq, the reason for it being as follows: The taxes (*kharāj*) of Fārs had been delivered to [Muḥammad b. Ibrāhīm]. Now Muḥammad b. Isḥāq complained to al-Mutawakkil about the hostility of his uncle, Muḥammad b. Ibrāhīm, whereupon al-Mutawakkil gave the former latitude to treat his uncle as he saw fit.

At that, Muḥammad b. Isḥāq appointed al-Ḥusayn b. Ismā'īl b. Ibrāhīm b. Muṣ'ab governor of Fārs and deposed his uncle.[352] Then Muḥammad b. Isḥāq approached al-Ḥusayn b. Ismā'īl about killing his uncle Muḥammad b. Ibrāhīm. It is reported that when al-Ḥusayn b. Ismā'īl went to Fārs, he presented his uncle with gifts, including sweets, on the day of Nayrūz.[353] Muḥammad b. Ibrāhīm

350. Text: *al-bāb.* Ibn al-Athīr, *Kāmil,* VII, 36, says more explicitly *bāb al-khalīfah.*

351. Muḥammad b. Ibrāhīm, uncle of Muḥammad b. Isḥāq, was the brother of Isḥāq b. Ibrāhīm b. Muṣ'ab; above, n. 98. See Table 3.

352. Al-Ḥusayn b. Ismā'īl b. Ibrāhīm b. Muṣ'ab was a cousin of Muḥammad b. Isḥāq b. Ibrāhīm and (like him) a nephew of Muḥammad b. Ibrāhīm; Zambaur, *Manuel,* 46, 197, 198. He was very active as a military commander in the ensuing period; see Saliba, Index, 176.

353. Nayrūz is the Arabic form of the Persian Nawrūz, the ancient Iranian (Achaemenid) New Year, which was celebrated into Islamic times, and with particular enthusiasm in the period of al-Mutawakkil. On the days of Nawrūz, sweets were prepared and given as presents, for instance, *ṣābūniyyah* and *lawzīnaj* (basically, sugar and almonds); *EI*[1], s.v. Nawrūz; Ahsan, *Social Life,* 99–100, 287.

partook of them. Then al-Ḥusayn b. Ismāʿīl entered and ordered that he be brought into another place and that sweets be offered to him again. Muḥammad b. Ibrāhīm ate more of them so that he became thirsty and wanted to drink, but water was withheld. He tried to leave the place where he was brought, but was denied exit. Muḥammad survived for two days and nights, and then he died. His property and family were carried to Sāmarrā on one hundred camels.

When al-Mutawakkil heard the announcement of Muḥammad b. Ibrāhīm's death, he ordered that a letter concerning him be written to Ṭāhir b. ʿAbdallāh b. Ṭāhir expressing condolences, and it was written as follows:

> Now then. The Commander of the Faithful offers you, [1406]
> with every benefit and favor, felicitation for the gifts of God and consolation for the calamities of His destiny. God has determined for Muḥammad b. Ibrāhīm, *mawlā* of the Commander of the Faithful, His decree for mankind (*ʿibād*) so that they have transience and He have permanence. The Commander of the Faithful consoles you for [the loss of] Muḥammad, as God gives His rich reward and recompense to whoever acts according to His command in his misfortunes. May God and what brings you near Him take precedence in all your circumstances. With thanks to God comes His abundance; and with submission to God's command, His pleasure. And God gives success to the Commander of the Faithful. Peace.

In this year, al-Ḥasan b. Sahl died, according to one informant, on the first of Dhū al-Ḥijjah (June 5, 851).[354] The informant who stated this said that Muḥammad b. Isḥāq b. Ibrāhīm died on the twenty-fifth of this month (June 29, 851).

Al-Qāsim b. Aḥmad al-Kūfī reportedly said: I was in the service of al-Fatḥ b. Khāqān in 235 (849–50), while al-Fatḥ held administrative offices for al-Mutawakkil, including intelligence (*akhbār*) concerning the elite and commoners in Sāmarrā and the Hārūnī [Palace] and what was adjacent to it.[355]

---

354. Al-Ḥasan b. Sahl had been finance minister and governor under al-Ma'mūn; see above, n. 196.

355. He is al-Fatḥ b. Khāqān, son of Khāqān b. ʿUrṭūj (Ghurṭūj). The Khāqānids were of Turkish stock, and were the ruling dynasty in Farghānah (see Zambaur,

A dispatch came from Ibrāhīm b. 'Aṭā', supervisor of Intelligence in Sāmarrā, reporting the death of al-Ḥasan b. Sahl, stating that he took an overdose of medicine on the morning of Thursday, 25 Dhū al-Qa'dah (May 20, 851), that he died at noontime on this day, and that al-Mutawakkil ordered that his funeral equipment be furnished from his treasuries. When he was placed on his litter (*sarīr*), a number of merchants who were creditors of al-Ḥasan b. Sahl hung onto it, holding up his burial. Yaḥyā b. Khāqān,[356] Ibrāhīm b. 'Attāb, and a man known as Barghūth mediated their case.[357] They resolved the matter, and he was buried.

[1407] The next day a dispatch arrived from the chief of Intelligence in Baghdad (Madīnat al-Salām) with an announcement of the death of Muḥammad b. Isḥāq b. Ibrāhīm on the afternoon of Thursday, 5 Dhū al-Ḥijjah (June 9, 851). Al-Mutawakkil grieved deeply over him. He said, "May God be great and exalted. How fate has overtaken al-Ḥasan [b. Sahl] and Muḥammad b. Isḥāq at the same time!"

In this year, al-Mutawakkil ordered that the grave of al-Ḥusayn b. 'Alī and the residences and palaces surrounding it be destroyed. The site of his grave was to be ploughed, sown, and irrigated, and people were to be prevented from visiting it.[358] It is reported that

---

Manuel, p. 12—Khāqānids). His father was chief of the Turkish troops from Central Asia who formed part of the royal guard of al-Mu'taṣim. Al-Fatḥ was educated, from the age of seven, along with al-Mutawakkil, in the court of the caliph, who adopted him. Thus, he was the adopted brother of al-Mutawakkil, and became his secretary and close confidant. He was governor of Egypt, 242 (856–57)–47 (861–62); Zambaur, *Manuel,* 27. Al-Fatḥ was friend and patron of the great Jāḥiẓ (Pellat, *Milieu,* 66), as well as other writers and poets, and was himself an author. Al-Fatḥ assembled a large library at Sāmarrā, containing many philosophical works, and had an impressive command of Arabic; see, for instance, Yāqūt, *Irshād,* VI, 116ff; and see O. Pinto, "al-Fatḥ B. Ḥāqān"; *EI*², s.v. Al-Fatḥ died while protecting al-Mutawakkil on the night he was assassinated (see below, 1460, p. 180). See Table 2.

356. Yaḥyā b. Khāqān was the brother of al-Fatḥ and Ja'far (Zambaur, *Manuel,* 12).

357. For *qaṭa'a amrahum* in this sense, see Glossarium, CDXXVIII.

358. The grave of al-Ḥusayn b. 'Alī (Qabr al-Ḥusayn, Mashhad al-Ḥusayn) is located at Karbalā', where al-Ḥusayn and his followers were massacred by the Umayyads in 680. Al-Mutawakkil's obliteration of the site was part of his anti-Shī'ite policy. By 366 (977), when Ibn Ḥawqal visited Karbalā', during the rule of the Shī'ite Buwayhid dynasty, he found a large shrine over the tomb; it had once again become an attraction for pilgrims; see Ibn Ḥawqal, *Masālik,* p. 166; *EI*², s.v. Karbalā'. According to a tradition, the caliph was punished for destroying the tomb in such a way that after his death hardly a trace remained of Sāmarrā; see Qazvīnī, *Nuzhat al-qulūb,* 32, 42; tr. 39, 49.

an agent of the chief of security police announced in the area: "Whomever we find near al-Ḥusayn's grave after three days we shall send to the Maṭbaq [Prison]." People fled and refrained from going to the grave. This place was ploughed, and the area around it was sown.

In this year, al-Mutawakkil appointed as secretary ʿUbaydallāh b. Yaḥyā b. Khāqān and dismissed Muḥammad b. al-Faḍl al-Jarjarāʾī.[359]

In this year, Muḥammad al-Muntaṣir went on the pilgrimage. His grandmother, Shujāʿ, mother of al-Mutawakkil, went on the pilgrimage with him, al-Mutawakkil accompanying her as far as al-Najaf.

In this year, Abū Saʿīd Muḥammad b. Yūsuf al-Marwazī al-Kabaḥa Fāhu perished.[360]

It is reported that Fāris b. Bughā al-Sharābī—he was the deputy of his father—appointed this Abū Saʿīd, a *mawlā* of Ṭayyiʾ, as governor of Ādharbayjān and Armenia. He encamped in al-Karkh, that is, Karkh Fayrūz.[361] He died suddenly on 7 Shawwāl (June 28, 851) while he was in al-Karkh. He had put on one of his shoes and reached out to put on the other when he fell over dead.

---

359. Al-Jarjarāʾī had followed Ibn al-Zayyāt in the wazīrate. ʿUbaydallāh's appointment (Zambaur, *Manuel,* 6) indicates the growing power and influence of the Khāqānids.

360. The cognomen al-Kabaḥa Fahu, if correct, means "The One Who Bridled His Mouth." See Ṭabarī, Index, 235; al-Thaghrī al-Kabaḥa Fahu. Ms. C has al-Kakh (?). But the reading is uncertain. Cairo edition's text reads: *al-Kabaḥa fujāʾatan* (the second word appears in the text farther on). See *Fragmenta,* 546: *fujāʾatan* (after Yūsuf). He was an army commander from Khurāsān (Marw), who made his first appearance at the time of al-Maʾmūn, in 210 (816–17; Ṭabarī, III, 1093), when he participated in a campaign against the rebellious citizens of Qumm, along with (his uncle) ʿAlī b. Hishām (al-Marwazī). His cognomen there is given as al-K-ḥ-b-q-w-ṣ (see Bosworth, *Reunification,* 166). He executed his uncle Ḥusayn b. Hishām in 217 (832–33) in the name of al-Maʾmūn (Ṭabarī, III, 1107; and Ibn Ṭayfūr, *Baghdād,* 147). But Bosworth, 192, n. 598, does not identify him with our man. He was active under al-Muʿtaṣim and participated in the campaign against Bābak; Marin, *Reign,* Index, 133. See also Balādhurī, *Futūḥ,* 198; Iṣfahānī, *Aghānī,* XVIII, 47, 108, 169–70; Ibn Khallikān, *Wafayāt,* III, 658 (with Abū Tammām and al-Buḥturī< Iṣfahānī, *Aghānī,* 169–70). According to Yaʿqūbī, *Taʾrīkh,* II, 598, he died on his way to a campaign in Armenia.

361. The words "that is Karkh Fayrūz" appear to be a gloss. A Karkh Quarter existed in Baghdad, and a Karkh Fayrūz in the area of Sāmarrā, which was situated between the villages of Karkh Fayrūz (or Karkh Bājaddah) on the north and al-Maṭīrah on the southeast. Karkh Fayrūz was a military cantonment occupied by a number of the caliphal Turkish guards, who were isolated from the local citizens. See Yāqūt, *Muʿjam,* IV, 255; *EI*², s.v. al-Karkh.

[1408] Al-Mutawakkil appointed Abū Sa'īd's son Yūsuf over the security police (*al-ḥarb*), over which his father had been in charge. Following that, he assigned to him the taxes of the province [of Ādharbayjān and Armenia] and its estates. He went to the province, took control of it, and sent his administrative officers to every area.

Leading the pilgrimage this year was al-Muntaṣir Muḥammad b. Ja'far al-Mutawakkil.

The Events of the Year 237
(July 5, 851–June 22, 852)

One of the events was the revolt of the inhabitants of Armenia against Yūsuf b. Muḥammad.[362]

The Cause of the Revolt by the Inhabitants of Armenia against Yūsuf b. Muḥammad

We have previously mentioned the reason for al-Mutawakkil's appointing this Yūsuf b. Muḥammad governor of Armenia. The reason for the revolt of the inhabitants of Armenia against him was reportedly as follows:

When he went to his administrative prefecture in Armenia one of the Patrikioi named Buqrāṭ b. Ashūṭ, called the chief Patrikios,

362. Yūsuf, son of Abū Saʿīd Muḥammad b. Yūsuf al-Marwazī, was governor of Armenia in 235 (849–50) and of Ādharbayjān in 237 (851–52); Balādhurī, *Futūḥ*, 248; Zambaur, *Manuel*, 177, 178. Armenia was the scene of periodic insurrections in the ʿAbbāsid period; the rebellion against al-Mutawakkil reported here was the most serious; see also Yaʿqūbī, *Taʾrīkh*, II, 598, and in general, *EI*², s.v. Armīniya.

rebelled, seeking to take rule.[363] Yūsuf b. Muḥammad seized him, bound him, and deported him to the gate of the caliph.[364] Buqrāṭ and his son then converted to Islam.

It is reported that when Yūsuf deported Buqrāṭ b. Ashūṭ, the latter's nephew and a number of Armenian Patrikioi rallied against Yūsuf. Snow had fallen in the town where Yūsuf was situated. It is said to have been Ṭarūn.[365] When the snow settled, the Armenians besieged it from every side, surrounding Yūsuf and those who were with him in the town. Yūsuf went out to the
[1409] gate of the city and fought them. [The Armenians] killed him and all those who fought alongside him. Those who did not fight alongside him were told to strip and escape naked. Many of them discarded their clothing and escaped nude and barefoot. Most of them died from the cold, but some escaped, losing their fingers.

When Yūsuf deported Buqrāṭ b. Ashūṭ, the Patrikioi took an oath to kill Yūsuf and vowed to shed his blood. Mūsā b. Zurārah[366] went along with them in this. He was responsible for the daughter of Buqrāṭ.

Sawādah b. ʿAbd al-Ḥamīd al-Jaḥḥāfī[367] discouraged Yūsuf b.

---

363. The rulers of Armenia were called Biṭrīq (Patrikios) by the Arabs. Buqrāṭ b. Ashūṭ (Bagrat son of Ashot Bagratuni) refused to pay tribute to Abū Saʿīd Muḥammad b. Yūsuf in 849 and had resisted the caliph's forces sent in 850. Balādhurī, who reports these events (*Futūḥ*, 248), does not mention the present rebellion of Buqrāṭ b. Ashūṭ that led to his deportation, thus magnifying the offence to the Armenian Patrikioi. See Laurent, *L'Arménie*, 117ff.; Vasmer, *Chronologie*, 91ff.; and Vardan's *Universal History*, tr. J. Muyldermans, 122ff. See also Grousset, *Histoire*, 357f; Minorsky, *History*, 24f.; and "Caucasia IV," 510. Armenian chronicles, including an eyewitness account of some of these events by Thomas Ardzruni (Artsruni), taken together with reports in Muslim sources, give a fairly clear and detailed picture.

364. That is, the Caliphal Palace in Sāmarrā.

365. Ṭarūn (Taron) is the area west of Lake Van; Yāqūt, *Muʿjam*, III, 534; Le Strange, *Lands*, 115–17. The event took place in the town of Mūsh in Taron; Vasmer, *Chronologie*, 93. According to Balādhurī, *Futūḥ*, 248, the Khuwaythiyah participated in this attack, a detail that is confirmed by our text farther on.

366. On Mūsā b. Zurārah (of Arzan), see Balādhurī, *Futūḥ*, 248. In 849–50, he tried to take over Taron on the pretext that he would deliver tribute to the caliph. He was repulsed, however, by Bagrat of Taron and Ashot Ardzruni, after which he supported the Armenians against the Muslims. He came to negotiate with the Muslims but was seized and deported to Sāmarrā; see Laurent, *L'Arménie*, 119, 326. See also Yaʿqūbī, *Ta'rīkh*, II, 598.

367. The Arab amīr Sawādah b. ʿAbd al-Ḥamīd al-Jaḥḥāfī is mentioned in the *Universal History* of Vardan (tr. Muyldermans, 118) as having led 4,000 men in battle (in 823–24) against Ashot Msaker. Smbat, son of Ashot (Sunbāṭ b. Ashūṭ), made peace with him. See also Minorsky, "Caucasia, IV," 509.

Abī Saʿīd from remaining where he was and told him the news he heard concerning the Patrikioi. Yūsuf, however, refused to comply, and the [Armenians] caught up with him in the month of Ramaḍān. They surrounded the wall of the town, the snow being up to twenty *dhirāʿ* (ca. ten meters) in the vicinity of the town and as far as Khilāṭ and Dabīl.[368] Everything was snowed in.[369]

Before this, Yūsuf had divided his forces among the villages (*rasātīq*) of his province, groups of his forces heading [to be stationed in] each of its regions. A contingent of the Patrikioi and their allies were sent against each group and killed them in a single day. They had surrounded Yūsuf in the town for several days, at which point he went out to [confront] them. He fought until he was killed.

Al-Mutawakkil consequently sent Bughā al-Sharābī to Armenia, seeking vengeance for Yūsuf.[370] He headed for Armenia from the direction of the Jazīrah. He began in Arzan[371] [by attacking] Mūsa b. Zurārah[372]—he is Abū al-Ḥurr—and he had sisters and brothers, [namely] Ismāʿīl, Sulaymān, Aḥmad, ʿĪsā, Muḥammad, and Hārūn. Bughā deported Mūsā b. Zurārah to the gate of the caliph. He then proceeded to lay siege in the mountain of the Khuwaythiyyah.[373] They constituted the majority of the inhabitants of Armenia and were the killers of Yūsuf b. Muḥammad. [1410]
Bughā fought and defeated them, killing about 30,000 and taking

368. Khilāṭ (Akhlāṭ, Armenian Khlat') was a town and fortress immediately northwest of Lake Van; see *EI*², s.v. Akhlāṭ. Dabīl is Dvin, the capital of Armenia; *EI*², s.v. Dwin.

369. Literally, "The world was all snow" (*wa-l-dunyā kulluhā thalj*).

370. Ṭabarī says that it was Bughā al-Sharābī, that is, the Younger, who was dispatched, but other sources state that it was Bughā the Elder, governor of Ādharbayjān and Armenia in 237 (851–52); see, for instance, Balādhurī, *Futūḥ*, 248; Yaʿqūbī, *Taʾrīkh*, II, 598; *Fragmenta*, 547; Ibn al-Athīr, *Kāmil*, VII, 39; Abū al-Maḥāsin, *Nujūm*, I, 290. See also Vasmer, *Chronologie*, 94, n. 16. It is possible that Bughā al-Sharābī participated in the early stages of the campaign. See also Bar Hebraeus, *Mukhtaṣar*, 247, 253, 254.

371. The most important town by this name in eastern Anatolia is on the east bank of the Arzanṣū (modern Garzansu) River; *EI*², s.v. Arzan. Baladhuri, *Futūḥ*, 248, says that Bughā al-Kabīr began in Badlīs, where he seized Mūsā b. Zurārah.

372. There is a lacuna in the text. Cairo edition reads (Mss. A and D): "And he is Abū al-Ḥurr," and then has "and he had sisters." Leiden Ms. C is corrupt but may be construed to yield the same as Cairo edition. The words "and he had sisters" also appear in Ibn al-Athīr.

373. The Khuwaythiyyah were rugged mountain folk who lived in the region of Sāsūn. See Honigmann, *Ostgrenze*, 206; Canard, *Histoire*, 185f.

many captive. He sold them in Armenia. He then went to the territory of Aghbagh[374] and took prisoner Ashūṭ b. Ḥamzah, Abū al-ʿAbbās, ruler of Aghbagh. Aghbagh was a subdistrict of al-Busfurrajān. Bughā also built al-Nashawā.[375] He then went to the city of Dabīl in Armenia and stayed there for a month, after which he went to Tiflis.[376]

In this year, ʿAbdallāh b. Isḥāq b. Ibrāhīm was appointed governor of Baghdad and over the security police of the Sawād.[377]

In this year, Muḥammad b. ʿAbdallāh b. Ṭāhir[378] came from Khurāsān [to Sāmarrā] on 22 Rabīʿ II (October 2, 851), and was appointed over the security police, the poll tax (*jizyah*), and the administrative districts of the Sawād, and he was made the representative of the Commander of the Faithful in Baghdad (Madīnat al-Salām). He then proceeded to Baghdad.

In this year, al-Mutawakkil removed Muḥammad b. Aḥmad b. Abī Du'ād from the *maẓālim* courts and appointed Muḥammad b. Yaʿqūb, known as Abū al-Rabīʿ.

In this year, al-Mutawakkil showed favor to Ibn Aktham.[379] He

---

374. The text reads: Albaq. The note in the Leiden edition says Albaq = Armenian Aghbagh, located, as the next sentence states, in the district of al-Busfurrajān (Vaspurakan). It lies between Lake Van and Lake Urmiya. See Canard, *Histoire,* 191–92 (citing, *inter alia,* our passage). For Ashūṭ b. Ḥamzah, see also Balādhurī, *Futūḥ,* 248. He is Ashot Ardzruni, son of Hamazasp, whose son was Gregory; Vardan, *Universal History,* tr. Muyldermans, 123, n. 2. According to Yaʿqūbī, *Ta'rīkh,* II, 598, Ashūṭ was executed and suspended at the Public Gate.

375. The note in the Leiden edition suggests that some part of the text is lacking before the word *wa-banā* ("he built"). Al-Nashawā is a town north of the Aras River in Ādharbayjān; see Le Strange, *Lands,* 167.

376. On Tiflis, capital of Georgia, see *EI*[1], s.v. Bughā occupied all of Armenia systematically, beginning in the south with Taron, reaching the basins of the Araxes and the Kur Rivers, and going as far as Albania in the east and Georgia in the west (below, 1415; p. 122); Laurent, *L'Arménie,* 118–19.

377. ʿAbdallāh b. Isḥāq b. Ibrāhīm was apparently son of Isḥāq b. Ibrāhīm, the Ṭāhirid, but he does not appear in Zambaur, *Manuel,* 197, 198, or in other references to the Ṭāhirids.

378. For the Ṭāhirid Muḥammad b. ʿAbdallāh b. Ṭāhir, d. 253 (867–68), see *EI*[1], s.v. Muḥammad b. ʿAbdallāh; Zambaur, *Manuel,* 20, 25, 197, 198. See also Bosworth, "The Ṭāhirids and Their Culture," 46, 68; *idem,* "The Ṭāhirids and Ṣaffarids," 102, 103.

379. The judge Abū Muḥammad Yaḥyā b. Aktham was active under al-Ma'mūn and al-Mutawakkil; d. 242. See Bosworh, *Reunification,* Index, 281; Ibn Ṭayfūr, *Baghdād,* Index, 219; Khaṭīb, *Ta'rīkh Baghdād,* XIV, 191–204; Ibn al-Abbār, *Iʿtāb,* 97, 157; Massignon, "Cadis et naqībs," 107; Sourdel, *Vizirat,* I, 238–39. Yaḥyā b.

was in Baghdad, and was sent to Sāmarrā and made chief judge. He was then appointed also over the *maẓālim* courts. Al-Mutawakkil removed Muḥammad b. Aḥmad b. Abī Du'ād from the *maẓālim* courts of Sāmarrā on 19 Ṣafar this year (August 22, 851).

In this year, al-Mutawakkil became angry with Ibn Abī Du'ād and ordered that his estates be put in trust on 24 Ṣafar (August 27, 851). His son Abū al-Walīd Muḥammad b. Aḥmad b. Abī Du'ād was imprisoned on Saturday, 3 Rabīʿ I (September 4, 851), in the [1411] Bureau of Taxation; and his brothers were imprisoned in the custody of ʿUbaydallāh b. al-Sarī,[380] deputy chief of security police. On Monday (4 Rabīʿ [September 6]), Abū al-Walīd delivered 120,000 dīnārs and jewels valued at 20,000 dīnārs. A settlement was made thereafter in the amount of sixteen million dirhams. The sale of all their estates was witnessed. Aḥmad b. Abī Du'ād had been paralyzed. On Wednesday, 4 Shaʿbān (January 31, 852), al-Mutawakkil ordered that the children of Aḥmad b. Abī Du'ād be remanded to Baghdad.

Abū al-ʿAtāhiyah recited:[381]

If your judgment were sound,
Your decision apposite,

Jurisprudence, were you content, would have diverted you
From professing that God's Word is created.

How can you do this when the root of religion creates consensus,
And ignorance and foolishness make one follow a branch.

Aktham was a fervent proponent of Sunnism and enemy of Muʿtazilism, and his appointment was clearly related to the deposition of the pro-Muʿtazilite Ibn Abī Du'ād, which is reported immediately below. Ibn Kathīr, *Bidāyah*, X, 315–16, 319–29, records that Ibn Ḥanbal recommended Yaḥyā to the caliph. Indeed, in this year al-Mutawakkil invited Ibn Ḥanbal to visit Sāmarrā; see *Tarjamat al-Imām Aḥmad b. Ḥanbal*, in *Musnad*, ed. Shākir, 110ff.

380. For ʿUbaydallāh b. al-Sarī, see Ṭabari, III, 1086–87 (Bosworth, *Reunification*, 159–60, and Index, 280). He was chief of police and then governor of Egypt (820, 822). See also Zambaur, *Manuel*, 27. And see Crone, *Slaves on Horses*, 75; 255, n. 578.

381. See Abū al-ʿAtāhiyah, *Dīwān*, 354.

Al-Khalanjī was displayed in public in Jumādā II (November 30–December 28, 851).[382]

In this year, Ibn Aktham appointed Ḥayyān b. Bishr[383] over the judiciary of the East Side [of Baghdad], and he appointed Sawwār b. 'Abdallāh al-'Anbarī[384] over the West Side. Both of them were blind in one eye.

[1412] Al-Jammāz recited:[385]

I have seen among grave offenses two judges,
Who are the gossip of East and West.

They divided blindness into two equal halves,
As they divided the judgeship of the two sides [of Baghdad].

You would think the one of them who nods his head
To look into inheritances and debts

Were like someone upon whom you placed a wine jug[386]
Whose bung you opened for a single eye.

They augur the demise of Yaḥyā
If he begins his judgeship with two one-eyed men.

In this year, on the Day of Breaking the Fast, al-Mutawakkil

---

382. On al-Khalanjī, see also *Ṭabarī*, III, 1639 (Saliba, 104), 1641 (106), 1684 (143). For *uqīma li-l-nās*, see Glossarium, CDXXXIX.

383. Ḥayyān b. Bishr b. al-Mukhāriq, d. 237 (851–52) or 238 (852–53), had been a judge in Iṣbahān at the time of al-Ma'mūn. See Khaṭīb, *Ta'rīkh Baghdād*, VIII, 284–86; Massignon, "Cadis et naqībs," 108. The Khaṭīb cites (p. 285) our passage ('Alī b. al-Muḥassin [al-Tanūkhī]—[Abū al-Qāsim] Ṭalḥah b. Muḥammad b. Ja'far—Muḥammad b. Jarīr al-Ṭabarī). The following poem is said to have been recited by 'Ubaydallāh b. Muḥammad al-Kātib, and it is ascribed to Di'bil (b. 'Alī al-Khuzā'ī) rather than to al-Jammāz, as in our text. See also Tanūkhī, *Nishwār*, VI, 101–02.

384. Sawwār b. 'Abdallāh al-'Anbarī; d. 245 (below, 1440 [p. 157]); Mas'ūdī, *Murūj*, VII, 210; Khaṭīb, *Ta'rīkh Baghdād*, IX, 210–12 Guidi, *Tables*, 393.

385. On Muḥammad b. 'Amr al-Jammāz, see Guidi, *Tables*, 272; Ibn al-Jawzī, *Muntaẓam*, V, 18–19; Ibn al-Mu'tazz, *Ṭabaqāt al-shu'arā'*, 99, 373–75; Sezgin, *GAS*, II, 508. He died by 255 (868–69).

386. The word *dann* means wine jug, or jar; but as the *qalansuwa ṭawīlah*, the conical Persian hat, was also called *danniyyah* because of its resemblance to a *dann*, there may also be an allusion here to the headgear of the judges. We are led to picture an inverted jar (or hat) pulled over the eyes, having one eye opening.

ordered that the corpse of Aḥmad b. Naṣr b. Malik al-Khuzāʿī be taken down and turned over to his friends.

What Was Done with Aḥmad b. Naṣr and the Result of This

Al-Mutawakkil reportedly ordered that Aḥmad b. Naṣr's corpse be turned over to his friends for burial, and this was done. When al-Mutawakkil had become caliph, he prohibited debate concerning the Qur'ān and so on, and sent letters about this to distant regions.[387] When he was considering the removal of Aḥmad b. [1413] Naṣr from his gallows, the mob and riffraff assembled at the site, where they grew in number and talked [boldly] among themselves. When al-Mutawakkil heard about this, he sent Naṣr b. al-Layth to them. Naṣr seized about 20,000 of them, and flogged and imprisoned them. Al-Mutawakkil gave up the idea of removing Aḥmad b. Naṣr from his gallows when he learned of the growing involvement of the populace in his cause. Those who were seized on Aḥmad b. Naṣr's account remained in prison for some time, after which they were released.

When Ibn Naṣr's body was turned over to his friends at the time that I have mentioned, his nephew Mūsā brought it to Baghdad. It was washed and buried, and the head was brought together with the body. ʿAbd al-Raḥmān b. Ḥamzah brought his body in an Egyptian cloth[388] to his own residence, covered it in a shroud, and offered a funeral prayer. A merchant called al-Abzārī,[389] along with some members of Aḥmad b. Naṣr's family, undertook its burial.

The postmaster in Baghdad, who was named Ibn al-Kalbī, wrote from a place in the region of Wāsiṭ called al-Kaltāniyyah[390] to al-

---

387. This is Ṭabarī's only reference to al-Mutawakkil's anti-Muʿtazilite policy, and it is introduced *en passant* in connection with the report that the caliph gave a decent burial to the anti-Muʿtazilite, pro-Ḥanbalī rebel, Aḥmad b. Naṣr.

388. See Rosenthal, *Four Essays,* 74, who observes that Egyptian *mandīls* were popular in ʿAbbāsid Iraq.

389. The word *abzār* (or *ibzār* < Pers. *afzār*) means "food seasoning." Thus, an *abzārī* is a "seller of food seasoning." It was also the man's family name, as he is called Ibn al-Abzārī below.

390. So Leiden text. Leiden Mss. and Cairo edition: al-Kalbāniyyah; see Addenda, DCCLXXV; Yāqūt, *Muʿjam,* IV, 299 (al-Kaltāniyyah); Minorsky, *History,* 181.

Mutawakkil concerning the populace and how they had gathered, and their wiping the funeral bier, that is, the bier of Aḥmad b. Naṣr, and the wood where his head had been.[391] Al-Mutawakkil then asked Yaḥyā b. Aktham how Ibn al-Abzārī had been admitted to the grave despite the great number[392] of the Khuzā'ah. He replied, "Commander of the Faithful, he was Aḥmad's friend."

Al-Mutawakkil ordered that a letter be sent to Muḥammad b. 'Abdallāh b. Ṭāhir restraining the populace from assembling and agitating in this manner. Some(one) among them had nominated
[1414] his son to alarm the populace at the time of Aḥmad's death. Al-Mutawakkil consequently sent a dispatch prohibiting public assembly.

'Alī b. Yaḥyā al-Armanī led the summer campaign this year.[393]

Leading the pilgrimage this year was 'Alī b. 'Īsā b. Ja'far b. Abī Ja'far al-Manṣūr. He was governor of Mecca.[394]

---

391. Text: *wa-mijassat ra'sihi.* Cairo edition: *bi-khashabat ra'sihi,* which is followed here.

392. Text: *kibrah.* Cairo ed. vocalizes *kubrah* and cites variant (Ms. A) *kathrah,* which is accepted here. On the Khuzā'ah in early Islam, see the detailed article in *EI*², s.v. Aḥmad b. Naṣr was, of course, from this tribe.

393. 'Alī b. Yaḥyā al-Armanī ("the Armenian") engaged in several campaigns against the Byzantines. He was finally killed in battle in 249 (863–64); Ṭabarī, III, 1509 (Saliba 9–10). He had been governor of Egypt in 226 (840–41) and again in 234 (848–49); see Kindī, *Wulāh,* 195, 197; Abū al-Maḥāsin, *Nujūm,* II, 245, 246, 248, 257, 274, 278). 'Alī b. Yaḥyā was governor of Ādharbayjān and of Armenia, with his residence in Dabīl in 248 (862–63); Zambaur, *Manuel,* 27, 177, 178. See also Balādhurī, *Futūḥ,* 201, according to whom he built Sīsiyyah, the administrative center of 'Ayn Zarbah.

394. 'Alī b. 'Īsā was a Hāshimite, a great-grandson of the caliph al-Manṣūr; see Zambaur, *Manuel,* 20.

The
Events of the Year
238
(June 23, 852–June 11, 853)

One of the events was Bughā's defeat of Isḥāq b. Ismāʿīl, *mawlā* of the Umayyads, in Tiflis and Bughā's burning the town.[395]

Bughā's Role in the Defeat of Isḥāq b. Ismāʿīl

It is reported that when Bughā went to Dabīl because of the murder of Yūsuf b. Muḥammad by the inhabitants of Armenia, he stayed

395. Isḥāq b. Ismāʿīl, *mawlā* of the Umayyads, namely, of the caliph Marwān b. Muḥammad, was said to have been of Qurayshite descent. He governed Armenia from its capital, Tiflis. Yaʿqūbī, *Ta'rīkh,* II, 598, tells that, when Isḥāq once refused to answer Bughā the Elder's summons, the latter attacked him. ʿArīb, *Ṭabarī continuatus,* 153, refers to a *Risālah* on the killing of Isḥāq b. Ismāʿīl. Ibn Khurrādadhbih, *Masālik,* 63, reports that when he passed through Armenia, bearing a letter of commendation from al-Wāthiq, Isḥāq b. Ismāʿīl was the ruler there. Bughā's campaign against Isḥāq b. Ismāʿīl is actually a continuation of the campaign of 237 (851–52) described above, pp. 1408–10 (pp. 113–16). The reason for the break in narrative is simply the annalistic form of Ṭabarī's *History.* Isḥāq was an energetic ruler, who had subdued the Abasges, Georgians, and Khazars and defeated a Byzantine army in 837 near Kars, as well as two other armies in 842. See Laurent, *L'Arménie,* 320–21; and Grousset, *Histoire,* 359ff. And see Minorsky, *History,* 25, where it is stated that the revolt of Isḥāq lasted thirty-five years before he was finally executed.

there for a month. On Saturday, 10 Rabīʿ I, 238 (August 30, 852), Bughā sent Zīrak the Turk, who crossed the Kur [River]. It is a large waterway, the size of the Ṣarāt [Canal] in Baghdad, even larger, and it is between the town [of Dabīl] and Tiflis on the west side and Ṣughdbīl on the east side. The camp of Bughā was on the east side [of the river]. Zīrak crossed the Kur to the Hippodrome (*maydān*) of Tiflis. Tiflis had five gates: the Hippodrome Gate, the Qarīs Gate, the Small Gate, the Suburb Gate, and the Ṣughdbīl Gate. The Kur is a river that flows down along the town.

[1415] Bughā also sent Abū al-ʿAbbās al-Wāthī al-Naṣrānī[396] against the inhabitants of Armenia, Arab and non-Arab alike. Zīrak assaulted them near the Hippodrome [Gate],[397] and Abū al-ʿAbbās, near the Suburb Gate. Isḥāq b. Ismāʿīl went out to [confront] Zīrak and engaged him in battle, while Bughā stood on a hill overlooking the town near the Ṣughdbīl [Gate] to see what Zīrak and Abū al-ʿAbbās were doing. Bughā sent fire hurlers (*naffāṭīn*), who bombarded the town with fire. The [buildings in the] town [were made] of pine wood, and the wind fanned the flames, which ignited the pine.

When Isḥāq b. Ismāʿīl came to the town to observe [what was happening], he noticed that the fire, which had engulfed his palace and surrounding area,[398] had trapped him. Then the Turks and Maghāribah attacked him, took him captive, seized his son ʿAmr, and brought them to Bughā. Bughā ordered that Isḥāq be remanded to the Gate of Thorns, where he was decapitated. His head was brought to Bughā, and his body was suspended on a cross at the Kur [River].[399]

---

396. Text follows Ms. C. O: al-Wāritī; Ibn al-Athīr, *Kāmil*: al-Wārithī. The note in the Leiden edition suggests either al-Wānandī (Armenean Vanant) or al-Qārithī (Garouts = Kars). Cairo edition Ms. A: al-Wādī. On p. 1416, his name is said to be Sunbāṭ (Smbat) b. Ashūṭ.

397. It appears that the word *bāb* must be supplied or understood here and immediately below.

398. Text: *Wa-jawārīhi* ("and his female slaves"). The combination of palace and female slaves—or place where they were—is possible but rather odd. Read: *wa-jiwārīhi.*

399. The *History of Sharvān and al-Bāb*, tr. Minorsky, *History*, 25, says that Isḥāq was suspended at the gate of Ṣughd in Tiflis. His head, according to Ibn ʿAbd Rabbihi, *ʿIqd*, I, 136, was sent to the caliph in Sāmarrā. See also Yaʿqūbī, *Taʾrīkh*, II, 598. In Georgian (according to Minorsky) the name is Sagodebeli, meaning "place of lamentations." See above, 1414, where a Ṣugdhbīl Gate is mentioned.

Isḥāq b. Ismāʿīl was a stocky old man[400] and had a large head. He was tattooed with blue (indigo) markings, and was ruddy, bald, and cross-eyed. His head was raised over the Gate of Thorns. Barghāmush,[401] deputy of Bughā, supervised his execution. About 50,000 men were burned in the city. The fire burnt itself out in a day and a night,[402] for it was a pine-wood fire that does [1416] not last. The Maghāribah arrived in the morning. They took the living captive and plundered the dead.

The wife of Isḥāq lived in Ṣughdbīl. It is opposite Tiflis, on the east side, and is a town that Kisrā Anūshirwān built.[403] Isḥāq had fortified it, dug its defensive trench, and manned it with Khuwaythiyyah warriors and others. Bughā gave them a guarantee of safe-conduct, stipulating that they lay down their arms and go where they wished. The wife of Isḥāq was the daughter of the Lord of the Throne (Ṣāḥib al-Sarīr).[404]

Then Bughā reportedly sent Zīrak to the fortress of Jardmān,[405] which is between Bardhaʿah[406] and Tiflis, along with a contingent of his troops. Zīrak conquered Jardmān and took captive its Patrikios, al-Qitrīj,[407] on the Jardmān Road, and brought him to the army camp.

---

400. For *shaykh maḥdūr,* see Glossarium, CLXXXV.

401. Text: Ghāmish. The note *ad loc.* suggests Barghāmush (unpointed); see Yaʿqūbī, *Buldān,* 262 = Wiet, *Les pays,* 54.

402. Ms. O has on Wednesday through the night.

403. Yāqūt, *Muʿjam,* III, 396, describes Ṣughdbīl as a town on the east of the Kur River opposite Tiflis, and says that it was built by Kisrā Anūshirwān near the place where he founded Bāb al-Abwāb (Darband). Yāqūt also relates the account of Bughā's attack on Tiflis, his burning the city and killing Isḥāq. And he notes that Isḥāq had married the daughter of Ṣāḥib al-Sarīr. His report is presumably derived from Ṭabarī.

404. He is also called Wahrazān-Shāh. The district of Sarīr is named after him, in the middle of the Ḳoy-Su valley in southern Dāghistān; *EI*², s.v. al-Ḳabḳ. See also Minorsky, *Ḥudūd,* 447; and see especially the account in the *History of Sharvān and the Bāb,* tr. Minorsky, *History,* 97, 155.

405. For the fortress of Jardmān or Gardmān, see Vardan, *Universal History,* tr. Muyldermans, 123, n. 5. Ms. C: al-Khazarmān; ʿAynī and Ibn al-Athīr, *Kāmil*: al-Ḥarazmān.

406. Bardhaʿah (Armenian Partav and modern Barda) was the former capital of Arrān, 28 km. from the Kur river; *EI*², s.v. Arrān, the present-day Soviet republic of Azarbayjan, is ancient Caucasian Albania; *EI*², s.v.

407. He is Ktričn, prince of Gardmān; Vardan, *Universal History,* tr. Muyldermans, 123, n. 5.

Bughā then attacked ʿĪsā b. Yūsuf, the nephew of Stephanos.[408] He was in the fortress of Xtiš, belonging to the subdistrict of al-Baylaqān.[409] Xtiš is ten *farsakh*s (sixty km.) from al-Baylaqān and fifteen *farsakh*s (ninety km.) from Bardhaʿah. Bughā made war against him and conquered [his fortress]. He seized ʿĪsā b. Yūsuf and deported him along with his son and father. He deported Abū al-ʿAbbās al-Wāthī—his name was Sunbāṭ (Smbat) b. Ashūṭ—and along with him, Muʿāwiyah b. Sahl b. Sunbāṭ (Smbat),[410] Patrikios of Arrān, and Adharnarsē b. Isḥāq al-Khāshinī.[411]

[1417] In this year, 300 Byzantine vessels came, bringing Ooryphas, Nikētiatēs (?) and Martinakios (?).[412] They were naval commanders. Each of them commanded one hundred vessels.[413] Nikētiatēs besieged Damietta.[414] Between Damietta and the coast is a

408. See Ṭabarī, III, 1224, 1228 (Marin, *Reign*, 48, 51), where he is called ʿĪsā b. Yūsuf b. Iṣṭifānūs. Read perhaps: b. ukht Iṣṭifānūs. On p. 1232 (Marin, 56), ʿĪsā b. Yūsuf is said to be the *nephew* of Stephanos by the latter's sister. In the *History of Sharvān and the Bāb*, he is called Abū Mūsā; see Minorsky, *History*, 165; and "Caucasia IV," 512ff. He began to reign in 841, after the defeat of Bābak, and ruled for another thirteen years.

409. For the fortress Xtiš, Arabic Kithīsh, see Minorsky, *History*, 165, n. 4. For Baylaqān, the town and district of Arrān, south of the Caucasus, see *idem*, "Caucasia IV," 513; *EI*², s.v. Minorsky places the fortress, according to its location given here, in present-day Shusha (Shushi).

410. Muʿāwiyah's father, Sahl b. Sunbāṭ, had succeeded in dominating Arrān. See Ṭabarī, III, 1232 (Marin, *Reign*, 55), where Sahl sends Muʿāwiyah with Bābak to Afshīn. On Sahl b. Sunbāt, see Minorsky, "Caucasia IV," 506ff. Minorsky contends (p. 510), on the basis of Armenian sources, that it was rather Sahl b. Sunbāṭ who was deported, along with Armenian princes, and that his name was mistakenly replaced by that of his son.

411. On Adharnarsē (Adarnasē), see Minorsky, "Caucasia IV," 510, 514. The toponymic *nisbah* Khāshinī is from Khachen. See note in Leiden edition and Vardan, *Universal History*, tr. Muyldermans, 123; Minorsky, "Caucasia IV," 514, 526.

412. For the reading Ooryphas, see note on the text, and Vasiliev, *Byzance*, I, 214, n. 3. The second name is written clearly as Ibn Qaṭūnā. Vasiliev (*apud* Grégoire) proposes that it represents Greek Nikētiatēs (Ib[n] Nqaṭūnā), i.e. Sergios *ho* Nikētiatēs, who had commanded an expedition to Crete. Two other possibilities mentioned are Photinos (E. W. Brooks) and Kontomutēs. The third name, it is said (here and 315, n. 1), may be either Bardas (W-r-d) or Martinakios. See Grégoire, "Études," 516–17. And see Christides, *Conquest*, 164, n. 53; 165, n. 54. Christides rejects Grégoire's identification of Nikētiatēs and regards the others as mere guesswork.

413. Yaʿqūbī, *Taʾrīkh*, II, 596, says that there were eighty-five vessels.

414. Damietta is a well-known town in Lower Egypt, situated near the egress of the Nile. Its location exposed it to periodic naval raids. (Following the attack

kind of lake in which water reaches the chest of a man.[415] Whoever crosses it to the land is safe from sea vessels. A group of people crossed it to safety, but many of the women and children drowned. Those who were able to take ships escaped [by going] to Fusṭāṭ. Fusṭāṭ is a four-day journey from Damietta.

ʿAnbasah b. Isḥāq al-Ḍabbī[416] was the chief of the security police (*maʿūnah*) of Egypt. When the festival approached, he ordered the troops that were in Damietta to come to Fusṭāṭ to help celebrate it. Thus, Damietta was vacated of troops. The vessels of the Byzantines arrived from the direction of Shaṭā, where *shaṭawī* [cloth] is manufactured.[417] One hundred *shalandiyah* vessels[418] besieged Damietta, each carrying between fifty and one hundred men. The Byzantines attacked Damietta and burned whatever of its houses and reed huts they reached. They carted away the weapons there that the [Muslims] intended to ship to Abū Ḥafṣ, ruler of Crete—about 1,000 lances along with their equip-

---

described here, al-Mutawakkil constructed a fortress in Damietta as part of an overall strategy to fortify the coastal area.) The Byzantine attack on Damietta was an offshoot of the struggle between the Muslims and Byzantines for control of Crete. The Byzantines, led by the Logothete Theoktistos, had attacked that island, then ruled by Andalusian Muslims, and occupied it temporarily. See Christides, *Conquest,* 172. As the Muslims in Crete received their arms from Egypt, the Byzantine fleet besieged Damietta in order to capture arms there destined for Crete. The purpose of the invasion may have been also to relieve pressure on Sicily. See Maspéro-Wiet, *Matériaux,* 35, 92–93 *et passim.* And see Vasiliev, *Byzance,* I, 212ff., 315ff.; Bury, *History,* 292ff.; Grégoire, "*Études*"; Levi Della Vida, "A Papyrus Reference." And see accounts in Yaʿqūbī, *Taʾrīkh,* II, 596–97; Kindī, *Wulāh,* 201; and Maqrīzī, *Mawāʿiẓ,* IV, 40; Christides, *op. cit.,* 164–65; *EI*², s.v. Dimyāṭ.

415. Between Damietta and the coast is the northern part of Lake Manzala, where there are sandbars, inlets, and shallow water.

416. ʿAnbasah b. Isḥāq al-Ḍabbī was governor of Egypt as of 237 (851–52) or 238 (852–53); Yaʿqūbī, *Taʾrīkh,* II, 596—237; Kindī, *Wulāh,* 200–02; Abū al-Maḥāsin, *Nujūm,* II, 293 (*sub anno* 238); Maqrīzī, *Mawāʿiẓ,* V, 139; Zambaur, *Manuel,* 27. According to some of these sources he was accused of tyranny and ineffective strategy against the enemies of the Muslims. ʿAnbasah had also been sent to govern Sind by Ītākh, according to Yaʿqūbī, *Taʾrīkh,* II, 585. It is possible that the Byzantine attack was timed with ʿAnbasah's absence from Damietta, as he and his garrison had left for Cairo; see Christides. *Conquest,* 164 (citing J. Shayyāl, *al-Mujmal fī taʾrīkh Dimyāṭ* [Alexandria, 1949], 10).

417. Shaṭā, a few miles from Damietta on the western side of Lake Manzalah, was famous for its fine *shaṭawī* cloth, mentioned here.

418. *Shalandiyah* vessels, also called *Sharandī* and *Sharandiyah* (<Greek *chelandion*) were often used by the Byzantines as warships, particularly troop carriers, as in our text; see Kindermann, "*Schiff,*" 51 (where our text is cited).

[1418] ment.[419] They killed whomever of the men they could, and took furnishings, candy (*qand*)[420] and flax, which had been loaded for transport to Iraq. They took captive about 600 Muslim and Copt women. There were said to be 125 Muslim women, the rest being Copts.[421]

There were reportedly about 5,000 Byzantines in the *shalandiyah* vessels that besieged Damietta. They loaded their ships with furniture, property, and women, and burned the storehouse containing the sails—they are ship sails[422]—and set fire to the Friday Mosque and churches in Damietta. The women and children, who tried to escape and were thought to have drowned[423] in the lake of Damietta, outnumbered those whom the Byzantines took captive. The Byzantines thereafter withdrew from Damietta.

It is reported that Ibn al-Akshaf, who had been incarcerated in the prison of Damietta by ʿAnbasah, broke his bonds and went out to fight the Byzantines. A group of men helped him, and he killed a number of the Byzantines.

Following that, the Byzantines proceeded to Ushtūm [near] Tinnīs.[424] As they could not manage to sail [as far as Tinnīs], and were afraid of running aground, they proceeded to Ushtūm. It is an anchorage four *farsakh*s (twenty-four km.), or somewhat less, from Tinnīs. Ushtūm has a wall with two iron gates, which al-

---

419. During the caliphate of al-Maʾmūn, Abū Ḥafṣ ʿUmar b. ʿĪsā al-Andalusī raided Crete, gradually conquering its fortified places and expelling the Byzantines, and then setting up an "independent emirate" that recognized ʿAbbāsid authority; Balādhurī, *Futūḥ*, 279; Zambaur, *Manuel*, 70; *EI*^{2}, s.v. Iḳrītish; Christides, *Conquest*, 85ff. *et passim*. On the Muslim arsenals and shipyards in Damietta, see *ibid.*, 164, citing A. M. Fahmy, *Muslim Sea-Power in the Eastern Mediterranean* (London, 1950), 30ff.; M. Abbady and E. A. Salem, *Taʾrīkh al-baḥriyyah al-Islāmiyyah fī Miṣr wa-l-Shām* (Beirut, 1972), 46ff.

420. *Qand* is from Persian *qandī* ("sugar, sugar candy"), which is related to English "candy" < French (*sucre*) *candi* < Italian (*zucchero*) *candito*.

421. Yaʿqūbī, *Taʾrīkh*, II, 597, says that the Byzantines took captive 1,820 Muslim women, 1,000 Copt women, and 100 Jewish women, as well as weapons. Christides, *Conquest*, 165, prefers Ṭabarī's count, as the Christian population in Damietta was greater than that of the Muslims.

422. The statement "they are ship sails" is apparently a gloss on the word *qulūʿ*, which may be a plural of *qalʿah* = "fortress" but here is rather a plural of *qilʿ* = "sail"; Glossarium, CDXXXII. On shipyards in Damietta, see above, n. 419.

423. Text: *wa-kāna man ḥadhira minhum*. Cairo edition (Ms. A): *huẓira*.

424. Ushtūm is a fortified town situated between Tinnīs and Faramā on a branch of the Nile; Maspéro and Wiet, *Matériaux*, 17.

Muʿtaṣim had ordered to have built. The Byzantines destroyed all of it, burned the town with mangonels and ballistas, and carted away its two iron gates. They then headed for their own territory without any interference.

In this year, on Monday, 5 Jumādā II (November 22, 852), al-Mutawakkil left Sāmarrā, heading for al-Madā'in. He arrived at al-Shammāsiyyah[425] on Tuesday, 13 Jumādā II (November 30, 852), and stayed there until Saturday. He crossed in the evening to Quṭrabbul[426] and then returned, entering Baghdad on Monday, 18 Jumādā (December 5, 852). He went through its bazaars and thoroughfares and then halted at al-Zaʿfarāniyyah, thereafter going on to al-Madā'in.[427] [1419]

ʿAlī b. Yaḥyā al-Armanī led the summer expedition.

Leading the pilgrimage this year was ʿAlī b. ʿĪsā b. Jaʿfar b. Abī Jaʿfar.

---

425. Al-Shammāsiyyah is the well-known quarter in northeast Baghdad; Le Strange, *Baghdad,* 169–76, 199–216.

426. Quṭrabbul is a district northwest of the Round City, opposite the Shammāsiyyah Quarter. Al-Mutawakkil thus crossed the Tigris from east to west.

427. Al-Zaʿfarāniyyah is a village near Baghdad below Kalwādhā; Yāqūt, *Muʿjam,* II, 931. Herzfeld, *Samarra,* 201, identifies it with modern Zimberāniyyah. Al-Madā'in was the famous city, founded on the site of Ctesiphon and adjacent towns, along the Tigris, about 32 km. to the southeast of Baghdad; *EI*², s.v.

The
Events of the Year
239
(June 12, 853–June 1, 854)

In al-Muḥarram (June 12–July 11, 853) this year al-Mutawakkil ordered that the Dhimmīs affix two yellow sleeves to their outer cloaks.[428] Then in Ṣafar (July 12–August 9) he ordered that they restrict their mounts to mules and donkeys and avoid riding and pack horses.

In this year, al-Mutawakkil banished ʿAlī b. al-Jahm b. Badr to Khurāsān.[429]

In this year, the ruler of the Ṣanāriyyah was killed at the Public Gate in Jumādā II (November 7–December 6).[430]

---

428. This regulation follows the above edicts (p. 1389, p. 89) by about four years. The word *dhirāʿayn,* sg. *dhirāʿ,* means "forearm," "cubit," but also "sleeve," as is appropriate here; Lane, *Lexicon,* 962; Ahsan, *Social Life,* 62.

429. Ṭabarī typically does not give a reason for the dismissal. ʿAlī b. al-Jahm was a strong supporter of Aḥmad b. Ḥanbal and the Sunnite camp, and thus, he was welcomed as a court companion of al-Mutawakkil, but his loose tongue and the envy of rivals landed him in trouble and led to his imprisonment and banishment; *EI*², s.v.

430. The Ṣanāriyah (Armenian Tsanar-kʿ; Georgian Tsʿanar) were Christians of a martial bent who lived in the central Caucasus area north of Georgia; Minorsky, *Ḥudūd,* 400–02; *idem, History,* 162, and Index, 183; "Caucasia IV,", 506. According to Yaʿqūbī, *Taʾrīkh,* II, 598, Bughā was defeated by them.

In this year, al-Mutawakkil ordered that churches and synagogues newly built under Islam be destroyed.

In Dhū al-Ḥijjah (May 3–June 1, 854) this year Abū al-Walīd Muḥammad b. Aḥmad b. Abī Du'ād died in Baghdad. [1420]

In this year, ʿAlī b. Yaḥyā al-Armanī led the summer expedition.

Leading the pilgrimage this year was ʿAbdallāh b. Muḥammad b. Dāwūd b. ʿĪsā b. Mūsā b. Muḥammad b. ʿAlī. He was the governor of Mecca.

In this year, Jaʿfar b. Dīnār went on the pilgrimage. He was the supervisor of the Mecca Road near al-Kūfah, and he was appointed over the events of the festive season.

In this year, Palm Sunday of the Christians and the Day of Nayrūz coincided on Sunday, 20 Dhū al-Qaʿdah (April 22, 854). The Christians reportedly claimed that these two days would never coincide under Islam.[431]

---

431. See below, n. 508.

The Events of the Year 240

(June 2, 854–21 May 21, 855)

One of the events was the revolt of the inhabitants of Ḥimṣ against their chief of security police (*maʿūnah*).

The Cause for the Revolt of the Inhabitants of Ḥimṣ and Its Result

It is reported that their chief of security police (*maʿūnah*) killed a man who was one of their leaders. The chief at the time was Abū al-Mughīth al-Rāfiʿī Mūsā b. Ibrāhīm.[432] As a result, the inhabitants of Ḥimṣ revolted in Jumādā II (October 28–November 25) of
[1421] this year and killed a number of his men. They then expelled him along with the tax supervisor from their town. When al-Mutawakkil heard this, he sent against them ʿAttāb b. ʿAttāb, dispatching with him Muḥammad b. ʿAbdawayh Kirdās al-Anbārī.[433] The

---

432. Yaʿqūbī, *Taʾrīkh*, II, 599, describing this revolt, calls Abū al-Mughīth the *ʿāmil* (governor or fiscal administrator) of Ḥimṣ. See also Abū al-Maḥāsin, *Nujūm*, II, 249ff., 301.

433. ʿAttāb b. ʿAttāb al-Qāʾid appears in Ṭabarī, III, 1822, as a commander of the Shākiriyyah and is identified (p. 1826) as a Khurāsānian commander. See also

caliph ordered ʿAttāb to tell them that the Commander of the Faithful had replaced al-Mughīth by Muḥammad b. ʿAbdawayh and that, if they obeyed and acquiesced, then the latter would be appointed over them. But if they refused and persisted in opposition, then [al-Mutawakkil ordered ʿAttāb], "Stay put, and write to the Commander of the Faithful to send you Rajāʾ or Muḥammad b. Rajāʾ al-Ḥiḍārī or some other cavalryman to wage war against them."[434]

ʿAttāb b. ʿAttāb left Sāmarrā on Monday, 24 Jumādā II (November 20, 854).[435] They acquiesced to Muḥammad b. ʿAbdawayh, whereupon al-Mutawakkil appointed him over them, and he accomplished wonders with them.

In al-Muḥarram (June 2–July 1) of this year, Aḥmad b. Abī Duʾād died in Baghdad after his son Abū al-Walīd Muḥammad, his son having died there twenty days before him, in Dhū al-Ḥijjah (May 3–June 1, 854).

In this year al-Mutawakkil removed Yaḥyā b. Aktham from the office of judge in Ṣafar (July 2–30, 854).[436] He confiscated from him what he had in Baghdad, in the amount of 75,000 dīnārs.[437] He took 1,000 dīnārs from Yaḥyā's columned arcade in his palace, and he also seized 4,000 *jarībs*[438] of land in al-Baṣrah.

Yaʿqūbī, *Taʾrīkh*, II, 594 (where he appears as one of the commanders sent against Muḥammad b. al-Baʿīth); Masʿūdī, *Murūj*, VII, 291 (in charge of the *dīwān [al-]jaysh [wa]-l-shākiriyyah*); and Tanūkhī, *Faraj*, 89–90. As for Muḥammad b. ʿAbdawayh (b. Jabalah), see Yaʿqūbī, *Taʾrīkh*, II, 599. Yaʿqūbī mentions him earlier (p. 586) in connection with revolts in Damascus and Palestine.

434. Rajāʾ b. Ayyūb al-Hiḍārī, father of Muḥammad b. Rajāʾ al-Ḥiḍārī, had been an army commander at the time of al-Muʿtaṣim; Ṭabarī, III, 1194 (Marin, *Reign*, 27), and III, 1320 (Marin, 125). He was governor of Damascus in 226 (840–41); Zambaur, *Manuel*, 28. His son, Muḥammad b. Rajāʾ al-Ḥiḍārī (Leiden edition, Ms. O: al-Ḥiṣārī), was also an army commander. He led the rear guard of Waṣīf against the Byzantines in 248 (862–63). In 252 (866–67) he appears along with "Baghdadian commanders," including ʿAttāb b. ʿAttāb. In 254 (868) he was governor of al-Baṣrah (Ṭabarī, III, 1745); Zambaur, *Manuel*, 41, gives 255 (868–69).

435. Ms. C: Rabīʿ.

436. As usual, Ṭabarī does not give a reason for the dismissal. See Ṭabarī, III, 1139 (Bosworth, *Reunification*, 230), on the "infamous conduct" of Ibn Aktham; and Marzubānī, *Muʿjam*, 431, for a poem on the same. He was renowned for his licentious behavior and pederasty.

437. Ms. O: twenty-five thousand; ʿAynī: eighty thousand.

438. A *jarīb* = 1592 sq.m., according to Hinz, *Masse und Gewichte*, 65.

In Ṣafar (July 2–30, 854) of this year, al-Mutawakkil appointed Jaʿfar b. ʿAbd al-Wāḥid b. Jaʿfar b. Sulaymān b. ʿAlī as chief of the judiciary.

[1422] Leading the pilgrimage this year was ʿAbdallāh b. Muḥammad b. Dāwūd. Jaʿfar b. Dīnār went on the pilgrimage and was in charge of the events of the festive season.

The Events of the Year 241

(May 22, 855–May 9, 856)

Among them was the revolt of the inhabitants of Ḥimṣ against their chief of security police, Muḥammad b. ʿAbdawayh.[439]

The Role of the Inhabitants of Ḥimṣ in the Revolt against Muḥammad b. ʿAbdawayh and Its Consequence for Them

It is reported that the inhabitants of Ḥimṣ revolted in Jumādā II (October 17–November 14, 855) of this year against Muḥammad b. ʿAbdawayh, their chief of security police, with some of the Christians of Ḥimṣ supporting their revolt. Muḥammad b. ʿAbdawayh sent a dispatch about this to al-Mutawakkil.

Al-Mutawakkil then wrote ordering Muḥammad to resist them, and reinforced him with troops from the garrison[440] of

439. The population of Ḥimṣ was frequently restive from the time of Hārūn al-Rashīd. This was the second year in succession that they rebelled. The uprising this time included elements of the Christian population. The inhabitants of Ḥimṣ repeated in 250 (864–65); Ṭabarī, III, 1533 (Saliba, 27).

440. For *rātibah*, see Glossarium, CCLVIII.

Damascus, along with Ṣāliḥ al-'Abbāsī the Turk, who was governor there, and troops from al-Ramlah. Al-Mutawakkil ordered Muḥammad b. 'Abdawayh to seize three of their chiefs and flog them to death. And when they died, he was to suspend them on crosses at the doors [of their residences] and thereafter to take twenty of their notables and flog each of them thirty times and bring them in iron fetters to the gate of the Commander of the Faithful.

[The caliph also ordered Muḥammad to] destroy the churches and places of worship in Ḥimṣ, to join the house of worship[441] that was adjoined to the mosque of Ḥimṣ to it, to expel every single Christian from the city, and to make a prior announcement
[1423] among them to the effect that whoever he found there after three days would be severely chastised.[442]

Al-Mutawakkil ordered that Muḥammad b. 'Abdawayh be given 50,000 dirhams, and that his officers and eminent companions be given gifts. And he ordered that his deputy, 'Alī b. al-Ḥusayn, be given 15,000 dirhams and his officers 5,000 dirhams each. The caliph also ordered that robes of honor be presented [to them].

Muḥammad b. 'Abdawayh seized ten people from Ḥimṣ, and wrote that he had seized them, and that he had deported them to the palace of the Commander of the Faithful, but he did not flog them.[443] Al-Mutawakkil sent one of the associates of al-Fatḥ b. Khāqān by the name of Muḥammad b. Rizqallāh to restore to Ḥimṣ those whom Ibn 'Abdawayh had deported—Muḥammad b. 'Abd al-Ḥamīd al-Ḥaydī and al-Qāsim b. Mūsā b. Fū'ūs[444]—and to flog them to death and suspend them on crosses over the gates of the city. Muḥammad b. 'Abdawayh returned them, flogged them to death, and then suspended them over the Ḥimṣ Gate. He had the rest brought to Sāmarrā. There were eight of them. When they

441. The term *bī'ah* may refer to a synagogue, but here a Christian place of worship is intended.

442. Ms. O: *b-l-d-y-h*; superscript: *adabahu*; read: *ta'dībahu* (note *ad loc.*).

443. Text: *wa-lam yaḍribhum*. Ms. O: *wa-amara bi-ḍarbihim*, "and ordered that they be flogged."

444. The reading Fū'ūs follows Ms. C. Ms. O and 'Aynī: Far'ūsh. Read perhaps Qar'ūsh, or Turkish Qarghūsh (for Qarāqūsh; note *ad loc.*).

445. Cairo text adds bi-Naṣībīn.

arrived in Naṣībīn, one of them died,[445] whereupon al-Mutawakkil had them take his head, and had the seven others brought to Sāmarrā along with the head of the deceased. Muḥammad b. ʿAbdawayh thereafter wrote that he seized ten of the inhabitants of Ḥimṣ after this and flogged five to death. He then flogged five more, but they did not die.

Muḥammad b. ʿAbdawayh wrote afterward that he defeated one of their rebels by the name of ʿAbd al-Malik b. Isḥāq b. ʿImārah. He was reportedly one of the leaders of the rebellion (*fitnah*). He flogged him at the Ḥimṣ Gate until he died, and suspended him on a cross above a fortress called Tall al-ʿAbbās. [1424]

In this year, people in Sāmarrā reportedly had abundant rain in Āb (August, 855).

In this year, in Muḥarram (May 22–June 21, 855), al-Mutawakkil appointed Abū Ḥassān al-Ziyādī as judge of the Sharqiyyah [Quarter].[446]

In this year, al-Mutawakkil flogged ʿĪsā b. Jaʿfar b. Muḥammad b. ʿĀṣim, the proprietor of Khān ʿĀṣim in Baghdad.[447] He was flogged, it is said, 1,000 stripes.

The Reason for Flogging ʿĪsā b. Jaʿfar b. ʿĀṣim and the Caliph's Role in This

The reason for this was that seventeen men testified before Abū Ḥassān al-Ziyādī, judge of the Sharqiyyah [Quarter], against ʿĪsā b. Jaʿfar to the effect that the latter had defamed Abū Bakr, ʿUmar, ʿĀʾishah, and Ḥafṣah. Their testimonies reportedly differed in this regard.[448]

---

446. Abū Ḥassān al-Ziyādī, al-Ḥasan b. ʿUthmān, was a traditionist, historian, and judge under al-Mutawakkil. He died, according to Sezgin, *GAS*, I, 316, in 243 (857–68). But Ṭabarī, III, 1434, says that he died in Rajab, 242 (November 3–December 2, 856; see below, p. 147); see on him, Tanūkhī, *Faraj*, 159–63; *Nishwār*, II, 234; VI, 64; Ibn Kathīr, *Bidāyah*, X, 344; Massignon, "Cadis et naqībs," 108. For location of the Sharqiyyah suburb east of the Baṣrah Gate, see Lassner, *Topography*, 248, 275.

447. An alternative name given below, 1426 (p. 137), is Aḥmad b. Muḥammad b. ʿĀṣim. The Khān ʿĀṣim was a caravanserai in the Market of the Perfumers (Sūq al-Rayḥāniyyīn); Le Strange, *Baghdad*, 271. See also Abū al-Maḥāsin, *Nujūm*, I, 304.

448. The cursing of Abū Bakr, etc., indicates that ʿĪsā b. Jaʿfar was a Shīʿite.

The postmaster of Baghdad wrote about this to ʿUbaydallāh b. Yaḥyā b. Khāqān, and he transmitted it to al-Mutawakkil. Al-Mutawakkil then gave orders for ʿUbaydallāh to write to Muḥammad b. ʿAbdallāh b. Ṭāhir, instructing him to flog this ʿĪsā, and [to see to it that] when ʿĪsā died he should be tossed into the Tigris, and that his body not be handed over to his folk. ʿUbaydallāh replied to al-Ḥasan b. ʿUthmān's letter to him concerning ʿĪsā:[449]

In the name of God, the Merciful, the Compassionate.

May God give you long life, protect you and extend His
[1425] beneficence to you. Your letter has arrived concerning the man named ʿĪsā b. Jaʿfar b. Muḥammad b. ʿĀṣim, the proprietor of the caravanserais, and the witnesses' testimony as to his defaming the companions of the Messenger of God, cursing them, declaring them infidels, accusing them of grave sins and ascribing hypocrisy to them, and so on, by which he came out in opposition against God and His Messenger. [And the letter mentioned] your verification of these witnesses and their testimony, your validation of the probity of those who were qualified witnesses and their testimony that was evident to you, and your exposition of this in a note that went along with your letter.

You presented this to the Commander of the Faithful, may God give him power, whereupon he ordered that a letter be sent to Abū al-ʿAbbās Muḥammad b. ʿAbdallāh b. Ṭāhir, *mawlā* of the Commander of the Faithful, may God give him long life, concerning the ideas of the caliph, may God give him long life, about protecting the religion of God, reviving its tradition, and taking revenge upon those who deviate from it. And he ordered that the man (ʿĪsā b. Jaʿfar) be flogged as a fixed punishment (*ḥadd*)[450] for public defamation and be given 500 stripes beyond the

449. Al-Ḥasan b. ʿUthmān = Abū Ḥassān al-Ziyādī. He had apparently written a letter that was forwarded by the postmaster, who as chief of Intelligence included an account of his own.

450. The *ḥadd* punishments are those that are sanctioned in the Qurʾān for crimes committed against God (*EI*², s.v. Ḥadd). Defamation (*shatm*) is occasionally considered one of them.

fixed punishment for the grave things he dared to undertake. And, if he dies, he should be thrown into the river without a funeral prayer, thus deterring every deviant in religion who abandons the community of Muslims. I have informed you of this so that you shall know it, God—the exalted—willing. Peace upon you and the mercy and blessings of God.

It is reported that after this ʿĪsā b. Jaʿfar b. Muḥammad b. ʿĀṣim—one informant said that his name was Aḥmad b. Muḥammad b. ʿĀṣim[451]—was flogged; he was left in the sun until he died and was then thrown into the Tigris. [1426]

In this year, there was a meteor storm visible in Baghdad. This was on Thursday night, 1 Jumādā II (October 17, 855).[452]

In this year, an epidemic[453] took place, so that horses and cattle perished.

In this year, the Byzantines raided ʿAyn Zarbah and took captive the Zuṭṭ who were there along with their wives, children, buffaloes, and cattle.[454]

In this year, there was a prisoner exchange between the Muslims and Byzantines.[455]

---

451. Ms. O omits this comment, which may, in fact, be an intrusive gloss or a supplementary parenthetical remark. The confusion in Ms. C points in this direction.

452. Masʿūdī, *Murūj*, VII, 230, mentions the meteor storm immediately after noting the popular belief that after Ibn Ḥanbal's death the world darkened. See also Yaʿqūbī, *Taʾrīkh*, II, 600. Ṭabarī does not mention Ibn Ḥanbal's death. In fact, he generally overlooks Ibn Ḥanbal (see Translator's Foreword). Sensitive to the silence, Ibn Kathīr, *Bidāyah*, X, 325, observes that Ṭabarī did not mention the death of *any* Ḥadīth scholars this year (so as to avoid mentioning the death of Ibn Ḥanbal). Ibn Kathīr then gives a long eulogy of Ibn Ḥanbal.

453. See Glossarium, CCCCXXIII; Lane, s.v. *ṣidām*.

454. The Zuṭṭ (Zoṭṭ), arabicized form of Jāt (see *EI*², s.v. Djāt), were an Indian people who raised buffaloes. They were brought by Muʿāwiya or al-Walīd to Antioch and the area north of the city; see Balādhurī, *Futūḥ*, 192. Many were settled by al-Ḥallāj in the marshes (al-Baṭīḥah) in southern ʿIrāq, where they indulged in robbery and plunder, and eventually revolted in the area of al-Baṣrah from 205–20 (820–35). The caliph al-Muʿtaṣim defeated them and transplanted them (220/835) to ʿAyn Zarbah on the frontier, where they were occasionally raided by the Byzantines; see Ṭabarī, III, 1167–70 (Marin, *Reign*, 4–8). See also Vasiliev, *Byzance*, I, 223.

455. On the prisoner exchange of 241 (855–56), see Vasiliev, 222ff.; 317ff.

The Reason for the Prisoner Exchange

It is reported that Theodora, empress of Byzantium, mother of Michael, sent a man named George, son of Cyriac, to request an exchange of Muslims who were in the hands of the Byzantines.[456] The number of Muslims approached 20,000. Al-Mutawakkil sent a Shī'ite by the name of Naṣr b. al-Azhar b. Faraj[457] to determine the exact number of Muslim captives in the hands of the Byzantines, so as to order their exchange. This was in Sha'bān (December 15, 855–January 12, 856) of this year. [Naṣr returned],[458]
[1427] having remained with the Byzantines for some time.

It is reported that after Naṣr's departure, Theodora ordered that her prisoners be passed in review, and that conversion to Christianity be proposed to them. Those who converted were to be on an equal footing with those who had done so previously, but those who refused [to convert] were to be killed. She reportedly had 12,000 prisoners killed. Another view is that it was Theoktistos the Eunuch[459] who had them killed, without her having ordered this.[460]

The governors of the frontier towns of Syria and the Jazīrah

456. Ya'qūbī, *Ta'rīkh,* II, 599, states that the emperor (*ṭāghiyat al-Rūm*) initiated the prisoner exchange, sending gifts, and that the caliph reciprocated with twice as many. See also Mas'ūdī, *Tanbīh,* 191. The Leiden edition gives the name Cyriac half unpointed. The Cairo edition has *Q-r-y-ā-f-s.* Vasiliev suggests the reading Qiriyāqus or Karbeas; *Byzance,* I, 225, 317. Thus, Ṭabarī makes Theodora empress in 241 (855–56), which is compatible with her actual fall in 243 (857–58). Cf., however, above, where he places her fall in 233 (847–48); 1379 (p. 76) and n. 264.

457. Text: Faraj. Ms. O is unpointed. C has Qarkh or the like. Cairo edition, Ms. D, has Farūkh. Naṣr b. al-Azhar was also involved in the prisoner exchange of 246 (860–61) and gives his own personal account; below, 1449 (pp. 168–70).

458. The note in the Leiden edition suggests that some words are lacking, such as *fa-kharaja Naṣr.* See also Vasiliev, *Byzance,* I, 317. The Cairo edition does not take this into account. Without the addition, the sentence would read something like: "This was in Sha'bān of this year after he remained with them for some time."

459. Text: *Q-n-q-l-h.* Ms. O is unpointed. C: *F-n-q-l-h.* Cairo edition text is like the Leiden text. Ms. A has *Q-y-f-l-h.* Theoktistos the Eunuch (Kanikleios) is suggested by the note in the Leiden edition, *ad loc.*; and see Vasiliev, *Byzance,* 225. The form Nīqōlā in Bar Hebraeus, *Chronography,* 142, is simply a mistake for *Qaniqlā* (Vasiliev).

460. Vasiliev regards these reports by Arab choniclers as "fort douteuses" (*Byzance,* I, 225). On laws for prisoners of war, see E. Gräf, "Religiöse und rechtliche Vorstellungen."

received a letter from al-Mutawakkil stating that negotiations had taken place between Shunayf al-Khādim and George, emissary of the Byzantine emperor, concerning the prisoner exchange, and that an agreement had been reached between them. This George had requested an armistice from 5 Rajab, 241 (November 19, 855), until 22 Shawwāl of this year (March 5, 856), in order to assemble the prisoners and give the Byzantines sufficient time to get to their place of sanctuary. The letter concerning this arrived on Wednesday, 5 Rajab (November 19), and the prisoner exchange took place on the Day of Breaking the Fast this year [1 Shawwāl (February 12, 856)].[461]

George, the emissary of the Byzantine empress, departed for the region of the frontier towns on Saturday, 22 Rajab (December 6, 855) with seventy mules that were leased to him. Abū Qaḥṭabah al-Maghribī al-Ṭurṭūsī[462] went along with him, so that they might observe the time of the Breaking of the Fast.[463] A number of Patrikioi and pages belonging to George came with him, about fifty men.

Shunayf al-Khādim departed for the prisoner exchange in the middle of Shaʿbān (ca. 30 December, 855), along with one hundred horsemen, thirty Turks, thirty Maghāribah, and forty Shākiriyyah horsemen. Jaʿfar b. ʿAbd al-Wāḥid, who was chief judge,[464] requested that he be permitted to attend the prisoner exchange, and [1428]
that someone be deputized to take his place. He was given permission, and 150,000 dirhams were allocated for him as a subsidy and 60,000 for service allotments. He deputized Ibn Abī al-

461. The ʿĪd al-Fiṭr is celebrated at the conclusion of Ramaḍān.

462. An Abū Qaḥṭabah is said to be the emissary of Khāqān al-Khādim in the prisoner exchange of 231 (845–46); see above, 1352 (p. 38) and n. 135. The toponymic *nisbah* al-Ṭurṭūsī indicates a provenance from Tortosa, Spain. (Consider also the *nisbah* al-Maghribī.) But the reading "al-Ṭarsūsī" may also be considered.

463. Text: *al-fiṭr*. Ms. O *al-fidā'* = "the prisoner exchange." So Cairo edition (Ms. A).

464. Jaʿfar b. ʿAbd al-Wāḥid al-Hāshimī al-Qurayshī had been chief judge in Sāmarrā in 240 (854–55); al-Mustaʿīn later deposed him and exiled him to al-Baṣrah (249–50/863–65). He died in 258 (871–72). See also Masʿūdī, *Tanbīh*, 191; Khaṭīb, *Ta'rīkh Baghdād*, VII, 173; Ibn al-Jawzī, *Muntaẓam*, V, 11, 152; Yāqūt, *Irshād*, II, 258–59; Abū al-Maḥāsin, *Nujūm*, I, 330–331.

Shawārib,[465] who was then a young man. Jaʿfar departed and met Shunayf. And a group of leading Baghdadians[466] departed.

The exchange of prisoners reportedly took place in Byzantine territory, on the Lamos River, on Sunday, 12 Shawwāl, 241 (February 23, 856). The number of Muslim prisoners was 785 men and 125 women.[467]

In this year, al-Mutawakkil made the subdistrict of Shimshāṭ tithe (*ʿushr*) land, transferring [its inhabitants] from land tax (*kharāj*) to a tithe, and he sent them a letter to this effect.[468]

In this year, the Bujah[469] attacked a military guard (*ḥaras*)[470]

---

465. Al-Ḥasan b. Muḥammad b. Abī al-Shawārib al-Qāḍī belonged to the family of the Banū al-Shawārib (*EI*², s.v. Ibn Abī'l-Shawārib), which included Ḥadīth scholars, jurists, and judges. They were strong advocates of Sunnism. Ṭabarī studied Ḥadīth with Muḥammad b. ʿAbd al-Malik b. Abī al-Shawārib. Al-Ḥasan b. Muḥammad became chief judge in 252 (866–67; Ṭabarī, III, 1684, Saliba, 143). Ṭabarī says that he died in Mecca after going on the pilgrimage in 261 (874–75; III, 1891). Khaṭīb, *Ta'rīkh Baghdād*, VII, 410–11, notes that he was deputy chief judge in Sāmarrā as of 240 (854–55); and see Ibn al-Jawzī, *Muntaẓam*, V, 27; Massignon, "Cadis et naqībs," 108.

466. In today's Arabic *awsāṭ al-nās* means "the middle class." Here it means "important people"; see Glossarium, DLVI (*optimi*); and Dozy, *Supplément*, II, 801; "les grands."

467. Masʿūdī, *Tanbīh*, 191, says that there were 2,200 men and 100 women.

468. Shimshāṭ is ancient Greek Arsamosata, north of Āmid, on the Arsanas River. Yāqūt, III, *Muʿjam*, 319, warns the reader to distinguish it from Sumaysāṭ (Samosata). These two toponyms were indeed occasionally confused by scribes. See also Le Strange, *Lands*, 116–17; and see Minorsky, *Ḥudūd*, 393, on the confusion between Shimshāṭ and Sumaysāṭ, which is often spelled Shumayshāṭ. Balādhurī, *Futūḥ*, 219, says that al-Mutawakkil transformed the territory of Shimshāṭ from *kharāj* to tithe land so that the area would be on the same footing as other *thughūr*. See also Balādhurī, 203, on these *thughūr*. The *ʿushr* rate amounted to 1/10 of the produce; the *kharāj* from 1/5 to 2/3, most often 1/2; see Løkkegaard, *Islamic Taxation*, 72ff.

469. The Bujah, a people of Hamitic origin, were nomadic tribes that lived between the Nile and the Red Sea. They had submitted to Muslim control by treaty, but periodically withheld the annual tribute and mounted raids. See especially Masʿūdī, *Murūj*, III, 32–34; Maqrīzī, *Mawāʿiẓ*, III, 2, 267–80; Abū al-Maḥāsin, *Nujūm*, I, 295ff. Ibn Ḥawqal, *Masālik*, 53, gives an account of the episode described in our text. See Levtzion and Hopkins, *Corpus*, 21, 31, 40–41, 44, 184, 199, where classical sources concerning the Bujah and related groups are cited. See also *EI*², s.v. Bedja; Hasan, *The Arabs and the Sudan*, Index, 281. Abū al-Maḥāsin places the blame for the Bujah's effrontery at this time upon the weak governorship of ʿAnbasah b. Isḥāq al-Ḍabbī.

470. For *ḥaras*, see Glossarium, CLXXXIX.

from Egypt, and al-Mutawakkil dispatched Muḥammad b. ʿAbdallāh al-Qummī[471] to wage war against them.

The Affair of the Bujah and Its Consequences

It is reported that the Bujah did not raid the Muslims, nor did the Muslims raid them because of the long-standing armistice between them, which we have mentioned previously in our book.[472] They are of the stock of the Ḥabash (Abyssinians), in the West. Among the black peoples (*sūdān*) in the West are the Bujah, the Nūbah, and the people of Ghānah, al-Ghaf-r, ?-y-n-w-r, R-ʿ-wīn, F-r-ww-iyah, B-k-sūm, M-kār-h, ʾ-k-r-m and al-Khams.[473] 1429]
There are gold mines in the territory of the Bujah. They bind by oath those who work in them. The Bujah deliver annually from their mines to the agents of the Egyptian government 400 *mithqāls*[474] of gold ore, prior to smelting and refining. From the time of al-Mutawakkil's reign the Bujah refrained from delivering this tax for several consecutive years. Al-Mutawakkil reportedly appointed over the Egyptian Postal and Intelligence Service one of his servants (*khadam*) named Yaʿqūb b. Ibrāhīm al-Bādhghīsī, *mawlā* of al-Hādī. He was known as Qawṣarah.[475] Al-Mutawakkil assigned to him the Intelligence Service of Cairo, Alexandria, Barqah, and the provinces of the Maghrib.

Yaʿqūb b. Ibrāhīm wrote to al-Mutawakkil that the Bujah had broken the treaty between them and the Muslims. They advanced

471. Ms. O has ʿĪsā with ʿUbaydallāh as a superscript. He is mentioned, for instance, by Balādhurī, *Futūḥ*, 282; Kindī, *Wulāh*, 200; Maqrīzī, *Mawāʿiẓ*, III, 275; Abū al-Maḥāsin, *Nujūm*, II, 297.

472. See Ṭabarī, I, 2593. For the treaty, see also Maqrīzī, *Mawāʿiẓ*, III, 273–75; and see Hasan, *The Arabs and the Sudan*, 39–40.

473. The names in the text are uncertain. For *B-k-sūm*, O reads *Y-kshūm*, which the note says may be identified with Axum. (But cf. Minorsky, *Ḥudūd*, 474.) And the note compares *F-r-ww-iyah* with *bilād al-Faruwiyyīn* (citing Bakrī, *Muʿjam*, ed. De Slane, 174).

474. A *mithqāl* is a dīnār of full weight.

475. The cognomen Qawṣarah means "date basket." Ṭabarī, III, 1296 (Marin, *Reign*, 105), mentions him as chief of Intelligence. He is called there Yaʿqūb b. Ibrāhīm al-Būshanjī, *mawlā* of al-Hādī, known as Qawṣarah. Būshanj is a town, and Badhghīs (or: Badghīs) is a district, in Khurāsān. *Fragmenta*, 514, reads: Muṣʿab b. Ibrāhīm.

from their territory to the mines of gold and precious stones that were on the border between Egypt and the territory of the Bujah.[476] The Bujah killed a number of Muslims employed in the mines for mining the gold and precious stones, and took captive a number of the Muslim children and women. The Bujah claimed that the mines belonged to them and were in their territory, and that they would not permit the Muslims to enter them. This alarmed all the Muslims employed in the mines, so that they abandoned them in fear for their lives and for their children. The
[1430] assessment of a fifth of the gold, silver, and precious stones that was excavated from the mines and levied for the central government thereby ceased.

Al-Mutawakkil was dead set against this and greatly annoyed. He therefore sought advice concerning the circumstances of the Bujah. He was informed [as follows]: They were a nomadic people, tenders of camel and livestock. Getting to their territory was difficult, and it was inaccessible to troops, for it consisted of desert and steppe. It was a month's journey from the land of Islam to the territory of the Bujah, through wasteland, mountains, and barren country, lacking water, vegetation, refuge, or a fortified position. Any government representative who entered Bujah territory would have to be supplied with provisions for his entire intended stay until he returned to the land of Islam. If the extent of his stay was greater than estimated, he and all his comrades would perish. And the Bujah would simply overcome them without hostilities. Their land did not remit to the central government land tax or any other tax.

Al-Mutawakkil therefore refrained from dispatching anyone against them. But the situation only got worse, and the boldness of the Bujah against the Muslims intensified to the point that the inhabitants of Upper Egypt feared for their lives and for their children. As a result, al-Mutawakkil appointed Muḥammad b. ʿAbdallāh, known as al-Qummī, to wage war against them, and

476. The area was famous for its emeralds and other precious stones, mentioned by Masʿūdī and Maqrīzī, among others. The gold and emerald mines were between Qūṣ, Wādī al-ʿAllāqī, and the Red Sea.

appointed him chief of security police[477] for these subdistricts, namely, Qifṭ, Aqṣur, Isnā, Armant, and Uswān (Aswān).[478]

Al-Mutawakkil commissioned Muḥammad b. ʿAbdallāh to wage war against the Bujah and to correspond with ʿAnbasah b. Isḥāq al-Ḍabbī, the officer in charge of the Egyptian security forces. Al-Mutawakkil also wrote to ʿAnbasah, instructing him to supply Muḥammad with all the requisite regular troops and [1431] Shākiriyyah stationed in Egypt. Thus ʿAnbasah removed Muḥammad's pretext [that he lacked forces].

Muḥammad b. ʿAbdallāh departed for the land of the Bujah, and all those who had been employed in the mines and a large number of volunteers joined him. About 20,000 men[479] accompanied him, including horsemen and infantry. He sent to al-Qulzum[480] by sea seven vessels loaded with flour, olive oil, dates, *sawīq*,[481] and barley, ordering a contingent of his men to maneuver the vessels by sea so as to land at the coast of Bujah territory.

Muḥammad b. ʿAbdallāh al-Qummī forged on in Bujah territory until he traversed the mines, where gold was mined, and came to their fortresses and citadels. Their king encountered Muḥammad b. ʿAbdallāh al-Qummī—the king's name was ʿAlī Bābā, and the name of his son was Laʿīs[482]—with a great army, far outnumbering the men who were with al-Qummī. The Bujah were mounted on their camels, carrying their lances with them. Their camels were choice, of noble pedigree, like the camels of Mahrah.[483] The

477. The term *muʿāwin* is understood here as equivalent to *ṣāḥib al-maʿūnah*, which is similar to *ṣāḥib al-shurṭah* and *ṣāḥib al-ḥarb*; see Glossarium, CCCLXXXIII.

478. For these places in Upper Egypt, see Yaʿqūbī, *Buldān*, 333 = Wiet, *Les pays*, 188–89 (Qifṭ, Luqṣur, i.e., Luxor, Isnā and Aswān). See also Maspéro-Wiet, *Matériaux*, 185, for Qifṭ, Aqṣur, Asnā, Armant, and Aswān; and for Qifṭ, ancient Coptos, see 148–49; Luxor, 23, Armant, 7, 191, Aswān, 127–29 *et passim*. And see Maqrīzī, *Mawāʿiẓ*, III, 3, 5, 32, 194, 248, 249, 280, 295, 303, 304; and *EI*², s.v. Qifṭ.

479. In his account, Abū al-Maḥāsin gives 7,000 men.

480. See *EI*², V, 367, s.v. Ḳulzum (where the Buja rebellion is mentioned).

481. For *sawīq*. see above, n. 75.

482. For "his son" Ms C has rather "his father" (*abīhi*); the note suggests *ibn akhīhi*, "his nephew." For Laʿīs, the note refers to *Fragmenta*, 550, note c, and Ibn al-Athīr, *Kāmil*, 52, note 2.

483. Mahrī (cf. French *méhari*) camels are speedy riding camels from the area of the Mahrah tribe in southeastern Arabia; see *EI*², s.v. Mahra. These camels were

two sides began to confront each other on successive days. But they would only skirmish and not actually engage in combat. The Bujah king set about harassing[484] al-Qummī, so as to protract the time [of their stay] and exhaust the supplies and fodder that were with [al-Qummī and his men]. Thus they would lose strength and die from exhaustion, and the Bujah could then easily overcome them.

Just when the Bujah ruler figured that the supplies were ex-
[1432] hausted, the seven vessels that al-Qummī had sent landed on the coast at a place called Ṣanjah.[485] Al-Qummī dispatched there a group of his men to protect the vessels from the Bujah. Al-Qummī divided the ships' freight among his followers, so that they had adequate supplies of fodder.

Seeing this, 'Alī Bābā, the Bujah chief, went on to do battle with the Muslims, rallying troops against them. The two sides clashed and fought violently. The camels upon which the Bujah fought were unseasoned[486] and tended to be frightened and alarmed by everything. Noticing this, al-Qummī rounded up all the camel and horse bells in his camp. He then attacked the Bujah, stampeding their camels with the clanging of the bells. Their alarm was considerable. It drove them over mountains and valleys, totally splintering the Bujah forces. Al-Qummī and his men pursued and seized them, dead or alive, until night overtook him. This took place at the beginning of 241 (855–56). Al-Qummī then returned to his camp and could not count the dead they were so many.

When al-Qummī arose in the morning, he discovered that the Bujah had rallied a contingent of infantry and had proceeded to a place where they felt safe from al-Qummī's pursuit. But al-Qummī with his cavalry overtook them at night. Their king fled,

---

prized from ancient times for their fine, noble breed, and were valued by caliphs. Ibn Baṭṭūṭah, *Travels*, 69, who visited 'Aydhāb, took note of the superior camels of the Bujah. Maqrīzī, *Mawā'iẓ*, III, 268, notes the martial virtues of their camels and the effective use the Bujah made of lances while fighting from their backs.

484. For *taṭarrada* in this sense, see Glossarium, CCCXXXVIII. And see also Maqrīzī, *Mawā'iẓ*, III, 268.

485. Balādhurī, *Futūḥ*, 282, states that the place of landing was rather 'Aydhāb. See also Abū al-Maḥāsin, *Nujūm*, I, 297.

486. Text: *za'iratan* = "thin-haired." Ms O: *ghirratan*, i.e., "inexperienced," etc. Cf. Abū al-Maḥāsin, *Nujūm*, I, 298: *wa-hiya* [*al-ibl*] *'alā ghāyah min al-za'ārah wa-l-nifār* ("extremely peevish and timid").

taking his crown and furnishings. ʿAlī Bābā requested thereafter a guarantee of safe-conduct to return to his kingdom and territory. Al-Qummī granted him this, and ʿAlī Bābā delivered the taxes to him for the period of time for which he had withheld them, namely, four years, at 400 *mithqāl*s per year.

ʿAlī Bābā appointed his son Laʿīs as deputy over his kingdom. [1433]
Al-Qummī departed with ʿAlī Bābā for the gate of al-Mutawakkil, and arrived there at the end of 241 (855–56). He attired this ʿAlī Bābā with a silk brocade-lined robe and a black turban and covered his camel with a brocaded saddle and brocade horse cloths. At the Public Gate, along with a group of the Bujah, were stationed about seventy pages, upon saddled camels, carrying their lances, on whose tips were the heads of their warriors who had been killed by al-Qummī.[487]

Al-Mutawakkil discharged al-Qummī on the Day of Sacrifice, 241 (April 20, 856), and appointed Saʿd al-Khādim al-Ītākhī[488] over the Bujah and the road between Mecca and Egypt. And Saʿd appointed Muḥammad b. ʿAbdallāh al-Qummī. Al-Qummī departed with ʿAlī Bābā, who stuck to his religion. Some(one) of [the informants] reported seeing ʿAlī Bābā with a stone idol in the shape of a young boy to which he prostrated himself.

In this year, Yaʿqūb b. Ibrāhīm, known as Qawṣarah, died in Jumādā II (October–November 855).

Leading the pilgrimage this year was ʿAbdallāh b. Muḥammad b. Dāwūd.

Jaʿfar b. Dīnār went on the pilgrimage this year, and he was the supervisor of the Mecca Road and the events of the festive season.

---

487. Ms. O omits *qutilū min ʿaskarihim.*

488. Saʿd al-Khādim al-Ītākhī appears below (1465, p. 185) as a courtier of al-Mutawakkil.

The Events of the Year 242

(May 10, 856–April 29, 857)

Among the events that happened this year were the enormous earthquakes that took place in Qūmis and its surrounding villages in Shaʿbān (December 3–31, 856).[489] Homes were destroyed,
[1434] and many people died from collapsing walls and the like. Their number reportedly came to 45,096. The greatest effect of the earthquakes was in Dāmaghān. It is reported that there were earthquakes and shocking noises this year in Fārs, Khurāsān, and Syria. The same thing took place in the Yemen along with a lunar eclipse.

In this year, the Byzantines advanced from the area of Samosata, following the summer expedition of ʿAlī b. Yaḥyā al-Armanī, as far as Āmid.[490] They then advanced from the frontier

489. Qūmis is a small province between the Alburz mountains to the north and the Great Desert to the south. Its administrative capital was Damghān, or Madīnat Qūmis (the City of Qūmis); Le Strange, *Lands*, 364–68; *EI*², s.v. Ḳūmis. Yaʿqūbī, *Taʾrīkh*, II, 600, mentions the earthquakes that took place in Qūmis and Naysābūr and the surrounding area in 242 (856–57), in which about 200,000 people are said to have perished.

490. Leiden and Cairo editions: Shimshāṭ. The note in the Leiden edition cites the reading Sumaysāṭ (i.e. Samosata) of Ibn al-Athīr, *Kāmil*, VII, 53, and Abū al-

towns of the Jazīrah and plundered a number of villages, taking captive about 10,000 men. They entered from the direction of Tephrikē,[491] a village [in the control] of Karbeas. They then departed, returning to their territory. Karbeas, ʿUmar b. ʿAbdallāh al-Aqṭaʿ, and a contingent of volunteers pursued them but did not catch one of them.[492] ʿUmar wrote to ʿAlī b. Yaḥyā to make a winter expedition into their territory.

In this year, al-Mutawakkil had ʿUṭārid killed.[493] He was a Christian, who had converted to Islam, and remained a Muslim for many years, and then he apostatized. He was asked to recant, but he refused to return to Islam. He was executed on 2 Shawwāl (February 1, 857), and was burned at the Public Gate.[494]

In this year, in Rajab (November 3–December 2, 856), Abū Ḥassān al-Ziyādī, judge of the East Side [of Baghdad], died.

In this year, al-Ḥasan b. ʿAlī b. al-Jaʿd, judge of Madīnat al-Manṣūr, died.

Leading the pilgrimage this year was ʿAbd al-Ṣamad b. Mūsā b.

Maḥāsin, *Nujūm,* II, 307. It was Samosata that was, in fact, raided by the Byzantines during this campaign. For confusion in texts between Shimshāṭ and Sumaysāṭ, see above, n. 468. Āmid (or Amida), the most important city in Diyār Bakr, was located on the left bank of the Tigris; it was frequently attacked by the Byzantines in the tenth century. On this episode, see Vasiliev, *Byzance,* I, 233–34, 318–19.

491. Text: Abrīq. The note in the Leiden edition identifies Abrīq with Greek Tephrikē (citing *Theophanes continuatus,* p. 16). The name, it is pointed out, is also written Tibrikē, Brikē, and Aphrikē. See also Vasiliev, *Byzance,* I, 233; Bury, *History,* 278. The Arabic name appears to be derived from *Brikē.* Karbeas (Qarbiyās) belonged to the Paulician iconoclasts. On their beliefs, see Runciman, *Medieval Manichee,* 26–62. Persecuted by Theophilus and Theodora, who regarded them as Manichaeans, they took refuge in Muslim territory. Karbeas sought shelter with the amīr of Melitene (Malaṭiyah) and settled in the area of Tephrikē. Before the fall of Theodora, the Byzantines sent an army to raid Samosata and Āmid, and they thereafter attacked Tephrikē, the headquarters of Karbeas; Bury, *ibid.,* 278f.

492. ʿUmar b. ʿAbdallāh al-Aqṭaʿ ("the One-Armed") was a military commander who fought on several occasions against the Byzantines. He led a summer raid in 246 (860–61; below, 1449, p. 167). He was finally killed in a battle with the Byzantines in 249 (863–64); Ṭabarī, III, 1509 (Saliba), 9, where he is called b. ʿUbaydallāh.

493. Ms. O and Ibn al-Athīr, *Kāmil,* VII, 53, have *rajulan ʿaṭṭāran,* that is, a perfumer, pharmacist. ʿUṭārid is the planet Mercury.

494. Burning was occasionally used as a punishment for apostates (*murtaddūn*); see *EI*[1], s.v.

[1435] Muḥammad b. Ibrāhīm al-Imām b. Muḥammad b. ʿAlī, who was governor of Mecca.[495] Jaʿfar b. Dīnār went on the pilgrimage this year. He was the supervisor of the Mecca Road and the events of the festival season.

---

495. An ʿAbbāsid, he was governor of Mecca beginning with this year (Zambaur, *Manuel,* 20) and led the pilgrimage in 243, 244, and 249 (below, 1436, 1437, 1515 [Saliba, 14]).

The Events of the Year 243

(April 30, 857–April 18, 858)

In this year, al-Mutawakkil went to Damascus on 20 Dhū al-Qaʿdah (March 8, 858).[496] He observed the Day of Sacrifice in Balad. Yazīd b. Muḥammad al-Muhallabī recited when he departed [from Baghdad]:[497]

---

496. On Mutawakkil's move to Damascus, see, e.g., Yaʿqūbī, *Taʾrīkh,* II, 600; Masʿūdī, *Murūj,* VII, 257; Abū al-Maḥāsin, *Nujūm,* II, 315. The reason for transferring the capital from Sāmarrā to Damascus was evidently the caliph's desire to avoid the powerful influence of the Turks in Sāmarrā by moving to Arab Syria. Balad is a town in the Jazīrah slightly northeast of Mosul; Le Strange, *Lands,* 99, 125. On the way to Damascus, al-Mutawakkil followed the route along the Tigris passing through Mosul. This was the postal road. See Le Strange, *Lands,* 84. On the way back, he took the route along the Euphrates to Anbār (below, 1436, p. 152).

497. Yazīd b. Muḥammad b. Yazīd al-Muhallabī was a member of the famous Muhallabī family that supplied governors and wazīrs in the ninth and tenth centuries; Zambaur, *Manuel,* 11. He was a poet, a boon companion of al-Mutawakkil, and panegyrist of al-Muntaṣir; see Iṣfahānī, *Aghānī,* VIII, 176–77, XI, 165; Sezgin, *GAS,* II, 606. He wrote a fine elegy on the death of al-Mutawakkil; Ibn ʿAbd Rabbihi, *ʿIqd,* II, 26; Mubarrad, *Kāmil,* III, 1258. According to Abū Bakr al-Ṣūlī, Ibrāhīm al-Ṣūlī recited the poem quoting al-Muntaṣir (note *ad loc.*). Abū Bakr al-Ṣulī also preserves two additional lines of verse: Muḥammad (al-Muntaṣir) says: "Let my soul be ransom for you, pity me and refrain from leaving./ If you depart, abandoning me, I shall have no joy but meeting again." Se also Masʿūdī, *Murūj,* VII, 257; Abū al-Maḥāsin, *Nujūm,* II, 315.

I think that Syria gloats at Iraq,
 Now that the Imām has resolved to depart.

If you abandon Iraq and its people,
 Consider that a beauty may fade if divorced.

In this year, Ibrāhīm b. al-ʿAbbās [al-Ṣūlī] died.

Al-Ḥasan b. Makhlad b. al-Jarrāḥ, deputy of Ibrāhīm, supervised the Bureau of Estates in Shaʿbān (November 23–December 21, 857).[498]

Hāshim b. Bānījūr died in Dhū al-Qaʿdah (February 19–March 20, 858).[499]

[1436] Leading the pilgrimage this year was ʿAbd al-Ṣamad b. Mūsā.

Jaʿfar b. Dīnār went on the pilgrimage, and was supervisor of the Mecca Road and the events of the festival season.

---

498. Al-Ḥasan b. Makhlad b. al-Jarrāḥ was a secretary of Christian background who had recently converted to Islam. He later served al-Mutawakkil and became wazīr under al-Muʿtamid; Sourdel, *Vizirat,* Index, 766; *EI*², s.v. Ibn Makhlad.

499. Hāshim b. Bānījūr belonged to the family of Bānījūr that ruled Balkh from 233 (847–48) until 337 (948–49); Zambaur, *Manuel,* 27, 41, 202 (genealogical table), 204; *EI*², *Supplement,* s.v. Banīdjūrids.

The Events of the Year 244

(April 19, 858–April 7, 859)

Among these events was al-Mutawakkil's entrance into Damascus in Ṣafar (May 19–June 16, 858). From the time he left Sāmarrā until he entered Damascus ninety-seven days elapsed or, it is said, seventy-seven days. He decided to take up residence there, transferred the royal bureaus, and gave orders for building in Damascus. The Turks were in a state of foment over [the withholding of] their service allotments and the allotments for their families, and so al-Mutawakkil gave orders to placate them.

Al-Mutawakkil thereafter found Balad unpleasant. This was because its air was cool and humid, the water unwholesome, the wind blowing from afternoon and continuing to intensify throughout the entire night. It had many fleas; prices were high; and snow interfered with supply of provisions.

In this year, al-Mutawakkil dispatched Bughā from Damascus to raid the Byzantines in Rabīʿ II (July 17–August 14, 858). Bughā undertook the summer expedition and conquered Ṣamāluh.[500]

500. Ṣamāluh is written here with final *h*; Yāqūt, *Muʿjam*, III, 416, has final *w*. He places it at the Syrian frontier towns near Maṣīṣah (Mopsuestia) and Tarsus. Ṣamāluh = *Sēmalouos kastron*; Vasiliev, *Byzance*, I, 234; Minorsky, *Ḥudūd*, 220.

Al-Mutawakkil resided in Damascus for two months and a number of days. He then returned to Sāmarrā, staying along the Euphrates, turning off for al-Anbār, and then from al-Anbār taking the Ḥurf Road to Sāmarrā.[501] He entered Sāmarrā on Monday, 22 Jumādā II (October 5, 858).

In this year, some(one) of the informants allege(s), al-Mutawakkil[502] appointed Abū al-Sāj[503] supervisor of the Mecca Road in place of Jaʿfar b. Dīnār. What is correct, in my view, is that he appointed him as supervisor of the Mecca Road in 242 (856–57).

[1437] In this year, a lance that had belonged to the Prophet, called al-ʿAnazah, was reportedly brought to al-Mutawakkil.[504] It is said to have belonged to the Najāshī, king of Abyssinia, who gave it to al-Zubayr b. al-ʿAwwām. Al-Zubayr gave it to the Messenger of God, and it remained in the possession of the muezzins. Someone marched with it before the Messenger of God on the two festivals. It was implanted before him in the courtyard,[505] and people prayed toward it.[506] Al-Mutawakkil ordered that it be carried before him. The chief of the security police would bear it before the caliph, and the deputy chief of security police would carry his lance.

In this year, al-Mutawakkil became angry with Bukhtīshūʿ, confiscated his property, and banished him to al-Baḥrayn.[507]

---

501. Al-Mutawakkil stayed along the Euphrates road and headed southeast until Anbār instead of heading directly east from Ḥadīthah, which would have brought him straight to Sāmarrā. He then headed back north to Sāmarrā, thus doubling the distance he had to travel. Ḥurf is a village in the area of al-Anbār (Yāqūt, *Muʿjam,* II, 243) after which this route is presumably named.

502. Ms. C and Cairo edition Ms. D have al-Muntaṣir instead of al-Mutawakkil.

503. Abū al-Sāj Dīwdād b. Dīwdast was an army commander who had supported Afshīn in his campaign against Bābak (Ṭabarī, III, 1222, 1228, Marin, *Reign,* 46, 52). He was commander of the Mecca Road until the struggle between al-Mustaʿīn and al-Muʿtazz erupted in 251 (865–66). He then continued to engage actively in warfare and politics; d. 266 (879–80); Ibn al-Jawzī, *Muntaẓam,* V, 56; Zambaur, *Manuel,* 32 (governor of Aleppo in 254/868–69), 43 (governor of al-Kūfah in 252/866–67), 179 (genealogy of Sājites in Ādharbāyjān); *EI*², Abū'l-Sādj Dīwdād.

504. On the famous lance called al-ʿAnazah, see *EI*², s.v. It was an emblem of prophetic and caliphal authority.

505. Text: *al-fanāʾ*. ʿAynī: *fī al-asfār* ("on journeys").

506. Ms. O adds *fī al-faḍāʾ* = "in the open space."

507. Bukhtīshūʿ b. Jibrīl, of the famous family from Jundaysābūr, died in 256 (869–70); Sezgin, *GAS,* III, 243. Bukhtīshūʿ was a court physician for al-Mutawak-

An Arab tribesman recited:

O anger that came with fateful force,
When the lion sprang upon him with might and main.

Bukhtīshūʿ was deluded
When he intrigued against the lords, the moons,

The amīrs, the pure leaders,
Heirs apparent of the chosen lord,

And against the *mawlā*s and the free.
He cast him to an isolated wasteland,

The shore of al-Baḥrayn, for his baseness.

In this year, the Festival of Sacrifice of the Muslims, Palm Sunday of the Christians, and Passover of the Jews coincided.[508]

Leading the pilgrimage this year was ʿAbd al-Ṣamad b. Mūsā.

---

kil. He had been dispossessed and banished previously by al-Wāthiq, in 230 (844–45), but his situation improved under al-Mutawakkil, until the physician took liberties with the caliph, and was then banished on several occasions; Ibn Abī Uṣaybiʿah, *ʿUyūn,* I, 138. In the poem here, he is said to have intrigued against the crown princes and the Turks (*mawlās*).

508. Gil, *Palestine,* I, 385, n. 700, mentions that Muslim chroniclers (citing Ibn al-Athīr, Sibṭ b. al-Jawzī, Abū al-Maḥāsin) recorded an unprecedented occurrence in the year 244, namely, that the Day of Sacrifice, the Jewish Passover, and the Christian Palm Sunday (al-Shaʿānīn < Heb. *Hōshaʿnōt*) fell on the same day. The coincidence, as Gil shows, does not work out, as the Festival of Sacrifice was on March 19, 859, whereas Passover was on March 23.

The
Events of the Year
245
(April 8, 859–March 27, 860)

[1438] In this year al-Mutawakkil gave orders to build al-Māḥūzah, and he called it the Jaʿfarī.[509] He granted there fiefs to his army commanders and companions. Al-Mutawakkil expended great effort in building it and withdrew to al-Muḥammadiyyah so that the construction of al-Māḥūzah could be carried out.[510] The caliph or-

509. The Jaʿfarī Palace complex, or al-Jaʿfariyyah, was named after al-Mutawakkil whose name (*ism*) was Jaʿfar. It is not to be confused with the Jaʿfarī Palace in Baghdad, built by Jaʿfar al-Barmakī. Yaʿqūbī (*Buldān*, 266–76 = Wiet, *Les pays*, 60–61) observes that al-Mutawakkil lived in the palaces of the Jaʿfarī for only nine months and three days before his assassination there. Al-Muntaṣir then ordered that al-Māḥūzah be abandoned and destroyed, and that the building material be brought back to Sāmarrā. According to Yaʿqūbī, *Taʾrīkh*, II, 601, al-Māḥūzah was 3 *farsakhs* (18 km.) from Sāmarrā. Yāqūt, *Muʿjam*, III, 17, says that the renovation of the Jaʿfarī cost ten million dirhams. See also *Muʿjam*, III, 18 (poem of ʿAlī b. al-Jahm). The remains of the Jaʿfariyyah complex occupy about 1⅓ sq. km. between the Nahr al-Raṣāṣ canal and the Tigris (Creswell, *Early Muslim Architecture*, II, 277, and Plate 70a). See Herzfeld, *Samarra*, 125; Creswell, II, 277f.; Sāmarrāʾī, *Taʾrīkh*, I, 95–96; Rogers, "Samarra," 130, 136, 148, 150; al-ʿAmid, *Architecture*, 202ff.

510. Herzfeld, *Samarra*, 125, cites Ibn Serapion to the effect that the Muḥammadiyyah (named for Muḥammad al-Muntaṣir) was in al-Qāṭūl al-Kisrawī. According to Yāqūt, *Muʿjam*, IV, 430, it was formerly the monastary of Dayr Abū Ṣufrā, then the Ītākhiyyah (after Ītākh al-Turkī). See also Herzfeld, 72.

dered that the palaces of al-Mukhtār and al-Badīʿ be demolished and had their teak wood transferred to the Jaʿfarī.[511] It is said that he spent more than two million dīnārs on the Jaʿfarī.[512] He assembled therein Qur'ān readers, who recited the Qur'ān; and entertainers, to whom he gave two million dirhams, also attended. Al-Mutawakkil and his followers called it al-Khāṣṣah al-Mutawakkiliyyah.[513] And he constructed within it a palace which he named Lu'lu'ah. A taller structure had never been seen.[514]

Al-Mutawakkil ordered that a canal (*nahr*) be dug, beginning at a place called Karmā, five *farsakh*s (thirty km.) above al-Māḥūzah.[515] The canal would feed into the mouths[516] of the canals around it, providing drinking water. And he ordered the expropriation of Jabiltā, Upper and Lower al-Khaṣāṣah,[517] and Karmā,

511. Yaʿqūbī, *Ta'rīkh,* II, 600, mentions the Badīʿ; Yāqūt, *Muʿjam,* III, 17, mentions only Mukhtār (which he says cost five million dirhams to construct); see also Herzfeld, *Samarra,* 132–33; Samarrā'ī, *Ta'rīkh,* I, 135–36.

512. If this is the renovation that Yāqūt had in mind, the sum was ten million dirhams; *Muʿjam,* III, 17 (above, n. 509).

513. The administrative center al-Mutawakkiliyyah thus equals al-Jaʿfariyyah; see Herzfeld, *Samarra,* 124–25. Baladhuri, *Futūḥ,* 240, 364, states that al-Mutawakkil built a new administrative center (*madīnah*), calling it al-Mutawakkiliyyah between al-Karkh Fayrūz and al-Qāṭūl, in which al-Māḥūzah was included. He also takes note of the great mosque that he built there, which Ṭabarī does not mention in our text.

514. The Lu'lu'ah (Pearl) Palace, situated within the Jaʿfariyyah administrative center, according to Herzfeld, *Samarra,* 128, was either identical with the Jaʿfarī Palace or was its main building; see also 104, 132, 147. Rogers, "Samarra," 148, suggests that the Lu'lu'ah was not a vast building but most probably a kiosk or courtyard. According to Yāqūt, *Muʿjam,* III, 17, five million dirhams were spent on the Lu'lu'ah; it was built by al-Muʿtaṣim for Afshīn (Ṭabarī, III, 1307 and 1315; Marin, *Reign,* 114, 120). Masʿūdī, *Murūj,* VII, 365, calls it Lu'lu'at al-Jawsaq to distinguish it from Lu'lu'at al-Jaʿfarī. He notes that al-Muʿtazz and al-Mu'ayyad were imprisoned there (see below, pp. 210f.). Both these Lu'lu'ahs are to be distinguished, of course, from the town Lulon in Asia Minor that the Arabs called Lu'lu'ah (below, n. 551).

515. On al-Mutawakkil's irrigation project, see Yaʿqūbī, *Ta'rīkh,* II, 601; *Buldān,* 267 = Wiet, *Les pays,* 67. Herzfeld, *Samarra,* 125, and n. 2, says that Karmā (Syriac Karmē) had been a Nestorian bishopric from A.D. 486 to 554. See also Rogers, "Samarra," 145.

516. For the expression *fūh al-nahr* in the sense of "mouth of the canal," see Glossarium, CDVIII; Lane, *Lexicon,* 2465.

517. Jabiltā or Jabultā is on the east bank of the Tigris slightly northeast of Takrīt and opposite it on the post road from Baghdad to Mosul. It is sometimes mispointed as Ḥabiltā; Le Strange, *Lands,* 91, 92, n. 1, 125. For upper and lower Khaṣāṣah, Ms. O and ʿAynī have al-Khaṣāṣiyyah; see also Herzfeld, *Samarra,* 67, 125.

forcing their inhabitants to sell their residences and land. They were compelled to do this so that the land and residences in all these villages would be turned over to the custody of al-Mutawakkil, who would then evict the inhabitants. He allocated 200,000 dīnārs for expediture on the canal and assigned the money to Dulayl b. Yaʿqūb al-Naṣrānī, secretary of Bughā.[518] This was in Dhū al-Ḥijjah, 245 (February 27–March 28, 860). He held 12,000 men responsible for the job of digging the canal. Dulayl
[1439] continued to work at it, allocating ever increasing sums of money, dispersing all of it among the secretaries, until al-Mutawakkil was killed, whereupon the canal fell into disuse. Al-Jaʿfariyyah was laid waste and demolished, and the canal project went uncompleted.

In this year, the territory of the Maghrib suffered an earthquake, which destroyed fortresses, residences, and bridges. Al-Mutawakkil ordered that three million dirhams be distributed among those whose residences were afflicted. ʿAskar al-Mahdī in Baghdad suffered an earthquake this year, as did al-Madā'in.[519]

In this year, the Byzantine ruler sent Muslim prisoners and communicated a request for a prisoner exchange for those he still held.[520] The person who came to al-Mutawakkil as an emissary on behalf of the Byzantine sovereign was an elder named Triphylios.[521] With him were seventy-seven Muslim prisoners whom Michael, son of Theophilus, the Byzantine ruler, presented to al-Mutawakkil. Triphylios came to al-Mutawakkil on 24 Ṣafar (May 31) of this year (859). He resided with Shunayf al-Khādim. Then al-Mutawakkil dispatched Naṣr b. al-Azhar al-Shīʿī with the emissary of the Byzantine sovereign. He set out during this year, but the prisoner exchange did not take place until 246 (March 28, 860—January 16, 861).

518. Dulayl b. Yaʿqūb al-Naṣrānī, a Christian secretary, served Bughā al-Turkī and al-Mutawakkil. He is first mentioned in Ṭabarī, III, 1184 (Marin, *Reign*, 1, 19, 20). Dulayl later served as supervisor of the ministry of estates (III, 1513; Saliba, 12). He still appears as Bughā's secretary in 251 (865–66; 1535, Saliba, 28); and see Saliba, Index, 174. See also Yāqūt, *Irshād*, II, 30.

519. ʿAskar al-Mahdī is the older name of Ruṣāfah in Baghdad; Le Strange, *Baghdad*, 42, 189; Lassner, *Topography*, 150.

520. See Vasiliev, *Byzance*, I, 234–35, 319.

521. Text: Aṭrūbaylīs. The note in the Leiden edition identifies the elder as Triphylios (citing *Theophanes continuatus*, 122.8). Vasiliev, *Byzance*, I, 234, n. 5, cites Bar Hebraeus (*Chronography*, 144), where the reading is Aṭrōphilos (or Aṭrōphīlōs).

It is reported that in Shawwāl (December 30, 859–January 27, 860) an earthquake and tremor killed many people in Antioch. Fifteen hundred homes and about ninety towers along its walls collapsed as a result. Dreadful indescribable noises were heard emanating from the openings of the residences. The inhabitants of Antioch fled to the desert. [Part of] Mount al-Aqraʿ shook loose and sank into the sea.[522] The sea was stormy on that day, and black, murky, putrid vapors rose from it. A river in Antioch disap- [1440] peared the distance of a *farsakh* (six km.), and it was not known where the waters vanished.

It is said that in this year the inhabitants of Tinnīs[523] in Egypt heard a continuous, dreadful clamor, from which many people died.

In this year, an earthquake effected Bālis, al-Raqqah, Ḥarrān, Ra's ʿAyn, Ḥimṣ, Damascus, Edessa, Tarsus, Mopsuestia, Adana,[524] and the coasts of Syria. Laodicea was convulsed. Not a residence remained there, and only a few of its inhabitants escaped. Jabalah[525] and its inhabitants perished.

In this year, the level of Mushāsh—the spring of Mecca—declined, so that the price of a waterskin in Mecca reached eighty dirhams.[526] The mother of al-Mutawakkil sent funds that were disbursed for it.[527]

In this year, Isḥāq b. Abī Isrā'īl, Sawwār b. ʿAbdallāh, and Hilāl al-Rāzī died.[528]

In this year, Najāḥ b. Salamah perished.

---

522. Mount al-Aqraʿ is classical Casius. Earthquakes and seismic shocks were quite common in the Antioch region throughout history.

523. Ibn al-Athīr, *Kāmil*, VII, 56: Sīs; Abū al-Maḥāsin, *Nujūm*, I, 752: Bilbays.

524. Text: Adanah, Addenda, DCCLXXVI and Cairo edition, Ms. D: Adhanah.

525. Jabalah is a port on the coast of Syria, about 30 km. south of Laodicea. Its citadel had been built by Muʿāwiyah; see Yāqūt, *Muʿjam*, II, 25; *EI*², s.v. Djabala.

526. Mushāsh is a canal near Mt. ʿArafāt that reaches Mecca; Yaʿqūbī, *Buldān*, 316 = Wiet, *Les pays*, 154; Yāqūt, *Muʿjam*, IV, 536. On the price of a waterskin, see above, 1330 (p. 6) and n. 10.

527. Ms. O has *fa-baʿatha* and omits *umm*, that is, "Al-Mutawakkil sent. . . ."

528. Isḥāq b. Abī Isrā'īl Ibrāhīm al-Marwazī, a Ḥadīth scholar, died this year in Shawwāl (December 30, 859–January 27, 860) in Baghad, at the age of ninety-five, according to Dhahabī, *ʿIbar*, 444. For Sawwār b. ʿAbdallāh, see above, 1411 (p. 118) and n. 384. A Hilāl b. Yaḥyā, Abū Yaḥyā, called al-Rā'ī (not al-Rāzī), a Ḥanafī scholar, died in al-Baṣrah in 245; Ibn al-Nadīm, *Fihrist*, 507; Sezgin, *GAS*, I, 435. (The *Fihrist* gives his surname as Abū Bakr.) The identification is uncertain.

The Cause of Najāḥ b. Salamah's Demise

I have received an account on the authority of al-Ḥārith b. Abī Usāmah, some of which I report on the basis of information from him and some from other informants:[529] Najāḥ b. Salamah was responsible for the Bureau of Registering and Supervising Government Officals (*dīwān al-tawqīʿ wa-l-tatabbuʿ ʿalā al-ʿummāl*). Before this he had been secretary of Ibrāhīm b. Rabāḥ al-Jawharī and was responsible for estates. The government officials all feared
[1441] him and carried out his wishes, unable to deter him from doing whatever he wanted. Al-Mutawakkil often took him as a drinking companion.

Al-Ḥasan b. Makhlad and Mūsā b. ʿAbd al-Malik were associates of ʿUbaydallāh b. Yaḥyā b. Khāqān, who was wazīr of al-Mutawakkil. They would carry out for ʿUbaydallāh whatever he ordered them to do. Al-Ḥasan b. Makhlad was responsible for the Bureau of Estates (*dīwān al-ḍiyāʿ*) and Mūsā for the Bureau of Taxation (*dīwān al-kharāj*).

Najāḥ b. Salamah wrote a note to al-Mutawakkil concerning al-Ḥasan and Mūsā, in which he reported that they had acted in bad faith and had been derelict in their duties, and that he would expropriate from them forty million dirhams [which they had allegedly embezzled].

Al-Mutawakkil invited Najāḥ to drink with him that evening. He said, "O Najāḥ, may God forsake whoever forsakes you, come to me early tomorrow so that I may turn al-Ḥasan and Mūsā over to you." Early in the morning Najāḥ organized his men, saying, "So-and-so, you seize al-Ḥasan; so-and-so, you seize Mūsā."

When Najāḥ came to al-Mutawakkil early in the morning, he came across ʿUbaydallāh. The latter had ordered that Najāḥ be kept away from the caliph. ʿUbaydallāh said to him, "O Abū al-Faḍl, take leave so that we and you can look into this matter, and let me give you advice that will redound to your benefit." Najāḥ asked, "What might it be?" ʿUbaydallāh replied, "I shall conciliate between you and the two of them (al-Ḥasan and Mūsā). Write a note stating that while you were drinking you divulged things

529. For al-Ḥārith b. (Muḥammad) Abī Usāmah, who died in 282 (895–96) at the age of ninety-six, see Khaṭīb, *Ta'rīkh Baghdād,* VIII, 218–19; Sezgin, *GAS,* I, 160.

that you would rather reconsider. And I shall settle the matter with the Commander of the Faithful."

Thus ʿUbayadallāh tricked Najāḥ into writing a note as he requested.[530] [When Najāḥ had written a note in his own hand, ʿUbaydallāh took it with him. He then summoned al-Ḥasan and Mūsā. Informing them of the situation, he ordered them to draft two million dīnārs to the credit of Najāḥ and his colleagues. They did so, and ʿUbaydallāh took both notes] and brought them to al-Mutawakkil.

ʿUbaydallāh said, "O Commander of the Faithful, Najāḥ has reconsidered what he said yesterday. And this is a note of Mūsā and al-Ḥasan stating that they guarantee [to pay Najāḥ] the [1442] amount that they have stipulated. Take the sum which they guarantee, but be considerate to them and take approximately what Najāḥ guaranteed to give you from them."[531]

Al-Mutawakkil was delighted and consented to do as ʿUbaydallāh had suggested. He said, "Hand Najāḥ over to the two of them." They took him along as they departed, ordering that his cap be removed from his head. It was silk. He was chilled as a result, and said, "Woe to you, O Ḥasan, I am cold." Ḥasan ordered that his cap be put back on his head. Mūsā then went with Najāḥ to the Bureau of Taxation.

They then went to Najāḥ's two sons, Abū al-Faraj and Abū Muḥammad. Abū al-Faraj was seized, and Abū Muḥammad b. bt. Ḥasan b. Shunayf fled.[532] And they also seized his secretary, Isḥāq

---

530. The bracketed material that follows is from Ibn al-Athīr, *Kāmil,* VII, 57, 11.5–8. The segment was omitted in our text due to homoeoteleuton. *Fragmenta,* 553, adds that ʿUbaydallāh threatened al-Ḥasan and Mūsā that, if they failed to comply with his advice, he would turn them over to the caliph, who would have them killed. The threat appears in the second version of the story, which is related by Ṭabarī below.

531. The drift of this account is that Najāḥ was tricked into writing a note informing the caliph that he did not take money from Mūsā and al-Ḥasan, but they wrote a note stating that he did, and thus *he* appears to be an embezzler. ʿUbaydallāh suggests that the caliph not take from Mūsā and al-Ḥasan all the money that Najāh was to receive from them but the lower sum that he was to turn over to the caliph. According to Ashtor, *Prix,* 40, in the mid-tenth century the ratio of dirhams to dīnārs was 25:1.

532. Najāḥ had two sons. The first, called here Abū al-Faraj, is named Muḥammad on 1443. The second son, called here Abū Muḥammad b. bt. Ḥasan b. Shunayf, is named Aḥmad on 1443.

b. Saʿd b. Masʿūd al-Quṭrabbulī, and ʿAbdallāh b. Makhlad, known as Ibn al-Bawwāb—he was devoted to Najāḥ.

Najāḥ and his son (Abū al-Faraj) confessed to al-Ḥasan and Mūsā to having about 140,000 dīnārs, aside from the value of their palaces, furnishings, and income-producing properties[533] in Sāmarrā and Baghdad, and from the many estates they had.

Al-Mutawakkil ordered that all this be confiscated. Najāḥ was repeatedly beaten with whips, about 200 lashes, in a place other than that used for flogging. He was smothered and suffocated. Mūsā al-Furāniq and al-Maʿlūf suffocated him.[534]

Al-Ḥārith, however, maintained that Najāḥ's testicles were
[1443] crushed until he died. He expired on Monday, 22 Dhū al-Qaʿdah, of this year (February 18, 860). Al-Mutawakkil ordered that he be washed and buried, and he was interred at night.[535]

Najāḥ's son Muḥammad, ʿAbdallāh b. Makhlad, and Isḥāq b. Saʿd were beaten about fifty-five stripes. Isḥāq confessed to having 50,000 dīnārs, and ʿAbdallāh b. Makhlad confessed to having 15,000 or, it is said, 20,000 dīnārs. Najāḥ's son Aḥmad b. bt. Ḥasan had fled. Aḥmad was caught after the death of Najāḥ and imprisoned in the Bureau [of Taxation]. All the furnishings in the palace of Najāḥ and his son Abū al-Faraj were seized; their palaces and estates were confiscated wherever they were; their families were evicted. His representative in the region of the Sawād was seized—he was Ibn ʿAyyāsh. The latter confessed to having 20,000 dīnārs. Ibn ʿAyyāsh sent to Mecca, seeking al-Ḥasan b. Sahl b. Nūḥ al-Ahwāzī and Ḥasan b. Yaʿqūb al-Baghdādī. Because of Ibn ʿAyyāsh a group of people were seized and imprisoned.

It is reported that the reason for Najāḥ's demise was different from what we have mentioned. Accordingly, he was antagonistic toward ʿUbaydallāh b. Yaḥyā b. Khāqān. Now, ʿUbaydallāh had great influence with al-Mutawakkil and was in charge of the wa-

533. Text: *wa-mustaghallātihimā.* Ms. O *wa-mustaʿmalātihimā.* Glossarium, CCCLXXVII: "products," citing Yāqūt, *Muʿjam,* II, 603.

534. Mss. C and O: without points and add *ibn* after Mūsā. Ṣūlī omits *ibn.* The note identifies him with Mūsā b. ʿAbdallāh al-Iṣfahānī (citing Ibn Khallikān; see *Wafayāt,* III, 59). *Furāniq* (< Pers. *parwanak*) means "courier, messenger." Al-Maʿlūf is apparently identical with Jaʿfar al-Maʿlūf, mentioned below on 1444.

535. See also Ibn Khallikān, *Wafayāt,* III, 59, where this account is given.

zīrate and all of its administrative functions. Najāḥ was in charge of [the Bureau of] the Public Registry (*tawqīʿ al-ʿāmmah*).

When al-Mutawakkil decided to build the Jaʿfarī [Palace], Najāḥ said to him—he was among the boon companions—"Commander of the Faithful, I shall name some men for you. Turn them over to me so that I can expropriate money from them with [1444] which you can build your administrative center, because you need to lay out quite a sum for its construction." He replied, "Name them." Najāḥ then sent a note in which he mentioned: (1) Mūsā b. ʿAbd al-Malik; (2) ʿĪsā b. Farrukhānshāh, deputy of al-Ḥasan b. Makhlad;[536] (3) al-Ḥasan b. Makhlad; (4) Zaydān b. Ibrāhīm, deputy of Mūsā b. ʿAbd al-Malik; (5) ʿUbaydallāh b. Yaḥyā and his two brothers (6) ʿAbdallāh b. Yaḥyā and (7) Zakariyyā'; (8) Maymūn b. Ibrāhīm;[537] (9) Muḥammad b. Mūsā al-Munajjim[538] and his brother (10) Aḥmad b. Mūsā; (11) ʿAlī b. Yaḥyā b. Abī Manṣūr;[539] and (12) Jaʿfar al-Maʿlūf, accountant (*mustakhrij*) of the Bureau of Taxation, and others—about twenty men.

This favorably impressed al-Mutawakkil, who bade Najāḥ to come early the next day. When al-Mutawakkil arose, he had no doubts about this. But ʿUbaydallāh b. Yaḥyā argued with al-Mutawakkil, saying, "O Commander of the Faithful, Najāḥ wants to assault every single secretary and army commander. Who, O Commander of the Faithful, will perform the administrative functions?"

---

536. Zambaur, *Manuel*, 6, says that ʿĪsā was wazīr for al-Muʿtazz in 252 (866–67), but this is not mentioned by Ṭabarī, according to whom he was head of the Bureau of Taxation; III, 1513 (Saliba, 13), 1640 (Saliba, 105); see Saliba, Index, 177.

537. According to Ibn al-Nadīm, *Fihrist*, 271, he was a secretary in charge of correspondence under al-Mutawakkil; Hilāl al-Ṣābī, *Wuzarā'*, 203–04, 250; Sourdel, *Vizirat*, 338, 738.

538. Text: Muḥammad b. Mūsā. Ms. C: Mūsā b. Mūsā; Ms. O: Muḥammad b. ʿĪsā. Muḥammad b. Mūsā was one of the famous Banū Mūsā b. Shākir. See, for instance, Ibn al-Nadīm, *Fihrist*, 645–46; Sezgin, *GAS*, V, 246; VI, 147–48. Muḥammad had two brothers, Aḥmad (mentioned here) and Ḥasan. Muḥammad, the eldest, died in 259 (872–73).

539. ʿAlī b. Yaḥyā, of the famous Banū al-Munajjim, was a protégé of Muḥammad b. Isḥāq b. Ibrāhīm and a close associate of al-Fatḥ b. Khāqān, for whom he assembled a great library. He was a leading boon companion of al-Mutawakkil; Ibn al-Nadīm, *Fihrist*, 255, 313; Yāqūt, *Irshād*, V, 459–77; Ibn Khallikān, *Wafayāt*, II, 312–13; Stern, "*Chronography*," 437–38.

Najāḥ came early the next day, and 'Ubaydallāh let him take his place in his audience hall (*majlis*), but did not present him to the caliph.

'Ubaydallāh had Mūsā b. 'Abd al-Malik and al-Ḥasan b. Makhlad presented and said to them, "If Najāḥ gets to see the Commander of the Faithful, he will turn the two of you over to him, and he will kill you and confiscate your property. So write a note to the Commander of the Faithful in which you stipulate that you guarantee [to pay] two million dīnārs."

They wrote a note in their hand, and 'Ubaydallāh b. Yaḥyā brought it to al-Mutawakkil.[540] 'Ubaydallāh began to go back and forth among the Commander of the Faithful, Najāḥ, Mūsā b. 'Abd
[1445] al-Malik and al-Ḥasan b. Makhlad. He kept going in and out [of the caliphal audience], keeping an eye on Mūsā and al-Ḥasan.[541]

Then 'Ubaydallāh brought Mūsā and al-Ḥasan in to al-Mutawakkil, and they guaranteed this amount. He went out with the two of them and handed Najāḥ over to them. All the people, including the inner circle of notables and the commoners, as well as Mūsā and al-Ḥasan, were certain that they two and 'Ubaydallāh b. Yaḥyā would be handed over to Najāḥ in view of the discussion between Najāḥ and al-Mutawakkil.

They seized Najāḥ. Mūsā b. 'Abd al-Malik supervised his torture and imprisoned him in the Bureau of Taxation in Sāmarrā and flogged him severely.

Al-Mutawakkil ordered that his secretary Isḥāq b. Sa'd—he supervised his private affairs and the estates of some(one) of his sons—be fined 51,000 dīnārs. He was made to swear an oath on this.

Al-Mutawakkil said, "He appropriated from me fifty dīnārs in the days of al-Wāthiq, when he replaced 'Umar b Faraj, until he freed my pay allotments. Take one thousand dīnārs for every dīnār [he appropriated] and then another thousand beyond that, just as he seized an exorbitant amount of money."

Isḥāq b. Sa'd was imprisoned, and three installment payments were arranged for him.[542] He was not released until he paid

540. The words "to al-Mutawakkil" are added in Ms. O.

541. Ms. O omits this sentence, which is not entirely clear.

542. *Wa-nujjima 'alayhi fī thalāthati anjum.* For the sense of "to discharge a debt through payments," see Glossarium, DII.

17,000 dīnārs in cash and only after guarantors were secured from him for the balance.

ʿAbdallāh b. Makhlad was seized and fined 17,000 dīnārs. ʿUbaydallāh [b.] al-Ḥusayn b. Ismāʿīl[543]—he was one of the chamberlains of al-Mutawakkil—and ʿAttāb b. ʿAttāb were directed by a letter of al-Mutawakkil to flog Najāḥ fifty times if he did not confess and deliver the wealth he was reported to own.[544] He flogged him and then repeated the same a second and third day. [1446]

Najāḥ said, "Inform the Commander of the Faithful that I am dying." Mūsā b. ʿAbd al-Malik ordered Jaʿfar al-Maʿlūf, along with an officer from the Bureau of Taxation, to crush his genitals, [which they did] until he turned cold and died.

Mūsā rode early in the morning to al-Mutawakkil and informed him that Najāḥ had died. Al-Mutawakkil said to Mūsā and al-Ḥasan, "I want my money which you two guaranteed." They used artful means to confiscate all [Najāḥ's] property and that of his sons. They imprisoned Abū al-Faraj—he was responsible for the Bureau of Control of Estates on behalf of Abū Ṣāliḥ b. Yazdād[545]—confiscated all his possessions and all his landed property, and assigned his estates over to the Commander of the Faithful, seizing what they did from his companions.

Al-Mutawakkil would often say to them when he was drinking, "Bring my secretary back to me; if not, bring the money." He assigned the Bureau of Public Registry[546] to ʿUbaydallāh b. Yaḥyā, and appointed as deputy over it his cousin, Yaḥyā b. ʿAbd al-Raḥmān b. Khāqān. Mūsā b. ʿAbd al-Malik and al-Ḥasan b. Makhlad were dilatory in this matter, and al-Mutawakkil kept demanding from them the money that they had guaranteed from Najāḥ.

Only a small amount of the money had been delivered before Mūsā b. ʿAbd al-Malik rode out accompanying al-Muntaṣir from the Jaʿfarī [Palace]. Al-Muntaṣir was heading for Sāmarrā to his

543. Ms. O: ʿAbdallāh b. al-Ḥasan.

544. For this translation of *mā wuṣifa ʿalayhi,* see Glossarium, DLVII.

545. Abū Ṣāliḥ al-Marwazī b. Yazdād ʿAbdallāh b. Muḥammad later became wazīr under al-Mustaʿīn in 249 (863–64); III, 1513 (Saliba, 13); Zambaur, *Manuel,* 6.

546. Text: *dīwān tawqīʿ al-ʿāmmah.* O: *dīwān al-tawqīʿ al-ʿāmmah.*

residence in the Jawsaq [Palace].[547] Mūsā arrived there with him [and stayed for][548] an hour, and then departed, heading back. While he was on the way, he cried out to someone who was with
[1447] him, "Grab me." They rushed to him, and he fell paralyzed into their arms. He was carried to his residence. He held out that day and night and then died.

Al-Mutawakkil appointed ʿUbaydallāh b. Yaḥyā also over the Bureau of Taxation. He appointed as deputy Aḥmad b. Isrāʾīl, secretary of al-Muʿtazz. Aḥmad was also his deputy over the secretariat of al-Muʿtazz.

Al-Qiṣāfī recited:[549]

Najāḥ did not fear the assault of fate,
Until his power passed to Mūsā and al-Ḥasan.

He came wresting the benefits of the noble,
And he left deprived of purse and limb.

In this year, in Rajab (October 2–31, 859), Bukhtīshūʿ the physician was flogged one hundred and fifty times, and then shackled in irons and incarcerated in the Maṭbaq [Prison].

In this year, the Byzantines raided Samosata,[550] killing and

547. The Jawsaq al-Khāqānī was named for al-Fatḥ b. Khāqān. Yāqūt, *Muʿjam,* III, 17, says that al-Mutawakkil spent 500,000 dirhams on it. See Herzfeld, *Samarra,* 94–95, 104, 115, 132; Creswell, *Early Muslim Architecture,* II, 232ff., and figure 194; Rogers, "Samarra," 147. It is identified with the Caliphal Palace; see above, n. 125.

548. The note in the Leiden edition suggests that *aqāma* be added here.

549. For Abū al-Fayḍ ʿAmr b. Naṣr al-Qiṣāfī, panegyrist of Hārūn and his successors, d. ca. 247 (861–62), see Sezgin, *GAS,* II, 526. Ms. C: al-Qunāfī; Ṣūlī: al-Quḍāfī al-Shāʿir. Ṣūlī omits the last verse and adds four others:

His havoc befell people, crushing them
As though he were a rough-taloned lion.

Oppression has removed him humbly from this world
For it casts one from power to impotence.

He did not thank God for the health and benevolence
That embraced him.

Ingratitude brings one
From joy to misery and grief.

550. Text: Sumaysāṭ. Ms. O: Simshāṭ; Ms. C: Shimshāṭ. Ibn al-Athīr, *Kāmil,* VII, 57; Abū al-Maḥāsin, *Nujūm,* II, 320: Sumaysāṭ. See above, n. 468. On the events, see Vasiliev, *Byzance,* I, 235f., 319f.

taking captive about 500 persons. ʿAlī b. Yaḥyā al-Armanī led the summer expedition.

The inhabitants of Lulon prevented their governor from entering the town for thirty days.[551] The Byzantine ruler sent to them [1448] a Patrikios who was to guarantee each of them 1,000 dīnārs if they would deliver Lulon to him. They let the Patrikios come up to them, and then, once they were given their back allotments and what they wished, they handed over Lulon and the Patrikios to Balkājūr in Dhū al-Ḥijjah (February 27–March 27, 860).[552] The Patrikios whom the Byzantine emperor dispatched to them was called "Logothete."[553]

When the inhabitants of Lulon handed him over to Balkājūr, [he brought the Patrikios to al-Mutawakkil.][554] Others say that ʿAlī b. Yaḥyā al-Armanī brought him to al-Mutawakkil. Al-Mutawakkil handed him over to al-Fatḥ b. Khāqān, and he proposed Islam to him, but the Patrikios refused. When they said, "We'll kill you," he responded, "You know better." The Byzantine ruler wrote offering to exchange him for 1,000 Muslims.

Leading the pilgrimage this year was Muḥammad b. Sulaymān b. ʿAbdallāh b. Muḥammad b. Ibrāhīm al-Imām.[555] He was known as al-Zaynabī, and he was governor of Mecca.

The Nayrūz of al-Mutawakkil, which the supervisors of the land tax cooperated with him in postponing, fell this year on Saturday, 11 Rabīʿ I (June 16, 859), corresponding to 17 Ḥazīrān (June 17) and 28 Ordīwihisht.[556]

---

551. Lulon, Arabic Lu'lu'ah, was strategically located, having a fortress that overlooked the northern end of a pass that led over the Cilician Gates, from Podandos to Tyana; Le Strange, *Lands*, 134, 135, 139, 150. Lulon was under Byzantine control.

552. Balkājūr was the commander for the Muslims.

553. Text: Lughuthīṭ. For the title Logothete, see Bury, *History*, 210; *idem*, *Imperial Administrative System*, 111.

554. The words "he brought the Patrikios to al-Mutawakkil" are added from Ibn al-Athīr, *Kāmil*, VII, 57: *fa-sayyarahu ilā al-Mutawakkil.*

555. See Zambaur, *Manuel*, 20.

556. Nayrūz (Nawrūz) is the first day of the Persian solar year on which the land tax (*kharāj*) was collected. As the intercalation of one day per four years was disregarded under Islam, the date of Nawrūz and collection of the *kharāj* continued to advance so that by the time of al-Mutawakkil it fell two months early, permitting tax agents to collect taxes prematurely before crops were harvested. The new date fixed by al-Mutawakkil was meant to correspond with the old time. Bīrūnī, *Chronology*, 32, says that the fiscal reform of al-Mutawakkil took place in

Al-Buḥturī al-Ṭāʾī recited:[557]

The Day of Nayrūz has returned to the time
    That Ardashīr enacted.

Muḥarram, 243 (April 30, 857–May 29, 857). Bīrūnī notes that the planned reform was not actually put into effect, so that al-Muʿtaḍid had to address himself to the problem later. See Ṭabarī, III, 2143 (Rosenthal, *Return,* 19 and n. 103). Yāqūt, *Irshād,* II, 128–29, relates an account, going back to Balādhurī, concerning the letter, drafted by Ibrāhīm b. al-ʿAbbās al-Ṣūlī, announcing the reform. He had made an error that was detected by the astronomers ʿAlī b. Yaḥyā al-Munajjim and Muḥammad b. Mūsā. Ordīwihisht stands for Ordībihist (Ordībehesht), the second month of the Persian (Zoroastrian) calendar.

557. The famous poet Buḥturī died 284 (897–98); *EI*², s.v.; Sezgin, *GAS,* II, 560. He was companion and panegyrist of al-Mutawakkil and of later caliphs. Cairo edition cites his *Dīwān,* II, 57. Bīrūnī (see previous note) cites three additional verses of the poem.

The Events of the Year 246

(March 28, 860–January 16, 861)

One of the events was the summer expedition of ʿUmar b. ʿAbdallāh al-Aqṭaʿ. He brought back 7,000 head of livestock.[558] There was also the raid of Karbeas, who brought back 5,000 head of livestock. And then there was the raid of al-Faḍl b. Qārin.[559] He conquered the fortress of Anṭālya,[560] traveling by sea in twenty vessels. [1449]

There was the raid of Balkājūr; he brought back livestock and captives.

Finally, there was the summer expedition of ʿAlī b. Yaḥyā al-Armanī. He brought back 5,000 head of livestock and about 10,000 horses, mares, and donkeys.

---

558. Ms. O: 15,000 heads.

559. Balādhurī, *Futūḥ*, 159, says that al-Faḍl b. Qārin was governor (*ʿāmil*) of Ḥimṣ. In 248 (862–63) he was again sent to put down a rebellion there (III, 1508, Saliba, 7). He was eventually killed, while he was governor, by the inhabitants of Ḥimṣ, supported by the Banū Kalb, in 250 (864–65); III, 1533 (Saliba, 27).

560. Mss. Anṭākiyah, that is, Antioch. So Ibn al-Athīr, *Kāmil*, VII, 59, and Ibn Khaldūn, *ʿIbar*, III, 589. ʿAynī: Anṭālyah. Anṭālyah (Greek Attaleia) is a town on the southern coast of Anatolia; *EI*², s.v. Anṭālyah is easily confused with the more common Anṭākiyah. As Antioch is inland, and this was a sea raid, it is clear that Anṭālyah is meant.

In this year, al-Mutawakkil withdrew to the administrative center that he built in al-Māḥūzah and began to reside there on the Day of the ʿĀshūrāʾ (February 25, 861).

In this year, there was the prisoner exchange in Ṣafar (April 27–May 25, 860) administered by ʿAlī b. Yaḥyā al-Armanī.[561] Two thousand three hundred and sixty-seven persons were exchanged. Some authorities say that the prisoner exchange this year was carried out in Jumādā I (July 24–August 22, 860).

The following is reported on the authority of Naṣr b. al-Azhar al-Shīʿī, who was the emissary of al-Mutawakkil to the Byzantine ruler for the prisoner exchange:[562] When I went to Constantinople, I visited [Emperor] Michael's palace with my black robe, sword, dagger, and cap. I had a discussion with the maternal uncle of the ruler, Bardas, who was in charge of the affairs of the realm.[563] They refused to let me enter with my sword and black robe, whereupon I said that I was leaving, which I did. But I was
[1450] brought back while I was on my way. I had gifts with me, including about 1,000 musk bags, silk garments, much saffron, and exquisite pieces. The emperor had permitted delegations from Burjān to attend and others who had come to him.[564] The gifts that I brought were carried in to him.

When I was admitted into his presence, he was on an elevated throne,[565] with the Patrikioi standing around him. I greeted him and then sat down at the edge of the large dais where a seat had been prepared for me.[566] I placed the gifts before him.

In front of Michael there were three interpreters: a valet

561. On this prisoner exchange, and the mission of Naṣr b. al-Azhar, see Vasiliev, *Byzance,* I, 237ff., 320ff.; Bury, *History,* 279–81.

562. See also the description in Bar Hebraeus, *Chronography,* 144–45.

563. The Mss. are unpointed. The text has *B-t-r-n-ā-s*; ʿAynī: *B-t-r-y-ā-s.* Petronas was a brother of Theodora. Bury, *History,* 279, suggests that Bardas is intended. This makes sense in view of the fact that Bardas, also a brother of Theodora, was by 861 virtually the supreme authority in the empire, wielding power in his nephew's name. Bury suggests that Naṣr had written in his report "his uncle" and Ṭabarī added the explanatory "Petronas." But cf. Vasiliev, *Byzance,* I, 238, n. 1.

564. Burjān is the area of the Bulgars; *EI*², s.v. Bulghar; Minorsky, *Ḥudūd,* Index, 488.

565. Text: *fa-idhā huwa ʿalā sarīr fawqa sarīr,* lit. "he was on a throne above a throne." The bottom *sarīr* must have been a dais. For *sarīr* ("seat, bench, sofa, royal seat/throne, bier"), see Sadan, *Mobilier,* 32ff.

566. That is, at the edge of the platform or elevation on which the royal throne was placed.

(*ghulām farrāsh*) of Masrūr al-Khādim,[567] a page of ʿAbbās b. Saʿīd al-Jawharī, and a veteran interpreter of his named Sergius.[568] They asked me how they should translate my words to him, and I answered, "Don't add anything to what I say to you." They set about translating what I was saying. The emperor accepted my gifts and did not give orders that any of them be handed on to anyone else. He was congenial to me and honored me, and had a house prepared for me close by him. I went out and took up residence there.

Inhabitants from Lulon approached the emperor expressing their desire to convert to Christianity and join up with him. They sent along two Muslims from there to serve as hostages.

Naṣr said: Michael disregarded me for about four months until he received a letter about the revolt of the inhabitants of Lulon, their seizing his emissaries, and the Arab conquest of the town. The Byzantines resumed speaking with me, and the negotiations between us concerning prisoner exchange led to the surrender of all the prisoners in their possession and all those whom I brought. There were a little over one thousand. And all the prisoners who were in their hands came to more than two thousand, including twenty women, along with ten children.

They accepted my request for a mutual oath. I asked that the emperor's maternal uncle swear, whereupon he did so on behalf of Michael. I said, "O king, your maternal uncle has sworn an [1451]
oath to me. Does this oath bind you?" He responded affirmatively with a nod.[569] I did not hear him utter a word from the time I entered Byzantine territory until I left. Only the interpreter would speak, and he would listen and then nod yes or no without talking. His maternal uncle administered his affairs.

I then left him, along with the prisoners, who were in excellent condition. When we came to the place for the prisoner exchange, we released our respective groups of prisoners. More than two

567. A Masrūr al-Khādim al-Kabīr first appears at the time of Hārūn al-Rashīd; see Crone, *Slaves on Horses*, 192–93; and see Ṭabarī, III, 1166 (Marin, *Reign*, 4). According to Jahshiyārī, *Wuzarā'*, 254, he survived until the time of al-Mutawakkil. See above, n. 242.

568. Text: Surḥūn. Read perhaps Sarjūn, that is, Sergius; Vasiliev, *Byzance*, I, 238, n. 3.

569. For *qāla bi-ra'sihi* in the sense of gesturing, see Glossarium, CDXXXVII, where Ṭabarī, III, 1251, is also cited (Marin, *Reign*, 72).

thousand Muslims came into our hands, including a few who had converted to Christianity. The Byzantines received a few more than a thousand.

A number [of Muslim prisoners] had converted to Christianity. The emperor said to them, "I will not accept you until you reach the site of the prisoner exchange. Whoever wishes me to receive him into Christianity should return from this place. If not, let him rejoin his companions and go off with them."

Most of those who had converted to Christianity were inhabitants of the Maghrib. The majority had converted in Constantinople. There were two goldsmiths who had converted, and they were friendly toward the [other] prisoners. Only seven Muslims remained in Byzantine territory of those whom the [Byzantine] ruler had taken captive. Five had been brought from Sicily, and I paid their ransom so that they could be sent back there. Two men were hostages from Lulon, whom I left, saying, "Accept these two,[570] for they wish to convert to Christianity."

The inhabitants of Baghdad had rain this year for twenty-one days in Sha'bān (October 21–November 18, 860) and Ramaḍān (November 19–December 18). It rained so much that the grass grew beyond the roofs of houses.

[1452] Al-Mutawakkil performed the prayer of Breaking the Fast this year in al-Ja'fariyyah. 'Abd al-Ṣamad b. Mūsā prayed in its Friday Mosque, but no one led public prayer in Sāmarrā.

In this year, information was received concerning a neighborhood in the area of Balkh belonging to the *dihqāns*, where it rained pure blood.[571]

Leading the pilgrimage this year was Muḥammad b. Sulaymān al-Zaynabī.

In this year, Muḥammad b. 'Abdallāh b. Ṭāhir went on the pilgrimage, and supervised the events of the festival season.

The inhabitants of Sāmarrā observed the Day of Sacrifice this year (10 Dhū al-Ḥijjah [February 25, 861]) on Monday, on the basis of sighting the new moon, and the inhabitants of Mecca observed it on Tuesday.

---

570. Text: *uqtuluhumā* = "Kill these two." Addenda, DCCLXXVI: *iqbaluhumā*, which is followed here.

571. Balkh was the principal city in Khurāsān. The *dihqāns* were in this period hereditary rulers of a given area; Minorsky, *Ḥudud*, 523; *EI*[2], s.v. Dihḳān.

The Events of the Year 247[572]
(July 5, 861–June 22, 862)

One of the events was the murder of al-Mutawakkil.

The Reason for al-Mutawakkil's Murder and How It Took Place

Abū Jaʿfar said:[573] It was reported to me that the reason for this was that al-Mutawakkil ordered that letters be drawn up concerning the confiscation of Waṣīf's estates in Iṣbahān and the Jabal so as to grant them as fiefs to al-Fatḥ b. Khāqān. The appropriate letters were written, and they were transmitted to the [Office of the] Seal to be executed[574] on Thursday, 5 Shaʿbān (October 14, 861). Waṣīf learned of this and then confirmed that this was indeed al-Mutawakkil's order.

Al-Mutawakkil planned to lead the public prayer on the last Friday of Ramaḍān (December 5, 861). On the first day of Ramaḍān

572. Text: *wa-thalāthīn.* Addenda, DCCLXXVI: *wa-arbaʿīn.*

573. That is, Ṭabarī. The following account is translated by Sauvaget, *Historiens,* 24–31 ("Une tragédie de palais"); and see pp. 45–50 for a translation of Masʿūdī's account.

574. Text: *ʿalā an tataqaddama.* Cairo edition (Mss. A and D): *ʿalā an tunfadha.*

(November 8, 861) it became common knowledge that the Commander of the Faithful would lead the public prayer on the last Friday of the month. The people assembled for this purpose,
[1453] thronging together. The Hāshimites left Baghdad [for Sāmarrā] to present petitions to him and to speak with him when he went out riding.[575]

When Friday arrived, al-Mutawakkil decided to ride to the prayer service, whereupon ʿUbaydallāh b. Yaḥyā and al-Fatḥ b. Khāqān said to him, "O Commander of the Faithful, the people have assembled, and there are many, from your family and others, some registering grievances and some petitioning. As the Commander of the Faithful is complaining of dejection and indisposition,[576] if he wishes to order that one of the heirs apparent lead the prayer, and that we should all support him, let him do so."

The caliph replied that he agreed and ordered al-Muntaṣir to lead the prayer.

When al-Muntaṣir rose to ride to the prayer service, ʿUbaydallāh and al-Fatḥ said, "O Commander of the Faithful, we have an idea—but the Commander of the Faithful is more perceptive [than we]." He asked, "What is it? Propose it to me." They replied, "O Commander of the Faithful, give orders that Abū ʿAbdallāh al-Muʿtazz bi-llāh lead the public prayer, so as to honor him on this exalted day." The members of his household and all the notables gathered together, for God has caused him to reach his appointed time.[577] Abū Jaʿfar said: A child had been born to al-Muʿtazz a day before this.

Thus al-Mutawakkil ordered al-Muʿtazz to ride out and lead the public prayer, while al-Muntaṣir remained in his residence, which was in al-Jaʿfariyyah.[578] This only exasperated al-Muntaṣir further. When al-Muʿtazz had completed his sermon, ʿUbaydallāh b. Yaḥyā and al-Fatḥ b. Khāqān rose in his honor and kissed his hands and feet. Having finished praying, al-Muʿtazz departed, the two leaving with him, along with the notables, in the caliphal

---

575. Text: *rakaba*. Leiden Ms. C: *rākib*.

576. Text: *wa-waʿkah*. Leiden Mss. *w-ʿ-l-a*. Cairo edition, Mss. A and D; Ibn al-Athīr, *Kāmil*, VII, 60: *wa-ʿillah bihi*.

577. Text: *balagha 'llāhu bihi*; see Lane, s.v. *balagha*, I, 250a.

578. Text: *fī manzilihi wa-kāna bi-l-Jaʿfariyyah*. Ms. O: *bi-dārihi fī al-Jaʿfariyyah*.

procession. He marched with the insignias before him, until he was admitted into his father's presence, 'Ubaydallāh and al-Fatḥ [1454]
accompanying him.

Dāwūd b. Muḥammad b. Abī al-ʿAbbās al-Ṭūsī, who entered with him, said, "O Commander of the Faithful, permit me to say something." He replied, "Speak." Dāwūd then said, "By God, O Commander of the Faithful, I have known al-Amīn, al-Ma'mūn, al-Muʿtaṣim, and al-Wāthiq bi-llāh as well. But, by God, I have never witnessed anyone occupy a pulpit who was superior in imposing stature, spontaneous speech, sonorous voice, mellifluous tone, and eloquence to al-Muʿtazz bi-llāh. May God give him power, O Commander of the Faithful, by your abiding survival, and may God give you and us pleasure by giving him life." Al-Mutawakkil replied, "May God let you hear glad tidings and delight us through you."

On Sunday—this was the Day of Breaking the Fast (December 8, 861)—al-Mutawakkil felt weak and requested that al-Muntaṣir be given orders to lead the public prayer. 'Ubaydallāh b. Yaḥyā b. Khāqān then said to him, "O Commander of the Faithful, the people had anticipated seeing the Commander of the Faithful on Friday and thronged together, but the Commander of the Faithful did not ride out. We fear that if he does not ride out [this time] people will spread alarming news about his illness. It would be best for the Commander of the Faithful to cheer his friends and daunt his enemies by doing so. Al-Mutawakkil then ordered them to make the necessary preparations for him to ride out. He did so and led the public prayer, and then turned back to his residence, remaining there on this day and the next without inviting any of his boon companions.

It is reported that, when he rode out on the Day of Breaking the Fast, lines had been formed for him for about four *mīl* (eight km.).[579] The people passed before him on foot, and he led the public prayer. He returned to his palace, took a handful of earth, and sprinkled it upon his head. Asked about this, he said, "I saw this mighty throng, and realizing that they were under my power, [1455]
I wished to humble myself before God."

579. The following section on al-Mutawakkil's murder is translated by Lewis, *Islam*, 30–34; see also the reference by Goldziher, *Muslim Studies*, II, 63.

On the day after the Day of Breaking the Fast, he did not invite any of his boon companions. On the third day, which was Tuesday, 3 Shawwāl (December 10, 861), in the morning, he was vivacious and cheerful. He commented, "I feel as though I have recovered my pulse."[580]

Al-Ṭayfūrī and Ibn al-Abrash, who were his physicians, said to him, "O Commander of the Faithful, may God determine what is good for you, go ahead [and summon your boon companions]."[581] And so he did. He craved camel meat and gave orders that it be served to him, and then grasped it with his own hand.

It is reported that Ibn al-Ḥafṣī the Singer attended the audience.[582] Ibn al-Ḥafṣī said: None of those who usually dined with him attended[583] except for me, ʿAthʿath,[584] Zunām,[585] and Bunān,[586] the page of Aḥmad b. Yaḥyā b. Muʿādh,[587] who came with al-Muntaṣir. Ibn al-Ḥafṣī went on: Al-Mutawakkil and al-

---

580. Text: *mass al-dam*. Masʿūdī, *Murūj*, VII, 274: *harakat al-dam*.

581. Al-Ṭayfūrī is Isrāʾīl b. Zakariyyāʾ al-Ṭayfūrī; Sezgin, *GAS*, III, 91, 97. An Ibn al-Ṭayfūrī is mentioned below, 1496 (p. 219), who may be his son. Al-Ṭayfūrī is a family name. The word *ṭayfūr* means "bird, winged insect"; Steingass, *Dictionary*, s.v. Al-Ṭayfūrī was the physician of al-Fatḥ b. Khāqān, who presented him to al-Mutawakkil; Ibn Abī Uṣaybiʿah, *ʿUyūn*, I, 107–8. For Ibrāhīm b. Ayyūb al-Abrash, son of the translator-physician Ayyūb al-Abrash, see *ibid.*, I, 158.

582. Ibn al-Ḥafṣī al-Mughannī was a court singer of al-Mutawakkil; Shābushtī, *Diyārāt*, 153; Neubauer, *Musiker*, 181. Ibn al-Zubayr, *Dhakhāʾir*, par. 143, mentions him among a group of singers.

583. Text: *mimman yaʾkul ḥāḍiran*. Cairo edition, Ms. A, adds *bayn yadayhi* after *yaʾkul*.

584. ʿAthʿath al-Aswad was a black slave of Muḥammad b. Yaḥyā b. Muʿādh. See also below, 1459–61; Ibn Ṭayfūr, *Baghdād*, 106; Iṣfahānī, *Aghānī*, XIII, 30–32; Shābushtī, *Diyārāt*, 154; Farmer, *History*, 140, 161.

585. Zunām al-Zamīr ("the Reed Pipe Player") was a musician who specialized on the *mizmār*, or reed pipe, and entertained in the courts of Hārūn, al-Muʿtaṣim, al-Wāthiq, and al-Mutawakkil; Ṭabarī, III, 1323 (Marin, *Reign*, 127); Shābushtī, Diyārāt, 154; Ibn al-Zubayr, *Dhakhāʾir*, par. 143; Farmer, *History*, 131; Neubauer, *Musiker*, 209–210; Stigelbauer, *Sängerinnen*, 67, 131.

586. Bunān b. ʿAmr al-Ḍārib, Raʾs al-Baghl ("Mule Head") was a court singer at the time of al-Mutawakkil and al-Muntaṣir and a close confidant of the latter; Farmer, *History*, 158; Neubauer, *Musiker*, 176; Stigelbauer, *Sängerinnen*, 144, 147–49.

587. Aḥmad b. Yaḥyā b. Muʿādh followed his father Yaḥyā b. Muʿādh as governor of the Jazīrah under al-Maʾmūn, in 206 (821–22); Ṭabarī, III, 1045, 1075 (Bosworth, *Reunification*, 109, 147); Ibn Ṭayfur, *Baghdad*, 18, 101; Iṣfahānī, *Aghānī*, V, 104. See also Crone, *Slaves on Horses*, 184. He was a brother of Isḥāq b. Yaḥyā b. Muʿādh; above, n. 14.

Fatḥ b. Khāqān were dining together; we were nearby, across from them. The boon companions were dispersed in their chambers, as he had not yet invited any of them. The Commander of the Faithful turned to me and said, "You and ʿAthʿath dine before me, and let Naṣr b. Saʿīd al-Jahbadh dine with you."[588] I responded, "O my lord, Naṣr eats me out of house and home, by God. How can he be [permitted to] sit with us?" The caliph responded, "Go on and eat, by my life." And so we ate. Then we let our hands drop opposite him.[589] The Commander of the Faithful turned and looked at us with our hands dropped. He asked, "What is wrong with you that you are not eating?" I replied, "My lord, what was in front of us is gone." He ordered that more food be added. So [the [1456]
food] that was before him was ladled to us.

Ibn al-Ḥafṣī said that the Commander of the Faithful was never more cheerful than on that day. He added: Al-Mutawakkil convened his court, summoning his boon companions and singers, who then attended. Qabīḥah, the mother of al-Muʿtazz,[590] gave him a green, silk ornamented gown (*miṭraf*).[591] People had never seen anything quite as beautiful. He kept staring at it with approval, admiring it greatly. He then ordered that it be cut in half and returned to her, commenting to her messenger, "It will remind her of me."[592] He went on, "By God, my heart tells me that I shall not wear it, and I don't wish anyone after me to do so. I ordered that it be torn only so that no one wears it after me." We said to him, "Our lord, this is a happy day, O Commander of the Faithful. God forbid that you should say this, our lord." Then he began to drink and revel while repeating,[593] "By God, I am leav-

---

588. Naṣr b. Saʿīd al-Jahbadh, a government banker, is apparently not the same as Naṣr b. Saʿīd al-Maghribī, an army commander, mentioned below, 1481 (pp. 205–6).

589. The expression *ʿallaqa yadayhi* means to drop one's hands at a banquet when nothing more remains on the table, as opposed to raising the hands as a sign of satisfaction; Glossarium, CCCLXXII.

590. For Qabīḥah, mother of al-Muʿtazz, see, for example, Iṣfahānī, *Aghānī*, Index, 550; Ibn al-Jawzī, *Muntaẓam*, V, 48 (d. 264/877/78). She was called Qabīḥah ("Ugly") by al-Mutawakkil by way of antiphrasis; see Thaʿālibī, *Laṭāʾif*, 63.

591. A *miṭraf* is a garment with a (silk) embroidered border on either end; Ahsan, *Social Life*, 40–41; *EI*², s.v. Libās, V, 737.

592. Text: *adhkaratnī bihi*. ʿAynī: *qul lahā tadhkurīnī bihi* = "Tell her to remember me by it."

593. For *lahija bi-qawl* in this sense, see Glossarium, CDLXXIII.

ing you soon." He went on being frivolous and merry until the evening.

It is reported by some(one) of the informants that al-Mutawakkil decided—he and al-Fatḥ—that they would have lunch with ʿAbdallāh b. ʿUmar al-Bāzyār[594] on Thursday, 5 Shawwāl (December 12, 861), and arrange for him to assassinate al-Muntaṣir, and kill Waṣīf and Bughā, as well as other Turkish commanders and notables.

According to what Ibn al-Ḥafṣī reported, al-Mutawakkil's
[1457] ridicule of his son al-Muntaṣir increased on Tuesday, one day earlier. He would alternately vilify him, get him drunk, give orders that he be cuffed, and threaten to have him killed.

It is reported on the authority of Hārūn b. Muḥammad b. Sulaymān al-Hāshimī: I was informed by some(one) of the women who was in the curtained-off area that al-Mutawakkil turned to al-Fatḥ and said to him, "I am acquitted of God and my relationship to the Messenger of God[595] if you do not cuff him," that is, al-Muntaṣir. Al-Fatḥ got up and cuffed him twice on the back of his neck. Al-Mutawakkil then said to those present, "All witness that I have deposed the Impatient One."[596] Then al-Mutawakkil turned to him and said, "I named you al-Muntaṣir ("the Victorious"), but because of your folly the people named you al-Muntaẓir ("the Expectant"), and now you have become al-Mustaʿjil ("the Impatient")."

Al-Muntaṣir replied, "O Commander of the Faithful, if you had given orders that I be decapitated, it would have been more bearable than your present treatment of me." The caliph said, "Let him drink." Al-Mutawakkil then ordered that supper be served, and it was brought in, this being in the middle of the night.

Al-Muntaṣir left the caliph's company and ordered Bunān, Aḥmad b. Yaḥyā's page, to accompany him. When he exited,

594. Shābushtī, *Diyārāt*, 7–8, mentions a *Muḥammad* b. ʿUmar al-Bāzyār as a boon companion of al-Mutawakkil. The cognomen al-Bāzyār means "the Falconer" or more correctly "the Ostreger"; see *EI*², s.v. Bayzara.

595. See Qurʾān 9:1.

596. Leiden text adds at this point: *Fa-qāla al-Muntaṣir, yā Amīr al-Muʾminīn* ("Al-Muntaṣir replied, "O Commander of the Faithful"). But no reply follows (see two lines below). Cairo edition indeed omits these words, retaining only the name "al-Muntaṣir," according to which we would translate ". . . the Impatient One, al-Muntaṣir" as a gloss (see also Ibn al-Athīr, *Kāmil*, VII, 62: *yaʿnī al-Muntaṣir*).

food[597] was placed in front of al-Mutawakkil, which he set about eating, devouring it while drunk. It is reported on the authority of Ibn al-Ḥafṣī that, when al-Muntaṣir went out to his chamber, he took the hand of Zurāfah,[598] saying to him, "Come with me." He replied, "My master, [I cannot, for] the Commander of the Faithful has not yet risen." Al-Muntaṣir then said, "The Commander of the Faithful has been overcome by wine, and right now [1458] Bughā and the boon companions are leaving. Now, I would like you to place the responsibility for your children with me. Ūtāmish[599] requested that I marry off his son to your daughter and your son to his daughter." Zurāfah said to him, "We are your slaves, my master. Command us as you please." Al-Muntaṣir took him by the hand and departed with him.[600]

Ibn al-Ḥafṣī said: Zurāfah had commented to me before this, "Take care, for the Commander of the Faithful has become drunk and is just now awaking. Tamrah[601] summoned me and requested that I ask you to come to him, and we shall all go to his chamber." I said to him, "I shall precede you to him." He added: Zurāfah had gone with al-Muntaṣir to his chamber.

Bunān, the page of Aḥmad b. Yaḥyā, reported that al-Muntaṣir said to him, "I have matched the son of Zurāfah with the daughter of Ūtāmish and the son of Ūtāmish with the daughter of Zurāfah." I said to al-Muntaṣir, "My master, where is the wed-

---

597. *Mā'idah,* the common word for "table," has the sense of "food" here (cf. English "spread"), as is evident from the word *ya'kuluhā*; see Glossarium, CDXCVII.

598. A fellow named after Zurāfah (or Zarāfah = "Giraffe") is mentioned by Ṭabarī, III, 1504 (Saliba, 4); and see 1511 (Saliba, 11), where he leads a contingent of *mawlās* against attackers of the Sāmarrā prison. Mas'ūdī, *Tanbīh,* 362, says that he was a chamberlain (*ḥājib*) of al-Mutawakkil. See also Shābushtī, *Diyārāt,* 7, 40.

599. Ūtāmish later became wazīr under al-Musta'īn; Ṭabarī, III, 1502–03 (Saliba, 2). He was an army commander and nephew of Bughā the Elder. According to Ya'qūbī, *Ta'rīkh,* II, 601–02, Ūtāmish, called '*ṣāḥib* al-Muntaṣir,' took part in the plot to assassinate al-Mutawakkil. The note *ad loc.* gives his teknonym as Abū Mūsā and his patronymic as Khaṭarkīn. Mas'ūdī, *Murūj,* VII, 273, says that he was a page of al-Wāthiq, and that he was close to al-Muntaṣir, who cultivated the Turks, for which reason al-Mutawakkil hated him. See also Tanūkhī, *Faraj,* 157, 159; Sourdel, *Vizirat,* 289–91, 294, 303, 673, 726, 735.

600. Al-Muntaṣir tried to cajole Zurāfah to be loyal to him, and thus he hoped to build up a coterie of followers.

601. Text: Tamrah ("date"). Ṣūlī and Iṣfahānī, *Aghānī,* XIV, 52 (cited in note *ad loc.*) have Thamarah ("fruit").

ding felicitation?[602] It will enhance the betrothal [ceremony]." He replied, "Tomorrow, God willing, for this evening has already passed." Zurāfah departed for the chamber of Tamrah, and when he entered he called for food, which was brought in. He had eaten just a bit when we heard a clamor and screaming, at which point we got up.

Bunān continued: It was only after Zurāfah left Tamrah's residence that Bughā met al-Muntaṣir, who asked, "What is this clamor?" Bughā replied, "It's all right, Commander of the Faithful," whereupon al-Muntaṣir inquired, "What are you saying, woe unto you?" To which Bughā answered, "May God magnify your reward [for the loss of] our lord, the Commander of the Faithful. He was the Lord's servant, and when God summoned him, al-Mutawakkil responded."

Bunān said: Al-Muntaṣir held audience and gave orders that the
[1459] door of the house and the audience hall in which al-Mutawakkil had been killed be locked. It and all the other doors were then locked. He thereafter sent a message to Waṣīf ordering him to bring al-Muʿtazz and al-Mu'ayyad on the pretext that the message was from al-Mutawakkil.

It is reported on the authority of ʿAthʿath that al-Mutawakkil called for the repast after al-Muntaṣir had risen and left along with Zurāfah. Bughā the Younger, called al-Sharābī, was standing at the curtain [of the harem]. That day it was the turn of Bughā the Elder's patrol to guard the palace. His deputy in the palace was his son Mūsā, who was the son of al-Mutawakkil's maternal aunt.[603] Bughā the Elder was then away in Samosata.

Bughā the Younger entered the audience hall and ordered the boon companions to leave for their chambers. Al-Fatḥ said to him that it was not yet time for their departure, and that the Commander of the Faithful had not yet risen. Bughā then replied, "The Commander of the Faithful ordered me not to let anyone

602. *Nithār* is the strewing of fruits, nuts, sugar, or money on a festive occasion; Lane, *Lexicon*, 2764. The well-known sprinkling of coins on the head of a poet is mentioned below, 1466 (p. 186).

603. Mūsā, son of Bughā the Elder, died in Muḥarram, 264 (September 13–October 12, 877), and was buried in Sāmarrā, according to Ibn al-Jawzī, *Muntaẓam*, V, 49; and see Tanūkhī, *Nishwār*, IV, 110; VIII, 79–82; Sourdel, *Vizirat*, Index, 775.

remain in the audience hall after [he had imbibed] seven [*raṭl*s], and he has already drunk fourteen." Al-Fatḥ still did not want the guests to rise. Bughā now said to him that the female relatives of the Commander of the Faithful were behind the curtain, and that he had become drunk, in which case they should get up and leave. They all went out except for al-Fatḥ, ʿAthʿath, and four of the caliph's personal servants (*khadam al-khāṣṣah*)—Shafīʿ, Faraj the Younger, Mu'nis, and Abū ʿĪsā Mārid al-Muḥrizī.[604]

ʿAthʿath said: The cook placed the repast before al-Mutawakkil, whereupon he set about eating voraciously, inviting Mārid to eat with him. The caliph was drunk, and when he finished part of his food he recommenced drinking.

ʿAthʿath reported that Abū Aḥmad b. al-Mutawakkil [al-Muwaffaq], brother of al-Mu'ayyad on his mother's side, was with them in the audience hall. He rose to go to the privy, but Bughā al-Sharābī had locked all the doors except the one that led to the riverbank, through which the group that was designated to kill the caliph entered. Seeing them, Abū Aḥmad bellowed at them, "What is this, low lifes!" At that point their swords were already [1460]
drawn.

ʿAthʿath went on: At the head of the band that set about to assassinate the caliph were Baghlūn, the Turk; Bāghir; Mūsā b. Bughā; Hārūn b. Suwārategin; and Bughā al-Sharābī.[605] When al-Mutawakkil heard the cry of Abū Aḥmad, he raised his head, and seeing the group he asked, "What is this, Bughā?" The latter replied, "These are the men of the patrol who have put up for the night at the door of my lord, the Commander of the Faithful." The group withdrew to the rear when they heard al-Mutawakkil

604. For *al-khadam al-khāṣṣah* (*khawāṣṣ*), see Hilāl al-Ṣābī, *Rusūm*, 27, 80, 91; tr. Salem, 26, 65, 73. *Inter alia* they stand around and behind the caliphal throne. A Mārid al-Khādim is mentioned, *op. cit.*, 73; tr., 60.

605. For Baghlūn the Turk, see *Fragmenta*, 556; Herzfeld, *Samarra*, 208. Bāghir, or Bāghar, the Turk, Abū Muḥammad, was killed in 251 (865–66; Ṭabarī, III, 1535–38 [Saliba, 28ff.]. The story connects with events in our text. See also Masʿūdī, *Murūj*, VII, 263, 268, 269, 271–72; *Tanbīh*, 362. Bāghir is often singled out as the main assassin. The assassination scene is described, for instance, by Yaʿqūbī, *Ta'rīkh*, II, 601–02; Masʿūdī, *Murūj*, VII, 271–74; *Tanbīh*, 362; *Fragmenta*, 554–57; Yāqūt, *Irshād*, VI, 117. Yaʿqūbī mentions among the assassins Bughā the Younger, Ūtāmish, Bāghir, Baghlūn, Wājin, Kindāsh (and two other names that are unclear). Masʿūdī, *Murūj*, VII, 271, mentions only Bāghir, accompanied by ten anonymous Turks.

speak to Bughā. Neither Wājin[606] and his companions nor the sons of Waṣīf were with them as yet.

ʿAthʿath reported: I heard Bughā say to them, "Low lifes, you are as good as dead, so at least die with honor," whereupon the group [of assassins] returned to the audience hall. Baghlūn rushed over to al-Mutawakkil and struck him with a blow upon his shoulder and his ear, cutting it off. Al-Mutawakkil cried out, "Hold it! May God cut off your hand!" Then the caliph tried to throw himself upon Baghlūn. The latter blocked him with his hand, which the caliph removed. Bāghir then came to Baghlūn's support.

Al-Fatḥ called out, "Woe to all of you! [This is the] Commander of the Faithful." To this Bughā replied, "Why don't you shut up, you idiot!" Al-Fatḥ then shielded al-Mutawakkil, but Hārūn slit him open with his sword, whereupon he cried out "Death!" Hārūn and Mūsā b. Bughā pounced upon al-Mutawakkil with their swords. They killed him and sliced him to pieces. ʿAthʿath was struck by a blow on his head. A young servant (*khādim*) who was with al-Mutawakkil slipped under the curtain [of the harem] and thus was saved. The rest fled.[607]

[1461] Bunān reported: [The assassins] had approached Waṣīf and said to him, "Be with us. We fear that our plan will not work and we'll be killed." He replied, "Have no fear." They went on, "So send with us some of your sons," whereupon he sent with them five of his sons—Ṣāliḥ, Aḥmad, ʿAbdallāh, Naṣr, and ʿUbaydallāh[608]—so that they were able to accomplish their plan.

It is reported on the authority of Zurqān, the deputy of Zurāfah over the gatekeepers, and others that, when al-Muntaṣir took Zurāfah by the hand and led him from the palace and the group of assassins entered, ʿAthʿath looked at them and said to al-Mutawakkil, "We have gotten rid of the lions, snakes, and scorpions only to fall prey to the swords." The basis for this comment was

606. Ṣūlī adds al-Ṣughdī; cf. III, 1306 (Marin, *Reign*, 113), where he is called Wājin al-Ushrūsanī. Herzfeld, *Samarra*, 208, vocalizes Wājan.

607. Text: *wa-taharraba*. Leiden Ms. O, Cairo edition, Mss. A and D: *wa-taṭayyara* = "dispersed, vanished, disappeared."

608. Ṣāliḥ b. Waṣīf continued to play a role as a military figure in the following decades; d. 256 (III, 1832). Aḥmad b. Waṣīf is mentioned once again (Ṭabarī, III, 1833).

that al-Mutawakkil occasionally [amused himself] by inciting[609] snakes, scorpions, and lions [against prey].

When ʿAthʿath mentioned swords, al-Mutawakkil asked him, "Woe to you, what are you saying?"[610] He had just finished making his remark when the assassins burst in. Al-Fatḥ confronted them,[611] "Get out of here, you dogs, get out!" Bughā al-Sharābī rushed over to him and split open his belly with a sword. The others pounced upon al-Mutawakkil. ʿAthʿath fled headlong. Abū Aḥmad was in his chamber, and when he heard the commotion he came out and shielded his father. Baghlūn rushed up to him and struck him twice. When Abū Aḥmad saw the swords overtaking him, he exited, abandoning them.

The group of assassins went out to al-Muntaṣir and hailed him as caliph, informing him that the Commander of the Faithful had died. Brandishing swords over Zurāfah, they urged him to render the oath of allegiance, whereupon he did so. At this point, al-Muntaṣir sent a message to Waṣīf saying, "Al-Fatḥ assassinated my father, so I killed him in turn. Come with your eminent companions," whereupon Waṣīf and his companions presented themselves and rendered the oath of allegiance.

ʿUbaydallāh b. Yaḥyā was in his chamber executing affairs and [1462]
thus knew nothing of the [assassination by] the group.

It is reported, however, that a Turkish woman delivered a note disclosing what the group had planned. Accordingly, the note came to the attention of ʿUbaydallāh, who consulted al-Fatḥ about it. The matter [first] came to the attention of Abū Nūḥ ʿĪsā b. Ibrāhīm,[612] secretary of al-Fatḥ b. Khāqān, who communicated it to al-Fatḥ. They concurred that al-Mutawakkil should be kept in the dark so as to preserve his cheerfulness, being loath to spoil his day. They did not take the plot of this group seriously, confident that no one would dare or be able to carry it out.

It is also reported that Abū Nūḥ planned to flee on that very

609. For the verb *ashlā* in this sense, see Lane, *Lexicon,* 1592; Ahsan, *Social Life,* 214–16.

610. Leiden Ms. O and Cairo edition Ms. A add: *ay suyūf* = "that is, swords," and then *qāla* "He said"), as though resuming the narrative.

611. Text: *fa-qāla lahum*; Ms. O: *fa-ṣāḥa bihim* = "He shouted at them."

612. See *Fragmenta,* 556, l. 4: Ibn Nūḥ. He died in 255 (868–69); Ṭabarī, III, 1723. And see Sourdel, *Vizirat,* 297–99, 304, 317, n. 4; 323, n. 6; 735.

night, while ʿUbaydallāh was poring over his work, executing affairs.[613] Jaʿfar b. Ḥāmid[614] was in front of him when one of the servants (*khadam*) suddenly intruded and said, "Why are you sitting, my master?" He asked, "What's the matter?" The servant replied, "The palace is a single sword."

ʿUbaydallāh ordered Jaʿfar to go out, which he did.[615] He then returned and informed ʿUbaydallāh that the Commander of the Faithful and al-Fatḥ had been assassinated, whereupon ʿUbaydallāh left with his servants (*khadam*) who were with him and his personal entourage (*khāṣṣah*). He discovered that the doors were locked, and so headed in the direction of the riverbank, but the doors [leading to it] were also locked. He ordered that the [doors] on the side of the riverbank be forced open, whereupon three doors were forced, permitting him to exit to the riverbank. He went down into[616] a skiff[617] and took his place in it, accompanied by Jaʿfar b. Ḥāmid and a page of his. ʿUbaydallāh then traveled to the residence of al-Muʿtazz and asked for him, but did not find
[1463] him. He remarked, "We belong to God and to Him we return."[618] It is my death and the caliph's. And he lamented for him.

ʿUbaydallāh's companions rallied to him on Wednesday morning, including the Abnāʾ,[619] Persians, Armenians, street thugs (*zawāqīl*), Arab tribesmen, outlaws (*ṣaʿālīk*) and others. [There was a difference of opinion concerning their number.][620] Some(one) of the informants said that there were about 20,000 horsemen. Others stated that he had 13,000 men with him, and still others claimed that he had 13,000 bridles (horses) with him. Those who gave a low count put it somewhere between 5,000 and 10,000 men.

---

613. Ms. O adds *al-sulṭān* (that is, affairs of the central government), probably as explanation.

614. See Sourdel, *Vizirat,* 284, n. 4 (concerning our text).

615. Ms. O has: "He went out, looked and then returned . . . ," which makes the text clearer.

616. Text: *fa-ṣāra ilā.* Leiden Ms. O: *fa-nazala fī,* which is preferred here.

617. The *zawraq* is a popular small craft that was often used in the rivers and canals of Iraq; Kindermann, *"Schiff,"* 37.

618. See Qurʾān 2:151 and parallels.

619. The Abnāʾ (al-Dawla) were a military contingent in Baghdad; see *EI*², s.v.; and especially Lassner, *Shaping,* 129–36.

620. The bracketed words are added from Ms. O and from Cairo edition Ms. A.

They said to ʿUbaydallāh, "You have taken us as your protégés precisely for this kind of day; order us, then, to assail the group of assassins and kill al-Muntaṣir, the Turks, and his other associates. He refused this, commenting, "This is not the way of handling the situation, as our man is in their hands," meaning al-Muʿtazz.

It is reported on the authority of ʿAlī b. Yaḥyā al-Munajjim:[621] I was reading to al-Mutawakkil, a few days before he was killed, one of the books of the *Malāḥim*.[622] Coming to a passage in the book stating that the tenth caliph would be killed in his audience hall, I stopped reading and put the book aside. The caliph asked me, "What is the matter that you have stopped?" I answered that it was all right. He said, "By God, you must read it." I then read it but refrained from mentioning the caliphs. Al-Mutawakkil commented, "I wish I knew who this poor fellow is who is going to be killed."

It is reported on the authority of Salamah b. Saʿīd al-Naṣrānī[623] that al-Mutawakkil saw Ashūṭ b. Ḥamzah al-Armanī a few days before he was killed. The caliph grumbled about having an audience with Ashūṭ and ordered that he be evicted. When asked [1464]
whether he was satisfied with Ashūṭ's service, he replied, "Yes, indeed, but I dreamt a few nights ago that I had been riding him, when he turned to me, his head becoming like that of a mule,[624] and said to me, 'How much longer [do you suppose] you will molest us? Only a few days remain until the end of your appointed time of fifteen years.'" Salamah said: It tallied with the number of days [remaining of] his caliphate.

It is reported on the authority of Ibn Abī Rabʿī as follows: I dreamt that a man entered by way of the Rastan Gate[625] on a

621. See above, n. 539.

622. On *Malāḥim* books of prognostications concerning the length of rule of dynasties, see, for instance, Ibn Khaldūn, *Muqaddimah*, II, 187, 200, 202; Goldziher, *Muslim Studies*, II, 77; *EI*², s.v. Malāḥim, Malḥama.

623. Salamah b. Saʿīd al-Naṣrānī was a Christian who later became secretary to al-Mustaʿīn's mother (III, 1512, Saliba, 12); Sourdel, *Vizirat*, 304.

624. Text: *al-baghl*. Ms. O: *al-baʿīr* = "camel" and omits "to me."

625. Text: Bāb al-Rastan (cf. Yāqūt, *Muʿjam*, II, 335.18). Ms. O: al-Rastīn; C: al-Rassīn. There was a Rastan Gate in Ḥimṣ. In both dreams, representatives of groups the caliph had suppressed (Armenians, citizens of Ḥimṣ) appear.

heifer, his face to the desert steppe and his back to the town, reciting:

O eyes, woe to you, shed copious tears.[626]
The killing of al-Mutawakkil means resurrection is nigh.[627]

Ḥubshī b. Abī Rab'ī reportedly died two years before al-Mutawakkil was assassinated.

It is reported on the authority of Muḥammad b. Sa'īd—Abū al-Wārith, the judge of Naṣībīn: I dreamt that someone came to me saying:

O sleepy-eyed in a body that is awake,
Why do your eyes not weep copiously?[628]

Have you not seen what fate's trials have done
With the Hāshimite and al-Fatḥ b. Khāqān?

[1465] They will be succeeded by their own people who betrayed them
Until they too disappear like yesterday.[629]

After a few days, the postal courier conveyed the news that both the caliph and al-Fatḥ had been assassinated.

Abū Ja'far said: Al-Mutawakkil was assassinated an hour after dark on Wednesday night, 4 Shawwāl (December 11, 861). It is also said that he was killed on Thursday night. His caliphate had lasted fourteen years, ten months and three days at the time when he was assassinated. On the day of his murder, he was allegedly forty years old. Al-Mutawakkil was born in Fam al-Ṣilḥ[630] in Shawwāl 206 (February 27–March 27, 822). He had a light tan complexion, attractive eyes, and a sparse beard; he was slender.[631]

---

626. The second hemistich reads in the Leiden text: *bi-l-dam' saḥḥan wa-'sbilī* (for *wa-asbilī*). Ṣūlī and Ibn Badrūn, *Sharḥ*, 257: *bi-l-dam' minki wa-asbilī.*

627. Text: *al-qiyāmah.* Ṣūlī has *al-maniyyah* = "fate," "death."

628. Text and Cairo edition: *bi-tahtāni.* Cf. Ibn al-Athīr, *Kāmil*, VII, 64: *bi-buhtāni* ("in dismay").

629. Ms. O, Ibn al-Athīr, and Ṣūlī omit this verse.

630. Fam al-Ṣilḥ is on the east bank of the Tigris River, at the mouth (*fam*) of the Ṣilḥ Canal, north of Wāsiṭ; Le Strange, *Lands*, 28, 38.

631. For *asmar* as light-brown complexion, see Fischer, *Farb- und Formbezeichungen*, 36ff. The term is probably used to depict the color of skin expressed below (see n. 656) by *aṣfar.* A portrait of al-Mutawakkil, from a coin or medallion

Some Things about al-Mutawakkil and His Way of Life

It is reported on the authority of Marwān b. Abī al-Janūb Abū al-Simṭ:[632] I recited to the Commander of the Faithful a poem about him in which I mentioned the Rāfiḍah.[633] He appointed me as governor of al-Baḥrayn and al-Yamāmah and bestowed four robes upon me in the Public Audience Hall. Al-Muntaṣir bestowed a robe upon me and ordered that I be given 3,000 dīnārs, whereupon they were sprinkled on my head. Al-Mutawakkil ordered his son al-Muntaṣir and Saʿd al-Ītākhī to collect them for me so that I would not handle any of them. They collected them, and I departed with the coins.

Marwān said that the poem which he recited about the caliph was:[634]

The kingdom of the caliph Jaʿfar
    Bodes well-being for this world and the next.

Yours is the heritage of Muḥammad,
    And by your justice oppression is banished.

The daughters' sons[635] hope for the heritage, [1466]
    But they do not have a whit of it.

The son-in-law[636] is not an heir,
    And the daughter does not inherit the caliphate.

---

dated 855, preserved in the Vienna Kunsthistorisches Museum, is printed by Creswell, *Early Muslim Architecture*, II, 277 (fig. 221). It is also shown in a large plate in Sourdel, *Civilisation*, plate no. 28. An "effigie hiératique," it depicts the caliph's coiffure, and shows him without crown or turban. He wears instead a large cap as a kind of diadem, from which a veil falls similar to those worn by Umayyad rulers. He has a large moustache and a double-pointed beard. See also the description of his garb in Shābushtī, *Diyārāt*, 26. See above, p. 59.

632. Marwān b. Abī al-Janūb Abū al-Simṭ was a panegyrist who served in the courts of al-Ma'mūn, al-Muʿtaṣim, al-Wāthiq, and al-Mutawakkil; d. 240 (854–55); Iṣfahānī, *Aghānī*, XI, 2-6; Sezgin, *GAS*, II, 582.

633. That is, Imāmi Shīʿites.

634. On this important poem, see C. E. Bosworth, *Al-Maqrīzī's "Book of Contention,"* 21; Goldziher, *Muslim Studies*, II, 98–101.

635. That is, the descendants of Fāṭimah (and ʿAlī).

636. That is, ʿAlī, cousin and son-in-law of the Prophet.

Those who pretend to your legacy
Have only regret.

The deserving have received the inheritance,
So what does your reproach indicate?[637]

If you had a right to the caliphate,[638]
The resurrection would come to mankind.

The heritage is not for any but you,[639]
No, by God, and neither is honor,

I have come to show
The distinction between those who love and those who hate you.

After this, he sprinkled upon my head 10,000 dirhams for a poem I recited in the same vein.

It is related on the authority of Marwān b. Abī al-Janūb: When al-Mutawakkil became caliph, I sent to Ibn Abī Du'ād a panegyrical ode in which I eulogized him. At the end of the ode were two verses in which I mentioned the affair of Ibn al-Zayyāt, namely:

I was told that al-Zayyāt met his fate,
So I said that God has brought me conquest and victory.

Al-Zayyāt dug a pit with treachery
And was cast into it by falseness and betrayal.[640]

Marwān b. Abī al-Janūb continued: When Ibn Abī Du'ād received the ode, he mentioned it to al-Mutawakkil and recited the two verses to him. Al-Mutawakkil ordered that Marwān be presented to him. Ibn Abī Du'ād replied that he was in al-Yamāmah, where al-Wāthiq had banished him because of his affection for the Commander of the Faithful [al-Mutawakkil]. Al-Mutawakkil

637. "Your" here refers to the ʿAlids.

638. Text: *lahā*. Ms. O; Cairo edition, Ms. A; Ibn al-Athīr: *lamā*. See also Addenda, DCCLXXVI, and Glossarium, CDXL. The verse is addressed to the ʿAlids. I take *lahā* as referring to the caliphate.

639. Here "you" refers to the ʿAbbāsids in general.

640. Ṣūlī has: "The betrayal, which he intended, cast him into it."

called for Marwān to be presented. Ibn Abī Du'ād replied that Marwān was in debt, and al-Mutawakkil then asked how much it was. He answered that it amounted to 6,000 dīnārs. Al-Mutawakkil then gave orders that the money be given to Marwān, and so it was. After that, Marwān was brought from al-Yamāmah to Sāmarrā, where he eulogized al-Mutawakkil in an ode: [1467]

Youth has departed, would that it had not.
Old age has come, would that it had not.

And when he came to the following two verses of the ode, al-Mutawakkil ordered that he be given 50,000 dirhams:

The caliphate of Jaʿfar resembles prophecy,
It came without his seeking it or laying claim.[641]

God gave him the caliphate as
He gave prophecy to the apostle.

It is reported on the authority of Abū Yaḥyā b. Marwān b. Muḥammad al-Shannī al-Kalbī[642]—Abū al-Simṭ Marwān b. Abī al-Janūb: When I went to the Commander of the Faithful al-Mutawakkil ʿalā-llāh, I eulogized the heirs apparent and recited to him:[643]

May God water Najd, and peace be upon Najd,
How lovely is Najd in spite of distance.[644]

I looked to Najd, and Baghdad is far away.
Perhaps I shall see Najd, but O Najd!

In Najd there is a group who desire my visit, [1468]
And nothing is more pleasant than their visiting me.[645]

641. That is, borrowing from another people.
642. Ms. O: Abū Yaḥyā Ḥammād b. Muḥammad. Ṣūlī: "I was informed by Fatūḥ b. Maḥmūd b. Marwān—his father (Maḥmūd)—his father Marwān." Fatūḥ was thus the grandson of the poet Marwān b. Abī al-Janūb. Fatūḥ—or rather Mutawwaj?—was a poet in the court of al-Muktafī; Ibn al-Nadīm, *Fihrist,* 354; Sezgin, *GAS,* II, 582 (Marzubānī, *Muwashshaḥ,* 303).
643. See Iṣfahānī, *Aghani*, XI, 2.
644. Ṣūlī has "from near and far."
645. Ṣūlī omits the last verse but gives nineteen others, according to the note in the Leiden edition.

Marwān said: When I finished reciting the poem he ordered that I be given 120,000 dirhams, fifty gowns, and three mounts: a horse, a mule, and a donkey. I did not depart before reciting in gratitude:[646]

The Lord of mankind has chosen Jaʿfar for them,
Electing him to rule over them.

Marwān continued: When I came to the following verse, that is,

Restrain your generosity,
I fear I shall become overweaning—

Al-Mutawakkil exclaimed: "No, by God, I shall not hold back until I flood you[647] with my bounty, nor shall you depart[648] without stating a wish." I said: "O Commander of the Faithful, Ibn al-Mudabbir noted that the estate in al-Yamāmah, which you gave orders to present me as a fief, is *waqf* property[649] that al-Muʿtaṣim gave to his offspring, and thus it may not be bestowed as a fief." Al-Mutawakkil replied, "I'll hold you responsible for [payment of] a dirham a year for one hundred years."[650] I replied, "It is not proper, O Commander of the Faithful, that one dirham be paid to the bureau." Ibn al-Mudabbir then asked if 1,000 dirhams [could be paid over one hundred years], and I said yes, whereupon al-Mutawakkil handed it over to me and to my descendants.

Following that, the caliph remarked, "This is not [the fulfillment of] a wish; it is a liability." I replied, "Al-Wāthiq ordered that the estates that I owned be granted to me as fiefs, but Ibn al-
[1469] Zayyāt banished me, preventing me from taking possession of them, so deliver them to me." The caliph then ordered that they be handed over for one hundred dirhams per annum. They are the Suyūḥ.[651]

646. See Iṣfahānī, *Aghānī,* XI, 3.

647. Text: *uʿarrifaka* = "make you familiar with." The note in the Leiden edition suggests the reading *ugharriqaka,* which is followed here.

648. Text: *bariḥta.* O: *tabraḥ.*

649. *Waqf* is property that is inalienable, the profits from which go to charitable purposes.

650. He would thereby be paying a symbolic rent, and the *waqf* property would not be alienated.

651. The Suyūḥ were villages in al-Yamāmah that did not accept a peace treaty with Khālid b. al-Walīd when Musaylimah was defeated; Yāqūt, *Muʿjam,* III, 222.

It is reported on the authority of Abū Ḥashīshah:[652] Al-Ma'mūn used to say, "The caliph after me will have an *ʿayn* in his name." It was assumed that it was his son al-ʿAbbās, and it turned out to be al-Muʿtaṣim.[653] He would say that after him there would be a *hā'*. It was thought that it was Hārūn,[654] and it turned out to be al-Wāthiq. He would say that after him would be someone with yellow legs. It was surmised that it was Abū al-Ḥa-?-ā'iz al-ʿAbbās,[655] and it turned out to be al-Mutawakkil. I have seen him expose his legs when he sat on the throne, and they were yellow like the color of saffron.[656]

It is reported on the authority of Yaḥyā b. Aktham: I once attended the court of al-Mutawakkil when we mentioned al-Ma'mūn and his letters to al-Ḥasan b. Sahl. I went on quite a bit praising al-Ḥasan and depicting his merits, knowledge, learning, and intelligence, but none of those present concurred. Al-Mutawakkil asked what al-Ḥasan b. Sahl's view of the Qur'ān was.

I replied: He used to say, "Beyond the Qur'ān there is no need for further knowledge of precepts; beyond the Sunnah of the Messenger there is no need[657] for a single further action; and beyond clarification and exposition there is no need for further learning. And after rejection of demonstration and truth there are only swords to manifest proof." Al-Mutawakkil then said to Yaḥyā, "This is not what I wanted from you." To this Yaḥyā replied, "One who claims to be charitable should cite only the good qualities of someone who is absent."

The caliph now asked, "And what was al-Ḥasan accustomed to say during his discourse? For al-Muʿtaṣim bi-llāh—may God have [1470]
mercy upon him—used to recall it, but I have forgotten." Yaḥyā replied, "He used to say, 'O God, I praise you for the favors that

652. Abū Ḥashīshah Muḥammad b. ʿAlī b. Umayyah b. ʿAmr al-Ṭunbūrī was a court musician (a tunburist) and poet, who entertained in caliphal courts from the time of al-Ma'mūn to al-Muʿtamid; Farmer, *History*, 158; Neubauer, *Musiker*, 196; Sezgin, *GAS*, II, 608.

653. For al-ʿAbbās b. Ma'mūn, see Bosworth, *Reunification*, Index, 267. He died in prison at Manbij in 223; see Ṭabarī, III, 1257f. (Marin, *Reign*, 76f.); Zambauer, *Manuel*, 4, 28, 32. Al-Muʿtaṣim was al-Ma'mūn's brother.

654. Hārūn, son of al-Mā'mūn.

655. Ms. C: Abū al-ʿAbbās. His brother, Abū al-ʿAbbās Muḥammad?

656. Aṣfar means yellow or light-colored, and is the color by which the Arabs often described persons of Byzantine or European descent; See EI^2 s.v. It is probably intended to render what we call today "white." See also above, n. 631.

657. For *waḥshah* in the sense of necessity, see Glossarium, DLII.

only You can count, and I take refuge with You from sins that only Your pardon encompasses.'"

Al-Mutawakkil went on asking, "And what used he to say by way of approval or upon receiving some good news? Al-Mu'taṣim bi-llāh had ordered 'Alī b. Yazdād[658] to write it down for us. He did so and taught it to us, but we have forgotten." Yaḥyā replied that he would say, "Mentioning God's blessings and disseminating them, and counting his benefits and recounting them, is a precept which God has imposed upon their recipients, and is obeying His command regarding them and gratitude to Him for them. Praise be to God, Whose blessings are great and Whose favor is abundant, praise commensurate with His goodness that determines what is due Him and entails utmost gratitude to Him, thanks to His constant favor, kindness, and permanence—praise by someone who knows that this is from Him and gratitude to Him." Al-Mutawakkil said, "You are right. These are his very words, and all this is wisdom [which comes] from someone with experience and knowledge." The session then ended.

This year Muḥammad b. 'Abdallāh b. Ṭāhir came to Baghdad, having left Mecca in Ṣafar (April 16–May 14, 861). He complained that he was disturbed by the disagreement concerning the Day of Sacrifice. Al-Mutawakkil therefore ordered that a yellow mail pouch[659] be delivered from the gate [of the Caliphal Palace] to the celebrants of the festive season as to viewing the new moon of
[1471] Dhū al-Ḥijjah, and that it be sent, as is the mail pouch that comes at the farewell ceremony of the festive season. He also ordered that wax be used instead of olive oil and naphtha for the pilgrimage station of Muzdalifah and other pilgrimage shrines.

In this year, al-Mutawakkil's mother died in al-Ja'fariyyah on 6 Rabī' II (June 19, 861).[660] Al-Muntaṣir offered the funeral prayer, and she was buried at the Friday Mosque.

In this year, the caliphal oath of allegiance was rendered to Muḥammad b. Ja'far, on Wednesday, 4 Shawwāl (December 11,

658. In Ṭabarī, III 1272, 1273 (Marin, *Reign*, 88–89), he is called 'Alī b. Yazdād al-'Aṭṭār. See also Ibn al-Zubayr, *Dhakhā'ir*, 241.

659. A *kharīṭah* is a leather pouch or envelope used for official mail; Hilāl al-Ṣābī, *Rusūm*, 17, 126, 127; tr. Salem, 21, 103.

660. Ms. O has Rabī' I.

861) or, it is said, on 3 Shawwāl (December 10). He was twenty-five years old, and his teknonym was Abū Jaʿfar. This was in al-Jaʿfariyyah, where he stayed for ten days after the oath of allegiance was rendered. He then withdrew from there with his family, officers, and troops for Sāmarrā.

The Caliphate of al-Muntaṣir Muḥammad b. Jaʿfar

The Events of the Year 247 (cont'd)

(July 5, 861–June 22, 862)

Those whom we have mentioned previously gave al-Muntaṣir the oath of allegiance on Wednesday night. It is reported on the authority of some(one) of them: On Wednesday morning the notables were present in al-Jaʿfariyyah, including the army commanders, secretaries, eminent men, Shākiriyyah, regular troops, and others. Aḥmad b. al-Khaṣīb read to them a letter reporting in the name of the Commander of the Faithful al-Muntaṣir that al-Fatḥ b. Khāqān had assassinated al-Muntaṣir's father, Jaʿfar al-Mutawakkil, and that al-Muntaṣir therefore killed al-Fatḥ in turn. The notables gave the oath of allegiance. ʿUbaydallāh b. Yaḥyā b. Khāqān was present. He gave the oath of allegiance and then departed.

It is reported on the authority of Abū ʿUthmān Saʿīd the Younger: On the night that al-Mutawakkil was assassinated we were in the palace with al-Muntaṣir. Whenever al-Fatḥ went out, al-Muntaṣir accompanied him. And when he returned, al-Muntaṣir would rise or sit as al-Fatḥ did, and then exit in his wake. Whenever al-Fatḥ rode out, al-Muntaṣir held his stirrup and adjusted his attire on the saddle of his mount.

We received information that ʿUbaydallāh b. Yaḥyā had sta- [1472]

tioned a group of men along al-Muntaṣir's way to assassinate him when he departed. Al-Mutawakkil had reviled and vexed al-Muntaṣir before he left. Offended by the caliph, al-Muntaṣir went out in anger, we along with him. When al-Muntaṣir reached his palace, he sent a message to his boon companions and inner circle of notables—he had arranged with the Turks before he departed to kill al-Mutawakkil while he was intoxicated from the wine.

Saʿīd the Younger went on: It was not long before a messenger arrived to summon me, informing me that emissaries of the Commander of the Faithful had come to the amīr al-Muntaṣir while he was riding. Our previous discussion came to my mind, that is, they were going to assassinate al-Muntaṣir, and this is why he was being summoned. I rode along, armed and prepared, and came to the gate of the amīr, where I found the men agitated. For Wājin had come to him and informed him of al-Mutawakkil's demise,[661] at which point he rode off. Alarmed, I caught up with him on one of the roads.

Realizing the state I was in, al-Muntaṣir said, "Don't worry. After we departed, the Commander of the Faithful choked on his drinking cup and died, may God have mercy upon him." I was overwhelmed and distressed by this. We proceeded—Aḥmad b. al-Khaṣīb and a contingent of the commanders who were with us—until we entered al-Ḥayr,[662] and the news of al-Mutawakkil's murder followed us. The gates were seized and put in charge of guards.

I called out, "O, Commander of the Faithful," saluting al-Muntaṣir as caliph. I went on to say, "We should not leave you to the mercy of your *mawlās*[663] at this time."

He said, "By all means. You and Sulaymān al-Rūmī stay behind me." A piece of cloth was put down for him, which he then sat
[1473] on, while we stood about him. Aḥmad b. al-Khaṣīb and his secre-

661. Text: *qad faziʿa min amrihi.* Cairo edition: *qad faragha min amrihi* (lit. "had finished his task" or the like; followed here). See also Addenda, DCCLXXVI.

662. A *ḥayr* is a park, enclosure, or pleasure garden. The al-Ḥayr section of Sāmarrā was, according to Herzfeld, *Samarra,* 100, between the Jawsaq Palace, the Great Mosque of al-Mutawakkil, and the site of modern Sāmarrā. See Yaʿqūbī, *Buldān,* 258 = Wiet, *Les pays,* 50, 261–63/53–55, 265/58; Creswell, *Early Muslim Architecture,* II, 229f., 241, 254. Al-Ḥayr was also the name given to the outer thoroughfare of the city.

663. That is, the Turks.

tary Saʿīd b. Ḥamīd[664] were present so as to render the oath of allegiance.

It is reported on the authority of Saʿīd b. Ḥamīd that Aḥmad b. al-Khaṣīb said to him, "Woe to you, O Saʿīd, don't you have two or three words by which the oath of allegiance may be rendered?" I answered, "Yes, and still more words." So I drew up the document of the oath of allegiance and administered it to those who were present and to all who came until Saʿīd the Elder arrived.

[Al-Muntaṣir] then sent the oath of allegiance to al-Muʾayyad and told Saʿīd the Younger to go summon al-Muʿtazz.

Saʿīd the Younger reported: I said to him, "You shall not remain, O Commander of the Faithful, with less than the men who are [now] with you; and, by God, I shall not depart from behind you until the notables assemble." Aḥmad b. al-Khaṣīb then said, "There is someone here who is your equal, so go." I said, "I shall not go until enough men have assembled. I am at the moment more fit to serve him than you are." Then, when the number of army commanders rendering the oath of allegiance grew, I left in a state of despair. There were two pages with me. When I came to the gate of Abū Nūḥ,[665] the notables were coming and going in a state of agitation, for a great crowd with arms and equipment was at the gate.

When they became aware of me, one of their horsemen came over. He asked me who I was, for he did not know me. I gave him a cryptic reply about myself, telling him that I was one of al-Fatḥ's men. I proceeded to the gate of al-Muʿtazz, but did not find there any of the guards, gatekeepers or beggars,[666] nor any folk, until I came to the great gate. I knocked quite loudly but was answered only after some time. Asked who was there, I replied, [1474]
"Saʿīd the Younger, emissary of the Commander of the Faithful

---

664. Saʿīd b. Ḥamīd, secretary of Aḥmad b. al-Khaṣīb, was appointed over the Bureau of Correspondence in 249 (863–64; III, 1514; Saliba, 13); see Sourdel, *Vizirat*, 288, 293, 735.

665. Abū Nūḥ = ʿĪsā b. Ibrāhīm? See above, 1462 (p. 181). He was a secretary of al-Fatḥ b. Khāqān.

666. Text (and Cairo Ṭ): wa-l-muktarīn. Ms. C (and Cairo A, D): wa-l-mukabbirīn. Ms. O: wa-l-mukthirīn. The note in the Leiden edition suggests the reading al-muktadīn = "beggars," accepted here. See also *Wörterbuch*, p. 22a, where meaning of "human beings" is given for *mukabbirīn*. And see Addenda, DCCLXXVI; Glossarium, CDXLV.

al-Muntaṣir." The messenger went away and left me waiting. I felt rejected and at a loss. But he then opened the gate and Baydūn al-Khādim[667] came out, bade me enter, and locked the gate behind me. I thought to myself that I was surely finished.

Baydūn then asked me for news, and I informed him that the Commander of the Faithful had choked on his cup of drink and died on the spot, that the notables had assembled and rendered the oath of allegiance to al-Muntaṣir, and that he dispatched me to the amīr Abū ʿAbdallāh al-Muʿtazz bi-llāh to summon him to attend the oath-of-allegiance ceremony. He went in and then came out to me and said that I should enter, whereupon I was admitted to al-Muʿtazz.

Al-Muʿtazz said to me, "Woe unto you, O Saʿīd, what news is there?" So I told him more or less what I had told Baydūn. I offered condolences to him and wept. I said, "Attend, my lord, and be among the first to give the oath of allegiance, thus gaining your brother's good will." He replied, "Woe unto you, [let us wait] until the morning." I kept diverting him,[668] with Baydūn al-Khādim lending a hand, until he prepared himself for the public prayer. He called for his clothing, got dressed, and a horse was brought out for him. He rode off, I along with him, avoiding the main road. I set about talking to him, trying to ease the situation for him. I kept reminding him of things he knew about his brother until we arrived at the gate of ʿUbaydallāh b. Yaḥyā b. Khāqān. When al-Muʿtazz asked me about him, I replied that he would render the oath of allegiance with the notables, and that al-Fatḥ had already rendered the oath of allegiance, at which point he was relieved.[669]

[1475] A horseman caught up with us and went to Baydūn al-Khādim, confiding to him something I did not catch. Baydūn shouted at him, whereupon he went away, only to return three times. Each time Baydūn drove him away, shouting at him, "Leave us," until

667. See Iṣfahānī, *Aghānī,* IX, 118f. When Mutawakkil arrested ʿAlī b. al-Jahm, Baydūn went over to Qabīḥah. Herzfeld, *Samarra,* 212–13, says that he was the trusted servant of Qabīḥah and al-Muʿtazz.

668. For *fa-mā ziltu aftiluhu al-ḥabla wa-l-ghārib* in this sense, see Glossarium, CCCXCVII; Lane, *Lexicon,* 2333.

669. Text: *fa-taʾannasa.* Cairo edition, Mss. A and D: *yaʾisa* = "He then despaired."

we came to the gate of al-Ḥayr. I called for it to be opened. Asked who I was, I replied, "Saʿīd the Younger, with the amīr al-Muʿtazz," whereupon the gate was opened for me.

We went to al-Muntaṣir. Seeing al-Muʿtazz, he invited him to approach, embraced him, consoled him, and took the oath of allegiance from him. Then al-Mu'ayyad arrived with Saʿīd the Elder, and al-Muntaṣir did the same with him. When the notables arose in the morning,[670] al-Muntaṣir went to the Jaʿfarī [Palace] and ordered that al-Mutawakkil and al-Fatḥ be buried, and the notables[671] settled down.

Saʿīd the Younger said: I kept on demanding that al-Muʿtazz welcome the caliphate of al-Muntaṣir while he was immured in the palace until he gave me 10,000 dirhams.[672]

The text of the oath of allegiance that was rendered for al-Muntaṣir was as follows:[673]

> In the name of God, the Merciful, the Compassionate.
>
> You render the oath of allegiance to the servant of God, al-Muntaṣir bi-llāh, Commander of the Faithful, in obedience and contentment, with devotion, acceptance and sincere intention, not compelled but rather consenting, aware of what confirmation of this oath of allegiance entails, namely, obeying and fearing God and exalting the religion of God and His truth, the general welfare of God's servants, uniting the community, reforming affairs, tranquillity of the multitude, a secure future, power[674] of friends, repression of renegades.
>
> You are obligated to obedience and sincerity, and faithfulness to the rights and investiture of Muḥammad al-Imām, al-Muntaṣir bi-llāh, the Servant of God and his

670. Text: *wa-aṣbaḥa al-nās.* But this is strange and is unrelated to their settling down. One expects a verb such as *taḥarraka* or *iḍtaraba* ("were agitated"). See also below, 1479 (p. 202); and cf. Ibn al-Athīr, *Kāmil,* VII, 68, ll. 8–9.

671. Text: *li-nās.* Read *li-l-nās*; see also Addenda, DCCLXXVI.

672. Cairo edition, Ms. A, adds: "In this year al-Muʿtazz and al-Mu'ayyad abdicated, and [al-Muntaṣir] made public their abdication in the new Jaʿfarī Palace." But see below, 1485 (p. 210).

673. See the similar text in Ṭabarī, III, 1545f. (Saliba, 35f.).

674. Text: *wa-ʿizz.* O: *wa-ʿizzah* = "glory."

[1476] caliph. You shall not doubt, deceive, deviate, or have misgivings.

You shall heed him and give support, loyalty, and good counsel, secretly and openly, as well as ready devotion,[675] to all that the servant of God, al-Imām al-Muntaṣir billāh, Commander of the Faithful, orders.

You shall be allies of his friends and foes of his enemies, elite and common, far and near. You shall adhere to his oath of allegiance, in loyalty to [his] investiture, in responsibility for the covenant. Your heart shall be like your speech, your mind like your tongue, willing what the Commander of the Faithful wishes for you now and in the future.

After undertaking this oath of allegiance to the Commander of the Faithful on your souls, confirming it on your necks, you shall render him your solemn oath, willing, obeying, with integrity of heart and intention.[676]

You shall not be permitted to violate anything that God has enjoined upon you.

No one among you shall deviate in this from support, devotion, good counsel, and friendship.

You shall not substitute [anything for this], and no one among you shall go back on his intention and deviate from his public position.

Your oath of allegiance, which you have sworn, is such that God will examine your hearts [to ensure] your commitment[677] and loyalty to its promise and your devotion to supporting it and assisting its recipient.

No defect, circumventing, artifice, or interpretation on your part shall adulterate this until the time when you
[1477] meet God. You shall fulfill His covenant and carry out His claim upon you, not being presumptuous,[678] nor infringing [the oath of allegiance]. For those of you who render an oath of allegiance to the Commander of the

675. Text: *al-khufūf wa-l-wuqūf*; see Glossarium, CCXXVII.
676. Text: *niyyatihi*. See 1546, l. 20, in parallel text: *bayʿatihi*.
677. Text: *wa-iʿtiqādihā*. See 1547, l. 2; *wa-iʿtimādihā*.
678. Text: *mustashrifīn*. See 1547, l. 5: *mustaribīn*.

Faithful are actually rendering an oath of allegiance to God. God's hand is above your hands. Whoever violates [the oath] only violates his own interests. And whoever fulfills what God has imposed upon him shall be given a great award.

You are obligated by this, [namely] by this oath of allegiance that has been imposed upon you, through which you rendered your solemn vow, and by which loyalty, support, friendship, and sincerity are laid upon you. The divine covenant is incumbent upon you, for His covenant demands responsibility,[679] and the compact of God and His messenger. God has most strictly enjoined His prophets and messengers, and every one of His servants, in imposing His contracts,[680] that you heed this oath of allegiance, that you do not substitute [anything for this], that you obey and not disobey, that you are sincerely devoted without reservation, and that you adhere to what you promised, just as those bound to obedience obey, and those bound to a contract and loyalty remain steadfast in their loyalty and obligation. No whim or distraction shall divert you from this. And no error shall divert you from right guidance, while you expend your souls and effort, fulfilling the obligation of religion and obedience by means of your commitment. God will only accept from you loyalty to this oath of allegiance.

Whoever has rendered the oath of allegiance to the Commander of the Faithful and then violates what he has [1478]
affirmed, secretly or overtly, explicitly or deviously, deceiving with regard to his devotion to God, his commitment to the compacts of the Commander of the Faithful, and the divine covenants laid upon him,[681] using levity rather than seriousness, reliance upon falsehood rather than defending the truth, departing from the manner of

679. The words *inna ʿahdahu kāna masʾūlan,* according to the note *ad loc.*, are an intrusion from the margin. But cf. 1547, ll. 11–12.

680. Text: *min mutaʾakkadi wathāʾiqihi.* See 1547, l. 14; *min mawākīdihi wa-mawāthīqihi.*

681. Text: *mawāthīq Amīr al-Muʾminīn wa-ʿuhūd Allāh ʿalayhi.* See 1548, l. 9, which omits "the compacts of the Commander of the Faithful."

honorable men in their oaths—all that the betrayer owns who violates God's covenant in any way, whether money or immovable property, freely grazing livestock, or agriculture or stock farming, will become charity for the poor for the sake of God.[682] It is forbidden for him to restore deceitfully anything of this to his property. And whatever benefit he has for the rest of his life from property of little or great value shall be treated in this way, until his fate overtakes him and his appointed time comes upon him. Every slave (*mamlūk*) that he owns today up to thirty years of age, whether male or female, is free for the sake of God. And his wives on the day that the sin adheres to him and whomever he marries after them up to thirty years of age are divorced definitely by a legally approved[683] divorce, in which there is no exception or taking back. He is obligated to go to the sacred house of God for thirty pilgrimages. God will only accept from him fulfillment of this. He is quit of responsibility to God and His messenger, and God and His messenger are quit of responsibility to him.[684] God will not accept from him any substitute [for this].[685] God is your witness in this, and God is a sufficient witness.[686]

The following is reported: On the morning when al-Muntaṣir
[1479] was given the oath of allegiance, the news spread in al-Māḥūzah—it is the administrative center that Jaʿfar [al-Mutawakkil] had built—and among the inhabitants of Sāmarrā[687] concerning the murder of Jaʿfar. At that time, the troops and the Shākiriyyah, as well as others from among the rabble and commoners, came to the Public Gate in the Jaʿfarī[688] [Palace]. Many people gathered,

682. Text: *fī wujūh sabīl Allāh.* 1548, l. 12 adds *maḥbūs,* that is, "given as a religious bequest."

683. The word *wa-l-sunnah* in the text is omitted by Ms. O.

684. See Qur'ān 9:1.

685. Qur'ān 2:48/45, 123/117.

686. Qur'ān 13:43; 29:52/51, etc.

687. Text: *fī ahl Sāmarrā.* Read: *wa-fī ahl Sāmarrā*; see Ibn al-Athīr, *Kāmil,* VII, 68.

688. The Jaʿfarī Palace had a Public entrance where the Main Road (Shāriʿ al-Aʿẓam) met it. Yaʿqūbī, *Buldān,* 266 = Wiet, *Les pays,* 60, speaks of three monumental gates. Rogers, "Samarra," 150, states that the triple entrance of the Jaʿfarī

word got around among them, and they rode to one another discussing the oath of allegiance.

ʿAttāb b. ʿAttāb went out to them—or it is said that it was Zurāfah who did so—and told them something they would like concerning al-Muntaṣir, but they let him hear something offensive.[689] He then went in to al-Muntaṣir and informed him, whereupon the latter came out, with a number of Maghāribah before him. He shouted to them, "O those dogs, seize them." So they attacked the people and pushed them toward the three gates. The people were crushed and fell upon one another. They then scattered, [retreating] from several who had died from the crowding and trampling. Some said that six individuals [died], and some said that there were between three and six.

In this year, one day after the oath of allegiance was rendered to him, al-Muntaṣir appointed Abū ʿAmrah Aḥmad b. Saʿīd, *mawlā* of Banū Hāshim, to the *maẓalim* [court]. Someone recited:

O domain of Islam, when Abū ʿAmrah
Is appointed over public complaints

He is entrusted over a nation,
While he could not be entrusted even with dung.

In Dhū al-Ḥijjah, 247 (February 5–March 6, 862), al-Muntaṣir brought ʿAlī b. al-Muʿtaṣim[690] from Sāmarrā to Baghdad and placed him under custody.

Leading the pilgrimage this year was Muḥammad b. Sulaymān al-Zaynabī.

---

was merely a facade with decorative function. The Jawsaq Palace also had a Public Gate with a triple portico that took up the entire entrance, where the caliph held audience twice a week; Yaʿqūbī, *Buldān*, 261 = Wiet, *Les pays*, 63; Rogers, *loc. cit.*; Creswell, *Early Muslim Architecture*, II, 232, and Fig. 181. And see al-ʿAmid, *Architecture*, 207.

689. After *fa-asmaʿūhu* of the text ʿAynī adds: *mā yakrahuhu.*

690. ʿAlī b al-Muʿtaṣim was a brother of al-Wāthiq and al-Mutawakkil, and thus an uncle of al-Muntaṣir.

The Events of the Year 248

(March 7, 862–February 23, 863)

[1480] One of the events was al-Muntaṣir's dispatching Waṣīf the Turk on the summer expedition to Byzantine territory.

The Reason for Dispatching Waṣīf to Byzantium and His Role

It is reported that the reason for this was that there was rancor between Aḥmad b. al-Khaṣīb and Waṣīf. When al-Muntaṣir became caliph and Ibn al-Khaṣīb was his wazīr, the latter incited al-Muntaṣir against Waṣīf. Aḥmad advised al-Muntaṣir to get Waṣīf to leave his army camp and to mount a campaign at the frontier. Ibn al-Khaṣīb persisted until al-Muntaṣir summoned Waṣīf and ordered him to go off on the campaign.

It is reported that when al-Muntaṣir decided to send Waṣīf to campaign at the Syrian frontier, Aḥmad b. al-Khaṣīb said to him, "Who will be bold against the *mawlā*s until you order Waṣīf to march?"

Al-Muntaṣir told some(one) of the chamberlains to permit those present in the palace to enter. He did, and among them was

Waṣīf. The latter approached al-Muntaṣir, who said to him, "O Waṣīf, we have learned that the tyrant of Byzantium[691] is heading for the frontier towns. This is something that cannot be overlooked. Either you march, or I shall march." Waṣīf replied, "No, I shall march, O Commander of the Faithful," whereupon al-Muntaṣir said, "O Aḥmad, see to whatever he needs." When Aḥmad replied, "Yes, O Commander of the Faithful," al-Muntaṣir exclaimed, "What do you mean by 'yes?' Get going right now."

[Al-Muntaṣir went on to say] "O Waṣīf, order your secretary to [1481]
come to an agreement with Aḥmad as to what is required and stay with him until he settles matters with him."

Aḥmad b. al-Khaṣīb and Waṣīf then stood up [and left the caliph's presence]. Waṣīf continued to make preparations until he departed, but he nevertheless failed to carry out [his objective].

It is reported that when al-Muntaṣir summoned Waṣīf and ordered him to go on the campaign, he said to him, "The tyrant—that is, the Byzantine king—is on the move, and I fear that he will destroy whatever he touches in the territory of Islam, killing [people] and taking children captive. If you go on the campaign and wish to return, you may proceed forthwith to the gate of the Commander of the Faithful."

Al-Muntaṣir ordered a contingent of commanders and others to set forth with Waṣīf and selected elite soldiers for him. There were about 10,000 men accompanying him of the Shākiriyyah, the regular army, and the *mawlās*.[692] At the head of his advance guard was Muzāḥim b. Khāqān, brother of al-Fatḥ b. Khāqān.[693] Commanding his rear guard was Muḥammad b. Rajā'. On his right flank was al-Sindī b. Bukhtāshah.[694] And Naṣr b. Sa'īd al-

691. Ṭāghiyat al-Rūm is a common dysphemistic epithet for the Byzantine emperor.

692. Ms. O omits *mawlās* and has twelve thousand men.

693. Muzāḥim b. Khāqān, brother of al-Fatḥ, was governor of Egypt in 253 (867–68) and remained active as military commander in warfare and politics during the caliphates of al-Musta'īn and al-Mu'tazz. He was governor in Egypt as of 3 Rabī' I, 253 (March 16, 867); he died according to Ṭabarī (III, 1693, Saliba, 150) in Dhū al-Ḥijjah, 253 (December 2–31, 867); see also Kindī, *Wulāh*, 207–9, 211; Abū al-Maḥāsin, *Nujūm*, II, 337; Zambaur, *Manuel*, 27 (giving date of death as 9 Rabī' II, 254); Sourdel, *Vizirat*, 274, n. 5.

694. Al-Sindī b. Bukhtāshah is mentioned during the caliphate of al-Mu'taṣim; III, 1266 (Marin, *Reign*, 84).

Maghribī[695] was responsible for the siege machines. Waṣīf placed his deputy Abū ʿAwn at the head of the men and the camp. He was chief of the security policy in Sāmarrā.

When al-Muntaṣir sent his *mawlā* Waṣīf on the campaign, he forwarded a dispatch of Muḥammad b. ʿAbdallāh b. Ṭāhir, the text of which is as follows:

> In the name of God the Merciful, the Compassionate. From the Servant of God, Muḥammad al-Muntaṣir billāh, Commander of the Faithful, to Muḥammad b. ʿAbdallāh, *mawlā* of the Commander of the Faithful. Peace upon you. The Commander of the Faithful praises God for you—there is no God but He—and asks Him to pray for Muḥammad His servant and messenger, may God bless him and his family.
>
> [1482] Now then. God, to Him be praise for His blessings and gratitude for His favor, has chosen Islam, preferred and perfected it, and has made it a means to His approval and reward, an open road to His mercy and a way to the treasure of His glory. God has caused those who opposed Islam to incline toward it, and subjugated to it those who departed from its truth and preferred another way. He has favored Islam with the most complete and perfect of laws, the most excellent and just statutes. He has sent by way of Islam the best of mankind and the choicest of humans, Muḥammad, and has made the holy war the noblest of His precepts and the most expeditious means for reaching Him. For God has exalted His religion and has humbled the impudent polytheists.
>
> God says by way of commanding holy war and making it obligatory: "March out light or heavy (hearted), and strive with goods and person in the way of God; that will be better for you, if you have knowledge."[696] No mishap will befall the one who wages holy war for the sake of God. He will not suffer disease or harm as long as he is

695. Naṣr b. Saʿīd al-Maghribī later commanded the Maghāribah against the Turks, along with Muḥammad b. Rāshid, in 252 (866–67). They were both killed (Ṭabarī, III, 1680–81; Saliba, 140–41).

696. Qur'ān 9:41.

with God. He will not undergo the expense [of fighting], or clash with an enemy, or cross into a territory or tread on a land without having something written down [to his credit], abundant reward and hope for recompense.

God says: "That is because there befalls them not thirst or fatigue or lack of food in the way of God, nor do they make any invasion that rouses the anger of the unbelievers, nor do they wreak any stroke upon an enemy, but a good deed is thereby written down to their credit; verily God alloweth not to go lost the reward of those who do well. Nor do they make any contribution small or [1483] great, or cross a single wadi, but it is written down to their credit, that God may recompense them for the best they have been doing."[697]

Then God extols the superior rank of those who wage the holy war over those who refrain, His reward that He promised them and their proximity to Him. For He says: "Those of the believers who sit still—other than those who have some injury—are not on a level with those who strive with goods and persons in the way of God. God hath given preference in rank to those who strive with goods and persons over those who sit still, though to all God hath promised the good (reward). And God hath bestowed upon those who strive, in preference to those who sit still, a mighty hire."[698]

And through holy war God purchases the souls and property of the believers and makes His paradise a reward for them, His good pleasure a recompense for them for spending [their souls]. This is a promise from Him, truth in which there is no doubt, a fair judgment for which there is no substitute.

God says: "God has bought from the believers their persons and their goods at the price of the Garden (in store) for them, fighting in the way of God and killing and being killed—a promise binding upon Him in the Torah, the Evangel, and the Qur'ān; and who fulfills His cove-

697. Qur'ān 9:120–21/121–22.
698. Qur'ān 4:95/97.

nant better than God? So rejoice in the bargain you have made with Him; that is the mighty bliss."[699]

God has decided to revive those who strive for His victory and mercy, and has vouchsafed for those who die eternal life and proximity to Him, and an abundant share of His reward. He also says: "Count not those who have been killed in the way of God as dead, nay, alive with their Lord, provided for, delighting in what God has vouchsafed them of His bounty and rejoicing at (tidings
[1484] of) those who, left behind, have not yet joined them, that fear rests not upon them nor do they grieve."[700]

Holy war is more noble and suitable for triumph in this world and the next than any action by which the believers approach God and by which they may lay down their burdens, liberate themselves, and merit reward from their Lord. For those who profess it have sacrificed their souls so that the word of God be the highest, and they were generous with their souls, apart from their brothers behind them and the Muslim women. They have subdued the enemy by holy war.

The Commander of the Faithful desires to come close to God by waging holy war against His enemy, by carrying out His obligations in the religion that He entrusted him with, and seeking proximity to Him by strengthening His friends and permitting injury and revenge against those who deviate from His religion, deny His messengers, and disobey Him.

Pursuant to the above, he has seen fit to urge Waṣīf, the *mawlā* of the Commander of the Faithful, to march this year to the territory of the enemies of God, the Byzantine infidels, to mount a campaign, since God has informed the Commander of the Faithful of Waṣīf's obedience and good counsel, and his excellent disposition[701] and pure intention in all that brings him close to God and His caliph.

699. Qur'ān 9:111/112.
700. Qur'ān 3:169–70/163–64.
701. Text: *ta'bi'atihi.* Addenda, DCCLXXVI: *naqībatihi.*

The Commander of the Faithful—God is the sponsor of his help and success—has seen fit that Waṣīf, along with his *mawlās*, regular troops, and Shākiriyyah, whom the Commander of the Faithful has dispatched with him, arrive at the frontier of Malaṭyah[702] on 12 Rabīʿ II, 248, corresponding to 15 Ḥazīran of the months of the non-Arabs (June 15, 862), and that his invasion of the territory of the enemies of God take place on 1 Tammūz (July 1, 862).

Know this and send dispatches to the administrators in [1485] your provinces with the text of this letter of the Commander of the Faithful. Order them to read it to the Muslims before them and thus to motivate them for holy war, inciting and summoning them to it, and informing them of the reward that God has given those who wage it. This is so that those who have the intention, the readiness[703] and the desire for holy war will act in accordance with this letter by pouncing upon their enemy and speedily aiding their brothers, by defending their religion and protecting their territory when the army of Waṣīf, the *mawlā* of the Commander of the Faithful, arrives in Malaṭyah, at the time that the Commander of the Faithful has designated for them, God willing.

Peace upon you and God's mercy and blessings. Written by Aḥmad b. al-Khaṣīb on 7 al-Muḥarram, 248 (March 13, 862).

It is reported that someone by the name of Abū al-Walīd al-Jarīrī al-Bajalī was sent to take responsibility for the expenditures of Waṣīf's army, the booty, and the division of spoils. Al-Muntaṣir sent a dispatch with him to Waṣīf, ordering him to stay at the territory of the frontier when he had completed his expedition. He was to stay for four years, mounting [additional] campaigns at the usual times until word from the Commander of the Faithful arrived.

---

702. Malaṭyah (Greek Melitene) on the upper Euphrates, on the frontier of the Byzantines, was exposed to periodic Byzantine attacks; *EI*², s.v.

703. For *ḥisbah* in *jihād*, see Lane, *Lexicon*, 566, "reckoning, preparing, seeking, laying in store reward in world to come; reward."

In this year, al-Muʿtazz and al-Mu'ayyad abdicated, and al-Muntaṣir made public their abdication in the New Jaʿfarī Palace.

The Abdication of al-Muʿtazz and al-Mu'ayyad

It is reported that, when Muḥammad al-Muntaṣir bi-llāh's rule
[1486] had become stable, Aḥmad b. al-Khaṣīb said to Waṣīf and Bughā, "We have no guarantee against future events. The Commander of the Faithful may die, and al-Muʿtazz may assume rule, who then will wipe us out completely. The best course is to work toward deposing these two youths before they overcome us."

The Turks made every effort to accomplish this, urging it upon al-Muntaṣir by saying, "O Commander of the Faithful, depose them from [succession to] the caliphate and have the oath of allegiance rendered to your son ʿAbd al-Wahhāb." They importuned him to do this until he finally did so. The caliph went on paying respect to al-Muʿtazz and al-Mu'ayyad, strongly favoring al-Mu'ayyad. But then, forty days after he took office, he ordered that al-Muʿtazz and al-Mu'ayyad be summoned after they had departed. They were summoned and installed in a palace residence.

Al-Muʿtazz said to al-Mu'ayyad, "My brother, why do you think we were brought here?" He replied, "To depose us, O wretched one." Al-Muʿtazz said, "I don't think he will do this to us." Then, while they were going on this way, the messengers arrived with the deposition. Al-Mu'ayyad announced right then, "I heed and obey." But al-Muʿtazz stated, "I am not the person who would do such a thing, and, if you wish to kill me, it's your business."

The messengers returned to al-Muntaṣir and informed him [of what took place]. They then came back and carried on very roughly. Seizing al-Muʿtazz violently, they ushered him into the chamber, shutting the door behind him.

It is reported on the authority of Yaʿqūb b. al-Sikkīt[704]—al-Mu'ayyad: When I saw that, I said to them brazenly, "What is

---

704. He is Abū Yūsuf Yaʿqūb b. al-Sikkīt, a famous grammarian, tutor to al-Mu'ayyad; d. 246 (860–61); Ibn al-Nadīm, *Fihrist,* 159; Yāqūt, *Irshād,* VI, 300–302; Ibn Khallikān, *Wafayāt,* IV, 293; Sezgin, *GAS,* II, Index, 769; IV, 335; VII, 347; VIII, 129f.

this, you dogs? You are spilling our blood. Is this how you attack your lord? Stay away—God damn you—and let me talk to him." They now responded to me tentatively after they had been acting impetuously. They paused for a while and then said to me, "Go [1487]
meet with him if you like." I suspected that they had taken consultation [concerning this]. I rose and went to al-Muʿtazz, and found him in the chamber weeping. So I said to him, "Fool, in view of what they are known to have done to your father, and considering who he was, you still refuse to do what they want you to do! Abdicate, woe unto you, and don't discuss it any further with them."

Al-Muʿtazz said, "Praise God. Shall I divest myself of a right that I have already exercised, one that has come into effect in remote regions?"

I said, "This right killed your father. Would that it not kill you. Give it up, woe unto you! By God, if it is in God's prescience that you rule, then you surely will."

He then replied that he would [abdicate].

Al-Mu'ayyad said: I came out and said that he had responded favorably, and that the messengers should inform the Commander of the Faithful. They went off and then returned and congratulated me for it. A secretary whose name al-Mu'ayyad mentioned entered with them. He had with him an inkwell and a sheet of paper. He sat and then, turning to Abū ʿAbdallāh [al-Muʿtazz], he said, "Write your abdication with your own hand." When he hesitated, I said to the secretary, "Give me a sheet of paper and dictate what you wish."

He dictated to me a letter for al-Muntaṣir in which I informed him that I am incapable of ruling and I know that I cannot assume rule; that I am averse to having al-Mutawakkil held in error on my account if I am unsuitable; that I shall, therefore, ask the caliph for a deposition, and inform him that I abdicate and release the notables from their oath of allegiance to me. I wrote whatever he wanted. I then said, "Write, O Abū ʿAbdallāh." But al-Muʿtazz held back, so I said, "Write, woe unto you." At that point he wrote. The letter was then sent off.

After this the caliph summoned us. I asked, "Should we get new clothing or come in these?" He replied that we should get fresh clothes. I called for clothing and put it on, and Abū ʿAbdal-

lāh did the same. We left and entered [the caliph's presence.] He
[1488] was in his audience hall, the notables arrayed according to rank. We greeted them, and they returned our greeting, at which point he ordered that we be seated.

Al-Muntaṣir then asked, "Is this your letter?" Al-Muʿtazz was silent, so I took the initiative and said, "Yes, O Commander of the Faithful, this is my letter by my request and wish." I told al-Muʿtazz to speak up, whereupon he said something of this sort. Al-Muntaṣir then turned to us, with the Turks standing by, and said, "Do you think that I have deposed you, aspiring to live until my son grows up and then have the oath of allegiance rendered to him? By God, I do not covet this for even a minute! And, by God, as this is not my ambition, I prefer that my fathers' sons rule rather than my cousins. But these—and he gestured toward all the *mawlās*[705] standing and sitting—urged me to depose you. And I feared that, if I did not do so, one of them would attack you with an iron weapon and finish you off. What do you recommend that I do? Could I then kill him? By God, the blood of all the *mawlās* does not equal the blood of one of you. It is more expedient for me to yield to their demand." [Yaʿqūb b. al-Sikkīt] said: The two of them leaned over to him and kissed his hand. He embraced them, and they then departed.

It is reported that on Saturday, 22 Ṣafar 248 (April 27, 862), al-Muʿtazz and al-Muʾayyad abdicated. Each one wrote a document in his own hand, to the effect that he renounced the oath of allegiance that was rendered to him, that the notables were free to rescind it, and that they were incapable of executing any part of it. They then carried out the abdication in the presence of the notables, Turks, eminent men, companions, and judges—Jaʿfar b. ʿAbd al-Wāḥid was the chief judge. Also present were the army commanders; the Hāshimites; the administrators of the government bureaus; the officials;[706] the elite commanders of the guard; Muḥammad b. ʿAbdallāh b. Ṭāhir; Waṣīf; Bughā the Elder; Bughā
[1489] the Younger; and all those who were present in the Private Palace (Dār al-Khāṣṣah) and the Public Audience Hall (Dār al-ʿĀmmah).

705. That is, Turks.
706. For *shīʿah* in the sense used here, see above, n. 329.

The notables departed after this. The text that the two of them wrote was as follows:

> In the name of God the Merciful, the Compassionate.
>
> The Commander of the Faithful al-Mutawakkil ʿalā-llāh, may God be pleased with him, assigned to me this matter and had the oath of allegiance rendered to me, without my consent, while I was a minor. When I understood my circumstances, I realized that I could not execute what he assigned to me and would not be suitable as caliph of the Muslims. Whosoever is bound by the oath of allegiance to me is free to rescind it. I free you from it and I release you from your oath. I have no binding covenant or compact with you. You are released from it.

Aḥmad b. al-Khaṣīb read the documents aloud. Then each one of them rose and declared to those present: "This is my document and this is my statement. Witness for me. I release you from your oath and free you from it."

Al-Muntaṣir thereupon said to them, "God has blessed you and the Muslims." He arose and went inside. He had been sitting in the presence of the notables and had al-Muʿtazz and al-Mu'ayyad sit near him. Then he wrote a dispatch to government officials deposing al-Muʿtazz and al-Mu'ayyad. This was in Ṣafar, 248 (March 7, 862–February 23, 863).

The text of the letter of al-Muntaṣir bi-llāh to Abū al-ʿAbbās Muḥammad b. ʿAbdallāh b. Ṭāhir, *mawlā* of the Commander of the Faithful, pertaining to deposing Abū ʿAbdallāh al-Muʿtazz and Ibrāhīm al-Mu'ayyad was as follows:

> From the Servant of God, Muḥammad al-Imām al-Muntaṣir bi-llāh, Commander of the Faithful, to Muḥammad b. ʿAbdallāh, *mawlā* of the Commander of the Faithful.
>
> Now then. God—to Whom belongs praise for His blessings and gratitude for His favor—has made His caliphs governors, who carry out what His Messenger was sent with. They defend His religion, preach His truth, and [1490]
> execute His statutes. He has conferred His glory, by which He favored them, as support for His servants and

welfare for His land, and as mercy causing His creatures to thrive. He has imposed obedience toward them and related it to obedience to Him and to His Messenger, Muḥammad. He has imposed it as an obligation in His unambiguous (*muḥkam*) revelation, because obedience brings about tranquillity of the multitude, harmony of passions, the creation of order out of disorder, security of roads, repelling of the enemy, protection of women, sealing frontiers, and setting affairs straight.

He says: "O you who have believed, obey God and obey the Messenger and those of you who have the command."[707]

It is an obligation of God's caliphs, those whom He has rewarded with His great beneficence, favored with the highest rank of His glory and entrusted with a way to His mercy, good pleasure, and reward, to prefer obeying Him in every circumstance, to discharge what is His due, each one of them in order of proximity [to God].

May their role in striving for whatever draws one near to God match their rank in Islam and ruling Muslims. The Commander of the Faithful requests from God, seeking Him humbly before His greatness, to entrust to him rulership that brings welfare to his subjects; to ease his burdens that He placed upon him; and give him success in obeying Him; for He is attentive and nigh.

You know what you witnessed concerning the delivery to the Commander of the Faithful of two documents, in their handwriting, that is, by Abū ʿAbdallāh and Ibrāhīm, sons of the Commander of the Faithful al-Mutawakkil ʿalā-llāh, may God be pleased with him. They mention in these documents what God informed them of concerning the Commander of the Faithful's sympathy and compas-
[1491] sion, and his providing well for them. And they mention the investiture by the Commander of the Faithful al-Mutawakkil ʿalā-llāh of Abū ʿAbdallāh as heir apparent of the Commander of the Faithful and of Ibrāhīm as heir apparent after Abū ʿAbdallāh, and that when this investiture

707. Qur'an 4:59/62.

was made Abū ʿAbdallāh was an infant, not yet three years old, uncomprehending of his investiture and appointment. Ibrāhīm was young and had not yet reached puberty. They were not legally responsible, and the statutes of Islam therefore did not apply to them.

They mention that, when they reached puberty and understood their incapacity to carry out their investiture and the administrative functions assigned to them, it might become necessary for them to exhort God and the community of Muslims to let them extricate themselves from this matter with which they were invested, and relinquish the administrative functions to which they were appointed, releasing thereby all those under obligation of an oath of allegiance to them, for they were unable to carry out what they were nominated for and unsuited to be assigned to it.

And those who are associated with them, in their provinces, including commanders of the Commander of the Faithful, his *mawlā*s, pages, regular army, and Shākiriyyah, and all those who are with these officers in the court and in Khurāsān and all the other provinces shall be released from their service, and there shall cease to be any mention of association with the two of them. The two shall now become plebeians (*sūqah*) and commoners (*ʿāmmah*) among the Muslims.

They shall describe [themselves as such] whenever they mention this to the Commander of the Faithful and ask him about it from the time when God has brought His caliphate to him. They have abdicated and retired from the investiture. And they have released from their oath of allegiance, deposing them as they have deposed themselves, all those who have an oath of allegiance to them among the officers of the Commander of the Faithful, all [1492]
his close associates, his subjects, near and far, present and absent.

They granted the Commander of the Faithful the right to impose upon themselves the covenant of God and the most strict covenant and compact rendered to His angels, prophets, and servants. And they have acknowledged all the oaths that the Commander of the Faithful has imposed upon them to render obedience, sincere counsel, and friendship to him, secretly and openly.

They ask the Commander of the Faithful to publicize and disseminate what they have done, and to invite all his close associates to hear this from them. This they request, desire, and obey without being compelled or forced. The two documents that they presented in their handwriting shall be read to the caliph's close associates, to the effect that the investitute as heirs apparent came to them while they were young, and that they abdicated after they had reached puberty. They request dismissal from the administrative functions that they undertook, and that their associates in these provinces, including officers of the Commander of the Faithful, his regular troops, pages, Shākiriyyah, and all those who are with these officers in the court, in Khurāsān and all the rest of the provinces, shall be released from their service, and there shall cease to be any mention of association with the two of them. A dispatch pertaining to this should be sent to all the administrative officers of the provinces.

The Commander of the Faithful acknowledged the veracity of what they reported and presented, and proceeded to summon all his brothers and those in his court, including his family, his officers, his *mawlā*s, his adjuncts, the chiefs of his regular troops, his Shākiriyyah, secretaries, judges, jurists, and others, and all the rest of his close
[1493] associates to whom the oath of allegiance was rendered.

Present were Abū ʿAbdallāh and Ibrāhīm, the sons of the Commander of the Faithful al-Mutawakkil ʿalā-llāh, God be pleased with him. Their documents, in their own hand, were read aloud in their presence to the Commander of the Faithful, to them, and to all those present. They repeated the statement, once the two documents were read, in accordance with what they had written. Responding to this, the Commander of the Faithful decided to disseminate and publicize what they had done. He carried this out in accordance with three rights: (1) The right of God, insofar as He entrusted al-Muntaṣir with his caliphate and obligated him to provide for his friends by consolidating their community at all times and reconciling their hearts. (2) The right of subjects, who are entrusted to him by God, so that the one appointed over their affairs supervises, night and day, with care, justice and compassion, and carries out the statutes of God for mankind while assuming the responsibility of governance and right management. (3) The right of Abū ʿAbdallāh and Ibrāhīm, obliging the Commander of the Faithful because of their brotherhood and mutual kinship; for had they persisted in what they relinquished, despite their incapacity, this might have harmed Islam, and the adversity would have affected all Muslims. Thus, the heavy responsibility would have redounded to them.

The Commander of the Faithful has deposed them, as they deposed themselves, from the investiture as heirs apparent. And all the brothers of the Commander of the Faithful deposed them, as did the members of his family in his court. All those who attended deposed them, including the officers of the Commander of the Faithful, his [1494]
*mawlā*s, officials, commanders of his regular troops, Shākiriyyah, secretaries, judges, jurists, and his other close associates who rendered the oath of allegiance.

The Commander of the Faithful has ordered that the letters concerning this be drawn up and dispatched to all the administrative officials, so that their contents be made known in the provinces. They will depose Abū ʿAbdallāh and Ibrāhīm from the investiture as heirs apparent since they had deposed themselves and released the notables and commoners, those present and absent, the near and far. They will eliminate any reference to them as heirs apparent and remove from their letters and formulas any reference to the genealogy[708] of al-Muʿtazz bi-llāh and al-Muʾayyad bi-llāh, nor are they to invoke their names from the pulpits. In addition, they will eliminate all the old and new offices established by the two of them in their government bureaus, that is, offices pertaining to

708. Text vocalized: *nisab*. Addenda, DCCLXXVI: *nasab*.

their [former] associates. They will remove mention of them from emblems and flags,[709] and the officials are also obliged to remove their names where they were used to mark the horses of the Shākiriyyah and the frontier cavalry (*rābiṭah*).

Your station vis-à-vis the Commander of the Faithful will be determined by what God has chosen for him, namely, your obedience, sincere counsel and support, what God has granted your ancestors and yourselves, and what God has apprised the Commander of the Faithful of
[1495] concerning your obedience, discernment,[710] and endeavor to discharge [your] duty.

The Commander of the Faithful has assigned you independently to your office and has released you from service to Abū ʿAbdallāh and from those [others] in your provincial seat and in all the rest of the provincial areas. The Commander of the Faithful will not place between you and himself anyone who will govern over you. His order concerning this has gone out to the administrative officers of his government bureaus.

Know this and write to your administrative officers according to the text of this letter of the Commander of the Faithful to you. Suggest to them that they act in accordance with it, God willing. Peace.

Written by Aḥmad b. al-Khaṣīb on Saturday, 19 Safar, 248 (April 24, 862).

In this year, al-Muntaṣir died.

The Illness That Caused al-Muntaṣir's Death, the Time When He Died, and How Long He Lived

There is disagreement about the illness that caused his death. Some(one) of the informants said that he was afflicted by angina in his throat, on Thursday, 25 Rabīʿ I, 248 (May 29, 862), and that he died at the time of the afternoon prayer on Sunday, 5 Rabīʿ II (June 8, 862). Another view is that he died on Saturday afternoon,

709. Text: *maṭārid.* For the sense here, see Glossarium, CCCXXXIX.
710. Text: *wa-yumn naqībatika.* Ms. O: *wa-min tamyīz nafsika.*

4 Rabīʿ II (June 7, 862), and that the cause of his death was an inflammation in his stomach that moved to his heart, causing his death, and that his illness lasted for three days or so.

I have been informed by some(one) of our colleagues that al-Muntaṣir, having a fever, summoned a physician whom he or- [1496] dered to bleed him. He bled al-Muntaṣir with a poisoned lancet, from which he died.

The physician who bled the caliph returned to his residence, where he too was stricken with fever. He summoned one of his pupils and ordered him to bleed him, placing his lancets before the pupil, so that he might choose the best. The poisoned lancet with which he had bled al-Muntaṣir was among them. He had forgotten about it. The pupil did not find among the lancets placed before him any one better than the poisoned lancet. He therefore bled his teacher with it without being aware of what had taken place previously. When the pupil had bled his teacher with this lancet, his colleague noticed it and realized that he was about to die. The physician gave his bequest immediately and died the same day.

It is also reported that al-Muntaṣir was afflicted in his head. Ibn al-Ṭayfūrī[711] therefore put drops of oil in his ear. His head became inflamed, and he soon died. Another view is that Ibn al-Ṭayfūrī poisoned the caliph with his cupping glasses.

Abū Jaʿfar said: I often heard people say, when the caliphate passed to al-Muntaṣir, that from the time he acceded to rule until his death he would live for six months, as did Shīrawayh b. Kisrā after he killed his father. This [account] was spread among the populace and notables alike.[712]

It is reported on the authority of Yusr al-Khādim,[713] who was

---

711. See above, p. 174, and n. 581, for his father al-Ṭayfūrī. As son of a court physician of al-Mutawakkil, it is possible that he retained a residual loyalty to his father's patron. See also Ibn Badrūn, *Sharḥ*, 284.

712. Shīrawayh (Shīrūyah) b. Kisrā (591–628 A.D.) killed his father, Kisrā Parvīz. See the more elaborate account of Masʿūdī, *Murūj*, VII, 291, where it is told that the caliph saw a Persian inscription on a carpet telling the fate of Shīrawayh, which was translated for him; and see, for instance, Ibn Badrūn, *Sharḥ*, 283; Ibn al-Ṭiqṭaqā, *Fakhrī*, 239, Thaʿālibī, *Laṭā'if*, 72, and n. 2.

713. Yusr al-Khādim is mentioned again by Ṭabarī, *sub anno* 255 (869–69; III, 1743), with other members of al-Muntaṣir's entourage, including Saʿīd the Younger.

said to be in charge of al-Muntaṣir's treasury in the days of his amīrate, that one day during his caliphate, al-Muntaṣir awoke, after sleeping in his sitting room (*īwān*), weeping and lamenting. Yusr said: I respected him too much to ask him about his weeping and stood behind the door, when ʿAbdallāh b. ʿUmar al-Bāzyār arrived and heard his lamenting and sobbing. ʿAbdallāh asked me,
[1497] "What is wrong with him, woe to you, O Yusr." I informed him that the caliph had awakened from sleep in tears. ʿAbdallāh now approached al-Muntaṣir and said to him, "What is wrong with you, O Commander of the Faithful, that you are weeping, may God not let your eye shed tears?" Al-Muntaṣir replied, "Come close to me, O ʿAbdallāh." He did. The caliph then said to him, "I was sleeping and dreamt that al-Mutawakkil had come to me and said, 'Woe unto you, O Muḥammad. You killed me, wronged me, and usurped my caliphate.[714] By God, you will only enjoy the caliphate after me for a few days; then you are bound for hell.' I then awoke and could not control my weeping or anxiety."

ʿAbdallāh said to him, "This is a dream, and dreams may be either true or false. No, God will prolong your life and give you happiness. Now summon wine and entertainment and never mind dreams."

Yusr continued: The caliph did just that, but nevertheless went on being dejected until he died.

It is reported that al-Muntaṣir had consulted a group of jurists about killing his father, informing them about his doctrines and relating unseemly things about him, which I am reluctant to put down in writing. They advised al-Muntaṣir to kill him. We have mentioned in part what happened to him.

It is reported that, when al-Muntaṣir's illness became severe, his mother came to him inquiring about his condition. He replied, "By God, I have lost this world and the next."

[Ibrāhīm b. Jaysh said:[715] I have been informed by the secretary Mūsā b. ʿĪsā, secretary of my uncle Yaʿqūb and my cousin Yazīd, that when al-Muntaṣir acceded to the caliphate he would carry on quite a bit while intoxicated about the murder of his father al-

---

714. Text: *ghabantanī*. ʿAynī: *ghaḍibtanī*, i.e. *ghaṣabtanī* = "you have usurped me" (note *ad loc.* in Leiden edition).

715. The bracketed text appears only in the Cairo edition, on the basis of Ms. A.

Mutawakkil. He would say with reference to the Turks, "These are murderers of the caliphs." In such fashion he mentioned what they feared. The Turks gave one of his servants (*khādim*) 30,000 dīnārs to try and poison him. And they also gave a sum of money to ʿAlī b. Ṭayfūr.

When served fruit, al-Muntaṣir tended to favor pears. Ibn Ṭayfūr therefore chose a large, ripe pear, pierced the top, and poured poison into it. And the servant placed it on top of the pears that he served al-Muntaṣir. Setting eyes on the pear, al-Muntaṣir ordered the servant to peel it and feed it to him. The servant peeled and cut it, and then gave it to him, piece by piece, until he devoured it. When he had finished eating the pear, he felt faint and told Ibn Ṭayfūr that he felt feverish.

Ibn Ṭayfūr said, "O Commander of the Faithful, have yourself cupped, and you will recover from the illness in your blood." He expected that with the emission of blood the poison would take better effect. The caliph was cupped and became feverish, and his illness became worse. But Ibn Ṭayfūr and the Turks feared that his illness would last for a long time.

So Ibn Ṭayfūr said to al-Muntaṣir, "O Commander of the Faithful, the cupping has not had the beneficial effect that we expected. You require bleeding, which will be more effective in your case." When the caliph told him to go ahead, Ibn Ṭayfūr bled him with a poisoned lancet. The doctor, in a state of confusion, threw the instrument among his lancets. It was the sharpest and the best.

Then ʿAlī b. Ṭayfūr became feverish himself and summoned a pupil of his to bleed him. The pupil looked through the lancets and did not find any that was sharper or better, so he bled him, and Ibn Ṭayfūr died as a result.]

It is reported on the authority of Ibn Dihqānah: We were in al-Muntaṣir's audience hall one day after al-Mutawakkil was killed when al-Masdūd al-Ṭunbūrī related a story.[716] When al-Muntaṣir

716. Ibn Dihqānah al-Nadīm appears as a boon companion of al-Muʿtaṣim in Hilāl al-Ṣābī, *Rusūm,* 72; tr. Salem, 60. Abū ʿAlī al-Ḥasan al-Masdūd al-Ṭunbūrī was a composer and tunburist who performed in the courts of al-Wāthiq, al-Mutawakkil and al-Muntaṣir. See Iṣfahānī, *Aghānī,* XXI, 256–58; Farmer, *History,* 158–59; Neubauer, *Musiker,* 193–94.

asked, "When did this take place, he answered, "On a dangerous night."[717] This vexed al-Muntaṣir.

It is reported on the authority of Saʿīd b. Salamah al-Naṣrānī:
[1498] Aḥmad b. al-Khaṣīb came to us in a cheerful spirit, mentioning that the Commander of the Faithful al-Muntaṣir dreamt at night that he had ascended a flight of stairs until he came to the twenty-fifth step, whereupon he was told, "This is your dominion." Ibn al-Munajjim learned of this, so Muḥammad b. Mūsā and ʿAlī b. Yaḥyā al-Munajjim visited the caliph and congratulated him on the dream.

Al-Muntaṣir said, "The matter was not as Aḥmad b. al-Khaṣīb told you. Rather when I reached the end of the stairs I was told, 'Stop, this is the end of your life.'" He was extremely distressed and lived after this for some days, filling out a year, and then died when he was twenty-five years old.[718]

It is also said that he was twenty-five years and six months old when he died. Still another view is that he was twenty-four years old. According to the view of (some)one of the informants, his caliphate lasted six months and two days. Another version puts it at exactly six months. And still another view is that it lasted one hundred and seventy-nine days.

He died in Sāmarrā, in the renovated palace,[719] forty-four days after he came out publicly against his brothers.

It is reported that when death was upon him he said:

I never delighted in any worldly blessing I obtained,
But [I am joyous now that] I proceed to the noble Lord.

Aḥmad b. Muḥammad b. al-Muʿtaṣim[720] said the funeral prayer over him in Sāmarrā, where he was born.

He had wide eyes, an aquiline nose, and he was short and well endowed.[721] He is said to have been capable of inspiring respect for his authority. He was allegedly the first ʿAbbāsid caliph whose

717. Literally, "a night of no prohibition or impediment"; hence a night of anarchy or danger.

718. O adds: and six months, and omits the next sentence (by homoeoteleuton).

719. Text: *al-qaṣr al-muḥdath.* According to Herzfeld, *Samarra,* 105, it is the renovated Jawsaq Palace.

720. Aḥmad b. Muḥammad b. al-Muʿtaṣim became the caliph al-Mustaʿīn, succeeding al-Muntaṣir.

721. Text: *jayyid al-biḍʿah.* Addenda, DCCLXXVI: *al-biḍāʿah.* See also Glossarium, CXXXV; Dozy, *Supplément,* I, 92.

grave was known. This is because his mother requested that his grave be made public.[722] His teknomyn was Abū Jaʿfar and his mother's name was Ḥabashiyyah. She was a Byzantine concubine. [1499]

Something of al-Muntaṣir's Conduct

It is reported that when al-Muntaṣir assumed the caliphate the first thing he did was to remove Ṣāliḥ[723] from Medina and to appoint ʿAlī b. al-Ḥusayn[724] b. Ismāʿīl b. al-ʿAbbās b. Muḥammad as governor there.

It is reported on the authority of ʿAlī b. al-Ḥusayn: When I visited him to bid farewell, he said to me: "O ʿAlī, I am sending you to my flesh and blood." He pinched the skin of his forearm and said, "I am sending you to this. Watch how you are with these people and how you deal with them, that is, the family of Abū Ṭālib." I replied, "I hope to follow the opinion of the Commander of the Faithful, may God support him, concerning them, God willing." He said, "You will then thrive thereby[725] with me."

It is reported that Muḥammad b. Hārūn,[726] secretary of Muḥammad b. ʿAlī Bard al-Khiyār[727] and his deputy over the Bureau of Estates of Ibrāhīm al-Mu'ayyad, was struck dead on his bed

722. ʿAynī comments, citing al-Sibṭ [b. al-Jawzī], that Ṭabarī's statement here is surprising since the tombs of the ʿAbbāsid caliphs are in fact known, e.g., the tomb of al-Saffāḥ is in Anbār beneath the *minbar*; and those of al-Mahdī in Māsabadhān, Hārūn in Ṭūs, al-Ma'mūn in Ṭarsūs, and al-Muʿtaṣim, al-Wāthiq, and al-Mutawakkil in Sāmarrā.

723. O adds Ibn ʿĪsā; Ibn al-Athīr *Kāmil,* VII, 76 and Ṣūlī have Ibn ʿAlī. He is Ṣāliḥ b. ʿAlī b. ʿĪsā.

724. Text and Cairo edition: al-Ḥusayn. Ms. O and Ibn al-Athīr, *Kāmil,* VII, 76: al-Ḥasan.

725. Ṣūlī adds *ʿinda Allāh wa-,* that is, "You will then thrive in this with God and with me." On al-Muntaṣir's new orientation in favor of the Shīʿah and policy of détente with the ʿAlids, see Ibn al-Athīr, *Kāmil,* VII, 75–76; and Sourdel, "La politique religieuse," 6–8. Among other things, he permitted visiting the site of al-Ḥusayn b. ʿAlī's grave and restored Fadak to the descendants of al-Ḥusayn and al-Ḥasan, sons of ʿAlī b. Abī Ṭālib.

726. Ms. O: Hārūn. Ms. C: *Fragmenta,* 561.5; Ṣūlī: Dāwūd.

727. Text: Muḥammad b. ʿAli Bard (or: Burd) al-Khiyār. C: Ibn Bard al-Ḥanār (?); O: Ibn Bard al-Khiyār. *Fragmenta*: Ibn Bard al-Khabbāz. Ṣūlī says that Muḥammad b. Hārūn al-Anbārī (?) was a secretary of Bard (?) al-Kh-?-ār, that is, Muḥammad b. ʿAlī al-Ṣūlī. And elsewhere he mentions Muḥammad b. ʿAlī al-Ṣūlī, known as Bard (?) al-Khiyār.

[1500] with a number of blows by a sword. His son summoned a black servant (*khādim*) of his and also Waṣīf. Waṣīf reportedly tried to get the black to confess. He was then brought before al-Muntaṣir, and Jaʿfar b. ʿAbd al-Wāḥid was summoned, and questioned him about his murdering his patron. The black confessed, describing what he had done to Muḥammad and the reason for his killing him.

Al-Muntaṣir asked him, "Woe to you, why did you kill him?" The black replied, "Why did you kill your father, al-Mutawakkil?" Al-Muntaṣir then queried the jurists about the black's case, and they advised that he be killed, whereupon he had him decapitated and suspended near the gallows of Bābak.

In this year, Muḥammad b. ʿAmr al-Shārī (the Khārijite) rebelled in the region of Mosul.[728] Al-Muntaṣir sent against him Isḥāq b. Thābit al-Farghānī. He took Muḥammad captive with a number of his men, and they were killed and suspended.

In this year, Yaʿqūb b. al-Layth al-Ṣaffār moved from Sijistān and proceeded to Herat.[729]

It is reported on the authority of Aḥmad b. ʿAbdallāh, son of Ṣāliḥ, the prefect of the oratory: My father had a muezzin. Some(one) of our family saw him in a dream summoning [the people] to one of the [daily] prayers. Then he approached a house where al-Muntaṣir was and called out, "O Muḥammad, O Muntaṣir, your Lord is waiting in ambush."[730]

It is reported on the authority of Bunān the Singer—he was allegedly the person most intimate with al-Muntaṣir during the life of his father (al-Mutawakkil) and after he assumed the caliphate: I asked al-Muntaṣir to give me a brocade robe when he was caliph. He said, "I have something better for you than a brocade robe." I asked what it was. He replied: "Feign illness so that I will visit you, and more than a brocade robe will be given to you."
[1501] Bunān said: He died during these days and did not give me anything.

728. See also above, 1351 (p. 37).

729. Yaʿqūb b. al-Layth al-Ṣaffār was one of the two brothers who founded the Ṣaffārid dynasty; Bosworth, *Dynasties*, 103.

730. See Qurʾān 89:14.

Bibliography of Cited Works

Abbott, N. "Arabic Papyri of the Reign of Ǧaʿfar al-Mutawakkil ʿala-llāh." *ZDMG*, 92 (1938): 88–135.

Abū al-ʿAtāhiyah. *Dīwān*. Ed. L. Cheikho. 4th ed., Beirut, 1927.

Abū al-Ḥusayn, Muḥammad b. Abī Yaʿlā b. al-Farrāʾ. *Ṭabaqāt al-Ḥanābilah*. Ed. M. Ḥāmid al-Fiqī. 2 vols., Cairo, 1371 (1952).

Abū al-Maḥāsin b. Taghrībirdī. *al-Nujūm al-zāhirah fī mulūk Miṣr wa-l-Qāhirah*. Cairo, 1348ff. (1929ff.). Reprinted ca. 1967.

Abū Yūsuf, Yaʿqūb b. Ibrāhīm. *Kitāb al-kharāj*. Cairo, 1352 (1933–34).

Addenda: see Ṭabarī.

Aghānī: see Iṣfahānī.

Aḥmad b. Ḥanbal. *Musnad*. Ed. A. M. Shākir. 15 vols., Cairo, 1342 (1923), Cairo, 1375 (1956).

Ahsan, M. M. *Social Life under the Abbasids*. London and New York, 1979.

ʿAlī b. al-Jahm. *Dīwān*. Ed. Khalīl Mardam Bak. Damascus, 1949.

Amedroz, H. F. "Tales of Official Life from the 'Tadhkira' of Ibn Hamdun." *JRAS*, 1908: 408–70.

al-ʿAmid, T. M. *The ʿAbbasid Architecture of Samarra in the Reign of both al-Muʿtasim and al-Mutawakkil*. Baghdad, 1973..

ʿArīb b. Saʿd al-Qurṭubī. *Ṭabarī continuatus*. Ed. M. J. de Goeje. Leiden, 1897 (reprinted Cairo, 1977).

Ashtor, E. "The Social Isolation of *Ahl Adh-Dhimma*." *P. Hirschler Memorial Book*. Budapest, 1949. Reprinted in *The Medieval Near East: Social and Economic History*. London, 1978.

———. *Histoire des prix et des salaires dans l'Orient Médiéval*. Paris, 1969.

Ayalon, D. "Preliminary Remarks on the Mamlūk Military Institution in Islam." In *War, Technology and Society in the Middle East*. London, 1975: 44–58. Reprinted in *The Mamlūk Military Society*. London, 1979.

———. "The Eunuchs in the Mamlūk Sultanate." *Studies in the Memory of Gaston Wiet*. Jerusalem, 1977: 267–95. Reprinted in *The Mamlūk Military Society*. London, 1979.

al-Bakrī, ʿAbdallāh b. ʿAbd al-ʿAzīz. *Muʿjam mā istaʿjam*. 4 vols., Cairo, 1364–1371 (1945–51).

Balādhurī, Aḥmad b. Yaḥyā. *Futūḥ al-buldān*. Ed. Ṣalāḥ al-Dīn al-Munajjid. Cairo, 1956–58. tran. P. K. Hitti. *The Origins of the Islamic State*. 2 vols. New York, 1968.

Bar Hebraeus. *Chronography*. Ed. and tran. E. A. Wallis Budge. 2 vols. London, 1932 (reprint 1976).

———. *Taʾrīkh mukhtaṣar al-duwal*. Ed. A. Ṣāliḥānī. Beirut, 1890.

Barthold, W. "To the Question of Early Persian Poetry." *BSOAS*, 2 (1923):836–38.

Beckford, William. *Vathek*. Ed. R. Lonsdale. London, 1970.

Bell, R. *The Qurʾān*. 2 vols. Edinburgh, 1937.

Bīrūnī, Abū Rayḥān. *Chronology: al-Āthār al-bāqiyah ʿan al-qurūn al-khāliyah*. Ed. C. E. Sachau. Leipzig, 1878.

Bosworth, C. E. *Islamic Dynasties*. Edinburgh, 1967.

———. "Abū ʿAbdallāh al-Khwārazmī on the Technical Terms of the Secretary's Art." *JESHO*, 12 (1969): 113–64. Reprinted in *Medieval Arabic Culture and Administration*. London, 1982.

———. "The Ṭāhirids and Arabic Culture." *JSS*, 14 (1969): 45–79. Reprinted in *Medieval Arabic Culture and Administration*. London, 1982.

———. "The Ṭāhirids and Ṣaffarids." *The Cambridge History of Iran*, IV. Cambridge, 1975: 90–135.

———. "Al-Maqrīzī's 'Book of Contention and Strife Concerning the Banū Umayya and the Banū Hashim.'" *Journal of Semitic Studies Monograph*, 3. Manchester, 1981.

Bury, J. B. *The Imperial Administrative System in the Ninth Century*. New York, n. d. Originally: *The British Academy. Supplemental Papers*. I, 1911.

———. *A History of the Eastern Roman Empire*. London, 1912.

Canard, M. *Histoire de la dynastie des H'amdanides de Jazīra et de Syrie*, Vol. I. Publications de la Faculté des Lettres d'Alger, IIe Série, Tome XXI, Algiers, 1951.

Caskel, W. *Ǧamharat an-nasab: Das genealogische Werk des Hišām Ibn Muḥammad al-Kalbī*. Leiden, 1966.

Chejne, A. *Succession to the Rule in Islam*. Lahore, 1960.

Christides, V. *The Conquest of Crete by the Arabs* (ca. 824). Athens, 1984.
Creswell, K. A. C. *Early Muslim Architecture.* 2 vols. New York, 1940.
Crone, P. *Slaves on Horses. The Evolution of Islamic Polity.* Cambridge, 1980.
Daniel, E. *The Political and Social History of Khurasan under Abbasid Rule 747–820.* Minneapolis and Chicago, 1979.
al-Dhahabī, Muḥammad b. Aḥmad. *al-ʿIbar fī khabar man ghabar.* Ed. Ṣalāḥ al-Dīn al-Munajjid and Fuʾād Sayyid. 5 vols. Kuwait, 1960–66.
———. *al-Mushtabih fī al-rijāl.* Ed. ʿAlī M. al-Bajāwī. 2 vols. Cairo, 1962.
Dozy, R. *Dictionnaire détaillé des noms des vêtements chez les Arabes.* Amsterdam, 1845.
———. *Supplément aux dictionnaires arabes.* 2 vols. Leiden, 1881.
Dussaud, R. *Topographie historique de la Syrie antique et médiévale.* Paris, 1927.
Farmer, H. G. *A History of Arabian Music.* London, 1967.
Fattal, A. *Le statut légal des non-musulmans en pays d'Islam.* Beirut, 1958.
Fischer, W. *Farb- und Formbezeichnungen in der Sprache der altarabischen Dichtung.* Wiesbaden, 1965.
Fragmenta historicum arabicorum. Ed. M. J. de Goeje. Leiden, 1871.
Geyer, R. *Zwei Gedichte von al-ʾAʿšâ.* 2 vols. Vienna, 1905, 1919.
Gil, M. *Palestine during the First Muslim Period* (in Hebrew). 3 vols. Tel Aviv, 1983.
Glossarium: see Ṭabarī.
Goitein, S. D. *A Mediterranean Society.* 5 vols. Berkeley, 1967–88.
Goldziher, I. *Muslim Studies (Muhammedanische Studien).* Ed. S. M. Stern. tr. C. R. Barber and S. M. Stern. 2 vols. London, 1967–71.
———. "Historiography in Arabic Literature," *Gesammelte Schriften.* Ed. J. De Somogyi. 6 vols. Hildesheim, 1967–73.
Gräf, E. "Religiöse und rechtliche Vorstellungen über Kriegsgefangene in Islam und Christentum." *Die Welt des Islams,* 8 (1963): 89–139.
Grégoire, H. "Études sur le neuvième siècle." *Byzantion,* 8 (1933): 515–50.
Grousset, R. *l'Histoire de l'Arménie des origines à 1071.* Paris, 1947.
Guidi, I. *Tables alphabétiques du Kitāb al-Aġānī.* Leiden, 1895, 1900.
Hamdānī, Abū Muḥammad. *Ṣifat Jazīrat al-ʿArab.* Ed. D. H. Müller. Leiden, 1884–91; reprinted Amsterdam, 1968.
Ḥarīrī, Abū Muḥammad al-Qāsim. *Maqāmāt. Les Séances de Ḥarīrī.* Ed. S. De Sacy. 2d ed. 2 vols. Paris, 1847.
Hasan, Y. F. *The Arabs and the Sudan.* Edinburgh, 1967.

Herzfeld, E. *Geschichte der Stadt Samarra.* Hamburg, 1948.

Hilāl al-Ṣābī. *Rusūm dār al-khilāfah.* Ed. M. 'Awwād. Baghdad, 1383 (1964).

———. *Tuḥfat al-umarā' fī ta'rīkh al-wuzarā'.* Ed. 'A. A. Farrāj. Cairo, 1958.

———. *Rusūm dār al-khilāfah (The Rules and Regulations of the 'Abbāsid Court).* Tr. E. A. Salem. Beirut, 1977.

Hinz, W. *Islamische Masse und Gewichte.* Leiden, 1955.

Honigmann, *Ostgrenze:* see Vasiliev.

Ḥudūd al-'ālam. Tr. V. Minorsky. E. J. W. Gibb Memorial Series, N.S., 11. 2nd ed. Ed. C. E. Bosworth. London, 1970.

Ibn al-Abbār, Muḥammad b. 'Abdallāh. *I'tāb al-kuttāb.* Ed. S. Ashtar. Damascus, 1380 (1961).

Ibn 'Abd Rabbihi, Abū 'Umar. *al-'Iqd al-farīd.* 4 vols. Cairo, 1321 (1903).

Ibn Abī Uṣaybi'ah, Aḥmad b. al-Qāsim. *'Uyūn al-anbā' fī ṭabaqāt al-aṭibbā'.* Ed. A. Müller. 2 vols. Cairo, 1299 (1882).

Ibn al-'Adīm, 'Umar b. Aḥmad. *Zubdat al-ḥalab fī ta'rīkh Ḥalab.* Ed. S. Dahan. 3 vols. Damascus, 1370 (1951).

Ibn al-Athīr, 'Izz al-Dīn. *al-Kāmil fī al-ta'rīkh.* Ed. C. J. Tornberg. Leiden, 1853–74.

Ibn Badrūn, Abū al-Qāsim. *Sharḥ Qaṣīdat Ibn 'Abdūn.* Ed. Muḥyī al-Dīn Ṣabrī al-Kurdī. Cairo, 1340 (1921).

Ibn Baṭṭūṭa, Shams al-Dīn. *The Travels of Ibn Battuta.* tr. H. A. R. Gibb. Cambridge, 1958.

Ibn Ḥawqal, Abū al-Qāsim. *Kitāb al-masālik wa-l-mamālik.* Ed. M. J. de Goeje. Leiden, 1897.

Ibn al-Jawzī, 'Abd al-Raḥmān. *al-Muntaẓam fī ta'rīkh al-mulūk wa-l-umam.* Hyderabad, 1357–59 (1938–40).

Ibn Kathīr, Abū al-Fidā'. *al-Bidāyah wa-l-nihāyah.* 14 vols. Cairo, 1351–58 (1932–39).

Ibn Khaldūn, 'Abd al-Raḥmān. *Kitāb al-'ibar.* Beirut, 1957.

———. *The Muqaddimah.* Tr. F. Rosenthal. 3 vols. Princeton, 1967.

Ibn Khallikān, Aḥmad b. Muḥammad. *Kitāb wafayāt al-a'yān.* Tr. M. G. de Slane, *Ibn Khallikān's Biographical Dictionary.* Paris and London, 1843–71.

Ibn Khurradādhbih, Abū al-Qāsim. *Kitāb al-masālik wa-l-mamālik.* Ed. and tr. M. J. de Goeje. Leiden, 1889.

Ibn al-Mu'tazz, Abū al-'Abbās. *Ṭabaqāt al-shu'arā' al-muḥdathīn.* Ed. A. A. Farrāj. Cairo, 1956.

Ibn al-Nadīm, Muḥammad b. Abī Ya'qūb. *The Fihrist of al-Nadīm.* Ed. and tr. B. Dodge. 2 vols. New York and London, 1970.

Ibn al-Qifṭī, Jamāl al-Dīn. *Ta'rīkh al-ḥukamā'*. Ed. J. Lippert. Leipzig, 1903.

Ibn Qutaybah, ʿAbdallāh b. Muslim. *ʿUyūn al-akhbār*. Cairo, 1925–30.

Ibn Ṭayfūr, Aḥmad b. Ṭāhir. *Baghdād fī ta'rīkh al-khilāfah al-ʿAbbāsiyyah*. Baghdad, 1388 (1968).

Ibn al-Ṭiqṭaqā, Muḥammad b. ʿAlī. *Kitāb al-Fakhrī*. Beirut, 1386 (1966). Tr. C. E. J. Whitting. London, 1947.

Ibn al-Zubayr, al-Qāḍī al-Rashīd. *al-Dhakhā'ir wa-l-tuḥaf*. Ed. M. Ḥamīd-Allāh and Ṣalāḥ al-Dīn al-Munajjid. Kuwait, 1959.

Index: see Ṭabarī.

al-Iṣfahānī, Abū al-Faraj. *Kitāb al-aghānī*. 20 vols. Bulaq, 1868–69. vol. 21. Cairo, 1905.

al-Jāḥiẓ, Abū ʿUthmān ʿAmr b. Baḥr. *Fī manāqib al-Turk wa-ʿāmmat jund al-khilāfah*. In *Tria opuscula*. Ed. G. van Vloten. Leiden, 1903 (reprinted 1968), 1–56.

al-Jahshiyārī, Abū ʿAbdallāh, *Kitāb al-wuzarā' wa-l-kuttāb*. Ed. M. al-Saqqā', I. al-Ibyārī, and ʿA. Shilbī. Cairo, 1357 (1938).

Kaḥḥālah, ʿU. R. *Muʿjam qabā'il al-ʿArab*. 3 vols. Damascus, 1368 (1949).

Kennedy, H. *The Early Abbasid Caliphate, a Political History*. London and Totowa, NJ, 1981.

al-Khaṭīb al-Baghdādī, Aḥmad b. Thābit. *Ta'rīkh Baghdād*. 14 vols. Cairo, 1349 (1931).

Kindermann, H. *"Schiff" im Arabischen*. Bonn, 1934.

al-Kindī, Muḥammad b. Yūsuf. *Wulāh Miṣr. Histories of the Governors and Judges of Egypt*. Ed. Rhuvon Guest. E. J. W. Gibb Memorial Series, 19. Leiden and London, 1912.

Lane, E. W. *An Arabic-English Lexicon*. 8 vols. London and Edinburgh, 1863–93.

Laoust, H. *La profession de foi d'Ibn Baṭṭa*. Damascus, 1958.

———. *Les schismes dans l'Islam*. Paris, 1965.

Lapidus, I. "Separation of State and Religion in Early Islamic Society." *IJMES*, 6 (1975): 363–85.

Lassner, J. *The Topography of Baghdad in the Early Middle Ages*. Detroit, 1970.

———. *The Shaping of ʿAbbāsid Rule*. Princeton, 1980.

Laurent, J. *L'Arménie entre Byzance et l'Islam*. Paris, 1919.

Le Strange, G. *Baghdad during the Abbasid Caliphate*. London, 1900.

———. *Lands of the Eastern Caliphate*. Cambridge, 1905.

Levi Della Vida, G. "A Papyrus Reference to the Damietta Raid of 853 A.D.," *Byzantion* (American Series, III), 17 (1944–45): 212–21.

Levtzion, N., and J. F. P. Hopkins. *Corpus of Early Arabic sources for West African History*. Cambridge, 1981.

Lewis, B. *Islam from the Prophet Muhammad to the Capture of Constantinople.* 2 vols. New York, 1974.
Lichtenstädter, I. "The Distinctive Dress of Non-Muslims in Islamic Countries." *Historia Judaica,* 5 (1943): 35–52.
Løkkegaard, F. *Islamic Taxation in the Classic Period.* Copenhagen, 1950.
McCarthy, R. J. *The Theology of al-Ashʿarī.* Beirut, 1953.
Madelung, W. "The Origins of the Controversy Concerning the Creation of the Koran." *Orientalia Hispanica sive studia F.M. Pareja octogenario dicta.* Ed. J. M. Barral, I.1. Leiden, 1974: 504–25. [Reprinted in *Religious Schools and Sects in Medieval Islam.* London, 1985.]
Mango, C. "When Was Michael III Born?" *Dumbarton Oaks Papers,* 21 (1967): 253–58. Reprinted in C. Mango, *Byzantium and Its Image.* London, 1984.
Maqrīzī, Aḥmad b. ʿAlī. *al-Mawāʿiẓ wa- l-iʿtibār fī dhikr al-khiṭaṭ wa-l-āthār.* Ed. G. Wiet. Cairo, 1922. 3 vols. Cairo, 1967–68.
———. *al-Nizāʿ wa-l-takhāṣum fī mā bayna Banī Umayya wa Banī Hāshim.* See also Bosworth, "Al-Maqrīzī's 'Book of Contention and Strife.' "
Marin, E. *Abū Jaʿfar Muḥammad B. Jarīr al-Ṭabarī's The Reign of al-Muʿtaṣim* (833–842). New Haven, 1951.
Marzubānī, Muḥammad b. ʿImrān. *Muʿjam al-shuʿarāʾ.* Ed. F. Krenkow. Cairo, 1354 (1935–36).
Maspéro, Jean, and G. Wiet. *Matériaux pour servir à la géographie de l'Égypte.* Première série. Paris, 1919.
Massignon, L. "Cadis et naqībs baghdadiens," *WZKM,* 51 (1948): 106–15.
al-Masʿūdī, ʿAlī b. al-Ḥusayn. *Murūj al-Dhahab.* Ed. and tr. C. A. C. Barbier de Meynard and B. M. M. Pavet de Courteille. 9 vols. Paris, 1861–77.
———. *al-Tanbīh wa-l-ishrāf.* Ed. M. J. de Geoje. Leiden, 1894 (Reprinted Beirut, 1965).
Mercier, L. *La chasse et les sports chez les Arabes.* Paris, 1927.
Miah, M. S. *The Reign of al-Mutawakkil.* Dacca, 1969.
Minorsky, *Ḥudūd:* see *Ḥudūd al-ʿālam.*
———. "Caucasia IV." *BSOAS,* 15 (1953), 504–29.
———. *A History of Sharvān and Darband.* Cambridge, 1958.
Mottahedeh, R. P. *Loyalty and Leadership in an Early Islamic Society.* Princeton, 1980.
Mubārak, Abū al-ʿAbbās. *al-Kāmil.* Ed. Z. Mubārak. 3 vols. Cairo, 1355–72 (1936–52).
Muyldermans: see Vardan.

Neubauer, E. *Musiker am Hof der frühen ʿAbbāsiden.* Frankfurt/Main, 1965.
Ostrogorski, G. *History of the Byzantine State.* Oxford, 1956.
Paret, R. *Der Koran. Kommentar und Konkordanz.* 2d ed. Stuttgart, 1977.
Patton, W. M. *Aḥmed ibn Hanbal and the Miḥnah.* Leiden, 1897.
Pauly-Wissowa: *(Paulys) Real encyclopädie der classischen Altertumswissenschaft.*
Pellat, C. "Ǧaḥiẓ à Baġdād et à Sāmarrā." *RSO,* 27 (1952): 47–67.
———. *Le milieu baṣrien et la formation de Ǧāḥiẓ.* Paris, 1953.
———. "Une charge contre les secrétaires d'état attribuée à Ǧāḥiẓ." *Hesperis,* 1956: 29–50.
Pinto, O. "Al-Fatḥ B. Ḫāqān, favorito di al-Mutawakkil." *RSO,* 13 (1931): 133–49.
Pseudo-Tanūkhī. *al-Mustajād min faʿālāt al-ajwād.* Ed. Muḥammad Kurd ʿAlī. Damascus, 1946.
Qazvīnī, Ḥamdallāh Mustawfī. *Nuzhat al-qulūb. The Geographical Part of the Nuzhat-al-Qulūb.* Ed. G. Le Strange. London, 1915. Tr. Le Strange. London, 1919.
Qudāmah b. Jaʿfar, Abū al-Faraj. *Al-Kharāj wa-ṣināʿat al-kitābah.* Ed. Muḥammad Ḥusayn al-Zubaydī. Baghdad, 1981.
Qummī, al-Ḥasan b. Muḥammad. *Ta'rīkh Qumm.* Ed. J. Ṭihrānī. Tehran, 1313 (1934).
Rogers, J. M. "Sāmarrā: A Study in Medieval Town-Planning." *The Islamic City.* Ed. A. H. Hourani and S. M. Stern. Oxford, 1970: 119–55.
Rosenthal, F. *A History of Muslim Historiography.* Leiden, 1952, 1968.
———. *Four Essays on Art and Literature in Islam.* Leiden, 1971.
———. (Tr.). *The History of al-Ṭabarī.* Vol. XXXVIII. *The Return of the Caliphate to Baghdad.* Albany, 1984.
Runciman, S. *The Medieval Manichee.* Cambridge, 1947.
Sadan, J. *Le mobilier au Proche-Orient médiéval.* Leiden, 1976.
Saliba, G. (tr.). *The History of al-Ṭabarī,* Vol. XXXV. *The Crisis of the ʿAbbāsid Caliphate.* Albany, 1985.
Sāmarrā'ī, Yūnus I. *Ta'rīkh Madīnat Sāmarrā.* Baghdad, 1973.
Samhūdī, Jamāl al-Dīn. *Wafā' al-wafā'.* 2 vols. Cairo, 1326 (1908).
Sauvaget, J. *Historiens arabes.* Paris, 1946.
Schwarz, P. *Iran im Mittelalter nach den arabischen Geographen.* 9 vols. Stuttgart and Berlin, 1896–1936.
Sezgin, F. *Geschichte des arabischen Schrifttums.* Leiden, 1967–.
Shaban, M. *Islamic History: A New Interpretation.* 2 vols. Cambridge, 1971, 1976.
Shābushtī, Abū al-Ḥasan. *Kitāb al-diyārāt.* Ed. G. Awad. Baghdad, 1951.

Sourdel, D. *Le vizirat ʿAbbāside de 749 à 936.* Damascus, 1959–60.

———. "La politique religieuse des successeurs d'al-Mutawakkil." *SI,* 13 (1960). 5–20.

——— and J. Sourdel-Thomine. *La civilisation de l'Islam classique.* Paris, 1968.

Steingass, F. *Persian-English Dictionary.* London, 1930.

Stern, S. M. "Abū ʿĪsā Ibn al-Munajjim's *Chronography." Islamic Philosophy and the Classical Tradition: Essays presented . . . to Richard Walzer.* Ed. S. M. Stern *et al.* Oxford, 1972: 437–66.

Stigelbauer, M. *Die Sängerinnen am Abbasidenhof um die Zeit des Kalifen al-Mutawakkil.* Vienna, 1975.

Stillman, N. A. *The Jews of Arab Lands.* Philadelphia, 1979.

Ṣūlī, Ibrāhīm b. al-ʿAbbās. *Dīwān.* In *al-Ṭarā'if al-adabiyyah.* Ed. ʿAbd al-ʿAzīz al-Maymūnī. Cairo, 1937.

al-Suyūṭī, Jalāl al-Dīn. *Kitāb Bughyat al-wuʿāh.* Cairo, 1326 (1908). Ed. M. Abū al-Faḍl Ibrāhīm. 2 vols. Cairo, 1384 (1964–65).

———. *Ta'rīkh al-khulafā'.* Ed. M. Muḥyī al-Dīn ʿAbd al-Ḥamīd. Cairo, 1389 (1969). Tr. H. S. Jarrett. *Jalalu'ddin a's Suyuti. History of the Caliphs.* Amsterdam, 1970.

———. *al-Aḥādīth al-ḥisān fī faḍl al-ṭaylasān.* Ed. A. Arazi. Jerusalem, 1983.

al-Ṭabarī. Index, Introductio, Glossarium, Addenda et Emendanda: refer to Vols. 14 and 15 of Leiden edition. Leiden, 1901. *Ta'rīkh al-rusul wa-l-mulūk.* Ed. Muḥammad Abū al-Faḍl Ibrāhīm. vol. IX. Cairo, 1968.

Tanūkhī, Abū ʿAlī al-Muḥassin b. ʿAlī al-Tanūkhī. *al-Faraj baʿd al-shiddah.* Cairo, 1375 (1955).

———. *Nishwār al-muḥāḍarah.* Ed. ʿAbbūd al-Shālijī. Cairo, 1391–93 (1971–73). Ed. and tr. D. S. Margoliouth. *The Table-Talk of a Mesopotamian Judge,* Part I. London, 1921. Oriental Translation Fund, N.S., 27–28, trans. parts II & VIII. Hyderabad. n.d.

Thaʿālibī, Abū Manṣūr. *The Laṭā'if al-maʿārif of Thaʿālibī.* Tr. C. E. Bosworth. Edinburgh, 1968.

Theophanes (Confessor). *Chronographia.* Ed. C. de Boor. 2 vols. Leipzig, 1883–85 (reprinted Hildesheim, 1963).

Theophanes continuatus. Ed. I. Bekker. Bonn, 1838.

Thilo, U. *Die Ortsnamen in der altarabischen Poesie.* Wiesbaden, 1958.

Tritton, A. S. *The Caliphs and Their non-Muslim Subjects.* London, 1970.

Tyan, E. *Histoire de l'organisation judiciaire en pays d'Islam.* 2d ed. Leiden, 1960.

ʿUmar b. Abī Rabīʿah. *Dīwān*. Beirut, 1380 (1961). Ed. P. Schwarz, Leipzig, 1902–08.

ʿUmar, F. *Buḥūth fī al-taʾrīkh al-ʿabbāsī*. Beirut, 1977.

Vardan. *La domination arabe en arménie: extrait de l'histoire universelle de Vardan*. Tr. J. Muyldermans. Louvain and Paris, 1927.

Vasiliev, A. A. *Byzance et les Arabes*. Vol. I (trans. H. Grégoire and M. Canard). Brussels, 1935. Vol. II/2. M. Canard. *Extraits des sources arabes*. Brussels, 1950. Vol. III. E. Honigmann. *Die Ostgrenze des byzantinischen Reiches von 363 bis 1071*. Brussels, 1935.

Vasiliev, A. A. *A History of the Byzantine Empire*. 2 vols. Madison, Wisconsin, 1961.

Vasmer, R. *Chronologie der arabischen Statthalter von Armenien unter den Abbasiden, von as-Saffach bis zur Krönung Aschots I., 750–887*. Vienna, 1931.

Wakīʿ, Muḥammad b. Khalāf b. Ḥayyān. *Akhbār al-quḍāh*. Ed. ʿAbd al-ʿAzīz Muṣṭafā al-Maghārī. Cairo, 1366–69 (1947–50).

Wensinck, A. J. *et al. Concordance et indices de la tradition musulmane*. Leiden, 1936–69.

Wörterbuch der klassischen arabischen Sprache. Ed. J. Kraemer, H. Gätje *et al.* Wiesbaden, 1970ff.

al-Yaʿqūbī, Aḥmad b. Abī Yaʿqūb. *Taʾrīkh (Historiae)*. Ed. M. Th. Houtsma. 2 vols. Leiden, 1883.

———. *Kitāb al-buldān*. Ed. M. J. de Goeje. Leiden, 1892. Tr. G. Wiet. *Les pays*. Cairo, 1937.

Yāqūt b. ʿAbdallāh al-Ḥamawī. *Muʿjam al-buldān*. Ed. F. Wüstenfeld. 6 vols. Göttingen, 1866–73. Beirut, 1376 (1957).

———. *Irshād al-arīb ilā maʿrifat al-adīb (Muʿjam al-udabāʾ)*. Ed. D. S. Margoliouth, E. J. W. Gibb Memorial Series, 6. 7 vols. Leiden and London, 1907–27.

Zambaur, E. de. *Manuel de généalogie et de chronologie pour l'histoire de l'Islam*. Hannover, 1927.

Index

A

al-ʿAbbās, sons of 55
al-ʿAbbās b. Aḥmad b. Rashīd 70
al-ʿAbbās b. al-Maʾmūn 189
al-ʿAbbās b. Muḥammad b. Jibrīl al-Qāʾid al-Khurāsānī 30
al-ʿAbbās b. Saʿīd al-Jawharī 169
ʿAbbāsid caliphs xii–xiii, xxvi; regime 27–28; court 16 n. 40
ʿAbd al-ʿAzīz b. Zurārah 24
ʿAbd al-Malik b. Isḥāq b. ʿImārah 135
ʿAbd al-Raḥmān b. Ḥamzah 119
ʿAbd al-Raḥmān b. Isḥāq al-Qāḍī 32
ʿAbd al-Ṣamad b. Mūsā b. Muḥammad b. Ibrāhīm al-Imām 147–48, 150, 153, 170
ʿAbd al-Wahhāb, son of al-Muntaṣir 210
ʿAbdallāh b. al-ʿAbbās b. al-Faḍl b. Rabīʿ 54
ʿAbdallāh b. Aḥmad b. Dāwūd al-Hāshimī 23
ʿAbdallāh b. Isḥāq b. Ibrāhīm 116
ʿAbdallāh b. Makhlad (Ibn al-Bawwāb) 160, 163
ʿAbdallāh b. Muḥammad b. Dāwūd 129, 132, 145
ʿAbdallāh b. Ṭāhir, Abū al-ʿAbbās 21
ʿAbdallāh b. ʿUmar al-Bazyār 176, 220
ʿAbdallāh b. Waṣīf 180
ʿAbdallāh b. Yaḥyā 161
Abnāʾ 182
Abrīk, see Tephrikē
Abū al-ʿAbbās al-Wāthī al-Naṣrānī 122, 124
Abū ʿAbdallāh b. al-Aʿrābī al-Rāwiyah 44
Abū ʿAbdallāh al-Armanī 32
Abū ʿAbdallāh b. Qabīḥah, see al-Muʿtazz bī-llāh
Abū al-Agharr xvi, 80, 86, 88
Abū Aḥmad b. al-Mutawakkil, see al-Muwaffaq bi-llāh
Abū ʿAmrah Aḥmad b. Saʿīd 203
Abū al-ʿAtāhiyah 117
Abū ʿAwn 206
Abū Bakr, caliph xix, 135
Abū al-Faraj Muḥammad b. Najāḥ 159–60, 163
Abū al-Ghuṣn al-Aʿrābī 97
Abū Ḥafṣ ʿUmar b. ʿĪsā, ruler of Crete 125
Abū Hārūn al-Sarrāj 28, 29, 30, 35
Abū al-Ḥasan Isḥāq b. Ibrāhīm al-Madāʾinī 6
Abū al-Ḥasan Isḥāq b. Thābit b. Abī ʿAbbād 86
Abū Ḥashīshah, see Muḥammad b. ʿAlī b. Umayyah

Abū Ḥassān al-Ziyādī, see al-Ḥasan b. ʿUthmān
Abū Ḥa-?-ā'iz al-ʿAbbās 189
Abū al-Ḥurr, see Mūsā b. Zurārah
Abū ʿIsa Mārid al-Muḥrizī 179
Abū Jaʿfar, see Muḥammad b. ʿAbd al-Malik
Abū Jaʿfar al-Ṭabarī xiii–xxiv, 45 n. 168, 140 n. 465, 171–72, 184, 219
Abū Khaythamah Zuhayr b. Ḥarb 27
Abū Manṣūr, see Ītākh
Abū al-Mughīth al-Rāfiʿī Mūsā b. Ibrāhīm 130
Abū Muḥammad Aḥmad b. bt. Ḥasan b. Shunayf 159–60
Abū Naṣr Aḥmad b. Ḥātim 44
Abū Nūḥ ʿĪsā b. Ibrāhīm 9 n. 14, 181, 197
Abū Qaḥṭabah al-Maghribī al-Ṭurṭūsī 41, 139; see also Aḥmad b. Abī Qaḥṭabah
Abū Saʿīd, see Muḥammad b. Yūsuf al-Marwazī
Abū Saʿīd b. Salm 41
Abū al-Sāj Dīwdād b. Dīwdast 152
Abū Ṣāliḥ al-Marwazī b. Yazdād 163
Abū Ṭālib (family of) 223
Abū Tammām Ḥabīb b. Aws al-Ṭā'ī 6, 9 n. 18
Abū al-ʿŪd 14, 15
Abū ʿUthmān, see Saʿīd al-Ṣaghīr (the Younger)
Abū Wahb 38
Abū al-Walīd, see Muḥammad b. Aḥmad
Abū al-Walīd al-Jarīrī al-Bajalī 209
Abū al-Wārith 184
Abū al-Wazīr, Aḥmad b. Khālid 10, 15, 61, 66, 69–70, 74–75
Abū Yaḥyā b. Marwān b. Muḥammad al-Shannī al-Kalbī 187
abyaḍ (complexion) 52 n. 195
al-Abzārī 119–20
Adana 157
Ādharbayjān xiv, xvi, xxix, 77, 79, 96, 104, 111
Adharnarsē (Adarnasē) b. Isḥāq al-Khāshinī 124
Africa xvi
al-Afshīn 9 n. 14
Afterlife 40
Aghbagh (Albaq) 116
Aḥmad, brother of Mūsā b. Zurārah 115
Aḥmad b. ʿAbd al-Wahhāb 56
Aḥmad b. ʿAbdallāh b. Sāliḥ 224
Aḥmad b. Abī Du'ād, Abū ʿAbdallāh 10, 28, 31, 35, 40, 52, 61–64, 66–67, 70, 75, 117, 131, 186–87
Aḥmad b. Abī Qaḥṭabah 38, 40
Aḥmad b. Ḥanbal 31 n. 105, 32 nn. 107–8, 116 n. 379, 128 n. 429, 137 n. 452
Aḥmad b. al-Ḥārith, Abū Jaʿfar xvii, 40–41
Aḥmad b. Ibrāhīm b. Kathīr al-Dawraqī, Abū ʿAlī 27
Aḥmad b. Isrā'īl 8, 164
Aḥmad b. Khālid, see Abū al-Wazīr
Aḥmad b. al-Khaṣīb al-Jarjarā'ī xviii, 10, 15, 195–97, 204, 205, 209–10, 213, 218, 222
Aḥmad b. al-Mudabbir 95 n. 326
Aḥmad b. Muḥammad b. ʿĀṣim, see ʿĪsā b. Jaʿfar
Aḥmad b. Muḥammad b. Makhlad xv–xvi, 24
Aḥmad b. Muḥammad b. al-Muʿtaṣim, see al-Mustaʿīn bi-llāh
Aḥmad b. Mūsā 161
Aḥmad b. Naṣr b. Malik b. Haytham al-Khuzā'ī xvi, 27–35, 119–20
Aḥmad b. Saʿīd b. Salm b. Qutaybah al-Bāhilī 39, 41, 43
Aḥmad b. Waṣīf 180
Aḥmad b. Yaḥyā b. Muʿādh 174, 176
Aḥmad b. Yūsuf, Abū al-Jahm 72
al-Ahwāz 72–73, 96
ʿĀ'ishah (wife of Muḥammad) xix, 135
ʿAkk 96
al-ʿAlā' (son of Ibn al-Baʿīth) 87
Alexandria 141

ʿAlī b. Abī Ṭālib 185
ʿAlī Bābā (king of the Bujah) 143–45
ʿAlī b. al-Ḥusayn b. Ismāʿīl b. al-ʿAbbās b. Muḥammad 223
ʿAlī b. ʿĪsā b. Jaʿfar b. Abī Jaʿfar al-Manṣūr 120, 127
ʿAlī b. al-Jahm b. Badr xvi, 54–55, 74, 87–88, 94, 128
ʿAlī b. Muḥammad b. ʿAlī al-Riḍā b. Mūsā b. Jaʿfar, tenth *imām* of the Shīʿites 76
ʿAlī b. al-Muḥassin al-Tanūkhī 118 n. 383
ʿAlī b. Mūsā al-Riḍā, eighth *imām* of the Shīʿites 44
ʿAlī b. al-Muʿtaṣim 203
ʿAlī b. Ṭayfūr (Ibn al-Ṭayfūrī) 219, 221
ʿAlī b. Yaḥyā b. Abī Manṣūr al-Munajjim 161, 165 n. 556, 183, 222
ʿAlī b. Yaḥyā al-Armanī 120, 127, 129, 146–47, 165, 167–68
ʿAlī b. Yazdād 190
Āmid (Amida) 146
al-Amīn, Muḥammad, caliph 40, 173
Amorian (Phrygian) dynasty 3 n. 3
ʿAmr b. Abī ʿAmr al-Shaybānī 44
ʿAmr b. Aṭāʾ (suburb of) 26
ʿAmr b. Isfandiyār 35
ʿAmr b. Isḥāq b. Ismāʿīl 122
ʿAmr b. al-Maʿdī Karib al-Zubaydī, Abū Thawr 33
ʿAmr b. Naṣr al-Qiṣāfī 164
ʿAmr b. Saysil (?) b. Kāl 79–80
ʿAnat 96
ʿAnazah (lance) 152
al-Anbār 84, 152
ʿAnbasah b. Isḥāq al-Ḍabbī 125–26, 143
Anqās (Ayqās)? (Byzantine officer) 41
Anṣār 18, 19
Anṭālya (Attaleia) 167
Antioch 157, 167 n. 560
al-Aqraʿ (Mount Casius) 157
Aqṣur (Luqṣur, Luxor) 143
Arab(s) 122, 169
Ardashīr 166
Ardzruni (Artsruni), Thomas 114 n. 363
ʿArīsh Miṣr 96
Armant 143
Armenia, Armenians xiv, xvi, xxix, 96, 104, 111, 113–16, 121–22, 182
Arrān xxix, 124
Arzan 115
aṣfar (complexion) 189 n. 656
al-Aʿshā, Maymūn b. Qays 54 n. 205
Ashhab b. Duwaykil b. Yaḥyā b. Ḥimyar al-ʿAwfī 18–20
Ashjaʿ (tribe) 26
Ashnās, Abū al-Jaʿfar al-Turkī xi, xii, 5, 21
Ashras (army commander) 29
Ashūṭ b. Ḥamzah al-Armanī (Ashot Ardzruni) 114 n. 366, 116, 183
Asia Minor xiv
ʿAskar al-Mahdī 156
al-Aṣmaʿī 44
asmar (complexion) 184 n. 631
Athamina, Khalil 49 n. 183
ʿAthʿath al-Aswad xix–xx, 174–75, 178–79, 180–81
ʿAttāb b. ʿAttāb 130–31, 163, 203
ʿawāṣim and *thughūr* 38–39, 96, 139
ʿAwn al-Khayyāṭ 12, 14
awsaṭ al-nās 140 n. 466
Ayalon, David 13 n. 35
ʿAyn Zarbah 137
al-ʿAynī, Maḥmūd b. Aḥmad, *ʿIqd al-jumān* xxiv
Ayyūb b. al-Junayd al-Naṣrānī 74
Azd (tribe) 75
ʿAzzūn b. ʿAbd al-ʿAzīz al-Anṣārī xv, 11, 12, 13, 15

B

Bābak (enclosure of) 34, 37; see also Khashabat Bābak
Badīʿ (palace) 155

Baghdad (Madīnat al-Salām), Baghdadians xii–xiii, xix–xx, 28, 29, 31, 35, 39, 51, 69, 73–74, 84–85, 88, 95, 110, 116–17, 119, 122, 131, 140, 149, 170, 172, 187, 190, 203
Bāghir (Bāghar) al-Turkī, Abū Muḥammad 179
Baghlūn al-Turkī 179–80
Bāhilah (tribe) 18, 47, 50
al-Baḥrayn 36, 96, 108, 152–53, 185
Baʿīth (son of Ibn al-Baʿīth) 88–89
Bājarmā 96
Balad 149, 151
Bālis 157
Balkājūr (army commander) 165, 167
Balkh 170
al-Balqāʾ 25
Bānījūrids 150 n. 499
Banū ʿAbdallāh b. Numayr 49
Banū Abī Bakr b. Kilāb 24
Banū ʿAdī 46
Banū ʿĀmir b. Numayr 49
Banū ʿAwf 18, 20
Banū Bilḥajjāj 49
Banū Busrah 49
Banū Ḍabbah 46
Banū Fazārah 25, 26, 51
Banū Hāshim 203
Banū Hilāl 21, 22
Banū Ḥubshī 20
Banū Kalb 167 n. 559
Banū Khāqān, Khāqānids 75 n. 261, 89 n. 302, 109 n. 355, 110 n. 356, 111 n. 359
Banū Kilāb 26, 51
Banū Kinānah 18
Banū Labīd b. Sulaym 19
Banū al-Munajjim 161 n. 539
Banū Murrah 23, 25, 51
Banū Numayr (Numayrī) xv, 45–51
Banū Qaṭan 49
Banū Qushayr 36
Banū Salāh 49
Banū Shurayḥ 49
Banū Sulaym xv, 17–25
Banū Tamīm 46
Banū Ṭayyiʾ 51, 111
Banū Thaʿlabah 26, 51
Banū Wahb 9 nn. 16 and 18
Banū Zayd b. Taghlib 37
Bardas xvii, 168
Bardhaʿah (Partav, Barda) 123–24
Barghāmush, deputy of Bughā the Elder 123
Barghūth 110
barīd 99 n. 334
Barmakids xii, 8 n. 13, 14, 15
Barqah 36, 50, 96, 131, 141
al-Baṣrah 36, 50, 96, 131
Baṭn Nakhl 46
Baṭn al-Sirr 47–48
Baydūn al-Khādim 198
al-Baylaqān 124
biʿah 134
Biṭrīq 114 n. 363, see Patrikios
B-k-sūm(?) 141
Bughā al-Kabīr, Abū Mūsā al-Turkī xi, xiv–xvi, 17, 19–20, 22, 26, 36, 45–51, 115 n. 370, 116, 121–24, 151, 156, 176, 178, 210, 212
Bughā al-Ṣaghīr al-Sharābī xi, xiv, 34, 62, 68, 78–81, 86–88, 105, 115–16, 178–81, 212
al-Buḥturī al-Ṭāʾī 9 n. 18, 166
Bujah xvi, 140–45
Bukhtīshūʿ b. Jibrīl 152–53, 164
Bunān b. ʿAmr al-Ḍārib xx, xxii, 174, 176–78, 180, 224
Buqrāṭ b. Ashūṭ (Bagrat son of Ashot) 113–14
būriyyān 69
al-Busfurrajān (Vaspurakan) 116
al-Bustān (the Garden) 21
Byzantine(s), Byzantium xvi–xvii, xx, 38–43, 124–27, 137–40, 146, 156, 164–65, 169, 170, 204, 205, 208

C

Cairo 141
Caliphal Palace (Sāmarrā) xiv, 36, 82, 114, 190

Christian(s) 39 n. 140, 41 n. 151, 89, 129, 133–34, 153, 170
Christianity 138, 169–70
Constantinople xvii, 41, 168, 170
Copt(s) 126
Crete 10 n. 19, 125

D

Dabīl (Dvin) 115–16, 121–22
Dākharraqān (Dihkharghān, Tukharghan) 78
Damaghān 146
Damascus xiii, 25, 97, 149, 151–52, 157
Damietta xvi, 124–26
al-Dandānī (?) xvii, 70
dann, danniyyah 118 n. 386
Darabādh 96
Ḍariyyah 26
Dāwūd b. ʿĪsā b. Mūsā b. Muḥammad 4
Dāwūd b. Muḥammad b. Abī al-ʿAbbās al-Ṭūsī 173
Day of the ʿĀshūrāʾ (Yawm al-ʿĀshūrāʾ) 39
Day of Sacrifice (Yawm al-Naḥr) 6, 153
Dhāt ʿIrq 20, 21, 22
Dhimmīs xviii, 41–42, 89–90, 93, 128
dhirāʿ 12 n. 30
Dhū al-Qarnayn xix, 95
Dhū al-Thafināt 61
Diʿbil b. ʿAlī al-Khuzāʿī 118 n. 383
*dihqān*s 170
dīnār 9 n. 15
Diyār Muḍar 96
Diyār Rabīʿah 37, 96
Dome of the Girdle (Hārūnī Palace) 12
duʿafāʾ (sg. *daʿīf*) 25 n. 77, 47
Dulayl b. Yaʿqūb al-Naṣrānī 156
durrāʿah 62, 69

E

East Side (Baghdad) 28, 29, 30, 34, 118
Edessa 157
Egypt xiv, 108, 141–43, 145, 157
Egyptians 141
Euphrates 152
Euphrates Road 84
Evangel 207

F

Fadak 25
al-Faḍl b. Isḥāq al-Hāshimī 52–53
al-Faḍl b. Marwān Abū al-ʿAbbās 75
al-Faḍl b. Qārin 167
al-Faḍl b. Sahl 53
al-Faḍl b. Yaḥyā b. Khālid 13 n. 15
Fam al-Ṣilḥ 184
al-Fārābī, Abū Naṣr xiii
Faraj al-Ṣaghīr (the Younger) 179
farajiyyah 73
Fāris b. Bughā al-Sharābī 111
Farj Bayt al-Dhahab 96
Fārs 37, 51, 96, 104, 107–8, 146
al-Fatḥ b. Khāqān xi, xiii, xviii, xx, 109, 134, 165, 171–75, 178–82, 184, 195, 197, 199, 205
Fāṭimah 185
Fatūḥ b. Maḥmūd b. Marwān 187 n. 642
Filasṭīn 97
Fragmenta historicorum arabicorum xxiv
Friday Mosque (in al-Jaʿfariyyah) 170
F-r-ww-iyah (?) 141
Fusṭāṭ 125

G

Gabriel (angel) 95
Gate of Thorns (Tiflis) 122–23
George, son of Cyriac 138–39
Ghaf-r (?) 141
Ghānah 141
Ghānim b. Abī Muslim b. Ḥumayd al-Ṭūsī 37
Ghaṭafān (tribe) 26
Gold Palace (Baghdad) 88

Great Mosque of al-Mutawakkil 67 n. 230
Greek science and philosophy xiii

H

Ḥabash (Abyssinians) 141
Ḥabashiyyah (mother of al-Muntaṣir bi-llāh) 223
ḥadd (punishment) 136
Ḥadīth scholars xxi–xxii, 27, 28
Ḥaḍramawt 96
Ḥafṣah (wife of Muḥammad) xix, 135
Halān 50
ḥalbah 67 n. 230
Ḥalbas (son of Ibn al-Baʿīth) 88–89
Ḥamdawayh b. ʿAlī b. al-Faḍl al-Saʿdī 79–80
Ḥammād b. Jarīr al-Ṭabarī 18
Ḥanbalī(s) xxi, 119 n. 387
al-Ḥārith b. Abī Usāmah xviii, 158, 160
al-Ḥārrah (Ḥārrat Banī Sulaym) 19
Ḥarrān 157
ḥarrāqah (fast boat) 85
Ḥārrat Banī Sulaym 19
Harthamah Shār Bāmiyān 16
Hārūn, brother of Mūsā b. Zurārah 115
Hārūn b. al-Maʾmūn 189
Hārūn b. Muḥammad b. Sulaymān al-Hāshimī xix, 176
Hārūn al-Rashīd xii, 12–15, 38
Hārūn b. Suwārategin 179–80
Hārūnī Palace (Sāmarrā) xix, 11, 52, 69, 109
al-Ḥasan b. ʿAlī b. al-Jaʿd 147
al-Ḥasan b. al-Ḥusayn (Ṭāhirid) 44
al-Ḥasan b. Makhlad b. al-Jarrāḥ 150, 158–63
al-Ḥasan b. Muḥammad b. Abī al-Shawārib 139–40
al-Ḥasan b. Sahl xviii, 53, 109–10, 189
al-Ḥasan b. Sahl b. Nūḥ al-Ahwāzī 160
al-Ḥasan b. ʿUthmān 135–36, 147
al-Ḥasan b. Wahb 9
Ḥasan b. Yaʿqūb al-Baghdādī 160
Hāshim b. Bānījūr 150
Hāshimites xi–xii, 63, 84, 104, 172, 184, 212
al-Ḥayr 196, 199
al-Haytham b. Khālid al-Naṣrānī 75
Ḥayyān b. Bishr 118
Herat 224
al-Ḥijāz xv, 18, 25
Hilāl al-Rāzī 157
Ḥimṣ xvi, 97, 130, 133–35, 157
Ḥimṣ Gate 135
Hind bt. al-Ḥārith 14
hippodrome (Sāmarrā) 67 n. 230
Hippodrome Gate (Tiflis) 122
hippodrome (*maydān*) of Tiflis 122
al-Ḥīrah 4
ḥisbah (in *jihād*) 209
Hīt 96
holy war xvii, 206–9
Ḥubshī b. Abī Rabʿī 183–84
Humphreys, Stephen xxiii–xxiv
Ḥunayn b. Isḥāq xiii
Hurayrah (singing girl, beloved of al-Aʿsha) 54
Ḥurf Road 152
al-Ḥusayn b. ʿAlī (grave of) 110–11
al-Ḥusayn b. al-Ḍaḥḥāk xix, 53–54
al-Ḥusayn b. Ismāʿīl b. Ibrāhīm 108–9
Ḥuẓẓayyān 46

I

ʿibād 35 n. 119
Ibn Abī Duʾād, see Aḥmad b. Abī Duʾād
Ibn Abī Rabʿī, see Ḥubshī b. Abī Rabʿī
Ibn al-Abrash, see Ibrāhīm b. Ayyūb
Ibn al-Abzārī, see al-Abzārī
Ibn al-Akshaf 126
Ibn Aktham, see Yaḥyā b. Aktham
Ibn Asbāṭ al-Miṣrī 70
Ibn al-Athīr, ʿIzz al-Dīn, *al-Kāmil fī al-taʾrīkh* xxiv

Ibn ʿAyyāsh, see Muḥammad b. ʿAyyāsh
Ibn al-Baʿīth, see Muḥammad b. al-Baʿīth
Ibn al-Dawraqī, see Aḥmad b. Ibrāhīm
Ibn Dihqānah al-Nadīm xx, 221
Ibn al-Ḥafṣī al-Mughannī xix, 174–77
Ibn Ibrāhīm, see Isḥāq b. Ibrāhīm b. Muṣʿab
Ibn al-Kalbī 119
Ibn Kathīr, Abū al-Fidāʾ, *al-Bidāyah* xxi
Ibn al-Zayyāt, see Muḥammad b. ʿAbd al-Malik
Ibrāhīm, Abū al-Faḍl, edition of Ṭabarī, *Taʾrīkh* xxiii
Ibrāhīm, son of al-Mutawakkil, see al-Muʾayyad bi-llāh
Ibrāhīm b. al-ʿAbbās b. Muḥammad b. Ṣūl (al-Ṣūlī) xviii, 72, 75, 104, 150
Ibrāhīm b. ʿAṭāʾ xix, 110
Ibrāhīm b. ʿAttāb 110
Ibrāhīm b. Ayyūb al-Abrash 174
Ibrāhīm b. Jaysh xx, 220
Ibrāhīm b. al-Junayd al-Naṣrānī 74
Ibrāhīm b. al-Mahdī 54
Ibrāhīm al-Muʾayyad bi-llāh, see al-Muʾayyad bi-llāh
Ibrāhīm b. Muḥammad al-Mudabbir xvii, 83–85, 188
Ibrāhīm b. Rabāḥ (Riyāḥ) al-Jawharī 10, 12, 15, 158
ʿĪd al-Fiṭr 139
Ightibāṭ, see Qalam
inquisition (*imtiḥān*) 31, 38
Iraq 126, 150
ʿirq 20 n. 62
ʿĪsā, brother of Mūsā b. Zurārah 115
ʿĪsā al-Aʿwar (bathhouse attendant) 30
ʿĪsā b. Farrukhānshāh 161
ʿĪsā b. Ibrāhīm, see Abū Nūḥ
ʿĪsā b. Jaʿfar b. Muḥammad b. ʿĀṣim xix, 135–37
ʿĪsā b. al-Shaykh b. al-Salīl al-Shaybānī 80
ʿĪsā b. Yūsuf 124
iṣbaʿ 90 n. 307
Iṣbahān 37, 96, 171
Isḥāq b. Abī Isrāʾīl 157
Isḥāq b. Ibrāhīm b. Abī Khamīṣah 36
Isḥāq b. Ibrāhīm b. Muṣʿab xvii–xviii, 11, 21, 29, 32, 35, 73, 78, 81, 83–86, 105, 107–8
Isḥāq b. Ismāʿīl, *mawlā* of the Umayyads xvi, 121–23
Isḥāq b. Saʿd b. Masʿūd al-Qutrabbulī 159–60, 162
Isḥāq b. Thābit al-Farghānī 224
Isḥāq b. Yaḥyā b. Muʿādh 8
Islam 129, 142, 206, 213
Ismāʿīl, brother of Mūsā b. Zurārah 115
Ismāʿīl b. Muḥammad b. Muʿāwiyah b. Bakr al-Bāhilī 30
Ismāʿīl b. Nawbakht 53
Isnā (Asnā) 143
Isrāʾīl b. Zakariyyāʾ al-Ṭayfūrī 174
Ītākh (Aytākh) Abū Manṣūr al-Khazarī xi–xii, xvii–xviii, xxi, 9, 15, 16, 37, 61, 68, 81–86
Iyād 35
izār 90

J

al-Jabal 96, 171
Jabalah 157
Jabiltā (Jabultā) 155
Jaʿfar b. ʿAbd al-Wāḥid b. Jaʿfar 132, 139–40, 212, 224
Jaʿfar b. Dīnār al-Khayyāṭ 36, 129, 148–50
Jaʿfar b. Ḥadhdhāʾ(?) 40, 43
Jaʿfar b. Ḥāmid 182
Jaʿfar al-Maʿlūf 160–61, 163
Jaʿfar b. Muḥammad b. al-Baʿīth 88–89
Jaʿfar b. Muʿtaṣim, see al-Mutawakkil ʿalā-llāh
Jaʿfar b. Yaḥyā b. Khālid 13 n. 15
Jaʿfarī Palace (al-Jaʿfariyyah) (Sāmarrā) 154–56, 161, 163, 170, 172, 190–91, 195, 199; the new 210, 222

al-Jāḥiẓ, ʿAmr b. Baḥr, *Fī manāqib al-Turk* xiii
Jamarat al-ʿAqabah 7
al-Jammāz, Muḥammad b. ʿAmr 118
Janafā' 25
al-Jār 18
Jardmān (Gardmān), fortress of 123; Road 123
jarīb 131 n. 438
al-Jarjarā'ī, family 10 n. 19
al-Jawsaq (al-Khāqānī) (palace) xi, 36 n. 125, 164, 222 n. 719
al-Jazīrah 96, 115, 138, 147
Jews 41 n. 151, 153
al-Jibāl 37, 96

K

kāfir 33 n. 111
al-Kaltāniyyah 119
Karbeas (Qarbiyās) 147, 167
al-Karkh Fayrūz 111
Karmā 155
al-Khābūr 96
al-khadam al-khāṣṣah 179 n. 604
khādim 13
al-Khalanjī 118
Khālid (brother of Ibn al-Baʿīth) 87
Khalīfah (slave of Ibn al-Baʿīth) 77, 86
al-Khams (?) 141
Khān ʿĀṣim (in Baghdad) 135
Khāqān al-Khādim xvii, 22, 38–43
Khāqānids xxvii
kharāj 140, 165 n. 556
kharīṭah 190
al-Khaṣāṣah (Upper and Lower) 155
Khashabat Bābak 34, 37, 95, 224
al-Khāṣṣah al-Mutawakkiliyyah 155
al-Khaṭṭāb b. Wajh al-Fals 44
Khaybar 25
Khazar(s) 81
Khilāṭ (Akhlāṭ, Khlat') 115
Khuld Palace (Qaṣr al-Khuld) (Baghdad) 13 n. 34
Khurāsān(ī) 21, 28, 96, 101–4, 116, 128, 146, 215–16
Khuwaythiyyah 115, 123; mountain of 115
Khuzāʿah 120
Kindāsh 179 n. 605
Kirmān 21
Kisrā Anūshirwān 123
al-Kūfah 4, 83, 129
Kur River 122
Kurds 37
kustīj girdles 94
kuttāb al-ʿarḍ 40

L

Laʿīs (son? of ʿAlī Bābā) 143
Lake Urmiya 78
Lamos River (Lamas-Ṣū) 38, 41–42, 140
Laodicea 157
Lassner, Jacob xxiv
Laylā bt. Saʿd (the beloved of Majnūn) 56
Lecker, Michael 17 n. 44
Leo (V) 39
Logothete (al-Lughuthīṭ) 76, 165
Lord of the Throne (Ṣāḥib al-Sarīr), Wahrazān-Shāh 123
Lulon (Lu'lu'ah) xvi, 165, 169
Lu'lu'ah (palace) 155

M

al-Madā'in 81, 127, 156
Madīnat al-Manṣūr 147
al-Maghāribah 19, 79, 81, 122–23, 139, 203
al-Maghrib 96, 141, 156, 170
Māh al-Baṣrah 96
Māh al-Kūfah 96
Maḥmūd b. al-Faraj al-Naysābūrī xix, 95
Mahrah (camels of) 143
al-Maḥūzah 154–55, 168, 202
mā'idah 177 n. 597
Main Bridge (Baghdad) 84

al-Majnūn ("the Madman") 50
Majnūn, see Laylā
al-Majūsī al-Quṭrabbulī 53
Makrān 96
Malāḥim 183
Malaṭyah (Melitene) 209
Malik b. al-Haytham 27
al-Ma'mūn, 'Abdallāh, caliph 28–29, 81, 173, 189
manāṭiq (sg. *minṭaqah*) 90
mandīl 68
Manṣūr (household manager of Ibn al-Ba'īth) 80
Manṣūr (son of Ītākh) 85–86
Manzala, Lake 125 n. 415
Marāghah 78, 88
Mar'ah 46
Marand 77–80
Martinakios (?), Byzantine naval commander 124
Marwān b. Abī al-Janūb Abū al-Simṭ 185–86, 188
Marwān b. al-Ḥakam (Gate of) 24
Māsabadhān 96
Masdūd al-Ṭunburī, Abū 'Alī al-Ḥasan 221
maslaḥah 18
Masrūr Sammānah al-Khādim 69, 73, 169
al-Mas'ūdī, 'Alī b. al-Ḥusayn xiii
Maṭbaq (prison of Baghdad) 37, 106, 111, 164
mawlā(s) 81, 99, 101–2, 153, 196, 204–5, 209, 212, 215, 217
Maymūn b. Ibrāhīm 161
maẓālim court(s) 11, 38, 116–17, 203
Mecca xvii, 19, 20, 21, 75–76, 81–83, 96, 129, 145, 148, 157, 160, 165, 170, 190
Mecca Road 6, 36, 53, 76, 108, 129, 148, 150, 152
Medina, Medinese 16, 17, 18, 19, 20, 22–24, 26, 75–76, 81
Messenger of God (Muḥammad, the Prophet) 31–32, 105, 136, 152, 185, 189, 206, 214; tomb of 23
Michael (II) 3 n. 3, 39
Michael (III), son of Theophilus xvii, 3, 39, 41, 76, 138, 156, 168
midra'ah 16
Mihrajān 96
al-Mihrizār 35
Minā 6
mithqāl 141 n. 474
miṭraf 175
M-kār-h (?) 141
Mopsuestia 157
Mosul 37, 96, 224
mu'āwin 143
Mu'āwiyah b. Sahl b. Sunbāṭ (Sm̄bat) 124
al-Mu'ayyad bi-llāh, Ibrāhīm xviii, 96, 97–104, 178–79, 197, 199, 210–18, 223
Mubārak al-Maghribī xvii, 71, 74
Muhallabī, family 149 n. 497
Muḥammad, see Messenger of God
Muḥammad, brother of Mūsā b. Zurārah 115
Muḥammad b. 'Abd al-Ḥamīd al-Ḥaydī 134
Muḥammad b. 'Abd al-Malik (b.) al-Zayyāt xvii, xxi, 10, 36, 38, 39, 52, 57, 61, 63, 65–73, 75, 81, 186, 188
Muḥammad b. 'Abdallāh al-Qummī 141–45
Muḥammad b. 'Abdallāh b. Ṭāhir, Abū al-'Abbās xvi–xviii, 116, 120, 136, 170, 190, 206, 212–13
Muḥammad b. 'Abdallāh al-Ṭarsūsī xvii, 41, 42
Muḥammad b. 'Abdawayh Kirdās al-Anbārī 130, 133–35
Muḥammad b. Aḥmad b. Abī Du'ād, Abū al-Walīd 116–17, 129, 131
Muḥammad b. al-'Alā' al-Khādim 65
Muḥammad b. 'Alī Bard al-Khiyār 223
Muḥammad b. 'Alī b. Umayyah 189
Muḥammad b. 'Amr al-Khārijī (al-Sharī) 37, 224
Muḥammad b. 'Ayyāsh 30, 160
Muḥammad b. al-Ba'īth b. Ḥalbas xvi, 77–80, 86–89

Muḥammad b. Dāwūd b. ʿĪsā b. Mūsā 7, 16, 21, 64, 76, 82, 106
Muḥammad b. al-Faḍl al-Jarjarāʾī 75, 111
Muḥammad b. Faraj 73
Muḥammad b. Hārūn 223–24
Muḥammad b. Ḥātim b. Harthamah 79
Muḥammad b. al-Haytham b. ʿAdī al-Ṭāʾī 53
Muḥammad b. Ibrāhīm b. al-Ḥusayn b. Muṣʿab xviii, 29, 30, 51, 107–9
Muḥammad b. Isḥāq b. Ibrāhīm xix, 109–10
Muḥammad b. Jaʿfar, see al-Muntaṣir bi-llāh
Muḥammad b. Karīm xvii, 42, 43
Muḥammad b. Khālid b. Yazīd b. Mazyad al-Shaybānī 78
Muḥammad b. Kunāsah, Abū Yaḥyā 55
Muḥammad b. Mūsā al-Khwarazmī 53
Muḥammad b. Mūsā al-Munajjim 161, 165 n. 556, 222
Muḥammad b. Rajāʾ al-Hiḍārī 131, 205
Muḥammad b. Rizqallāh 134
Muḥammad b. Saʿdān al-Naḥwī 44
Muḥammad b. Saʿīd 184
Muḥammad b. Ṣāliḥ b. al-ʿAbbās al-Hāshimī 16, 18, 25
Muḥammad b. Sulaymān b. ʿAbdallāh b. Muḥammad al-Zaynabī 165, 170, 203
Muḥammad b. al-Wāthiq (al-Muhtadī) 62
Muḥammad b. Yaḥyā b. Muʿādh 174 n. 584
Muḥammad b. Yaʿqūb, Abū al-Rabīʿ 116
Muḥammad b. Yūsuf al-Jaʿfarī 26, 46–47, 49–50
Muḥammad b. Yūsuf al-Marwazī 111–12
Muḥammad b. Zubaydah, see al-Amīn
al-Muḥammadiyyah 154
Mukhāriq al-Mughannī 44
al-Mukhtār (palace) 155
Muʾnis 179
al-Muntaṣir bi-llāh, Muḥammad, caliph xi–xii, xiv, xvii–xx, xxii, 75, 86, 95–104, 108, 111, 163, 172–74, 176–78, 180–81, 183, 185, 190–91, 195–224 *passim*.
murtadd(ūn) 33 n. 111, 147 n. 494
Mūsā, nephew of Aḥmad b. Naṣr 119
Mūsā b. ʿAbd al-Malik 75, 158–63
Mūsā b. Bughā al-Kabīr 178–79
Mūsā al-Furāniq 160
Mūsā al-Hādī 33
Mūsā b. ʿĪsā 220
Mūsā b. Zurārah 115
Mushāsh 157
Muslim(s) xvii, xx, xxi, 41–43, 91–92, 126, 137, 140–41, 153, 156, 169–70, 208–9, 213, 215
al-Mustaʿīn bi-llāh, Aḥmad, caliph 222
al-Muʿtaṣim bi-llāh, Muḥammad, caliph xi–xii, 3, 67, 81, 86, 127, 173, 188–90
al-Mutawakkil ʿalā-llāh, Jaʿfar, caliph xi, xiv, xviii, xxii, 4, 59, 61–191 *passim*, 195–96, 198–99, 202, 213–14, 220–21, 224
Muʿtazilism (Muʿtazilites) xx, 28 n. 94, 31 n. 106, 38 n. 133, 116 n. 379, 119 n. 387
al-Muʿtazz bi-llāh, Muḥammad, caliph xviii, 88, 96, 104, 108, 164, 172–73, 175, 178, 182, 197–99, 210–18
al-Muwaffaq bi-llāh, Abū Aḥmad 179, 181
Muẓaffar (son of Ītākh) 85–86
Muzāḥim b. Khāqān 205
Muzdalifah 190

N

al-Najaf 111
Najāḥ b. Salamah, Abū al-Faḍl xviii, 10, 73–74, 157–64

al-Najāshī (king of Abyssinia) 152
Najd 187
*naqīb*s of the ʿAbbāsids 27
al-Nashawā 116
Naṣībīn 135, 184
Naṣr, *mawlā* of ʿUmar b. Faraj 73
Naṣr b. al-Azhar b. Faraj al-Shīʿī xvii, 138, 156, 168–69
Naṣr b. Ḥamzah al-Khuzāʿī 44
Naṣr b. al-Layth 119
Naṣr b. Saʿīd al-Jahbadh xix, 175
Naṣr b. Saʿīd al-Maghribī 205–6
Naṣr b. Waṣīf 180
Nayrūz (Nawrūz) 108, 129, 165–66
Naysābūr 21, 95
Nikētiatēs (?), Byzantine naval commander 124
niʿmah 12
nithār 178 n. 602
Nūbah 141
Nukhaylah 46

O

Ooryphas, Byzantine naval commander 124

P

Palace of Isḥāq b. Ibrāhīm 85
Palace of Khuzaymah b. Khāzim 84–85
Palm Sunday(s) 91, 129, 153
Passover 153
Patrikios (-oi) 43, 113–15, 123–24, 139, 165, 168
Persians 182
Petronas, brother of Theodora 168 n. 563
Place for Standing (Mawqif) 6
Podandos (Bozanti [Pozanti]) River 43
Portico of the Dome of the Girdle (Hārūnī Palace) 12
prisoner exchange xvii, 38–43, 137–40, 156, 168–70
Private Palace (Audience Hall) (Sāmarrā) 212
the Prophet, see Messenger of God
Public Gate of the Caliph's Palace (Sāmarrā) 95, 128, 145, 147
Public Gate of the Jaʿfarī Palace 202
Public Palace (Audience Hall) (Sāmarrā) 36, 38, 62, 185, 212
Public Treasury (*bayt al-māl*) 36

Q

qabā' 84
Qabīḥah 175
Qadhaq 96
Qalam al-Ṣāliḥiyyah (slave girl) 55–57
qalānīs (sg. *qalansuwah*) 90; *qalansuwah Ruṣāfiyyah* 62
qamīṣ 34
qand 126
Qandābīl 96
Qarāṭīs 3–4, 53
Qarīs Gate (Tiflis) 122
al-Qarnayn 47
Qarqīsiyā 96
Qāshān 96
al-Qāsim b. Aḥmad al-Kūfī xviii, 109
al-Qāsim b. Mūsā b. Fūʿūs (?) 134
al-Qāṭūl al-Kisrawī 82, 154 n. 510
Qawsarah, see Yaʿqūb b. Ibrāhīm al-Bādhghīsī
Qazwīn 96
Qifṭ 143
Qinnasrīn 96
al-Qitrīj (Ktričn), prince of Jardmān 123
Qudāmah b. Jaʿfar 85 n. 293
Qudāmah b. Ziyād al-Naṣrānī 85
al-Qulzum 143
Qūmis 146
Qumm 96

Qur'ān xviii, xxii, 49, 91, 95, 119, 155, 189, 206–8, 224; created 27–28, 31, 34, 39–40
Quraysh 18, 19
Quṭrabbul 127

R

al-Rabadhah 51
Rabīʿah (tribe) 79–80
Rāfiḍah 185
Rajā' b. Ayyūb al-Hiḍārī 131
Rakhsh (a page [*ghulām*]) 29, 30
al-Rakkāḍ ("The Runner"), a chief of the Banū Fazārah 25
Rāmiyah (raid of) 42
al-Ramlah 134
al-Raqqah 39, 157
Ra's Aḥmad b. Naṣr (place) 34
Ra's ʿAyn 157
al-Rashīd, see Hārūn al-Rashīd
Rāshid al-Maghribī 69, 72
Rastan Gate (Ḥimṣ) 183
rātibah 133
raṭl 6 n. 10
Rawḍat al-Abān 47
Rawḥ 73
Rawwādid dynasty 78 n. 271
al-Rayy 21, 96
Rosenthal, Franz xxiv
Rukhkhaj (Rukhkhajī) 74
al-Ruwaythah 18, 19
ru'yat Allāh 31 n. 106
R-'-wīn (?) 141

S

ṣaʿalīk 182
Saʿd al-Khādim al-Ītākhī 145, 185
Sadan, Joseph xxiv
Saʿdūn b. ʿAlī 75
ṣāḥib al-jisr 105; see also Isḥāq b. Ibrāhīm b. Muṣʿab
Ṣāḥib al-Sarīr, see Lord of the Throne
Saʿīd b. Ḥamīd 197
Saʿīd al-Kabīr (the Elder) 197
Saʿīd al-Ṣaghīr (the Younger), Abū ʿUthmān xix–xx, 64, 195–96, 199
Saʿīd b. Salamah al-Naṣrānī xx, 222
Saʿīd b. Ṣālih 83
Sājites, in Ādharbayjān 152 n. 503
al-Sajjād 61
Salamah b. Saʿīd al-Naṣrānī 183
Salamah b. Yaḥyā 19
Ṣāliḥ al-ʿAbbāsī al-Turkī 51, 134
Ṣāliḥ b. ʿAbd al-Wahhāb 55
Ṣāliḥ b. ʿAlī b. ʿĪsā 223
Ṣāliḥ b. ʿUjayf 81
Ṣāliḥ b. Waṣīf 180
Sallām al-Abrash 81
Salm b. ʿAmr al-Khāṣir 33
Ṣamāluh (Semalouos kastron) 151
Sāmarrā xi–xii, xvi, xviii–xix, xxi, xxxi, 31, 35, 37, 50 n. 186, 51, 69, 72, 74, 78–79, 81, 84–85, 87–88, 95, 109, 116–17, 127, 131, 162, 202–3, 206
al-Ṣāmighān 96
Sammānah, see Masrūr
Sammānah (a servant) 57, 74
al-Ṣamṣāmah (name of a sword) 33, 34
Sanad (Sind) b. ʿAlī, Abū al-Ṭayyib 53
al-Ṣanāriyyah (Tsanar-kʿ, Ts'anar) 128
Ṣanjah 144
Ṣaqr (brother of Ibn al-Baʿīth) 87
Ṣarāt Canal 122
sarāwīl (sg. *sirwāl*) 34
Sarīr, district 123 n. 404
Sāsūn 115 n. 373
Sawād 21, 96, 116
Sawādah b. ʿAbd al-Ḥamīd al-Jaḥḥafī 114
Sawd (Sūd) 46, 50
sawīq 24, 143
Sawwār b. ʿAbdallāh al-ʿAnbarī 118, 157
Seleucia 38, 42
Sergius (Sarjūn) 169
al-Shaʿānīn 153 n. 508
Shafīʿ 179

Shāhī (fortress) 78
Shahrazūr 96
Shākiriyyah 18–19, 63, 79, 82, 84, 89, 99, 102, 139, 143, 195, 202, 205, 209, 215–18
shalandiyah vessels 125–26
al-Shammāsiyyah 127
Shaqq al-Ḥārrah 19
Shār Bāmiyān, see Harthamah
Shāriyah al-Jāriyah 54
al-Sharqiyyah Quarter (Baghdad) xix, 135
Shaṭā 125; *shaṭawī* cloth 125
shīʿah 97, 212
shibr 93 n. 321
Shīʿite 135 n. 448, 138
Shimshāṭ (Arsamosata) 140, 146 n. 489, 164 n. 550
Shīrawayh (Shīrūyah) b. Kisrā xiv, 219
Shīrwān, Shīrwānshāh 78 n. 274
Shujāʿ, mother of al-Mutawakkil 111
Shunayf al-Khādim 139–40, 156
al-Shurayf 46
shurṭah 21, 143 n. 477
Sicily 170
ṣidām 137
Sijistān 224
Sīmā al-Dimashqī xi, 33
Sind 96
Sindī, *mawlā* of Ḥusayn al-Khādim xvii, 42
Sindī b. Bukhtāshah 205
Small Gate (Tiflis) 122
Stephanos 124
Suburb Gate (Tiflis) 122
sūdān (black peoples) 141
sūdān (blacks) of Medina 19, 23
Sufyān b. ʿUyaynah b. Maymūn al-Hilālī 32
Ṣughdbīl 122–23; Ṣughdbīl Gate (Tiflis) 122
Sulaymān, brother of Mūsā b. Zurārah 115
Sulaymān b. ʿAbdallāh b. Ṭāhir 6
Sulaymān b. Muḥammad b. ʿAbd al-Malik 71
Sulaymān al-Rūmī 196
Sulaymān b. Wahb 9, 15, 85
Sulaymānī sugar 64
al-Ṣūlī, Abū Bakr, *Kitāb al-awrāq* xxiii–xxiv, 54 n. 203, 72 n. 248
sulṭān 28 n. 95
Sumaysāṭ (Samosata) xvi, 140 n. 468, 146, 164
Sunbāṭ (Smbat) b. Ashūṭ 124; see also Abū al-ʿAbbās
Sundus 81
Sunni, Sunnism xx, 116 n. 379, 128 n. 429, 140 n. 465
al-Suwāriqiyyah 19, 20
al-Suyūḥ 188
Syria, Syrian 25, 96, 102–3, 138, 146, 150, 157

T

Tabālah 50
al-Ṭabarī, Abū Jaʿfar, see Abū Jaʿfar
Ṭabaristān 21, 44, 96
Ṭāhir b. ʿAbdallāh b. Ṭāhir 21, 109
Ṭāhir b. al-Ḥusayn 44
Ṭāhirids xxviii, 6 n. 9, 11 n. 26, 21 nn. 65 and 68, 29 n. 98, 44 n. 160, 107–9, 116 nn. 377–378
al-Ṭā'if 75
Takrīt 96
Ṭalḥah b. Muḥammad b. Jaʿfar 118 n. 383
Ṭālib 28–30
Ṭālib b. Dāwūd 40
Tall al-ʿAbbās (a fortress) 135
Tamrah (Thamarah) 177–78
ṭanāfis (sg. *ṭinfisah, ṭanfasah*) 69
tanawwara 31
tannūr 70 n. 244
Ṭardūsh al-Turkī 19
Tarsus 38, 43, 157
Ṭarūn (Taron) 114
tashbīh 31 n. 106, 34
ṭawīlah 62
ṭayālisah (sg. *ṭaylasān*) 89

al-Ṭayfūrī, see Isrā'īl b. Zakariyyā'
Ṭayyi', see Banū Ṭayyi'
Telesios(?) (Byzantine officer) 41
Tephrikē (Abrīk) 147
Theodora (Byzantine empress) 3, 76, 138
Theoktistos 76 n. 264, 124 n. 414, 138
Theophilus (Byzantine emperor) 3
Tiflis xvi, 116, 121–23
Tigris River 105, 137; districts of 96
Tinnīs 126, 157
Torah 207
Traditionists xx
Treasury of the Bride (Bayt Māl al-'Arūs) 14
Triphylios (Aṭrūbaylīs) 156
Turk, *mawlā* of Isḥāq b. Ibrāhīm 85–86
Turkestan xiii
Turks xi–xiv, 8 n. 13, 10 n. 19, 19, 50, 63–64, 79, 81, 122, 139, 149 n. 496, 151, 181, 183, 196, 210, 212, 221; sons of 62
ṭuruz (sg. *ṭirāz*) 99

U

'Ubaydallāh b. al-Ḥusayn b. Ismā'īl 163
'Ubaydallāh b. Muḥammad b. 'Abd al-Malik 71
'Ubaydallāh b. Muḥammad al-Kātib 118 n. 383
'Ubaydallāh b. al-Sarī 117
'Ubaydallāh b. Waṣīf 180
'Ubaydallāh b. Yaḥyā b. Khāqān xiv, xix–xx, 89, 111, 136, 158–64, 172–73, 181–83, 195, 198
Uḍākh 36, 47
'Ujayf b. 'Anbasah 70
'ulūj 41
'umālāt 10 n. 23
'Umar (caliph) xix, 135
'Umar b. 'Abdallāh al-Aqṭa' 147, 167
'Umar b. Abī Rabī'ah
'Umar b. Faraj al-Rukhkhajī 35, 52, 61, 65–66, 73–74, 106, 162
'Umarah b. 'Aqīl b. Bilāl b. Jarīr b. al-Khaṭafī 45, 46, 49
Umm Abīhā bt. Mūsā (sister of 'Alī b. Mūsā al-Riḍā) 44
umm (al-)walad 3
Urdunn 97
Urmiya 78
'ushr 140
Ushrūsaniyya-Ishtīkhaniyyah 50
Ushtūm 126
Uswān (Aswān) 143
Ūtāmish, Abū Mūsā 177, 179 n. 605
'Uṭārid (an apostate) 147
'Uzayzah b. Qaṭṭāb al-Sulamī (al-Labīdī) 18, 19, 20, 23, 24

W

waḥshah 189 n. 657
Wājin (Wājan) al-Ushrūsanī al-Ṣughdī 50, 179 n. 605, 180, 196
waqf, property 188
Waṣīf al-Turkī xi, xvii, 37, 61, 64, 82, 171, 176, 178, 180, 205–6, 208–10, 212, 224
Water Gate (Marand) 80
al-Wāthiq bi-llāh, Hārūn, caliph xi–xii, xiv–xv, xix–xx, 3–57 *passim*, 61, 64, 65, 67–68, 81, 86, 162, 173, 186, 188–89
West Side (Baghdad) 29, 30, 32, 34, 118
wife of Isḥāq b. Ismā'īl 123
William Beckford, *Vathek* 52 n. 195
wishāḥ 5 n. 6, 69 n. 238

X

Xtiš (Kithīsh), fortress of 124

Y

Yaḥyā b. 'Abd al-Raḥmān b. Khāqān 163

Yaḥyā b. Ādam al-Karkhī, Abū Ramlah 40, 43
Yaḥyā b. Aktham, Abū Muḥammad 116, 118, 120, 131, 189–90
Yaḥyā b. Harthamah 76
Yaḥyā b. Khālid al-Barmakī 13, 14, 15
Yaḥyā b. Khāqān al-Khurāsānī 75, 110
Yaḥyā b. Maʿīn b. ʿAwn, Abū Zakariyyā' 27
Yaḥyā b. ʿUmar al-Ḥusayn b. Zayd b. ʿAlī 105–6
Yakdur (Bakdur), fortress 78
al-Yamāmah xvi, 36, 46, 50, 78, 96, 108, 185–88
Yaʿqūb, uncle of Ibrāhīm b. Jaysh 220
Yaʿqūb b. Ibrāhīm al-Bādhghīsī, *mawlā* of al-Hādī 141, 143, 145
Yaʿqūb b. Ibrāhīm al-Dawraqī xiv, xvi, 27 n. 91
Yaʿqūb b. al-Layth al-Ṣaffār 224
Yaʿqūb b. al-Sikkīt, Abū Yūsuf 210, 212
al-Yaʿqūbī, Aḥmad b. Abī Yaʿqūb xi, xiii
al-Yāsiriyyah 84; bridge 84
Yazīd, cousin of Ibrāhīm b. Jaysh 220
Yazīd b. ʿAbdallāh al-Ḥulwānī al-Turkī 37, 69
Yazīd b. Muʿāwiyah (palace complex of) 20, 23
Yazīd b. Muḥammad al-Muhallabī 149
the Yemen 36, 50, 75, 96, 146
Yusr al-Khādim 219–20
Yūsuf b. Abī Saʿīd, see Yūsuf b. Muḥammad
Yūsuf b. Muḥammad b. Yūsuf xvi, 112–15, 121

Z

al-Zaʿfarāniyyah 127
Zakariyyā', brother of ʿUbaydallāh b. Yaḥyā 161
zammām (*zimām*) 66 n. 229
zawāqīl 182
zawraq 182
Zaydān b. Ibrāhīm 161
al-Zaynabī, see Muḥammad b. Sulaymān
Zīrak al-Turkī 79–80, 122–23
al-Zubayr b. al-ʿAwwām 152
Zunām al-Zamīr 174
zunnār belts 89–90
Zurāfah xx, 177–78, 180–81, 203
Zurqān xx, 180
Zurzur b. Saʿīd al-Kabīr (the Elder) 56
Zuṭṭ 137

?-y-n-w-r (?) 141
'-k-r-m (?) 141